# The English Jewry
## under Angevin Kings

# THE ENGLISH JEWRY
# UNDER ANGEVIN KINGS

*by*

## H.  G.  Richardson

**GREENWOOD PRESS, PUBLISHERS**
WESTPORT, CONNECTICUT

**Library of Congress Cataloging in Publication Data**

Richardson, H. G. (Henry Gerald), 1884-
    The English Jewry under Angevin kings.

    Reprint. Originally published: London : Methuen, 1960.
    Bibliography: p.
    Includes indexes.
    1. Jews--Great Britain--History.  2. Great Britain--
History--Angevin period, 1154-1216.  3. Great Britain--
Ethnic relations.  I. Title.
DS135.F5R5  1983      942'.004924      83-18539
  ISBN 0-313-24247-X (lib. bdg.)

Igitur his gestis ab Hebraeis, ego
quoque in his faciam finem sermonis.
Et si quidem bene et ut historiae
competit, hoc et ipse velim: sin autem
minus digne, concedendum est mihi.

First published in 1960 by Methuen & Co., Ltd., London
© 1960 H. G. Richardson

Reprinted with the permission of Methuen & Co., Ltd. on behalf of
Associated Book Publishers, Ltd.

Reprinted in 1983 by Greenwood Press
A division of Congressional Information Service, Inc.
88 Post Road West, Westport, Connecticut 06881

Printed in the United States of America

10 9 8 7 6 5 4 3 2 1

# CONTENTS

v

# CONTENTS

# FOREWORD

THE PRESENT BOOK IS based upon three unpublished papers, which I have been privileged to read in recent years to the Jewish Historical Society of England, and upon some earlier contributions to the history of the English Jewry. Its purpose is to set in a clearer light the position of the Jewish community in England before the reign of Henry III, though I have on occasion overstepped the boundary of 1216. It has seemed desirable to print as appendices a number of unknown or little-known documents which illustrate important aspects of Jewish life and the relations between the Jewish community and the English society in which they lived. The texts available in print are not so numerous as to necessitate any apology for adding to them. With their aid, and by looking afresh at the original sources, not all of which have been used by others, some errors of long standing have, it is hoped, been dispersed and some fresh knowledge made available. The need for a corrective of current beliefs is manifest. I need but cite one sentence from Dr A. L. Poole's volume in the *Oxford History of England*.

> The ostentation which possession of great wealth enabled the Jews to display, and their unconcealed contempt for the practices of Christianity, made them an object of universal dislike; as usurers, moreover, they had gained a strangle-hold on the recently founded monastic houses whose splendid buildings they had financed, and on many of the smaller aristocratic families. . . .[1]

Mr Poole gives no references, but the ultimate sources are, without doubt, a few well-known picturesque monastic writers

[1] *From Domesday Book to Magna Carta* (1951), p. 353. The sentence remains unchanged in the second edition (1955).

vii

describing particular instances, which have served as the basis for modern generalizations. If, however, there is evidence that wealthy Jews were accustomed to display their wealth ostentatiously, the evidence, I must confess, has escaped me. The evidence, so far as I am acquainted with it, for Jewish unconcealed contempt of Christian practices does not seem to me very much better than the evidence for Jewish ritual murders, though there were doubtless some ill-mannered Jews as there were many ill-mannered Christians. 'Universal dislike' again is a phrase that needs so many qualifications as to be at least misleading: it is a phrase that might be applied with equal truth or untruth to Italian merchants. As for the relation of monastic houses to Jewish moneylenders, the sober facts of history show the monks as happy collaborators with them rather than as victims and, even so, victims of their own mismanagement and folly. And some of 'the smaller aristocratic families' owed not a little of their good fortune to their association with Jews.

It has not been my intention to write a full history of the English Jewry at this period and some matters in which I have no competence or on which I have nothing fresh to say, I have passed over. In Mr Cecil Roth's *History of the Jews in England*, the reader has an excellent guide to present knowledge, knowledge to which he has contributed so notably. My debt to him and to previous writers on the medieval Jewry is obvious and great. The footnotes will, for the most part, indicate my obligations. It is right, however, that I should mention here the name of Joseph Jacobs, whose *Jews of Angevin England* (London, 1893) put the study of the early history of the English Jewry upon a new basis. Doubtless he overlooked not a little and both repeated other men's errors and fell into some errors of his own contrivance. But the marvel is that he, who had no claim to be a professed medievalist, made accessible so much that was new and true. And what was new he had to find largely in difficult manuscripts that have since been put into print and adequately indexed to the profit of his successors. If these chapters on Jewish history were worthy of a dedication they would be dedicated to the memory of Joseph Jacobs.

There is another name I would mention. This book owes not a little to Albert Montefiore Hyamson, but for whom it would never have been conceived and who, as Honorary Editor, obtained the financial support of the Jewish Historical Society for its publication. It was still some way from completion when the news of his death came to me. I fear I tried his patience sorely as I demanded from him delay after delay, so that I might seek further information or elucidate some point that was obscure to me. Regretfully I shall never be able to show him the manuscript or submit the proofs to him for his advice and correction. I owe other debts to Mr. V. D. Lipman, Mr. Cecil Roth and Professor G. O. Sayles for help with the manuscript and proofs: I can but hope that the volume will repay their kindness.

H. G. R.

# I

# THE SETTLEMENT

THERE HAD BEEN JEWISH communities in Gaul from early in the Christian era, and they were of some importance under the Franks. Of their subsequent history very little can be recovered for some centuries in the darkness that falls upon Western Europe after the break-up of the Carolingian empire.[1] A community seems, however, to have been established in Normandy, at Rouen, at the beginning of the eleventh century.[2] Whether this was a survival from Gallo-Roman times or whether the Jews were recent immigrants into this barbaric and unsettled province is unknown. The city of Rouen was relatively peaceful and was a centre of trade. Merchants of Rouen already resorted to London, where they sold wine and whalemeat,[3] and it is possible that among the Rouennais a Jew may occasionally have come to England. But there is no suggestion of a permanent settlement in this country until after the Norman Conquest.[4] That the London

[1] For a summary of the evidence see Robert Anchel, *Les Juifs de France* (1946), pp. 19–39.     [2] Below, p. 23.

[3] IV Æthelred, 2. 5 (Liebermann, *Gesetze der Angel-Sachsen*, i. 232).

[4] In the Latin paraphrase of VI Æthelred 9, of the early eleventh century, there is a suggestion that Jewish slave–dealers dealt in English slaves, but that does not mean that they were resident in the country (*ibid.*, i. 251; ii. 527, *s.v.* Juden (4)). The reference to Jews in the so-called *Leges Edwardi Confessoris* reflects the conditions under Henry I or Stephen (below, p. 109). The tradition of the medieval Jewry was that it dated from the Conquest (Sayles, *Select Cases in the Court of King's Bench*, iii. cxiv). M. Bernhard Blumenkranz has argued in favour of the presence of Jews in small numbers in England from the seventh century onwards and particularly in the tenth century. The evidence is weak and depends largely upon the attribution to an English author of the *Altercatio Æcclesie contra Synagogam*, which he has edited and which he dates 938–66. This hypothesis is far from being proved. See, however, his critical edition in *Revue du Moyen Age Latin*, x, no. 1–2 (and separately), especially pp. 31–5.

community was an off-shoot of the community at Rouen is hardly open to dispute:[1] in any case, the Jews of England were so closely allied to those of Normandy that there can be no doubt of their country of origin. Not only were the privileges of the Jews of England and Normandy guaranteed by one and the same charter,[2] but in the case of at least one family we can trace its ties with both countries until the eve of John's expulsion from the duchy. Rabbi Josce, the most distinguished Jew of London under Henry I, had a house in the Jewry at Rouen. That house descended to his son Isaac; but another son Abraham had a house in the same quarter. Both Isaac and Abraham were prominent members of the London Jewry. Isaac retained his father's house at Rouen until his own death in 1199 or 1200. Soon afterwards Isaac's son Josce, who was to become 'priest' of the Jews in England, sold it,[3] though he still retained a connexion with Normandy. Perhaps his son, another Isaac (Hakelin), still lived in Rouen, for in 1200 Isaac was in debt to the Norman exchequer, and this debt Josce undertook to pay.[4] In much the same way a year or two before, Richard I had instructed Isaac, the son of the Rabbi, to pay 1,000 marks to Henry de Gray, who was at the time keeper of the Jews in Normandy.[5] These are not very picturesque details, but they are the best evidence available of the links that bound the Jewries of London and Rouen. There is other evidence for the presence in England of Jews whose place of origin was Normandy,[6] but this does not strengthen the more direct evidence afforded by the family of Rabbi Josce of the retention of interests and residence on both sides of the Channel. For Jews from several other parts of France are found in England,[7] though, with one or two exceptions, we

[1] In the first recension of his *Gesta Regum Anglorum* (ii. 371 n.), William of Malmesbury stated that the Conqueror brought the Jews of London from Rouen.　　　　　　　　　　　　　　　[2] Below, p. 109.

[3] *Rot. Chart.*, p. 105b; *Rot. Lib.*, p. 72.　　　　[4] *Memoranda Roll 1 John*, p. 71.

[5] *Ibid.*, p. 70: for Henry de Gray, see below, p. 208.

[6] For example, Deulebenie and Isaac of Juvigny (*Pipe Roll 3 Richard I*, p. 140) and Elias of Auffay (receipt roll of 1194 in Jewish Hist. Soc., *Miscellanies*, i. lxxi).

[7] Paris in particular (*Pipe Roll 3 Richard I*, p. 140; *Rot. Oblat.*, pp. 246, 296; M. D. Davis, *Shetaroth*, p. 288) and, among other places, Étampes, Pontoise and Saumur (*Pipe Roll 3 Richard I*, pp. 139, 140, 149), Bourges (*Miscellanies*, i. lxix),

cannot be sure that they left any material ties behind them in the homes from which they came.[1] What the evidence as a whole indicates is that there was much movement of Jews over all lands where French was spoken. Doubtless there was some movement beyond those boundaries, but it was trifling by comparison. The first Jews to settle in England were, then, French Jews, and French the Jews in England remained until their expulsion in 1290. When they felt that their lives were in danger, they fled, if they could, to France. After the massacre in London in 1264, 'divers Jews, taking alarm at the troublous state of the realm, went overseas . . . to Normandy'.[2] This was doubtless their refuge when, in the earlier troubles under John, those who could made good their escape.[3] It was to a 'chapter' of Jews in France that English Jews resorted to decide a question of law when it was impossible to obtain a decision in England.[4] It was to France that the Jews finally returned on their expulsion. This 'Frenchness' the English Jews shared with English nobles and the higher and more learned of the English clergy. They belonged to their world, even though they might be at enmity with them. We have here a fact of cardinal importance.

Had William the Conqueror's wishes been fulfilled, England would have had one line of rulers after his death and Normandy another, and indeed for forty years or so after the Conquest English institutions and English speech and writing lived on with very little change. Had the Norman Duke Robert been as able as his younger brothers, William and Henry, the ties that

---

Senlis (*Cal. Plea Rolls*, i. 119, 134, 150, 154–6 *et passim*) Nantes (below, p. 282), Rochelle (see following note). The most famous of these Jews from France is Yom-Tob of Joigny, who perished at York in 1190 (William of Newburgh, *Historia Rerum Anglicarum*, pp. 318–20; Roth, *History of the Jews in England*, pp. 23, 270).

[1] Benedict of Talmont is one of the exceptions (*Rot. Litt. Pat.*, pp. 14, 53*b*). He appears to have been domiciled in Rochelle, but to have had property in Oléron (*Rot. Litt. Claus.*, i. 44, 75).

[2] Rigg, *Select Pleas*, p. 75.        [3] Below, pp. 171, 178.

[4] *Close Rolls, 1237–1242*, p. 464. The issue appears to have been the validity of a divorce: one of the parties, David of Oxford, was contumacious and the king supported him, going to the length of forbidding chapters to be held in England.

bound Normandy to England would have been increasingly loosened and England would have remained English. But the battle of Tinchebray, which was fought in 1106, determined that England and Normandy should obey a single ruler whose intention was to pass both of his dominions on to his son. Though his intention was frustrated and though for a time under Stephen the duke of Normandy was not the king of England, Henry I's ambition was realized in his grandson Henry II and his two great-grandsons Richard and John. And though John was expelled from Normandy in 1204, the work of a century was not quickly undone. The greater landowners of England, the higher clergy and many of the lower clergy, the upper classes in the towns, had become French in speech and culture and so they remained. It was not until the fifteenth century that French came to be a foreign language in England and French influences dwindled to very little or nothing.

It is in this setting that we must picture the English Jewry. It was English only because it was in England. After the early years of the settlement, which may have been tentative and when numbers were certainly small, the Jews of London found themselves living in conditions almost exactly like those they had known in France. Their lives were patterned like the lives of the higher military, clerical and mercantile classes, with whom they had the closest contacts and with whom they shared a common speech. They adopted French names. All belonged to that aristocratic French society which governed Europe to the west of the Rhine and North of the Mediterranean and in some Mediterranean lands as well. Members of that society might travel thousands of miles in the expectation of finding relatives or friends and an opportunity of employment among people who spoke the same language and had the same way of life. To belong to that society did not imply riches or exalted status. Every great man or rich man—the terms are synonymous—had a great household which included very humble members who nevertheless were set apart from the general population. The differentiation was recognized by the law. Ordinary folk were required to be grouped in tithings and to be mutually responsible for the good conduct of their fellows. But for the members of his household, the lord was responsible: they were in his mainpast.[1] The humblest household servant, then, belonged to an aristocratic community and, as time went on, it became the practice to mark this membership with the outward sign of the lord's livery. There was no exact parallel in the Jewry. True, there were rich Jews who had Jewish dependents in their households,[2] but the wealthiest among them did not have establishments which, in numbers and display, would differentiate them from wealthy Christian merchants. Few Jewish households, however, can have been wealthy, and the lists of contributors to Jewish taxes show that there were many more poor Jews than rich.[3] But, poor or rich, all were bound together by their religion and their condition and none had any other purpose in England than to subserve the interests of the king and the rulers in Church and State.

From the general population the Jews, high and low, were set apart far more than was any lord's household, though with the great they might be on familiar terms. Yet even here we must make a qualification. Their religion and their ritual created a barrier between the Jews and the Gentile world around, and at the same time bound them to a wider community than the country of their settlement or the French society whose speech and way of life they shared. This truth is curiously illustrated by the falsehoods of the renegade Jew, who alleged that the rulers and rabbis of the Spanish Jews assembled yearly at Narbonne to determine by lot in which land a ritual murder was to be committed and that the lot had fallen upon England in the year that St William of Norwich was killed.[4] Moreover, the first Jew in England of whom we

[1] See Pollock and Maitland, *History of English Law*, i. 568.
[2] The following examples from the particulars of the Guildford tallage will suffice: all are from *Pipe Roll 3 Richard I.* Magister puerorum Ysaac (p. 32); Vivus scriptor Helye (p. 61); Coc de domo Abraham, Josce de domo Samsonis, Mosse de eadem domo, Biket de domo Ysaac (p. 140).
[3] See the particulars of the Guildford tallage (*ibid.*, pp. 32, 60–1, 139–40) and the receipt roll of 1194 (Jewish Hist. Soc., *Miscellanies*, i. lxii–lxxiv).
[4] Jessopp and James, *St. William of Norwich*, pp. 93–4.

5

know anything definite, though French in speech, had studied the Talmud at Mainz,[1] and later in the twelfth century England was visited by Jews from Italy, Spain and, apparently, Russia,[2] as well as from French-speaking lands. Their wider interests, the fact that Jews had a third language, Hebrew, which was not accessible even to the clergy, emphasized their separateness. At the same time, it is unlikely that many Jews could be readily distinguished from Gentiles by their appearance, though their neighbours knew them by their practices. The order given in 1218 and repeated in 1253 that Jews in England should wear a badge (*tabula*) on the breast, so that they might be plainly recognized, was the outcome of an openly discriminatory decree of the Fourth Lateran Council in 1215, but nevertheless it does point to the difficulty, throughout all the lands of Latin Christendom, of distinguishing Jew from Christian by their physical traits.[3] During their long sojourn in Gaul and elsewhere the Jewish communities had not maintained a racial purity and, though the elements may not have been the same, by the eleventh century they were of as mixed descent as the upper classes everywhere. But for their religion, they would have been easily assimilable.

It would seem evident that the Jewish community was established in London by the king himself. London, it must be remarked, was, in the eleventh century and until late in the twelfth, a city containing much vacant land within the walls. More room was made available for settlers when the Norman kings abandoned the royal residence in the city. Westminster, that had been favoured by

[1] Gilbert Crispin, *Disputatio Iudei et Christiani* (ed. Blumenkranz: 1956), p. 27: this edition has superseded that of Dom Gerberon (1675), reprinted among Anselm's works at Paris in 1721 and by Migne in 1863. That the Jew was French in speech is plain from the fact that he had prolonged conversations with Gilbert Crispin, the Norman abbot of Westminster. We can exclude the use of Latin, which was not a familiar language spoken in Benedictine houses.

[2] Ysaac de Russia (*Pipe Roll 27 Henry II*, p. 134); Moses of Spain (*Pipe Roll 3 Richard I*, p. 139). The fairly common name 'Lombard' indicates an Italian origin.

[3] Cap. 68 (Hefele, *Histoire des Conciles* (1913), v. 1386: inserted in the Gregorian Decretals, X. 5.6.15). For the successive orders and their enforcement in England see below, pp. 178–84, 191–3.

Edward the Confessor, was favoured also by his successors, who built for themselves as well a stronghold in the Tower of London. The king's soke, as it may be conveniently called, covered a large area in the middle of the city, lying approximately between the present Guildhall and the Mansion House.[1] After the Conquest it was gradually alienated and more gradually covered with houses and lanes. The northern portion became known as Aldermanbury, because some long-forgotten alderman acquired it and had a great house built there, while much of the southern portion was granted by Henry I to his illegitimate son Robert, whom he created earl of Gloucester. It was to the east of the future Gloucester Soke that the Jews had first settled, near a market place called Kingcheap,[2] perhaps in some buildings left vacant on the departure of the royal court. Although the community seems soon to have expanded beyond the capacity of the Old Jewry, they never spread very far from it. Presumably it was there that they had their first synagogue—and a small room would have sufficed for their needs. But the 'great' synagogue, which superseded it, was in what is now Ironmonger Lane, a very short distance away, being to the west, instead of to the east, of the present Mercers Hall.[3] The great synagogue was the focal point of the medieval Jewry[4] and no London Jew seems to have dwelt more than a few score yards from it. They were near enough to the Tower to obtain the protection of the constable in case of need and at no great distance from their burial ground outside the city walls, just beyond Cripplegate.

There was nothing of the ghetto about the London Jewry,

---

[1] For the history of this area see W. Page, *London: its origin and early development*, pp. 140-3. The map at p. 133 puts the Walbrook too far to the east. Kingcheap was midway between the Walbrook and Old Jewry.

[2] The name was preserved in the late twelfth century and survived into modern times as Conyhope (*Stow's Survey* (ed. Kingsford), ii. 331; below, p. 48, n. 3).

[3] Below, pp. 237-9.

[4] The synagogue was used not only for religious purposes or those directly affecting the community, but was employed for inviting claims against Christian debtors effecting a settlement of their debts (Rigg, *Select Pleas*, pp. 9, 12; *Cal. Plea Rolls, passim*) as well as for notifying the total acquittance of a debtor (Matthew Paris, *Chronica Majora*, v. 398-9). There is, however, no direct evidence for these practices in the twelfth century.

E.J.A.K.—B                    7

although it had well-recognized, though perhaps shifting, boundaries.[1] Synagogues were very near churches.[2] Jews dwell next door to the Guildhall.[3] Jewish houses that escheated to the Crown were granted to Christians,[4] while the reverse of this process is illustrated by a conveyance from about the middle of the twelfth century. One of the foremost of London citizens, Gervase of Cornhill, sold to a leading member of the London Jewry, Isaac, the son of Rabbi Josce, a house that had belonged to his uncle, a former sheriff of London: there is a covenant under which Gervase's licence is required if Isaac proposes to dispose of the house to any other than a member of his own family.[5] Another example points in the same direction. The London house of the wealthiest of twelfth-century Jews, Aaron of Lincoln, was in the Gloucester Soke: an area of vacant land lay between it and the Walbrook and this area was 'developed', as we should say, by Gervase of Cornhill and other Christian speculators, with financial help from Aaron.[6] The primitive settlement of the Jews in England was the pattern for the larger settlements elsewhere as they spread over England: while keeping close together, they were still interspersed among their Christian neighbours.[7]

There is no evidence of a Jewish settlement outside London in the reign of Henry I. Certainly in 1130, when we might expect to

---

[1] Thus, in an appeal of felony, Isabel Cooke relates how she came in the Jewry of London into Coleman Street (*Cal. Plea Rolls*, iii. 288). Clearly the court of the Constable of the Tower could not have exercised jurisdiction over Christians misbehaving in the Jewry if its boundaries were not recognized: a good many such cases will be found in the roll of 1275–8 (P.R.O., E. 101/249/22).

[2] The church of St. Mary Colechurch and St. Olave Upwell were in Old Jewry and St. Martin Pomary in Ironmonger Lane. St. Mary 'Conyhope' (i.e. Kingcheap) and St. Mildred were within a few yards of Old Jewry and St. Lawrence Jewry within a short distance of Ironmonger Lane. At various times there were synagogues in Threadneedle Street, Coleman Street, Basinghall Street and the present Gresham Street, as well as the Great Synagogue in Ironmonger Lane (see below, pp. 195, 197, n.1).   [3] *Cal. Plea Rolls*, ii. 280.

[4] For some examples see *Rot. Chart.*, pp. 193, 203b; *Rot. Litt. Claus.*, i. 88b, 198b. It was the same in other towns (*Rot. Chart.*, pp. 52, 55b, 201).

[5] Below, pp. 237, 240.   [6] *Pipe Roll 4 Richard I*, p. 306; below, p. 47.

[7] In Bedford, for example, the Jews had houses in the High Street (P.R.O., E. 101/249/27, no. 21), as also at Exeter (below, p. 18).

have some notice of the presence of Jews in other parts of England had they been there, the only Jewish community mentioned is that of London.[1] This does not mean that the members of that community did not travel outside the city in pursuit of business, but it is unlikely that any Jew had a permanent residence elsewhere. In the reign of Stephen, who is said to have favoured Jews, communities are, however, found at Norwich, Cambridge[2] and Oxford.[3] There were probably communities at a number of other places, for early in Henry II's reign they are found at Lincoln and Northampton, at Thetford and Bungay, in Gloucestershire, Hampshire and Wiltshire. The amounts contributed by each community to the tax (*donum*) levied by the king in 1159 indicate the relative importance of each community, in wealth, if not in numbers. London naturally comes first with a contribution of 200 marks and then, in order, Norwich ($72\frac{1}{2}$), Lincoln (60), Cambridge and Hampshire (50), Thetford (45), Bungay and Northampton ($22\frac{1}{2}$), Oxford (20), while at the end of the list come Gloucestershire (5) and Wiltshire (2), where there were inconsiderable settlements.[4] These last two items indicate that Jews had but recently taken up their residence in the west. Excluding these two recent settlements, it is clear that the established communities were in those parts of the country that had been more effectively controlled by Stephen, and the inference seems justified that, in those parts where the Empress and her son Henry had been able to maintain themselves or where most of the fighting took place between the contestants for the crown,[5] there had been no Jewish

---

[1] *Pipe Roll 31 Henry I*, pp. 146–9.

[2] Jessopp and James, *St. William of Norwich*, pp. 92, 95. This hagiography provides evidence for communities of Jews not only at Norwich but at Cambridge (p. 94). For the Jews at Cambridge see also Wharton, *Anglia Sacra*, i. 625, 645–6: Bishop Nigel of Ely pawns an antique cross and a copy of the Gospels with them.

[3] The evidence for Jews at Oxford under Stephen is contained in a late and corrupt source, but is inherently probable: see C. Roth, *The Jews of Medieval Oxford*, p. 3.      [4] *Pipe Roll 5 Henry II*, pp. 3, 12, 17, 24, 28, 35, 46, 53, 65.

[5] See the summary of the evidence, with map, in A. L. Poole, *From Domesday Book to Magna Carta*, pp. 150–3. Gloucestershire and Wiltshire saw most of the fighting.

settlements. On Henry's coming to the throne, he must have followed Stephen's policy of encouraging the Jews.[1] The movement of expansion in the early years of Henry's reign may be illustrated by Richard of Anstey's dealings with moneylenders. Anstey is in Hertfordshire, a few miles from the point where that county meets Cambridgeshire and Essex. Originally Richard had had recourse to Jews at Cambridge, but in 1160 he was able to find a Jewish moneylender much nearer home, just over the Essex border at Newport, a royal manor. Since Essex does not figure among the counties in which the Jews were collectively taxed in 1159, Jacob of Newport would seem to be a very recent arrival in 1160.[2] He was not long alone, for a few years later Richard was borrowing from Mirabelle of Newport.[3] We see here how Jewish settlements—for reasons which will appear we must avoid the word 'communities'—were forming in the second half of the twelfth century, and the process can be traced in many parts of the country by means of entries on the account rolls of the Exchequer. These same rolls also indicate how some settlements failed to persist. That at Newport, for example, does not seem to have long survived the death of Jacob in 1183.[4]

The most complete view of Jewish settlements in England is afforded by the receipt roll recording contributions to a tax in 1194. This shows that outside London Jews were resident in twenty counties, settled principally in the larger towns, but some scattered in small numbers over the countryside.[5] Settlements in lesser towns and villages were, of course, those likely to be temporary. That at Thetford, for example, which was of im-

---

[1] So, extolling the return to peace after Henry II's accession, William fitz Stephen writes 'exeunt securi ab urbibus et castris . . . ad creditores repetendos Iudei' (*Materials for the history of Thomas Becket*, iii. 19).

[2] Palgrave, *English Commonwealth* (1922), ii. 117.      [3] *Ibid.*, p. 118.

[4] Jacob was recently dead at Michaelmas 1183, when Peitevin of Eye had the custody of his son (*Pipe Roll 29 Henry II*, p. 71). A certain Moses was assessed to the Guildford tallage of 1187 in Newport, but the debt was not collected and he had presumably removed or died (*Pipe Roll 3 Richard I*, p. 32: there is no note of payment in subsequent rolls). There is no mention of any Jew of Newport in the receipt roll of 1194.

[5] Jewish Hist. Soc., *Miscellanies*, i. lxii–lxxiv.

portance in 1159, seems to have disappeared by 1194, and it is doubtful whether the smaller settlement at Bungay still survived. A number of Jews are, it is true, described as 'of Bungay', but they are distributed over Norwich, Lincoln, Northamptonshire and Hereford[1] and may have been dispersed fairly recently. It is clear from the lists of contributors at different towns and in different counties that there was a good deal of movement from place to place, some of it quite temporary, as in those cases where men are taxed in one town but pay in another.[2] Many of the settlements, however, have members who, like the Jews of Bungay, have come from elsewhere, even from overseas, but are taxed with the rest, and therefore are more than casual visitors.[3] A wealthy Jew might well have roots in more than one place. Aaron of Lincoln had, as we have seen, a house in London, where he died.[4] Another of the leading Jews under Henry II, Jurnet of Norwich, who founded a family that was prominent in that city for several generations, transacted much of his business in London and evidently had close connexions with the Continent, whither he resorted when in trouble in England.[5] Of the family of Rabbi Josce, who, for the best part of a century at least, retained residences in Rouen after they had settled in London, mention has already been made.[6] Benedict of Talmont, prominent in the royal service under Richard and John, came, as his name implies, from Poitou, and maintained close relations with that country while he was domiciled in England.[7] The lives of such men ran closely parallel to the lives of the knightly class, men like William Marshal, who had for lord not only King John but Philip Augustus

[1] *Ibid.*, pp. lxvii, lxix, lxxiii, lxxiv.

[2] Thus Slema of London and Belin of Gloucester, who are entered under Northampton, pay (or are credited) in their town of origin (*ibid.*, p. lxxiv).

[3] Thus Benedict of Rochester pays in Canterbury, as also does Benedict of Romney (*ibid.*, pp. lxv, lxvi). Hamon de Burges, in Lincolnshire, may come from Bourges (p. lxix); Samson de Rume, in Warwickshire, seems also to come from abroad (p. lxxi). There can be no doubt of Elias of Auffay (*ibid.*).

[4] Above, p. 8; below, p. 115, n. 3.

[5] Below, pp. 39–41.        [6] Above, p. 2.

[7] Above, p. 3, n. 1. For his relations with Richard I, see *Gallia Christiana*, ii, Instrumenta, 423–4, no. xviii, and below, pp. 135–6.

as well, or like those captains of King John's, Fawkes of Bréauté, Engelard of Cigogné and the rest, who came from the Loire country to pursue military and administrative careers in England. Jew or knight, their careers were of the pattern of the French-speaking world in which they lived and which, partitioned as it was by the boundaries of kingdoms and provinces, had a unity of manners and conditions that opened the widest prospects for the adventurous, especially perhaps when to transfer oneself from one country to another did not mean that one changed one's ruler. Doubtless there were local laws and customs, local conditions and prejudices, even local differences in language, that a newcomer had to face, but no more than is involved today in passing from North to South in the United States or from Ireland to England or England to Scotland.

Although they resided temporarily and precariously in many parts of the country, it was only in substantial towns that the Jews had permanent settlements; and this is doubtless to be explained, not only because moneylending—and the trading it implies—was their characteristic profession, but because, from the beginning, they were under the protection of the keepers of royal castles. Jews stood in a special relation to the king: they and their chattels were his, and anyone molesting a Jew ran in danger of the royal displeasure. But the king's peace was not always maintained without difficulty, and only in the neighbourhood of a royal castle could a recognizable Jew be safe in times of popular disturbances.[1] In the reign of Stephen, when the royal power was weak, Jews seem to have been encouraged to settle on the lands of great lords and under their protection. In this way we can explain the presence, early in Henry II's reign, of Jewish settlements at Bungay

[1] This is true up to the time of the Expulsion. One of the aptest illustrations is that of the settlement at Bridgnorth, of which more is said hereafter. In 1267 two Jews had obtained licence to reside in Bridgnorth and, in case of need, to take refuge in the castle (*Cal. Plea Rolls*, i. 150). In 1273 the Jews of Bridgnorth had been placed—of course, at their own instance—under the protection of the sheriff (*Cal. Close Rolls, 1272–1279*, p. 49). For a Jew belonging to the king's son Edmund, who was permitted to take refuge in the king's castle wherever he dwelt, see *Cal. Patent Rolls, 1266–1272*, p. 515.

and Thetford, towns belonging to Hugh Bigod, earl of Norfolk. By 1194 both settlements appear to have been dispersed. As we have seen, the Jews of Bungay are then scattered over several towns, and there is the ominous fact recorded in 1192 that Isaac of Saint Edmund's had been killed at Thetford, leaving an orphan heir, who seemingly is safe with a guardian at Bedford.[1] There would not seem much room for doubt that the risings against the Jews in 1190 put an end to both settlements. It may be perhaps assumed that the Jews of Bungay and Thetford had been granted to Hugh Bigod by the king, that the earl was their lord, for otherwise it is difficult to understand how they could have been protected by him or have obtained justice. No similar case is known in the twelfth century, and in the thirteenth century the grant of Jews to a magnate was a very rare occurrence. The commendation or granting of Jews to vassals was not uncommon on the Continent,[2] but in England it was difficult to accommodate with the system of royal *archae* and the jurisdiction of the Justices of the Jews.[3] Consequently this was not a factor in their dispersion over the country, though lords of towns may have welcomed their presence and to that extent have encouraged their residence, more or less temporary, outside royal cities and boroughs. Thus, in 1226, the earl of Chester intervened to prevent the disturbance, by the sheriffs, of the Jews who were residing, presumably without royal licence, in Coventry and Leicester.[4]

The many indications of the presence of Jews in small towns or villages in the twelfth and thirteenth centuries have attracted attention, and long lists of these places have been compiled,[5] lists that may be misleading. The subject, therefore, should not be dismissed without some further discussion. It would seem that these

---

[1] *Pipe Roll 4 Richard I*, p. 203.    [2] Below, pp. 141, 202.

[3] The transfer of the Jewry, as such, to Richard of Cornwall or Prince Edward was, of course, a very different matter.

[4] *Rot. Litt. Claus.*, ii. 123a. The earl was lord of Coventry and he was at the time in possession of the lands of the earldom of Leicester. Hence his interest in the Jews in both places.

[5] Jacobs, *Jews of Angevin England*, pp. 374–80; Roth, *History of the Jews in England*, pp. 274–5, 291.

13

apparent country-dwellers were not permanently resident in the place from which they acquired a surname—the principal reason for identifying them with places outside the chief towns—but that there they found it convenient to have a house of business and occasional residence. The best evidence seems to be provided by the documents which have survived from Dunstable.[1] This was a monastic borough, the lordship of which was held by Dunstable Priory, with the consequence that any Jew desiring to do business in the town required the prior's licence. The terms of a licence granted in the early years of the thirteenth century shows that the licensees had no intention of taking up permanent residence in the town: nor is there any evidence that any Jew did so, though Jews bore the distinguishing surname 'of Dunstable' as far back as the days of Henry II,[2] when, we must suppose, the prior was already granting licences. It is, in any case, inconceivable that individual Jews lived isolated in the country without liens that connected them with the larger urban communities, with which their business activities and social and religious duties were bound up. The Jews to whom the surviving licence was given to carry on their business in Dunstable were clearly members of the London community.[3]

At the beginning of Henry III's reign and, we may infer, earlier in the thirteenth century, there were recognized communities in seventeen of the larger towns. These were Bristol, Cambridge, Canterbury, Colchester, Exeter, Gloucester, Hereford, Lincoln, London, Northampton, Norwich, Nottingham, Oxford, Stamford, Winchester, Worcester and York. It was in these towns that the Jews were assessed for taxation,[4] and in these towns *archae* were set up for the registration of Jewish bonds.[5] In 1194, however,

---

[1] Below, pp. 259–63.

[2] Iheremias Iudeus de Dunestaple (*Pipe Roll 34 Henry II*, p. 127); Aaron frater Leonis de Dunestaple (*Pipe Roll 3 Richard I*, p. 111).

[3] They are described as Flemengus Iudeus de Londoniis et Leo filius suus (below, p. 262). The father's name suggests that the family came from Flanders.

[4] This list is that given in the particulars of the aid for the marriage of the king's sister in the receipt roll of 5 Henry III (Jewish Hist. Soc., *Transactions*, xi. 99–111).          [5] See below, p. 16.

there could have been no system of recognized communities, such as we find in the thirteenth century, since the *capitula Iudeorum* of that year provide for the institution of an *archa* at 'six or seven places',[1] while the receipt roll of the same year presents no indication of an organization restricting the assessment of Jews to taxation at a limited number of urban centres.[2] The receipt roll, we must remember, is for one only of the two terms of the financial year, and apparent omissions in the Easter roll may have been supplied in the Michaelmas roll, but some facts are plain on the evidence of a single roll. Payments are recorded sometimes under towns and sometimes under counties, and the same names may appear under both headings.[3] It is impossible to detect any system in this cross-classification. Payments are recorded from all the towns which were to have recognized communities in 1221, except Nottingham, Stamford, Worcester and York. The towns of Nottingham and Worcester are presumably concealed under these counties and Stamford may be concealed under Lincolnshire; but there is no entry for Yorkshire and it is probable that the community at York had not yet been re-established after the massacre of 1190.[4] In this way we can account tentatively for all the recognized communities of 1221; but we have, in addition, entries under Bedfordshire, Chichester, Coventry, Hertford, Wallingford, Warwick and Warwickshire, as well as under Lincolnshire, Hampshire, Kent, Northamptonshire, Nottinghamshire and Worcestershire, which may conceal small towns and villages as well as county towns. The inference is that the arrangements in the *capitula Iudeorum* of 1194 were both new and tentative and that experience soon showed that great inconvenience was

---

[1] R. de Hovedene, *Chronica*, iii. 266.

[2] The text is printed in Jewish Hist. Soc., *Miscellanies*, i. lxii–lxxiv.

[3] For some significant instances, see below, p. 128.

[4] While the massacre has left many traces in the pipe rolls of Richard I, the first signs of the revival of Jewish activity in Yorkshire appear in 1196, when Amiot, a Jew of Bristol, is seeking to recover a debt from Ralf of Émondeville (*Pipe Roll 8 Richard I*, p. 187). In the following year Gentilia offers four ounces of gold for an inquest to ascertain whether her father, Samson, died a Jew or a Christian and to have his bonds (*Pipe Roll 9 Richard I*, p. 59): she failed to pay (*Pipe Roll 1 John*, p. 46).

caused by attempting to limit Jewish transactions to half-a-dozen centres and that three times this number were required. Although the matter needs further investigation, it would seem obvious that in the thirteenth century the system of *archae* and the plan of assessment to taxation followed the same pattern. In any case the pattern was not rigid: we must expect exceptions to any rule of the kind.

By 1241 there had been added to the list of recognised communities of twenty years earlier Bedford, Dorchester, Marlborough and Warwick, making twenty-one in all.[1] In 1254 there were still twenty-one communities, but Wilton had displaced Dorchester.[2] There are not included among these twenty-one those that are supposed to have existed for a time at Berkhamsted and Wallingford. Some mention should, however, be made of them, for their story suggests with what caution we should draw inferences from the existence of an *archa* where we have no independent evidence of an established Jewish community. Doubtless, as a general rule, an *archa* implies a community of some size and considerable activity in moneylending, and in 1275 it was ordered that Jews should reside only in royal cities and boroughs in which there was an *archa*.[3] But *archae* were undoubtedly set up, and had at least a fitful existence, in quite inconsiderable places. An *archa* had been set up at Berkhamsted in 1235 for the convenience of Jews who were the tenants of the king's brother Richard, earl of Cornwall, and naturally for the benefit of the earl himself.[4] In 1242 the king agreed that Jews and *archa* should be removed to Wallingford.[5] This transfer may not have taken place: the *archa*, wherever it was, seems to have fallen into disuse. At all events, in

[1] *Close Rolls, 1237–1242*, pp. 353–5.

[2] The evidence is provided by a roll of receipts from a tallage of 10,000 marks assessed in 38 Henry III (P.R.O., E. 401/1566) and the writs in *Cal. Patent Rolls, 1247–1253*, pp. 439–40, 441–4. Marlborough does not appear in the roll of receipts, but this records a little less than two-fifths of the assessment.

[3] *Statutes of the Realm*, i. 221–221a. This enactment was only slowly and imperfectly enforced (*Foedera*, I. ii. 543; *Cal. Plea Rolls*, iii. 317, 319; below p. 194).

[4] *Close Rolls, 1234–1237*, p. 46.

[5] *Close Rolls, 1237–1241*, p. 392.

1255 an *archa* was again established at Wallingford for the undis-
guised purpose of facilitating transactions in the bonds of one of
the richest Jews in England, Abraham of Berkhamsted, who had
in that year been presented to the earl by the king. Abraham had
debtors in half the counties of England, as far distant as Devon and
Yorkshire, and at the earl's instance all Abraham's bonds were
transferred to the *archa* at Wallingford. Thereupon orders were
issued to the sheriffs to distrain the debtors to make immediate
payment of the sums in which they were bound and to remit the
money to the earl within a month of the following Easter.[1] The
new *archa*, like the old, was, in fact, purely for the earl's convenience. There had been at least a few Jews resident at Wallingford
in 1194,[2] but it is not certain that in 1255 there were any living
there, even members of Abraham's household. Every *archa* needed
four chirographers, two Christians and two Jews; but Jews, or at
least suitable Jews, were not available at Wallingford, and they
had to be brought from Oxford when occasion required.[3] Obviously in this instance an *archa* did not connote a community,
and it is to be presumed that Abraham himself was a member of
the Oxford Jewry.[4]

*Archae* were subsequently set up at Devizes, Huntingdon,
Ipswich and Sudbury;[5] but, with the dubious exception of
Ipswich,[6] all of these had a brief existence, and there is no reason
to suppose that at any time there were in these towns more than a
handful of resident Jews. Huntingdon, alone of recent intro-
ductions, appears in a list evidently intended to be a complete

[1] *Cal. Patent Rolls, 1247–1258*, pp. 393, 396, 403; *Close Rolls, 1254–1256*,
pp. 170–2.      [2] Jewish Hist. Soc., *Miscellanies*, i. lxiv.

[3] *Cal. Patent Rolls, 1247–1258*, p. 393.

[4] For Abraham of Berkhamsted, see Roth, *op. cit.*, pp. 46, 55–6, 272; N. Den-
holm Young, *Richard of Cornwall*, pp. 69–70.

[5] Since that at Wallingford was, in fact, a private *archa*, mention of it is not to
be expected in royal records. The *archae* at Ipswich and Sudbury were apparently
closed by 1273, while those at Devizes and Huntingdon, though not mentioned
in 1273, were in existence in 1275 (*Cal. Patent Rolls, 1272–1289*, pp. 6, 126–7).
The intermittent closing and re-opening of *archae* at this period makes any
succinct statement of the position impossible: see below, p. 228, n. 3.

[6] See p. 19, n. 3, below.

statement of the *archae* still in being in 1279: since, however, Colchester and Stamford, which seem to have survived until 1290, are also omitted, the list is almost certainly defective.[1] But it is by no means easy to determine the point at which a community became extinct, and certainly in the last fifteen years of the English Jewry the existence of an *archa* does not necessarily connote the continued existence of a Jewish community. Cambridge, one of the oldest of the communities, together with Gloucester, Marlborough and Worcester, had been formally suppressed in 1275;[2] but in 1279 there were still *archae* at the three towns last named and it is assumed that Jewish, as well as Christian, chirographers will be available to furnish information as to their contents.[3] Nothing is said of an *archa* at Cambridge in 1279, though Jews owned property there until the Expulsion and presumably visited it on occasion.[4] If, however, the Jewish communities in these towns were not wholly extinct, they were moribund. Nor is this true only of towns where the Jewry had been formally suppressed. Exeter may furnish an example. In 1276 there seem to have been only two Jews in that city actively engaged in money-lending.[5] In 1290 the formerly flourishing Jewish community was represented by a single household, that of a Jewess named Comtesse, who owned a house in the High Street. Nevertheless there were still two *archae* at Exeter:[6] the old *archa* for bonds executed up to 1275 and the new *archa* that had been opened in 1283.[7] Evidently some business had been done fairly recently and presumably two Jewish chirographers had been found in some way: but there was hardly a shadow of a community and there was

---

[1] *Cal. Close Rolls, 1279–1288*, p. 41. Since Northampton is mentioned twice' the scribe was obviously in error. For Colchester and Stamford see below' p. 19, n. 3.

[2] Rigg, *Select Pleas*, p. 85. The Cambridge Jews were to go to Norwich, those of Gloucester to Bristol, of Marlborough to Devizes, of Worcester to Hereford: the *archae* were to go with them.

[3] *Cal. Close Rolls, 1279–1288*, p. 41.

[4] Stokes, *Studies*, pp. 190–2, below p. 21, n. 2.

[5] P.R.O., E. 101/249/31: their names are Auntera, widow of Samuel, the son of Moses, and Isaac, the son of Moses, apparently members of the same family.

[6] E. 101/249/27, no. 32.     [7] Below, p. 228, n. 3.

certainly no synagogue.[1] The story is much the same at Devizes, where the Jewry had been united with that formerly at Marlborough. Here in 1290 only one house was in Jewish ownership, though two others were leased, and only two Jews are named as occupying these houses: Cok (Isaac) and Josce, the son of Solomon of Marlborough. No synagogue is mentioned. There were still, it is true, two *archae* and a forcer (casket), all presumably containing bonds; but this is quite compatible with the practical extinction of the community.[2]

At the time of the Expulsion the total number of living communities appears to have been reduced to fourteen or fifteen.[3] The particulars that have been given afford some idea of the ebb and flow of Jewish settlement. No more than thirteen communities were recognized continuously throughout the thirteenth century,[4] and the total number at any time can rarely, and then only temporarily, have exceeded twenty. The principal settlements remained as they had been under Richard I and doubtless in the later years of Henry II: and although a few settlements gained in importance, this was probably at the expense of others. Of the truth of the general picture here presented we can find confirmatory evidence in the frequent instructions given in the thirteenth century that creditors should be invited in the synagogue to submit claims against named Christian debtors. The synagogues

---

[1] Besides the house owned by Comtesse, there was, we are expressly told, no other house owned or leased by Jews in Exeter. We should not, therefore, expect the mention of a synagogue, and there is none.

[2] P.R.O., E. 101/249/30, m. 3; E. 101/249/27, nos. 7, 8.

[3] It is apparent from Hugh of Kendal's account of Jewish houses sold (Pipe Roll 22 Edward I (E. 372/139), m. 3) that it is fairly safe to infer the existence of communities at Bedford, Bristol, Canterbury, Colchester, Hereford, Lincoln, London, Northampton, Norwich, Nottingham, Oxford, Stamford, Winchester, York. In Bedford (£14. 6s. 8d.), Nottingham and Stamford (each £13. 6s. 8d.), their houses were very few: the aggregate values are given in parentheses. At Ipswich the houses sold realized no more than £7. 6s. 8d., and the existence of a Jewry seems extremely doubtful. The position at Devizes is stated in the text. For Jewish property at Cambridge and Sudbury see p. 21, n. 2, below. Outside the eighteen towns here named, the Jews no longer own houses.

[4] The towns named in the first sentence of the preceding note, with the exception of Bedford.

seem to have been invariably those in the larger towns—indeed, it is unlikely that any existed elsewhere—and the inference must be that all Jews were members of the communities of one or other of those towns and might be expected to be present in the synagogue on some occasion within a period of a few weeks.[1]

Whatever may have been the position in the twelfth century, in the thirteenth permanent residence outside one of these towns appears to have been illegal without the king's licence. The statutory provisions of 1239 and 1253[2] do not seem to have been more than an affirmation of what was already the rule. In 1237, for example, the sheriff of Northamptonshire had been instructed to see that no Jew resided outside the town of Northampton.[3] Unauthorized residence appears, moreover, to have been the reason why the bailiff of Sittingbourne was instructed in 1231 to arrest Isaac the Jew with his chattels,[4] for in 1266 a licence was needed for a Jew of Canterbury to depart and reside in Sittingbourne.[5] How the authorized communities established themselves in the twelfth century is uncertain: no charter is known which permits Jews to reside in the towns where there is later evidence for the existence of synagogues or *archae*. If, at first, there was some tacit understanding that in a certain royal borough they would be protected, later their right of residence appears to have been a matter of custom. When we read under Edward I of the expulsion of Jews from Winchelsea 'in qua nullus Iudeus aliquibus temporibus habitare consueverit aut morari',[6] it is plain that the right of residence is regarded as prescriptive. The important words are *habitare* and *morari*. What was in question was not a visit or temporary stay for the purpose of business—and it is evident that Jews travelled all over the country, as indeed their charter plainly

---

[1] Above, p. 7, n. 4.

[2] *Liber de Antiquis Legibus* (Camden Soc.), p. 237; *Close Rolls, 1251–1253*, p. 313.

[3] *Close Rolls, 1234–1237*, p. 425.

[4] *Close Rolls, 1231–1234*, p. 12.

[5] *Cal. Plea Rolls*, i. 134. For later cases see Rigg, *Select Pleas*, pp. 61, 82; *Cal. Plea Rolls*, ii. 163; iii. 5, 127.

[6] *Foedera*, i. II. 503. The same grounds are given for the expulsion from Bridgnorth (*Cal. Close Rolls, 1272–1279*, p. 130).

permitted them to do[1]—but the establishment of a permanent community. Jews might indeed own property in a town in which they did not reside, as at Cambridge, whence they had been expelled at the instance of the queen mother in 1275.[2] Similarly they had been expelled from Bridgnorth at the instance of the townsmen in 1274,[3] but to that town, as the townsmen complained shortly afterwards, 'they still have their repair, three or four days in the week, because they own a house in the town'. The fact that they repaired to Bridgnorth, the townsmen continued, 'caused more damage to the town and countryside than their residence did'.[4] This complaint is cited to emphasize the distinction between permanent residence (*demure*) and resort for purposes of business (*repeyr*). Perhaps a caveat should be added that the political climate had been deteriorating throughout the thirteenth century, so far as the Jews were concerned, and the conditions at Bridgnorth under Edward I are not likely to have been paralleled a century earlier, when kings were not remarkable for their complaisance towards townsmen.[5] Even if townsmen had been hostile in the twelfth century—and there are too many instances of this hostility to lead us to suppose that Jews were universally welcome—a well-behaved Jew could reasonably count upon the support of the king

[1] Liceat eis ire quocumque voluerint cum omnibus catallis eorum (*Foedera*, i. 51). Et ubicumque Iudei fuerint liceat eis ire quocumque voluerint cum omnibus catallis eorum (*Rot. Chart.*, p. 93).

[2] Rigg, *Select Pleas*, p. 85; Stokes, *Studies in Anglo-Jewish History*, pp. 188–92. At least one Jew, Josce the son of Samuelot, retained his property in Cambridge until 1290. After the Expulsion the houses formerly owned by Jews in Cambridge realized £16. 13s. 4d. Similarly at Sudbury houses in former Jewish ownership realized £5. 0s. 0d. These details are from Hugh of Kendal's account, as to which see above, p. 19, n. 3.           [3] *Cal. Close Rolls, 1272–1279*, p. 130.

[4] P.R.O. Ancient Petitions, no. 10901: ke uncore ount lour repeyr chescune semayne trois jours ou quatre, par la reson ke il ount une meson en la vile, dount plus est en damage à la vile ke ne fu de la demure. Apparently the Jewish owner was anxious to sell: see *Cal. Fine Rolls, 1272–1307*, p. 48, which suggests that the petition cannot be later than June 1275.

[5] It was at the instance of the townsmen that Jews were prohibited from dwelling in Newcastle in 1234 (*Close Rolls, 1231–1234*, p. 466) and in Derby in 1261 (*Cal. Patent Rolls, 1258–1266*, p. 153). At Romsey, in 1266, it was the nuns who obtained the right to license Jewish residents (*ibid.*, p. 613). Nothing of this kind is known before the reign of Henry III.

and the king's representatives. It has already been remarked, however, that only in the neighbourhood of a royal castle could a Jewish community be established in relative safety, and this was doubtless the principal factor in determining the centres of permanent residence. The experience of the Jewish community at Norwich under Stephen must have taught every Jew in England how necessary royal protection was, how easily religious passions could be aroused and how maliciously unscrupulous might the clergy be, even the highest among them. For it was the bishop of Norwich, William Turbe, who was most active in prosecuting the charge of ritual murder against the Jews of his city, up to the supreme tribunal, the court held before the king himself.[1] The massacres of 1190 came to enforce the lesson of Norwich and to teach the imperative necessity of a place of refuge from mob violence.

[1] Jessopp and James, *St. William of Norwich*, pp. 92–3, 103–10.

# II

# JEWS AND GENTILES

THE FIRST NEWS WE have of the Jewish communities in Rouen and London is news of violence and disputes. Under Robert the Pious, the Jews in several French cities were given the alternative of forcible conversion or exile. The year was apparently 1010.[1] Of the events at Rouen, we have no details, except of the death of a number of unfortunates who refused baptism, including a prominent rabbi. At Limoges, for which city we have more details, there was a period of grace, during which Christian doctors sought to persuade the Jews to renounce their religion. Most of those unwilling to accept baptism fled with their families to other cities, but a few sought refuge in suicide. It may be that, in the ruder province of Normandy, more brutal treatment was meted out to the Jews, but the tempest passed and the community was restored, to suffer massacre again in 1096 at the hands of crusaders who turned their swords upon the infidels near at hand before setting out for the East.[2] Medieval chroniclers are apt to give the impression of more widespread violence and killing than actually occurred, and the Jewish community at Rouen was certainly not destroyed. Eadmer, a monk of Canterbury, writing less than a generation later, gives another picture of Rouen under William Rufus. Eadmer's story concerns a young convert to Christianity whose father sought to reclaim him. The youth

---

[1] The Hebrew account of the happenings at Rouen, of which a summary is given in H. Gross, *Gallia Judaica*, pp. 71–3, should be related to the account of events in Limoges in the Chronicle of Adémar de Chabannes, *s.a.* 1010 (ed. Chavanon, p. 169). The Hebrew account alleges that the movement against the Jews was instigated by the French king.

[2] Gilbert de Nogent, *Vita* (ed. Bourgin), p. 118.

refused to abjure and the dispute finally came before the king, who is reproved by the chronicler for favouring the Jews.[1] William of Malmesbury, who was compiling his *Gesta Regum* about 1125, repeats Eadmer's story and adds one of his own, in which he speaks of a disputation between Jews and bishops in London, promoted by the king. It is here that there occurs the well-known anecdote of Rufus's swearing by the Holy Face of Lucca to join their sect, if the Jews prevailed.[2] Needless to say, this is no more than an idle tale. But while neither Eadmer nor William of Malmesbury is a reliable witness to events or conditions in Rouen or London in the eleventh century, they are both good evidence of the hostility with which churchmen of the twelfth century regarded the Jews, a hostility not founded on any personal experience but the fruit of intolerance and prejudice. There were, indeed, exceptions, and the example often cited is that of Gilbert Crispin, the Norman abbot of Westminster, who composed early in the 1090's a 'disputation', founded upon real discussions in which he himself had been involved with a learned Jew, apparently a frequent visitor to England, but not a member of the London community.[3] If, however, the tone of the controversy and of the dedicatory letter to Archbishop Anselm are sweetly reasonable, the opening sentences of the disputation are more revealing of the general attitude of Christians towards Jews. 'If the [Mosaic] law is one that should be observed,' Gilbert's Jew asks, 'why then should you treat those who observe it as though they were dogs, driving them forth and pursuing them everywhere with sticks?'[4] A later dialogue with a similar purpose, dedicated to Alexander, bishop of Lincoln (1123–48), which borrows heavily from Gilbert, significantly omits any question of this kind.[5] If a Jew was fair game for the London rabble under

---

[1] *Historia Novella*, pp. 99–101. This passage was probably written before 1112.

[2] *Gesta Regum*, ii. 371. The text of the first recension is in a footnote.

[3] Gilbert became abbot in the year 1085. The 'disputation' cannot have been written before Anselm became archbishop in 1093. Its latest editor inclines to a date not later than 1096 (Blumenkranz, *ut. supra*, p. 12).

[4] *Disputatio* (ed. Blumenkranz), p. 28.

[5] Migne, *Patrologia Latina*, clxiii. 1045–72.

Rufus, he was no longer so under Henry I. It was from his reign
that the Jews dated their liberties and customs.[1] William II may
have scandalized churchmen by affecting to favour the Jews, but
it was Henry I, of whom no such stories are told, who gave them
his protection.

By 1130, the first year from which we have any real information, the Jewish community of London was settled and prosperous.
They can bear a fine of £2,000.[2] Their moneylending is upon a
large scale. They pay the king for his help in recovering their
debts or, in other words, for permitting an action of debt to be
brought before the barons of the exchequer. One group of Jews
offers six marks of gold for the king's aid against Richard fitz
Gilbert, while Richard for his part offers the king 200 marks,
which gives some indication of the amount at stake.[3] Earl Ranulf
of Chester is another considerable debtor who is giving difficulty,[4]
and so is Osbert of Leicester.[5] Evidently the transactions of the
London Jews are spread widely over the country. There are indications, too, that they have been accommodating the king with
loans, for there are some substantial transfers of money to prominent Jews, which have the appearance of repayments.[6] The
only indication that there was any other occupation than moneylending in the Jewry is the purchase by the king of two silver cups
from a London Jew, by name of Abraham, who may have been
either a trader or a silversmith.[7] But we cannot, of course, argue
from the silence of the records that Jews did not pursue other
occupations than these, and it is almost inconceivable that any
medieval man and *a fortiori* any medieval community, Jewish or
Christian, could live by moneylending alone. Moneylending
and trade went together.

What occupations did the Jews in England follow? Our ignorance of the daily work of any trader or craftsman in the twelfth

---

[1] As shown by Henry II's charter (below, p. 109).
[2] *Pipe Roll 31 Henry I*, p. 149.    [3] *Ibid.*, pp. 53, 148.
[4] *Ibid.*, p. 149.    [5] *Ibid.*, p. 147.
[6] *Ibid.*, p. 149. The entry is defective: the two names that can be recovered
are those of Rubigotsce and Manasser.
[7] *Loc. cit.*

century is no greater in the case of a Jew than of a Christian. Although we are aware, in general, of the occupations then pursued in England, we should find it possible to give an account in any detail of the activities of few men except the highest in Church and State, on the one hand, and those engaged in agriculture on the other. Their lives followed a known pattern. Of the lives of town-dwellers we have to be content with glimpses, hints and inferences. Street names, surnames, incidental references to guilds, tell us something of the working life of the citizens of London. We know a little of the sources that supplied the city markets and a little of the commerce that throve there; but of the career of a single merchant or craftsman we could say hardly anything worth the telling. Since Jews were rarely given occupational names we lack, for the most part, this index to their callings. A few we know, from their descriptions or incidental references, to have been physicians,[1] goldsmiths,[2] soldiers[3] and vintners,[4] even fishmongers[5] and cheesemongers.[6] It is clear that Aaron

[1] *Pipe Roll 3 Richard I*, p. 140 (two named): for later instances see Roth, *History of the Jews in England*, p. 114.

[2] *Rot. Chart.*, p. 62b; *Rot. Litt. Pat.*, pp. 54b, 81b. Elias l'Eveske evidently dealt in jewels as well as gold (*Cal. Liberate Rolls*, iii. 264, 338; iv. 195–6, 466).

[3] *Miles* may sometimes be the equivalent of *Meir*, but not in the case of *Benedictus miles* in *Pipe Roll 3 Richard I*, p. 140: cf. *Benedictus miles* in *Pipe Roll 31 Henry II*, p. 149, and subsequent rolls. Abraham, the cross-bowman, *balistarius*, is found in *Pipe Roll 13 John*, p. 261, and *Rot. Litt. Claus.*, i. 220b: he remained a Jew, though other Jewish crossbowmen became converts (cf. Roth, *op. cit.*, p. 122). John the Jew, a serjeant-at-arms at Bamburgh, is mentioned in 1236 (*Close Rolls, 1234–1237*, p. 313): he may be identical with John the Jew, employed as a messenger in 1224 (*Rot. Litt. Claus.*, i. 628a, 653b) and described as the sumpter-man of the king's chapel in 1229 (*Cal. Lib. Rolls, 1226–1244*, p. 144). This John was presumably a convert, like the convert knighted by Henry III, who was accused of dealing in clipped silver in 1278 (*Foedera*, I. ii. 551). But these converts had presumably taken to the profession of arms before conversion. Benedict *le Chivaler* may bear only a nickname (*Cal. Plea Rolls*, ii. 280).

[4] *Pipe Roll 23 Henry II*, p. 176; *7 Richard I*, p. 76; *5 John*, p. 193.

[5] Abraham *le Peysoner* (*Cal. Plea Rolls*, i. 168).

[6] Isaac and Deulecresse *furmager* (Jewish Hist. Soc., *Miscellanies*, i. lxix): see below, p. 152. Not all apparently occupational names are easy to interpret. Mention may, however, be made of the surname *le Ronmangur*, which seems to mean ironmonger (P.R.O., E. 101/249/16 (2 Edward I); *Cal. Plea Rolls*, ii. 50; iii. 288, 289).

of Lincoln dealt extensively in corn[1] and he was certainly not singular in this.[2] It is probable that, like his Christian counterpart, William Cade, he may have been a wool merchant as well as a corn merchant.[3] Pawnbroking, probably the most extensively practised of Jewish trades, necessarily implies skill in the repair and furbishing of jewellery and plate, clothing and armour, to make them readily saleable.[4] But when we have run through this short list of occupations, we are at a loss to suggest additions. From craft guilds, which were at once religious and monopolistic, the Jews were automatically excluded, with the consequence that they would find it difficult to make a career in the majority of urban trades. The undoubted fact that a Jew might be a goldsmith or a vintner makes it difficult to say that any occupation was absolutely closed, though we are puzzled to know in what relation a Jewish goldsmith or a Jewish vintner stood in regard to his Christian fellows. That there was a *modus vivendi* is obvious, which might one day extend so far as the admission of a Jew to a merchant guild, though this was certainly exceptional.[5] And whatever occasions of ill-feeling there may have been between Christian and Jew, there seems to be no suggestion at all that one of them might be trade rivalry. To pursue their callings, even moneylending, with success, the Jews must necessarily have cultivated good relations with the community in which they were a small and unassimilable minority. And they were dependent upon Christian masons and carpenters for the houses in which they dwelt, upon Christian markets for the food they ate and the clothes they wore. At the beginning of Henry III's reign there are arresting references to one *Ricardus Iudeus* or *le Giu*, who was

[1] Below, p. 78.

[2] Asser is found dealing in corn in *Pipe Roll 25 Henry II*, p. 49.

[3] Below, p. 78.

[4] Cf. Wharton, *Anglia Sacra*, i. 625, 645-6 (cross); *Pipe Roll 28 Henry II*, p. 14 (altar-vessel); *32 Henry II*, p. 78 (armour). For pawnbroking generally see below, pp. 76-7.

[5] The only case known is that of Benedict, the son of Abraham, at Winchester in 1268, for whom see the paper by Michael Adler in Jewish Hist. Soc., *Miscellanies*, iv. 1-8.

reeve of Worcester.[1] His forename, however, suggests that he had been baptized and his surname that he was a convert, who was thus distinguished from other Richards. We cannot conclude that it was possible for a Jew, who remained faithful to his religion, to attain high civic office.[2]

Jews did not live their lives apart. Yet they lived uneasily, for there is a reverse side to the tapestry. They were in England because they were useful to the king, who protected them, and there is ample evidence that they were in need of protection, for there were always Christians willing to raise voice and hand against a Jew. To the Church the unconverted Jew was a standing reproach and there were never wanting zealots for the conversion of the Jews. The treatises that provided the arguments theologians thought convincing were, of course, written for the consumption of Christian readers. When cast in the form of a dialogue, they necessarily fail to do justice to the Jewish interlocutor, who must be shown to have the worst of the argument. To the modern mind it is difficult to understand how conversions could have been effected by biblical citations taken out of their context and theological commonplaces. There were, however, other and more compelling reasons to persuade those who were not strong in the Jewish faith to throw in their lot with the Gentile community around them, from which they differed by so little, and the marvel is perhaps, not that there seems to have been a steady flow of converts to Christianity, but that the Jewish community stood steadfast as a whole through good times and ill. Converted Jews were more numerous in the twelfth century than has sometimes been allowed. Doubtless the numbers of converts were never so large as seriously to diminish the Jewish community, but it is misleading to say, as Michael Adler said, that 'from the date of

[1] K.R. Memoranda Roll 2 Henry III (P.R.O.E. 159/2, mm. 6d. 15, 17, 17d); L.T.R. Memoranda Roll (E. 368/1, m. 3). On m. 2d of the latter roll his forename is given as *Radulfus*, but this must be an error.

[2] This had been forbidden by a decree of the Lateran Council of 1215, elaborating a canon of the Council of Toledo (589). The prohibition was incorporated in the body of canon law, but was not binding, in practice, on secular princes: see below, p. 181.

the coming of the Jew to England with the Norman Conquest until the year 1232, the name of only one Jewess is recorded who ... joined the Church' and that 'seven men in this period are known to have accepted baptism'.[1] These numbers are less than those that can easily be made up for the last twenty years of the twelfth century, for incidental references to converts are not uncommon in the public records and, in any event, these references cannot conceivably cover more than a fraction of the cases of conversion. Isabelle, a converted Jewess, is mentioned in the pipe roll of 1180 only because Jeremiah, Jew of Dunstable, was fined a mark for imprisoning her.[2] In the pipe rolls of 1188 and 1189 the names of three converts appear, Nicholas, John and Peter. They do so because for eighteen months the king was paying them alms through the sheriffs of Essex and Surrey.[3] But such entries are altogether unusual, and there is no reason to suppose that, when the king did assist converts, he arranged for payment by the sheriff rather than by the exchequer or by his own almoner. We must confess our ignorance in the absence of *liberate* rolls and wardrobe accounts of the twelfth century. What we are not entitled to do is to deduce that these three men were the only converts at this period to receive alms. Nor can we be certain whether or not the Nicholas of 1188–9 is identical with the convert of the same name who is mentioned in the pipe roll of 1180 as owing half a mark for a default.[4] This fine, it may be remarked, he managed to pay by 1182, so that he was evidently not without some means.[5] Continuing these gleanings of casual entries in the records, we come to Richard and Henry, two other converts, who appear in the pipe roll of 1191 in the invidious role of informers against Deulesalt of London:[6] Jewry doubtless was well

---

[1] *Jews of Medieval England*, p. 32. Further details, indicating higher numbers, are given at pp. 279–81.

[2] *Pipe Roll 26 Henry II*, p. 129. I assume the identity of the Jeremiah of this entry, under Buckinghamshire and Bedfordshire, with the Jeremiah of Dunstable of *Pipe Roll 34 Henry II*, p. 127.

[3] *Ibid.*, pp. 23, 30; *Pipe Roll 1 Richard I*, pp. 20, 216.

[4] *Pipe Roll 26 Henry II*, p. 147.

[5] *Pipe Roll 28 Henry II*, p. 152.        [6] *Pipe Roll 3 Richard I*, p. 208.

rid of them. Thomas, a convert of Canterbury, is assessed at one mark for tallage in 1198.[1] John, a convert of Gloucester, is, in the following year, associated with a number of Jews in an appeal against Elias the Jew.[2] In 1199, too, we hear of Constance the convert, who had married Gerin the tailor and who expected to obtain, on preferential terms, her father's property in York, which had escheated to the Crown.[3] Again, Emma the convert, widow of Reiner son of Viel (whom she presumably married in the twelfth century) had a dispute regarding her dower with Chera, the wife of Isaac the chirographer (a prominent Jew under King John), and Chera's son by a former marriage.[4] Another convert, who is known to us by the initial of his baptismal name R, but which presumably stands for Robert, has left an interesting story behind him. He was converted at the instance of a nobleman, who seems to have been Robert *ès Blanchemains*, earl of Leicester, on whose death (in 1190) he was left without resources. At last, in desperation, he went to Rome and besought the aid of the pope, Innocent III, who gave him a letter instructing the abbot and convent of Leicester to provide him with food and clothing 'out of reverence for him through whom he received the light of truth'; for the earl was the founder's son and his wife built the great choir of the abbey. The letter suggests that there were many converts who, because of the poverty into which they had sunk, repented of their action; but this language doubtless reflects Robert's own exaggerations, for he, understandably enough, had every wish to impress the pope with the importance of the cause of which he was the representative.[5] This evidence is from the late twelfth century. From the late eleventh or the early twelfth

[1] *Pipe Roll 10 Richard I*, p. 208.

[2] *Pipe Roll 1 John*, p. 32.

[3] *Memoranda Roll 1 John*, p. 24. The entry is defective, but the fact that the property was Constance's father's seems to be implied by the statement that 'terra illa nunc remanet hereditaliter eis'.

[4] *Curia Regis Rolls*, vii. 70-1, 245. The property in dispute consisted of six messuages in Winchester, which Emma claimed as dower by her husband's gift.

[5] Migne, *Patrologia Latina*, ccxiv. 792-3. The date is 5 November 1199. This letter gives no indication of the length of R's stay in Rome. He may have petitioned, without success, Innocent's predecessor, Celestine III (1191-8).

century we hear of a monk at Westminster who was a convert[1] and of a married convert who had been baptized Robert and who was dependent upon charity for his subsistence.[2] Late in Stephen's reign, or early in Henry II's, a monk of Norwich was a convert and a traducer of the Jews.[3] The evidence before the reign of Henry II is scanty, but its paucity is more likely to be due to the nature of the sources than to the rarity of conversions.

It is desirable to add that two supposed items of evidence which have been pressed into service will not stand scrutiny. The often-repeated statement, apparently originating with Tovey, that a hospital was built at Bermondsey Priory in 1213 for converts from the Jewish faith, is a patent mistake, due to the double meaning of *conversi* in medieval Latin.[4] Here the word means lay brethren, and the building was for them and the monastic children (*pueri*).[5] The statement by the monastic chronicler is of purely domestic interest: if the prior had really constructed a *Domus Conversorum* and had provided for the maintenance of converts, we may be sure that the chronicler would have enlarged upon this remarkable fact and that it would not have gone unnoticed by contemporary writers. The other supposed piece of evidence is more respectable, being at least medieval, though long after the event. There is a reference in the *Little Red Book of Bristol* to the foundation, early in Henry II's reign, of a school for teaching Jewish and other children.[6] When we remember that medieval schools were under ecclesiastical authority, it is difficult to believe, much as we might

[1] Gilbert Crispin, *Disputatio* (ed. Blumenkranz), p. 28.

[2] S. Anselmi *Opera Omnia* (ed. Schmitt), v. 323–4 (epp. 380, 381). These letters suggest that the way of a convert was hard.

[3] Jessopp and James, *St. William of Norwich*, p. 93.

[4] Tovey, *Anglia Judaica*, p. 94; Adler, *Jews of Medieval England*, p. 281; Roth, *History of the Jews in England*, p. 43 (corrected, p. 290); Moorman, *Church Life in England in the Thirteenth Century*, p. 359.

[5] The original entry runs: Hoc anno Ricardus prior huius monasterii cum consensu conventus aedificavit in fundo celerarii quandam domum contra murum domus predictae, vocatam eleemosynaria siue hospitale conversorum ac puerorum, in honore sancti Thomae martyris . . . Et est dicta eleemosynaria exempta ab omni iurisdictione episcopali, sicut et monasterium (*Annales Monastici*, iii. 452).

[6] F. B. Bickley, *Little Red Book of Bristol*, p. 208: 'scholae pro Iudeis et aliis parvulis informandis' (cited by Adler, *op. cit.*, pp. 183, 281).

like to do so, that Jews and Christians sat side by side in a Bristol school. In any case, no word is said of converts or conversion: indeed, if that were the intention, we may be sure that Jewish parents would keep their children well out of harm's way. *Scola Iudeorum* is, however, medieval Latin for synagogue, and it seems necessary to suppose that a reference to a synagogue at Bristol has been misunderstood, and embroidered, by a later writer. But when we have dismissed the story of the Bristol school, as founded upon a misunderstanding, and the story of the Bermondsey *Domus Conversorum* as purely imaginary, we have not weakened the solid evidence for a steady, if tenuous, stream of converts from Judaism to Christianity in the twelfth and thirteenth centuries. Yet the way of the convert might be hard. If he had any fortune he was likely to sacrifice the greater part of it, for a Jew who left the community was liable to surrender all his wealth to the king, and in the opinion of some this was the principal obstacle to widespread conversions.[1] It was, then, only those with nothing to lose or with slender means who were likely to seek baptism, such Jews indeed as were liable to be expelled from the country because they were unprofitable to the king.

Between the millstones of the *sacerdotium* and the *regnum*, it might be thought the Jews would be ground to nothing. But persecution and oppression were intermittent; and the Jews played so necessary a part in the economy of so much of the twelfth and thirteenth centuries that they enjoyed the protection of the king and the tolerance, if not the affection, of the rulers in Church and State. The place of the Jew, or at least the wealthy Jew, may perhaps be illustrated by the life-story of Jurnet of Norwich.

[1] This is stated in a sermon of about 1260, wrongly attributed to Thomas Brinton, bishop of Rochester 1373–89 (*Speculum*, xxx. 268–9). This opinion may have been inspired by the conversion of Elias l'Eveske and two other Jews in 1259 (Matthew Paris, *Chronica Majora*, v. 730). Elias was a man of wealth who had been archpriest: on conversion he appears to have lost all his landed property (Stokes, *Studies in Anglo-Jewish History*, pp. 30–3). It is impossible that he should be Elias l'Eveske of the Expulsion, for on baptism he would assume a Christian name. A pertinent example is 'Isaac l'Eveske filius Henrici conuersi' in the tallage roll of 1272 (P.R.O., E. 401/1567). Henry, the baptismal name presumably bestowed by the king, may well conceal the Jewish name of Elias.

There is a special reason for selecting Jurnet as a representative example, because he has become the subject of a legend that needs to be dispersed if we are to understand the relations of Jew and Gentile in medieval England.

In 1745 there appeared the second volume of the Reverend Francis Blomefield's monumental *Essay towards a Topographical History of the County of Norfolk*.[1] This volume contains some account of the parish of Earlham, in the course of which a very remarkable story is briefly told. It concerns Ralf de Hauville and runs as follows:

In 1199 this Ralf, being then a knight, purchased of Humfry, his brother, all his inheritance in Erlham for 100s. paid to Humfry for his pilgrimage to Jerusalem and a settlement made on Miryld, daughter of Humfry, who escheated her lands by marrying Jurnet the Jew.[2]

As a rule, Blomefield follows the excellent practice of giving references to the authorities on which he relies, but in this instance he does not do so, though the documents on which the story is based can be identified. No one, however, seems to have investigated the story until it attracted the attention of Joseph Jacobs, who thought that various records, which he translated in his *Jews of Angevin England*, not only lent support to Blomefield's account but enabled him to amplify it. The story as it was presented by Jacobs has to be pieced together from several scattered paragraphs,[3] and it would be unfair to suggest what shape it would have finally assumed had he set himself to give it literary form. This he did not do; but Jacobs' materials were taken up and refashioned by Michael Adler, who, in so doing, added some touches of his own. In his careful and instructive book on the

---

[1] Some copies have an additional title page bearing the date 1739, but there seems no doubt that the volume was published at Norwich in 1745.

[2] *Op. cit.*, p. 853. The passage will be found at p. 510 of volume iv of the new edition, published in 1806.

[3] *Jews of Angevin England*, pp. 64, 84, 90, 165, 216.

*Jews of Medieval England*,[1] the legend of Jurnet of Norwich is found in its fully developed form. These are Adler's words:

> Few marriages created such a stir in English Jewry as when Jurnet (Jacob), the son of Moses of Norwich, about the year 1170 married Miryld (Muriel), the heiress of Sir Humphrey de Herlham, and she became a Jewess. This is the only example known in medieval records of the admission of a Christian woman into the faith. As a result of her apostasy, Muriel was deprived of all her lands, and her daring husband was mulcted in the sum of 6,000 marks (equal in modern value to £120,000). Their romantic marriage reduced them to utter poverty, and they left England for a few years. As Jurnet had been unable to meet the extortionate royal demands, his marriage fine was levied upon the whole Jewish community, which must have been none too happy at the entry of the high-born convert into the fold of Israel. Later on, the circumstances of the family improved, and their son Isaac and their daughter Margaret both became well-known financiers.

This account has been accepted, at least in its main outlines—the marriage of Christian lady and Jew, her conversion to Judaism and forfeiture of her lands—and, if unchallenged, might become established as veritable history.[2] And yet it should be challenged. For when it is asserted that in the twelfth century a Christian lady married a Jew, we should, before we give assent, require to know more of the circumstances of the marriage and to put questions that those who have repeated or developed the story told by Blomefield seem not to have put to themselves or, at any rate, have not answered. If the marriage had indeed taken place as related, it might well affect our whole conception of the relations between Jews and Christians in England at this period.

[1] *Jews of Medieval England*, pp. 23–4. Mr. V. D. Lipman informs me that Jurnet's Hebrew name was Eliab: consequently he cannot be identified with Jacob son of Moses.

[2] Cf. Stokes, *Studies*, p. 70, and Roth, *History of the Jews in England*, p. 10 (but see p. 289).

A valid marriage between a Christian and a Jew, who both adhered to the faith of their fathers, seems to be out of the question in the Middle Ages in any Western land. Such a marriage would be abhorrent both to the Church[1] and to the Jewish community. There was perhaps a stronger reason. A text in Justinian's Code forbade such marriages,[2] and certainly in the later twelfth century this text would be known to the many students of Roman law in England and would be regarded as authoritative both by canonists and common lawyers. No doubt an unmarried Jew who was converted to Christianity might contract a Christian marriage; but such a marriage has not been suggested in the case of Jurnet. There might conceivably be a third possibility: a Christian might contract a Jewish marriage if she or he became a proselyte, and those who have developed Blomefield's story have indeed implied that Muriel was converted to Judaism. But while a marriage between a Jew and a proselyte might be recognized by Jewish law or custom, this was no more than a theoretical possibility in twelfth-century England. Muriel's conversion rests upon no documentary evidence. Tolerant as twelfth-century English society was in some respects, no English Christian could embrace Judaism without running grave risk, not only of losing property, but of losing life as well. It was held to be good law in the thirteenth century that an apostate should, on conviction, be burnt,[3] and there is one well authenticated case in 1222, that of the deacon who had fallen in love with a Jewess, had been degraded in the council of Oxford and had been put to death by the king's bailiffs.[4] True, this was after the fourth Lateran Council of 1215, which had incidentally prescribed a distinctive garb for Jews as a precaution against irregular intercourse with Christian women;[5] but there is no reason to suppose that an apostate would

---

[1] Decretum, cc. 10–17 c. xxviii, qu. 1.

[2] Code, 1.9.7: 'Ne quis Christianam mulierem Iudaeus accipiat neque Iudaeae Christianus coniugium sortiatur . . .'

[3] Bracton, fo. 123*b*–124. Bracton, however, seems to know no other precedent than the Oxford case of 1222.

[4] The evidence is reviewed by Maitland. 'The Deacon and the Jewess', in *Canon Law in the Church of England*, pp. 158–79.      [5] Below, p. 180.

have been in any better case before than after 1215.[1] Seemingly we hear nothing of apostasy in England at an earlier date because apostasizing Christians had been unknown.

And yet Jurnet's wife was undoubtedly named Muriel. Can it be, though no one has ever suggested it, that Jurnet embraced Christianity? The point of the story would be badly spoilt if that were the case, but we can be quite sure that to his life's end Jurnet remained true to the faith of his fathers. The argument is brief but conclusive. It is evident that on conversion a Jew or Jewess would receive a Christian name, conferred at baptism, and would be absorbed and, normally, become indistinguishable within the Christian community. If a Jew were married and his wife were converted with him, the marriage would subsist, even though it had been contracted within the degrees of consanguinity or affinity condemned by the Church.[2] Single women would normally marry Christians and men would normally find some means of gaining a livelihood without resort to charity. There are facts which suggest that converts did not necessarily break all association with the Jewish community,[3] but they are not in the least

[1] Witness the fate of the Albigensian, burnt in London in 1210 or 1211 (*Liber de Antiquis Legibus*, p. 3). There was an earlier case, in 1166, of some visiting heretics who, having been condemned by an ecclesiastical tribunal, were beaten, branded and exiled by the lay power, a punishment which brought death to some of them: for the authorities see Maitland, *op. cit.*, p. 161.

[2] The first authoritative statement appears to have been made by Clement III in a decretal included in the *Compilatio Secunda* (Jaffé, no. 16595). This allowed some exceptions, but a stricter view was taken by Innocent III, who held such marriages to be binding. Innocent's decretal was embodied in the *Compilatio Tertia* (1210: earlier than the *Compilatio Secunda*, which was designed to supplement it) and then in the Gregorian Decretals, x. 4.14.4. Two cases of the thirteenth century show that Innocent III's ruling was followed and illustrate the problems arising. The first case is in 1234: a Jewess Chera, widow of Augustine the convert, sued for her dower and was denied 'quia vero contra iusticiam est quod ipsa Chera dotem petat vel habeat de tenemento quod fuit ipsius viri sui, ex quo in conversione sua noluit ei adherere et cum eo converti' (*Close Rolls, 1231–1234*, p. 555). The second case is in 1299, long after the Expulsion. Henry of Winchester had married a wife 'sub lege Iudaica' and both had been converted. He had died, and the jurors returned that his son Thomas was his heir 'si matrimonium precontractum inter ipsos antequam conversi essent rite stare posset' (*Calendarium Genealogicum*, ii. 563; *Cal. Inq. Post Mortem*, iii. 391, no. 506).

[3] Above, pp. 29–30.

likely to have engaged in moneylending. Even if they had money
to lend—which few converts are likely to have had—it is improbable that they would have invited ecclesiastical censure by
overt usury. When therefore we find that Jurnet still passed by
that name at his death and that his son succeeded him in his
business of moneylending, we may be sure that he had never
been a convert to Christianity. With that conclusion, the story
of Jurnet and Muriel, as told by Blomefield and elaborated by
more modern writers, must be finally rejected.

But there is a story, a true story, to put in its place, one that is
worth telling, for Jurnet had in some ways a remarkable career
which illustrates the good and evil fortune that might befall a
wealthy Jew. To begin with, let us look at the documents upon
which Blomefield's story was based. They were two: a fine dated
18 March 1197 and an entry in an assize roll of the tenth year of
John. The fine records an agreement between Ralf and Humfrey
of Earlham. Humfrey recognized Ralf's right, as lawful heir, to
an estate of land in Earlham of a carucate in extent, on condition
that Humfrey should retain Earlham mill for his lifetime and that
Humfrey's daughter, Mirulda, should hold twenty acres of land of
Ralf at a yearly rent of sixpence. Besides this, Ralf gave Humfrey
a hundred shillings towards his expenses as a crusader. Clearly
this was a family settlement, arising out of the decision of one of
two brothers or cousins to go on a crusade, from which his return
was problematical. Clearly also the crusader's daughter, Mirulda,
was, at the date of the fine, unmarried, for the grant of the twenty
acres is to her and her heirs and there is no mention of a husband.[1]
Whether Mirulda should be called high-born is questionable,
though she was of respectable parentage; but certainly in this
document there is no suggestion that she was a convert to Judaism.
Nor is there any such suggestion in the assize roll which gives the
continuation of the story. The year being the tenth of John's
reign, the date of the action must lie between Ascension Day
(15 May) 1208 and Ascension Day (6 May) 1209. If Humfrey had
ever gone to the crusades, which is perhaps doubtful, he had by

[1] *Feet of Fines 7 and 8 Richard I* (Pipe Roll Soc.), pp. 75–6.

now returned. By this time the mill that had been reserved to him under the fine of 1197 had passed into the possession of Ralf of Earlham and another Ralf, the son of Alfred, who held it at a rent from Isaac, Jurnet's son. Humfrey brought an action against the two Ralfs, alleging that they had unlawfully disseised him. The defendants vouched Isaac to warranty. Isaac was not present in court but was represented by his bailiff, who claimed that he had entry into the mill by the king's order and by the sheriff. This means that the mill had been mortgaged to him, that the payments had not been kept up and that by judgement of the court (presumably of the Justices of the Jews) he had been put in seisin of the mill by the sheriff. He had, in turn, let it to the two Ralfs. Further, he produced a bond setting out that Humfrey had mortgaged all his land in Earlham to Jurnet, the Jew, his wife Muriel and his son Isaac, and had engaged himself to pay the principal, namely five shillings, and a farthing a week interest. Since interest was to run from the date when John of Coutances was consecrated bishop of Worcester,[1] that is from 20 October 1196,[2] we know the approximate date of the transaction and can deduce that this also arose from Humfrey's decision to take the cross. Humfrey alleged that he had paid interest from 1196 to the date of the action, but this statement is difficult to reconcile with his departure for the crusades, since, as a crusader, he would presumably have been protected from demands for interest.[3] Moreover, it is hardly possible that Isaac could have obtained possession of the land, although Humfrey admitted that he had not paid the principal, if the debtor had been an absent crusader.

[1] The record gives 'Walterus de Custance' as the name of the bishop: but Walter was never bishop of Worcester and John is evidently meant.

[2] R. de Diceto, *Opera Historica*, ii. 146; Gervase of Canterbury, *Opera*, i. 543.

[3] The rule, from 1188 onwards, was that 'debitum post susceptionem crucis, quamdiu debitor erit in peregrinatione, non usuret' (*Gesta Henrici*, ii. 32; R. de Hovedene, *Chronica*, ii. 337; Gervase of Canterbury, *Opera*, i. 410). The parallel ordinance of Philip Augustus reads, on this point: 'Usura autem non currit super aliquem, a die qua ipse crucem assumpsit, de debitis prius contractis' (*Actes de Philippe Auguste* (ed. Delaborde), i. 277). Innocent III reinforced this provision in a circular letter of 15 August 1198 (Hovedene, *Chronica*, iv. 70-5; Potthast no. 347).

Since Humfrey withdrew from the action, it is to be feared that he was not a reliable witness.[1] The record is of some interest as an illustration of the mortgaging of land to Jewish moneylenders, but its chief interest lies in the mention of Jurnet, his wife Muriel and Isaac his son. There are no grounds for identifying this Muriel with Humfrey's daughter Mirulda, and indeed it is difficult to imagine how anyone could leap to the conclusion that the unmarried Mirulda of 1197 could be the same person as the married Muriel of 1196 with a grown-up son.

The mortgaging of Earlham mill was but a trifling incident in Jurnet's life, for his dealings were many and on a grand scale. Jurnet first appears in the records in 1169. Evidently he was already making loans to Henry II, for he received 50 marks which the burgesses of Norwich paid on the king's behalf.[2] It was merely a question of administrative convenience whether a payment was made in this fashion instead of from the king's treasury or his chamber, and we cannot measure the extent of Jurnet's transactions by such entries as this on the pipe rolls. Jurnet received, for example, a like sum from the same source in 1174,[3] but although we have no information regarding other receipts in the intermediate years we have no reason to suppose that these two entries are the measures of his dealings with the Crown, which may well have been continuous over many years. Such notices are not systematic and it is by little more than accident that we learn anything of his financial transactions. It is purely by the accident that the Honour of Richmond was in the king's hand that we learn in 1175 that Jurnet had had dealings with Bertha, countess of Britanny,[4] who had died before August 1167.[5]

It was in 1175 that Jurnet and another prominent Jew, Isaac, the son of Rabbi Josce, agreed to pay four marks of gold to the

[1] P.R.O. Assize Roll no. 558, m. 3. The abstract in *Abbreviatio Placitorum*, p. 64a, is inadequate.

[2] *Pipe Roll 15 Henry II*, p. 101.

[3] *Pipe Roll 20 Henry II*, p. 47.

[4] *Pipe Roll 21 Henry II*, p. 3. A debt of £31. 17s. 4d. owing by the Countess is discharged: this sum is presumably the final balance.

[5] C. T. Clay, *Early Yorkshire Charters*, iv. 91, 110.

king for the privilege of entering into partnership.[1] Half of this
sum (the equivalent of 40 marks in silver) was paid, when misfortune overtook Jurnet, and the proposal, if it did not fall through,
was delayed for a good many years.[2] Jurnet's misfortunes arose
from another partnership, formed with his brother Benedict and
two others, Le Brun of London and Josce Quatrebuches. Perhaps
*consortium* is a better word than partnership to apply to this
association. Its purpose was to provide the king with loans, but in
1177 the *consortium* came to grief and was succeeded by another,
also of four members.[3] The members of the first group had to
purchase the king's pardon at the price of 6,000 marks, of which
Jurnet's share was 2,000 marks as compared with Le Brun's 3,000:
the other two partners were evidently minor figures.[4] By 1181
Jurnet had paid off the balance of his fine,[5] but in 1184 he was
again heavily amerced, in no less a sum than 6,000 marks.[6] This
is the supposed penalty for his marriage with a Christian. As we
have seen, the penalty did not arise from any such delict, and it
may well be connected with some financial dealings with the
Crown, though there can be no certainty of this. There is this
similarity with the earlier fine of 6,000 marks, imposed upon the
*consortium* of which Jurnet had been a member, that a large part
was charged to the English Jewry as a community. On this
occasion, however, we are specifically told that Jurnet's bonds
were transferred to the Jewry,[7] and it is fair to deduce that on both
occasions the fastening of responsibility upon the whole Jewish

---

[1] *Pipe Roll 21 Henry II*, p. 20: 'ut rex concedat societatem inter eos de catallis suis'.

[2] The payment is in *Pipe Roll 23 Henry II*, p. 200. The balance charged against Isaac appears in *Pipe Roll 29 Henry II*, p. 162, with the note: 'Sed nondum potuit eam [societatem] habere'. In *Pipe Roll 30 Henry II*, p. 141, the debt is discharged.

[3] For these *consortia*, see below, pp. 62–3.

[4] *Pipe Roll 23 Henry II*, p. 201.

[5] *Pipe Roll 27 Henry II*, p. 160. The pipe roll shows a small debt of £26. 12s. 3d.: this is never discharged in Jurnet's lifetime and in 1199 is transferred to Benedict of Talmont's account (*Memoranda Roll 1 John*, p. 69). It does not necessarily follow that this sum had not been paid, but the exchequer was not satisfied that this was so.

[6] *Pipe Roll 30 Henry II*, p. 9.     [7] *Pipe Roll 33 Henry II*, p. 44.

community was no more than a method of realizing the debtor's assets.[1] For at this period there was no Exchequer of the Jews and no ready means at the disposal of the Crown for turning bonds into cash. Jurnet himself paid direct no more than sixty-eight marks[2] and then apparently removed to the Continent. His departure, however, was but temporary and in 1186 he agreed to pay 2,000 marks to be allowed to reside in England with the king's good will.[3] So far as the pipe rolls record, Jurnet paid only 200 marks of this fine,[4] but the balance may quite well have been paid to the king elsewhere than at the exchequer. In 1194 he paid to Queen Eleanor 40 marks in respect of queen's gold still owing to her from the reign of Henry II, and this alone represents a payment to the king of 400 marks in the way of fines.[5] That his financial status was virtually unaffected by the great sum he had to pay to the Crown is shown by his contributions to tallages after his return to England. His contribution to the Guildford tallage —imposed at Christmas 1186, not very long, perhaps only a few months, after his return—was assessed at 9,000 marks, and though he managed to get this assessment reduced, it still stood at £1221.[6] On the occasion of the Northampton *promissum* of 5,000 marks, imposed on the Jewish community in 1194, he paid, in two sums, 82 marks, but he seems to have passed on to his son a debt of over

[1] There is a parallel in the treatment of Le Brun's fine: see *Pipe Roll 23 Henry II*, p. 201, *24 Henry II*, p. 130, *28 Henry II*, p. 161. The proceeds of the bonds had not, however, been satisfactorily accounted for in 1199, when 5,525½ marks were transferred to Benedict of Talmont's account (*Memoranda Roll 1 John*, p. 70).

[2] 20 marks in *Pipe Roll 30 Henry II*, p. 9, and £32 in *Pipe Roll 31 Henry II*, p. 35. He was personally charged with 473½ marks: the balance of 405½ marks was still recorded as due in 1199, when it was transferred to Benedict of Talmont's account (*Pipe Roll 1 John*, p. 264).

[3] *Pipe Roll 32 Henry II*, p. 69.

[4] The payment was made when the debt was put in charge: the balance was transferred in 1199 to Benedict of Talmont's account (*Pipe Roll 9 Richard I*, p. 228; *10 Richard I*, p. 80; *1 John*, p. 265).

[5] *Pipe Roll 10 John*, p. 15.

[6] *Pipe Roll 9 Richard I*, p. 233. There is no specific statement that the tallage was that of Guildford, but subsequent tallages were of much more moderate amount and an assessment of 9,000 marks on any individual would be entirely out of the question (see below, pp. 162–5).

£400.[1] At the same time he contributed four besants to the special levy that was imposed upon the wealthier Jews while the *promissum* was in collection.[2] He had not now many years to live, for he was dead by Michaelmas 1197,[3] and his son Hakelin (Isaac), who, as we have seen, was associated in business with his father, agreed to pay the king 1,000 marks for the right to recover Jurnet's debts.[4]

These figures will give some idea of the scale on which Jurnet operated. Whether it is useful to attempt to express the sums paid or owed by him in terms of modern currency, by multiplying by thirty, forty or fifty or some other factor, is questionable. No index numbers based on general prices will give reliable standards to help us make comparisons in such matters between the twelfth or any medieval century and the present. If the necessaries of life were cheap and wages very low, at the same time the records are full of large sums owing or paid to the Crown by Jews and Christians alike. It is the actual payment of large sums in cash, sometimes for what seem trivial advantages, that is so noteworthy. To multiply by a factor, which might well represent the rise in value of corn or meat or eggs, seems patently to exaggerate the material sacrifices imposed on the well-to-do when they paid, or agreed to pay, substantial penalties or fines to the Crown. This is a wide problem that is but mentioned here to justify the *caveat* that the large sums in which Jurnet habitually dealt should not be magnified beyond reason. Michael Adler's conversion of 6,000 marks into £120,000 in terms of money in 1939 seems excessive,[5] since it implies that the payment of 6,000 marks by Jurnet is equivalent to the payment of £120,000 by a city man just before the recent war or more than a third of a million today. Evidently a fine of 6,000 marks did not mean ruin to Jurnet, and evidently he had large resources (some perhaps abroad) which the Crown

[1] *Memoranda Roll 1 John*, p. 72.

[2] Jewish Hist. Soc., *Miscellanies*, i. lxvi.

[3] This must be inferred from the entry in *Pipe Roll 9 Richard I*, p. 233, where Jurnet's son asks for an inquiry into his father's indebtedness for tallage.

[4] *Pipe Roll 1 John*, p. 291.

[5] *Jews of Medieval England*, p. 24: this is Adler's constant equivalent.

either could not, or did not desire to, touch. Jurnet's misfortunes still left him a wealthy man, a man of large financial interests and undertakings. And yet the transactions of his which are known to us in actual detail are very small affairs. When Earlham mill was mortgaged to him the amount advanced was no more than five shillings and the interest a farthing a week.[1] In another case the loan was six pounds and the interest a shilling a week.[2] In a third case he accepted 32 marks in settlement from the prior of Hatfield Peverel, who had stood surety for a third party in a bond for £40.[3] The cellarer of St Edmund's Abbey appears to have borrowed a similar sum from Jurnet: the actual amount is uncertain, but with accumulated interest the debt reached a total of £60. After payment of sums amounting to £50, the debt still stood at £26 and the capital had seemingly not been reduced.[4] Jurnet's dealings with the Crown were on a much greater scale, though his personal capital may not have been drawn upon to any large extent. The recorded payments to the *consortium* of which he was a member amounted, for example, to just short of £600 in the financial year 1176–7.[5] This sum is the total of repayments through the sheriffs. What proportion of the total loan or loans was repaid in this way and what proportion direct by the exchequer we have no means of telling. Whatever the extent of the advances, it is unlikely that loans to the king were more than indirectly profitable. Kings get special terms, and lenders expect privileges in return which will put them in a favourable position for reaping profits elsewhere. The scattered and fragmentary facts suggest both that Jurnet's business was very extensive and that he accommodated private clients with much larger sums than any of which we have direct evidence. It may well be that Jurnet and a number of his more prominent contemporaries had businesses falling little short of the scale on which that of Aaron of Lincoln was conducted.[6] Jurnet's own brother, Benedict, made

[1] Above, p. 38.  [2] Below, pp. 257–8.
[3] *Feet of Fines 7 and 8 Richard I*, p. 130.
[4] So I interpret the rather obscure details in *Chronica Jocelini de Brakelonda* (Camden Soc.), pp. 4–5.
[5] Below, p. 62.  [6] Below, pp. 115–16.

loans of £1,200 to St Edmund's Abbey, though this sum included accumulated interest. Isaac, the son of Rabbi Josce (with whom Jurnet had contemplated partnership), held a bond from the same abbey for £400, but whether this included any interest is not known. It is instructive to note also that a prominent London citizen, William fitz Isabelle, held a bond from St Edmund's for £1,040, which would not be likely to include any overt usury.[1] This last item is of particular interest because it demonstrates conclusively that Christians as well as Jews were financiers in a large way and reinforces the caution regarding the scale of ready-money transactions at this period and the danger of exaggerating them beyond measure.

We have seen that in 1196 Jurnet's wife and son were associated with him in business. A bond of 1190 shows that Muriel, but not Isaac, was then associated with him,[2] and the two deeds together indicate, of course, that it was between these dates that Isaac attained manhood. It is a commonplace that Jews associated their wives and sons with them in business. There is evidence that Christian moneylenders did likewise.[3] In both cases the reason presumably was to facilitate the transfer of debts to the widow or heir on the death of the head of the household. This was not, however, the only form of business association, and the question arises whether it was possible to form other business associations —as when Jurnet became a member of the *consortium* of the 1170's or when he proposed to enter into a partnership with Isaac, the son of Rabbi Josce—at the same time as a family firm subsisted. To this question there is no certain answer. In the case of Jurnet, we do not seem able to point to evidence showing that he was at any time a member of more than one partnership or *consortium*.

---

[1] *Chronica Jocelini de Brakelonda*, pp. 2–3. It would seem that Benedict's loans, of which alone we have details, did not require from him advances of more than 40 marks, £100 and a few small sums. But we cannot regard these transactions as typical. [2] Below, p. 257.

[3] A striking example is that of the *Vicomtesse* of Rouen, as to whom see below, p. 51. For cases of Christian widows, fining with the king to have the debts of their husbands, see *Pipe Roll 25 Henry II*, p. 128; *28 Henry II*, pp. 46, 147: the implication is that they will be assisted in recovering the debts in the king's court.

Yet a network of connexions of this sort might conceivably be the explanation of the great accumulations of capital which, in the form of money, precious goods and bonds, a number of Jewish, and perhaps Christian, financiers were able to amass. There is, again, no certain evidence that Jurnet had agents or junior partners, such as those employed by Aaron of Lincoln: the only possible indication is an action by Jurnet against Benjamin of Oxford to recover £30.[1] Like Aaron, however, Jurnet seems to have had more than one place of business. The *consortium* of which he was a member evidently conducted its business from London,[2] but Jurnet certainly had a residence in Norwich. A few years after his return from abroad a fine, to which he was a party, shows him, early in 1189, either acquiring a house in Norwich or settling the terms of purchase,[3] and it was at Norwich that he was taxed in the latter years of his life.[4]

In gathering together the references in the records to any prominent medieval Jew, the inevitable impression is one of harsh and arbitrary exactions. If these exactions are described without reference to the conditions of twelfth-century England, they have the air of unreasonable oppression of a small and unpopular community that lay at the mercy of their royal protector. But it is very difficult to maintain that Jews, at least in the twelfth century, were, on the whole, more liable to arbitrary exactions than Christians. To both the king sold his favours and remitted his displeasure at a very high rate. Not only were all the opportunities offered by feudal custom open to the king, but he also had judicial remedies for which any who desired to use them must pay. The king was

[1] *Pipe Roll 31 Henry II*, p. 40. The fine of six marks seems never to have been paid and the action may have been dropped.

[2] This is indicated by the fact that the fines on all four members are entered under London (*Pipe Roll 23 Henry II*, p. 201). The four marks of gold for the projected partnership with Isaac and all entries connected with them (above, pp 39–40) appear under London. Jurnet's house in London may be the *masagium* which was the subject of an action brought against him in the king's court by William of St. Michael (*Pipe Roll 30 Henry II*, pp. 139–40).

[3] *Feet of Fines Henry II and Richard I*, p. 3. See also the bond with Robert Benne of 1190, printed below, pp. 257–8.

[4] *Pipe Roll 9 Richard I*, p. 233; Jewish Hist. Soc., *Miscellanies*, i. lxvi.

entitled to aids and tallages. If a son was to be given peaceable succession to his father, the king was entitled to a recompense. If a widow, Jew or Christian, was to have the benefit of the debts due to her husband, she must pay the king for them.[1] The king was entitled to make money out of the marriages of heiresses and widows and out of the guardianship of orphans. If his courts were used to collect debts, he was entitled to demand his share. Whatever favour were granted, it was worth its price. In principle there was no discrimination between Jew and Christian. Christians paid, or undertook to pay, enormous sums, as well as Jews. The circumstances made a little difference. The Jew's wealth was in money or bonds and articles of value, the Christian's mainly in land. Only a Jew was likely to be mulcted for imprisoning a convert to Christianity[2] or for making a bill of divorce without the king's leave.[3] And while it is hard to understand why some fines were imposed, we may well reserve judgement before suggesting caprice or malice, which there is little warrant for assuming.

That the Jews were sometimes treated with malice and that the royal power was sometimes ineffectual to protect them cannot be denied. The hatred of the unusual, the unassimilable, that was manifested in Rouen and London in the eleventh century, was never extirpated. If there were no real grounds for complaint, they might be imagined, and the repeated accusations of ritual murder tell their own tale. Of these and of the massacres of 1190 much has been written, which it is unnecessary to recapitulate. These incidents, atrocious as they were, are not inconsistent with a long, quiet history of friendly intercourse and business dealings between Jew and Gentile. There are not wanting glimpses of a kindlier world. More than one story tells of the close relations between Jews and Christians at Canterbury: the Jews even entered into the Christians' quarrels and actually sustained the cause of the Christchurch monks against the monks of Saint Augustine's.[4] A

---

[1] Below, pp. 115–16.    [2] *Pipe Roll 26 Henry II*, p. 129.
[3] *Ibid.*, p. 87.
[4] *Materials for history of Thomas Becket*, ii. 71; Adler, *Jews of Medieval England*, pp. 51–6.

well-known story of Gerald the Welshman tells of a Jew journeying in company with ecclesiastical dignitaries and exchanging jests with them.[1] And there is that distinguished Jewish physician, killed in the massacre at Lynn, who by reason of his skill and modesty was the familiar of Christians and was held in honour among them.[2] One of the most striking pieces of evidence is, however, of later date, when the condition of the Jewry had changed for the worse. It is evident that, in the troublous days of the Barons' War, under Henry III, many Jews confided their valuables to the safe-keeping of their Christian neighbours. We hear, naturally enough, only of those cases where the trust was abused or where the valuables were lost.[3] But it is not likely that things turned out ill in more than a small fraction of cases, and this small fraction is an index of a great fund of good will. The same conclusion is forced upon us by the extent of the business dealings between Jews and Christians, not as between creditor and borrower, but as between willing seller and willing buyer.

The familiarity of the Jews with the monks of some of the greater Benedictine houses scandalized those of the stricter sort, and doubtless it led at times to imprudent borrowings; but the stories told at Bury St Edmunds and St Albans must not be taken as typical.[4] Many religious houses had business dealings with moneylenders that were as profitable to themselves as to the Jews.[5] Exactly the same is true of laymen.[6] Business associations between Jews and Christians go back certainly to the days of Henry II. One instance of no little interest may be recounted. Three plots of land near the present Mansion House, including one that lay between the house of Aaron of Lincoln and Walbrook, were 'developed', as we should say, by Gervase of Cornhill and his son Henry and three brothers Alan, Gervase and Joscelyn, the sons of Peter fitz Alan. Each group had a half-interest in the property and each borrowed money from Aaron on that security.

---

[1] Itinerarium Cambriae in *Opera*, vi. 146.

[2] William of Newburgh, *Historia* (ed. Howlett), i. 310.

[3] *Cal. Plea Rolls*, i. 133, 139–40, 142, 145–6, 191.

[4] *Chronica Jocelini de Brakelonda*, pp. 8, 22; Walsingham, *Gesta Abbatum*, i. 193–4.     [5] Below, pp. 86–100.          [6] Below, pp. 100–3.

On Aaron's death Henry of Cornhill seems still to have owed £100 and the brothers £50.[1] Quite obviously this was not a case of needy landowners borrowing improvidently from a money-lender, for Gervase of Cornhill was a wealthy man and a money-lender himself.[2] It was a business deal financed, at least in large part, by Aaron.

Business and social relations continued in the thirteenth century. There was never a recurrence of the massacres of 1190, but the atmosphere changed. The necessities of King John drove him to severities which seem to have been unknown in the twelfth century. It was not, however, the necessities of Henry III and Edward I that were the ultimate cause of the mounting oppression to which the Jews were subjected, nor was it their failure to satisfy the exacting demands of their royal masters that led to their final banishment. It was, rather, the organized intolerance which, in the thirteenth century, was manifested equally against heretics and infidels. When kings, who had been their defenders, turned against the Jews, there was no place for them in the kingdom. But that the decision to expel them should have come when it did, in 1290, was due not to the unceasing propaganda of the Church and the increasing unpopularity of the Jews among the base and ignorant, but to the financial difficulties in which Edward I had involved himself. Various explanations have been advanced for the Expulsion, but all have been based upon an inadequate understanding of the realities of both the twelfth and the thirteenth centuries. As later chapters will show, though forms might change, the functions performed by Jewish moneylenders under Edward I did not differ in kind from their functions under Henry II, nor did the functions of foreign merchants who, unlike the Jews, acted as international financiers. Any hypothesis that

---

[1] *Pipe Roll 4 Richard I*, p. 306. Gervase had predeceased Aaron, dying in 1185 or thereabouts (below, p. 237). Two of the plots lay in the parishes of St. Olave Upwell, in Old Jewry, and St. Mary 'Conyhope' or, in the spelling of the pipe roll, Cuningchep, a rendering of Cyning-ceáp, i.e. Kingcheap, the site of which is approximately Grocers Hall Court. The pipe roll confuses the names of the two parishes.

[2] Below, p. 59.

seeks to explain the Expulsion on the assumption that the economic organization of England had radically altered falls to the ground, because the premises from which it originates are untenable.[1] Further discussion in this place would be too great a digression; but to leave the matter thus might seem unwarrantable dogmatism. More therefore is said in a later note, which seeks to place the tragedy in its historical setting.

[1] Since it is sometimes cited as authoritative, reference should perhaps be made to a brief paper attempting to show 'that the Jews were expelled from England because from an economic point of view they were no longer performing the function which was their sole *raison d'être* in the circumstances' (P. Elman in *Economic History Review*, 1st Ser., vii. 145–54).

# III

# THE KING'S BORROWINGS

THE ECONOMIC HISTORY OF the twelfth century has yet to be written. It must be pieced together from the fragmentary records that time has spared, nowhere so plentifully (though still sparsely) as in England. But, however defective our knowledge, one thing is certain: by the middle of the century credit and finance had developed upon a wide, an international, scale. The century was not only one of economic progress but one of endless warfare, and to wage war money was needed. In the larger towns of Western Europe there were financiers ready to advance money upon security and apparently ready also to take large risks. These financiers were Christians. To suppose that Jews were the predominant moneylenders of the time is an error. True, they did lend money to landed knights who had taken the cross, but their status limited their activities in a way that the activities of Christians could not be limited. Their dependence upon the sovereign of the land in which they dwelt meant that their lendings were ultimately subject to his control.

When the duke of Normandy decided to contest the crown of England with King Stephen he needed as ample supplies of money as he could command. The Norman Jewry, however, even as contrasted with the English Jewry, was small and certainly not outstandingly rich.[1] Doubtless Duke Henry got what he could from the Jews of Rouen, but there is nothing to suggest that he borrowed money from Jews outside his own dominions. Jews were not international financiers in the twelfth century. The close connexion between the Rouen Jewry and the London Jewry may have facilitated the transfer of credit when Normandy and Eng-

[1] Below, pp. 201- 12.

land were under one ruler, but any transactions of that sort were
very limited compared with those in which Lombard and Flemish
financiers engaged. If then Duke Henry was to finance his campaign, it was upon Christian moneylenders that he must mainly
rely, and, in fact, two lent him money generously, William
Trentegeruns of Rouen and William Cade of Saint Omer. Both
of these men are worthy of more than passing notice.

William Trentegeruns had his wife as an associate, and after his
death (in 1159) she succeeded to his assets and liabilities and
evidently carried on his business. This parallel to the association
of Jews and their wives in moneylending is noteworthy, for it is
a further indication that Jewish and Gentile practices did not
greatly differ. Of William Trentegeruns we know little more
than that he was a prominent citizen of Rouen, where he was
the *vicomte* and, as such, associated with the administration. His
widow was known by the title of *vicomtesse* of Rouen and presumably occupied her husband's office and performed, perhaps
by deputy, the functions that went with it. She certainly continued
to be responsible for farming the revenues of Southampton which
her husband had farmed for three years. Apart from this, we learn
no more of their business than that from early in 1156 to
Michaelmas 1163 large sums of money were being repaid to them
from English revenues. Nearly £2,000 appears from the pipe
rolls to have come into their hands, and there is no reason to
suppose that this was the total of their receipts from the king:
there are no surviving Norman pipe rolls to tell us what they
received from the revenues of the duchy and no surviving issue
rolls or chamber rolls to tell us what sums were paid to them
directly from the treasury or from the king's privy purse.[1]

But at this point it will be well to say some explanatory words
that must be borne in mind whenever information is derived from
the pipe rolls. To begin with, we must guard ourselves against the
belief that 'the Exchequer of the Norman kings was the court in
which the whole financial business of the country was transacted'[2]

---

[1] For these transactions see *English Historical Review*, lxix. 607–8.
[2] Stubbs, *Constitutional History* (6th ed.), i. 407.

or that 'the Great Rolls of the Pipe . . . contain the summaries and authoritative details of the national account'.[1] These are text-book clichés, loaded with anachronism, that obscure the truth. The pipe rolls record the result of the judicial examination of Crown debtors, principally sheriffs who were called upon to account for the revenues that passed through their hands. The balance of receipts, after the deduction of authorized local expenditure, was required to be paid into the treasury. But money once in the treasury did not, with rare and special exceptions, come under the scrutiny of the barons of the exchequer. It was used and expended as the king directed: but of this the exchequer at this period, and consequently the pipe rolls, know nothing. Nor does the exchequer know anything of the king's borrowings, except indirectly and quite incidentally when loans are being paid off, not from the chamber (which we may equate with the privy purse) or from the treasury, but from moneys in the hands of Crown debtors or, in other words, when revenue is anticipated and debts to the Crown are assigned to the king's creditors. The pipe rolls thus reveal only a part, and not the most important part, of the king's financial affairs.[2] What they tell us of the king's credit transactions is accidental and merely incidental to an inquiry that has nothing to do with the larger aspects of royal finance.

We may now return to William Cade. He lived, as we have said, at Saint Omer. He was a man of immense wealth, with agents in every region of the Western world.[3] In the eleven years 1155 to 1166 the pipe rolls record the payment to him of some £5,600[4] and, as in the case of William Trentegeruns, we have no reason to suppose that this was all that he received from the king. The counterpart of these payments was obviously very large borrowings before, and probably after, Henry II came to the throne. Fortunately much more is known of William Cade than is revealed by the pipe rolls, for some record of many of his

---

[1] Stubbs, *Constitutional History* (6th ed.), i, p. 641.
[2] *English Historical Review*, lxix. 610–11.
[3] *Ibid.*, xxviii. 730.          [4] *Ibid.*, pp. 215, 219.

private transactions in England has been preserved.[1] He lent
money to earls and barons, bishops, abbots and archdeacons and
to many much humbler folk in all parts of the kingdom. Bishop
Nigel, the king's finance minister, the treasurer and the chamberlains of the treasury were among his clients, as also were the king's
justices. He advanced money upon the Cistercians' wool crops, for
he dealt extensively in wool and wool-fells, as well as in corn of
all kinds.[2] He had dealings not only with residents in England but
with visitors from abroad, who would make repayment in France
or Flanders.[3] If many of his transactions were openly usurious,
others brought a less direct profit, as when he advanced money in
coins of light weight and the loan was repaid in coins of full
weight.[4] If, as a rule, he required valuable security, he was prepared to lend money on the sworn promise of the borrower or the
pledged word of a third party of substance,[5] and even the king
guaranteed some of his loans.[6] He would accommodate anybody
and he had terms to suit every sort and condition of men.

The king's borrowings from William Cade appear to have
come to an end in 1163 or 1164. Payments to him certainly seem
substantially to have ceased before Michaelmas 1164: only three
payments are recorded on the pipe rolls for 1165 and 1166,[7] and
the inference is that these represent the last repayments of borrowings of earlier years.

William Trentegeruns and William Cade were not the only
Christians from whom Henry II borrowed large sums at the
beginning of his reign. Another lender at the same time was
Robert fitz Sawin, whose origin is unknown, but who does not

[1] Brief particulars of the debts due to him at his death have been preserved
(*ibid.*, pp. 220–7). For his bonds see below, pp 70–1.

[2] *Ibid.*, pp. 221, 223–5.  [3] *Ibid.*, p. 226.

[4] *Ibid.*, p. 224.  [5] Below, p. 70

[6] *Ibid.*, p. 221. It should be noted that the king guaranteed other debts
besides those to Cade. When for the Toulouse campaign Becket borrowed 500
marks from a Jewish moneylender, the king became surety for the loan and on
Becket's default was required to pay (*Materials for the history of Thomas Becket*,
iii. 53–4).

[7] *Pipe Roll 11 Henry II*, pp. 63–72; *Pipe Roll 12 Henry II*, p. 118. The total is
a little over £117. The contrast with *Pipe Roll 10 Henry II* is striking.

seem to have been English born. As in the case of Trentegeruns and Cade, it was arranged that he should farm the revenues of an important town: while they were given Southampton[1] and Dover,[2] fitz Sawin was given Northampton, in each case doubtless as security for their loans. For two years, from Michaelmas 1155 to Michaelmas 1157, fitz Sawin was allowed very advantageous terms, for the standard ferm of £100 was reduced to a half.[3] This meant that, apart from the normal profit that any fermor would expect to make, he received an additional £50. Nor was there any actual payment of the ferm into the king's treasury, for this was allowed to him *in soltis*, that is, as a repayment on account of his loans.[4] Thereafter the ferm was increased to the normal £100, so that the profit from farming the town revenues was reduced, but this £100 was retained by him *in soltis*, year by year until 1171:[5] in the next year repayments to him ceased, so far as the pipe rolls show.[6] Not only did he enjoy the revenues of Northampton, but in several years substantial sums were paid to him from other sources, about £400 in 1158, £240 in 1162, £150 in 1165,[7] and so on, quite apart, that is, from any

---

[1] William Trentegeruns and the Vicomtesse of Rouen had the farm of Southampton from February 1156 until Michaelmas 1163 (*Pipe Roll 2 Henry II*, p. 55; *9 Henry II*, p. 56; and intermediate rolls).

[2] William Cade had the farm of Dover from the beginning of the reign until Michaelmas 1161 (*Red Book of the Exchequer*, p. 648; *Pipe Roll 3 Henry II*, p. 108; *5 Henry II*, p. 61; *6 Henry II*, p. 55; *7 Henry II*, p. 62).

[3] The ferm in 1154–5 had been £100 (*Red Book of the Exchequer*, p. 655). For fitz Sawin's grant see *Pipe Rolls 2–4 Henry II*, pp. 42, 106, 139.

[4] That these payments *in soltis* were repayments of loans is a deduction from the conclusion that similar payments to William Cade were of this character (*English Historical Review*, xxviii. 218–19). It is noteworthy that repayments to moneylenders are not infrequently grouped together: e.g. Cade and fitz Sawin in *Pipe Roll 7 Henry II*, p. 18; fitz Sawin and Ralf Waspail in *Pipe Roll 8 Henry II*, p. 17; Cade and Waspail in *Pipe Roll 4 Henry II*, p. 165; Waspail and Isaac, the son of the Rabbi, in *Pipe Roll 8 Henry II*, pp. 24, 62. Confirmatory evidence of the meaning of the formula *in soltis* is supplied by an entry in the pipe roll of 1158 relating to the repayment of a loan made by the citizens of Winchester: in soltis ciuibus Wintonie lxi. li' et vi. s' et viii. d' *de prestito regi* (*Pipe Roll 3 Henry II*, p. 105). [5] *Pipe Roll 17 Henry II*, p. 48. The previous rolls have like entries.

[6] *Pipe Roll 18 Henry II*, pp. 33, 35.

[7] *Pipe Rolls 4 Henry II; 8 Henry II; 11 Henry II*.

payments he may have received direct from the treasury or the chamber, which the pipe rolls do not reveal. Beyond the financial details given in the pipe rolls, little is known of Robert fitz Sawin. He settled down in Northamptonshire where the king granted him the manor of Upton in 1159[1] and he became sheriff of the county in 1170:[2] he may have been in business as a merchant, for in 1173–4 he was concerned with supplying robes on a fairly large scale.[3] A fourth moneylender in the early years of Henry II, who is otherwise unknown, was Ralf Waspail. To begin with, he was closely connected with the king's chamber, if not actually employed there, but this connexion was brief.[4] His transactions with the king were apparently on a relatively small scale: repayments to him were irregular,[5] though in one year those shown on the pipe roll amounted to nearly £600. He disappears in 1163.

It will perhaps help to get Henry's dealings with Christian moneylenders into perspective if they are related to the dealings with similar and perhaps, in some instances, the same moneylenders by Henry's great contemporary Alexander III, pope from 1159 to 1181. Two illustrations may be given, which come from the early years of Henry's reign and are therefore apt. In 1166 (as it would seem) the bishop of London, Gilbert Foliot, had collected the bulk of Peter's Pence due to the pope but awaited the king's permission to transmit it to Rome. Meanwhile Alexander had anticipated its receipt, at least to the extent of borrowing 300 marks from Flemish merchants; and eight of these had now come from Rome expecting repayment from

---

[1] *Pipe Roll 5 Henry II*, p. 16; *Rotuli Hundredorum*, ii. 9. For some (not very accurate) particulars of the later history of his family see G. Baker, *History of the County of Northampton*, i. 222, and J. Bridges, *History of Northamptonshire*, i. 538–9.

[2] *Pipe Roll 16 Henry II*, p. 19.

[3] *Pipe Roll 19 Henry II*, p. 34; *22 Henry II*, pp. 50, 52. It is possible that he may merely, as sheriff, have been an intermediary.

[4] *Pipe Roll 4 Henry II*, pp. 120, 131, where the only entries indicating a connexion with the chamber are found.

[5] There are ten entries in *Pipe Roll 4 Henry II*, pp. 120–83; two in *Pipe Roll 5 Henry II*, pp. 3, 13; and none in the two years following. It is in *Pipe Roll 8 Henry II* that many payments are recorded amounting to nearly £600; but there are only two entries in *Pipe Roll 9 Henry II*, p. 25, after which they cease.

the bishop. Foliot, however, could do nothing without the king's approval and the Flemings had been hanging on in London waiting for their money to be released.[1] We do not know, but we may suppose, that ultimately they got their money. The important point in the present connexion is, however, that here we see Flemish merchants acting as international financiers, providing funds in Italy and recouping themselves from the debtor's assets in England.[2] Of course, they did not provide this service for nothing, and a letter of Alexander's, written from Rome in January 1166 to the archbishop of Reims,[3] removes any doubts as to the terms on which a needy pope could borrow money. Whatever, he says, is given him by way of charity (seemingly he may be referring to Peter's Pence) is swallowed up by the maw of usury. The archbishop had already acted as an intermediary in borrowing £150 for the pope and another sum for the cardinals while Alexander was in France (as he was, for the most part, in the four years 1162–5), and he is now asked to borrow discreetly another 100 marks from the same source. What the source was is not indicated, but presumably such a man as William Cade, whose agents were very near at hand.

Henry's borrowings from Christian moneylenders seem to have ended abruptly. Of the four who have been mentioned, three seem to have ceased to lend in 1163 or 1164: the exception is Robert fitz Sawin, who was domiciled in England and who apparently continued to accommodate the king for some years still. The reason why the king ceased to have recourse to Christians and turned increasingly, as we shall see he did, to Jews is hard to guess. Why, having once ceased, he did not later turn to Christians,

---

[1] Foliot's letter is in *Materials for the history of Thomas Becket*, v. 211, and also *Gilberti Epistolae* (ed. Giles), ii. 3. The date ascribed to it is 1165, but the reference to the presence of Flemish merchants at Rome shows that it cannot be earlier than 1166, for Alexander did not return to Rome until 23 November 1165.

[2] Another example is provided by the abbot elect of St. Augustine's, Canterbury, who was borrowing from Flemings in 1178 for the expenses of his suit before the Curia against the archbishop of Canterbury (Peter of Blois, *Epistolae* (ed. Giles), ii. 101, no. 158).

[3] Migne, *Patrologia Latina*, CC. 405–6; Jaffé, no. 11256.

may be plausibly conjectured. It may well be that Christian financiers had little trust in him after his treatment of William Cade's heirs, for to all seeming the whole of William's possessions in England, and presumably also in Normandy, were confiscated on his death and his debtors were required to account to the Crown.[1] It may be that no agreement could be reached upon the amount of the fine that the sons should pay for the privilege of succeeding to their father's estate,[2] but the king's action certainly has an air of the arbitrary and dishonourable, for he himself had guaranteed some of the debts that he proceeded to turn to his own use. And though there were plenty of Christian moneylenders in Western Europe, there is no evidence that Henry resorted to them. It was otherwise with his sons. Richard had resort to Lombards, to a merchant of Montpellier and to another of Saint Omer.[3] During his absence on crusade Roman merchants provided, on his authority, 800 marks for his mother, Queen Eleanor, and the archbishop of Rouen, Walter of Coutances, on their way back to England from Messina.[4] His queen, Berengaria, borrowed from Pontio Arnaldi, who was presumably either a Roman or a Lombard.[5] John, while count of Mortain, had resort to Catalan merchants from Barcelona and, after he became king, to a Flemish merchant from Ypres and to Lombard merchants from

[1] This is inferred by Sir Hilary Jenkinson (*English Historical Review*, xxviii, 214, 217). With the possible exception of a trifling payment by the earl of Arundel (*Pipe Roll 11 Henry II*, p. 93), any receipts accruing were not accounted for at the usual sessions of the exchequer and no reference to Cade's bonds appears on the pipe rolls until 1211 (*Pipe Roll 13 John*, p. 60.)

[2] It has been suggested that Cade's property was seized on his death because he was a usurer (*English Historical Review*, xxviii. 217), but there is no evidence that it was yet law that the king was entitled to the goods of a deceased usurer (*ibid.*, xliii. 333–6).

[3] *Foedera*, i. 78; *Pipe Roll 3 & 4 Richard I*, p. 145; *6 Richard I*, p. 250; *10 Richard I*, p. 172; *Magni Rotuli Scaccarii Normanniae*, ii. 300–1; *Rotuli Chartarum*, p. 31.

[4] *Pipe Roll 3 & 4 Richard I*, p. 29. For the identity of the 'queen' of this entry cf. *Itinerarium Regis Ricardi*, p. 176. See also Landon, *Itinerary of Richard I*, p. 192. The money was borrowed in Rome, apparently in April, and repaid before Michaelmas, it would seem in England, by Gilbert of Vascoeil, who accompanied the queen and the archbishop.

[5] *Pipe Roll 8 Richard I*, p. 150.

Piacenza.[1] He had dealings, too, with the Templars, but these were much more in the nature of a modern banking account. It is true that on occasion the Templars made him advances; but it is evident that, broadly speaking, he kept them in funds for the payments they made on his behalf.[2]

From these fragmentary references we get the impression of widespread and international moneylending by Christian merchants, and this impression is confirmed by what we know of the steps taken by the Church to protect crusaders who raised money to enable them to fight Saracens or heretics. It is not only Jewish moneylenders who are to be restrained by their sovereigns from demanding payment of capital or interest, but Christian moneylenders who are to be restrained by ecclesiastical censures, that is, in the last resort, if admonition failed, by excommunication.[3] Though we hear most of Christian moneylenders from the Continent,[4] they were not lacking in England. If they avoided overt usury, they nevertheless advanced money at a profit and, though perhaps sometimes abused as usurers, they might enjoy

---

[1] *Memoranda Roll 1 John*, p. 75; *Pipe Roll 1 John*, p. 197; *Rot. Chart.*, pp. 11b, 13, 96b; G. Dept, *Les influences anglaise et française dans le comté de Flandre*, pp. 71–3. John undertook to repay Richard's indebtedness to Lombard merchants (*Rot. Chart.*, p. 31).

[2] The most significant document is his letter of 14 April 1216, to brother Gérard Brochard (*Rot. Litt. Pat.*, p. 177). Other references are collected by Léopold Delisle in *Mémoires de l'Académie des Inscriptions*, xxxiii. pt. 2: see especially pp. 11–12, 15–16, 20–1. Jewish finance in the Middle Ages was never of the same character as the Templars'.

[3] So Innocent III in 1198 and again in 1208 and 1209 (Migne, *Patrologia Latina*, CCXIV. 311–12; CCXV. 1170; CCXVI. 159). Christian and Jewish usurers are grouped together also in the decree for a new crusade promulgated at the Lateran Council of 1215 (Hefele, *Histoire des Conciles*, v. 1193).

[4] In particular Roman merchants, who enjoyed papal support and were prominent in financing religious houses, as, for example, St. Augustine's, Canterbury (Peter of Blois. *Epistolae*, no. 158), Evesham (*Chronicon Abbatiae de Evesham*, pp. 225, 230–1), and the higher clergy, like Roger of St. Edmund, archdeacon of Richmond, as to whom see especially Innocent III's letter of 2 May 1204 (Migne, *op. cit.*, CCXV. 298). Usury was probably usually cloaked as damages (*poenae*) and expenses, but sometimes the payment of interest (*usurae*) seems to have been openly stipulated, though it was not always recovered (Cheney and Semple, *Letters of Innocent III*, no. 33).

the highest reputation and consideration. Few men stood so high in the city of London as Gervase of Cornhill, who served periods of office as justiciar and sheriff and founded a family distinguished in Church and State. He was a moneylender and the associate of Aaron of Lincoln.[1] His younger contemporary, William fitz Isabelle, for long periods sheriff of London, was without doubt a moneylender, who is named along with Jewish moneylenders as one of those to whom Saint Edmund's Abbey was heavily indebted.[2] Both these men seem to have been associated with William Cade.[3] Financiers, whether Christian or Jewish, English or Flemish, doubtless found it advantageous to be mutually accommodating. *Pecunia non olet*. And though most of the prominent English moneylenders may have been leading citizens of London, they were doubtless to be found elsewhere. Extensive financial dealings have been attributed to Gervase of Southampton in the reign of Richard I.[4] But, so far as is known, the Angevin

[1] J. H. Round, *Geoffrey de Mandeville*, pp. 304–12. For the accusation of usury, see *Materials for the history of Thomas Becket*, iii. 100. This accusation is supported by Gervase's transactions with Stephen's Queen Maud, who failed to redeem the loan he had made to her and who forfeited the land gaged to him (Round, *op. cit.*, pp. 120–1). For his association with Aaron, see above, p. 47. His son Henry was joined with him in this transaction with Aaron and evidently in other transactions, for in 1202 Hugh de Neville produced a starr of acquittance for a debt to Aaron from Gervase and Henry (*Pipe Roll 4 John*, p. 289). Henry seems also to have been a moneylender: see his bonds in Round, *Ancient Charters*, no. 54, and P.R.O., D.L. 25/108. There is no mention of interest in either bond, but this was normal practice (below, pp. 70, 139).

[2] His bond was for £1,040 (*Chronicon Jocelini de Brakelonda*, p. 2). He was sheriff in 1162 and 1176, from 1178 to 1187 and again in 1193. St. Albans, too, borrowed from Christians, but it is not clear whether they were foreign or native (Walsingham, *Gesta Abbatum Monasterii Sancti Albani*, i. 183).

[3] In a list of Cade's debts there is an item 'de atornatione de Lundonia—quater xx. libras et xix. libras—per Willelmum filium Isabelle et Gervasium de Corhilla' (*English Historical Review*, xxviii. 227). This seems to mean that these two had advanced money and had then discounted their bond with Cade. Gervase's acquaintance with Cade is shown also by the attestation of a deed of Gervase's in favour of St. Peter's, Ghent (Round, *Cal. Documents France*, p. 505).

[4] *Pipe Roll 4 John*, pp. xxi–xxii. That his debts were in the king's hands after his death because he had been a usurer receives, however, no direct confirmation from the pipe rolls. If that were the reason we should expect a number of Londoners to be in like case: but this we do not find.

kings made no use of English moneylenders to finance their wars. They discovered that taxation was preferable to borrowing, and this discovery is disclosed in the history of Henry II's relations with the English Jewry.

Henry succeeded his father as duke of Normandy in 1150 and, though all the early Norman records have disappeared, we cannot doubt that, as his predecessors had done, he derived what profit he could from the Norman Jewry. Such information as we have regarding the Jews in Normandy later in the twelfth century and in the early thirteenth century shows that, though the details of administration might differ, they were treated as their brethren in England were treated.[1] This, of course, we should expect since the two communities enjoyed the same rights and privileges and could be covered by one and the same charter. When, therefore, Henry became king of England, he had little fresh to learn in the matter of making the Jewry profitable. At first his opportunities could not have been great. Though the English Jewry was considerably larger than the Norman Jewry, the prosperity of English Jews could not have failed to be impaired by the insecurity and unrest of Stephen's reign. It is not surprising, therefore, that—so far as they are disclosed by the pipe rolls—Henry's borrowings from English Jews were, to begin with, on a very modest scale. In 1157 there is a repayment of 71 marks to Isaac, the son of the Rabbi,[2] that is of Rabbi Josce, the head of the prominent family from Rouen which was settled in London under Henry I.[3] Five years later, sums amounting to £171. 10s. are repaid to him by the sheriffs of four counties, while his brother Abraham receives £121. 13s. 4d. in three payments from the sheriff of Essex.[4] In the two following years further repayments are made to Isaac, but the amounts are small.[5] In 1165 the repayments to Jews are much heavier than ever before, amounting to nearly £950. Isaac is still

---

[1] Below, pp. 201–12.      [2] *Pipe Roll 3 Henry II*, p. 72.

[3] Above, p. 2. For Rabbi Josce—Rubi Gotsce, as the name was rendered— see *Pipe Roll 31 Henry I*, pp. 148, 149.

[4] *Pipe Roll 8 Henry II*, pp. 18, 24, 41, 62, 69.

[5] *Pipe Roll 9 Henry II*, p. 61 (£26. 16s. 8d.); *Pipe Roll 10 Henry II*, p. 31 (£12. 12s. 3d.).

the chief lender, but Aaron of Lincoln appears in this year for the first time and is repaid £100.[1] In the following year repayments are again heavier, £730 going to Isaac and £320 to Aaron.[2] In the two years 1165 and 1166, therefore, repayments of over £2,000 are recorded in the pipe rolls, and the inference is that the king's borrowings from two leading Jews were on much the same scale as his borrowings from William Cade had been. Indeed it would seem that, well before Cade's death, he and other Christian moneylenders were being replaced. It is then virtually certain that it was in 1164 that the king turned from Christian to Jewish moneylenders.

It is significant that in the pipe roll of 1167, apart from those to William fitz Sawin, no payments are recorded either to Christians or to Jews that have the appearance of repayments of loans. The explanation seems to be that the king had obtained other sources of income in 1166. He had confiscated Cade's bonds, worth, at face value, about £5,000,[3] and vacant bishoprics were, for some years, to yield a handsome addition to the ordinary revenues of the Crown.[4] The silence of the pipe rolls does not necessarily mean that by Michaelmas 1166 the king had squared his accounts with his creditors: all that it implies is that they were not being paid by anticipating the revenue. Borrowing still continued to some extent, but in 1168 only trivial repayments to Isaac are recorded,[5] and it is not until 1169 that there is any indication that the king has been again borrowing upon a substantial scale. Repayments in that year to Aaron of Lincoln amount to over £500,[6] and two new names appear among the king's creditors, Benedict, the son of Sara, and Jurnet of Norwich.[7] But the following year there are recorded only trivial repayments to Aaron,[8] and for the next three years, 1171–3, no repayments at all appear

[1] *Pipe Roll 11 Henry II*, pp. 4, 7, 35.
[2] *Pipe Roll 12 Henry II*, *passim*: see index.
[3] *English Historical Review*, xxviii. 211.
[4] J. H. Ramsay, *Revenues of the Kings of England*, i. 91, 99, 101, 103, 110, 112.
[5] *Pipe Roll 14 Henry II*, pp. 10, 119.
[6] *Pipe Roll 15 Henry II*, pp. 33, 36, 96, 169.
[7] *Ibid.*, pp. 86, 96, 101.        [8] *Pipe Roll 16 Henry II*, pp. 29, 142.

upon the pipe rolls: the king is still drawing large sums from vacant bishoprics. It is quite clear that Henry's Irish expedition of 1171–2 was not financed by borrowing, and it is obvious that he was not in pressing need of ready money. In 1174 and 1175 the only repayments of any significance are 50 marks to Jurnet[1] and £200 to Aaron,[2] but then the pipe roll of 1176 witnesses to a fresh development in the financial relations between the king and the Jews. Borrowings from individuals are few and trivial: instead, groups of Jews, partnerships or *consortia*, are organized to provide the king with the money he needs. First, the two most prominent among the king's earlier creditors, Aaron and Isaac, appear in partnership, having apparently Isaac's brother Abraham as an associate. In 1176 they are repaid over £600.[3] This partnership did not last long and was replaced by a *consortium* of four members, Jurnet of Norwich, Benedict his brother, Le Brun of London and Josce Quatrebuches. Payments to them by the sheriffs of fifteen counties amounting to little short of £600 are recorded in 1177,[4] but in the course of the year they incurred the king's displeasure and were obliged to purchase his pardon. The fines they agreed to pay amounted to 6,000 marks, one half of this being charged against Le Brun, and 2,000 marks against Jurnet: the other two partners were evidently minor figures.[5] These two and Jurnet proceeded to pay off their fines, which they did remarkably quickly;[6] but Le Brun was treated in a different fashion. In his case, his assets were handed over to four sureties or trustees, all prominent Jews, three of them associated in the partnership of the previous year, Aaron of Lincoln, Isaac and Abraham, sons of the Rabbi, the fourth being Isaac of Colchester. Their task was to realize Le Brun's assets, and this they proceeded to do; but the whole English Jewry was also held responsible for the prompt payment of 1,000 marks, the first instalment of Le Brun's fine, and they did, in fact, find the greater part of it.[7]

---

[1] *Pipe Roll 20 Henry II*, p. 47.    [2] *Pipe Roll 21 Henry II*, pp. 207, 212.
[3] *Pipe Roll 22 Henry II*, pp. 10, 85, 87, 98, 121, 137, 138, 154, 190, 194.
[4] *Pipe Roll 23 Henry II, passim*.    [5] *Ibid.*, p. 201.    [6] Above, p. 40.
[7] *Ibid.*, p. 201; *Pipe Roll 24 Henry II*, p. 130; *Pipe Roll 28 Henry II*, p. 161.

The first *consortium* having failed, in circumstances of which the pipe rolls, naturally enough, give no dirèct information, a second *consortium* seems to have been immediately formed. This, too, consisted of four members: in the first place Benedict, the son of Sara, Josce, Dieudonné l'Eveske and Vives, though Josce seems soon to have dropped out and to have been replaced by Benedict's brother Moses, while a little later Dieudonné replaced Benedict as head of the *consortium*.[1] All the five associated with the concern appear to have belonged to the London community, though none was a very prominent number. The repayments made to them over three years were, however, very considerable: nearly £1,200 in 1177,[2] £530 in 1178[3] and £160 in 1179,[4] or £1890 in all. These figures are presumably the index of much larger transactions and, in view of the relative insignificance of the members of the *consortium*, it is difficult to believe that they found from their own resources the money the king required. The inference is that they were no more than agents, intermediaries between the king and the English Jewry. In this way, too, the punishment inflicted upon the members of the first *consortium* may be explained: they failed, presumably culpably, to satisfy the king, not as moneylenders, but as his servants: and the penalty they incurred was shared by the Jewish community as a whole. There is nothing to suggest that the second *consortium* incurred the king's displeasure, but after 1179 it disappears from the pipe rolls and we must conclude that it was dissolved. Thereafter a new phase begins in the relations between the English Jewry and the Crown: borrowings cease and, when the king needs money, he takes it in the form of a tax.

The subject of taxation requires to be treated separately, and we may turn to other aspects of Jewish moneylending. But before

---

[1] There are some confusions in the entries on the pipe rolls: Brunus has occasionally been substituted for Benedict (*Pipe Roll 23 Henry II*, pp. 86, 160) and there are occasional omissions of a name: cf. *ibid.*, p. 175, where the wrong *consortium* was named before the scribe realized the error.

[2] *Pipe Roll 23 Henry II, passim.*

[3] *Pipe Roll 24 Henry II*, pp. 5, 35, 39, 53, 58, 65, 73, 114, 128, 129.

[4] *Pipe Roll 25 Henry II*, pp. 4, 54, 58, 75, 102, 109, 123, 126.

we do so, some reflections upon Henry II's borrowings may be helpful. That his borrowings were related to the fluctuations in his revenue as a whole is an obvious assumption, and it has already been suggested that by keeping English bishoprics void he found it possible to dispense with loans for several years. With the filling of the vacant sees this adventitious source of income ceased in 1173 and, so far as the pipe rolls afford an index, the gross English revenues fell off. This was a period of unrest and rebellion, but with the restoration of order, and following the Assize of Northampton, the revenue increased again in 1176 and 1177, largely as the consequence of the judicial and forest eyres.[1] There is, however, no obvious correlation between these fluctuations in the revenue and the resort to borrowing in the period 1176–9. The truth is that the material available is inadequate to explain Henry's financial expedients. It is not always appreciated that the surviving English records provide but a fraction of the evidence and that most of it is lost. Nor is the problem an insular one. England was doubtless Henry's largest single source of income, but the revenues of his Continental dominions were very substantial by contemporary standards. At their amount we cannot, except perhaps in the case of Normandy, make even the vaguest guess. What we can affirm is that any happy windfall, any unexpected emergency, anywhere within the Angevin 'Empire', might move the king to relax or increase his demands elsewhere. It follows that whatever explanation we may offer of the course of the king's borrowings is subject to a *caveat*.

That they were short-term borrowings hardly admits of doubt. This seems to be evident from what we know of the history of the period 1176–9. There is little overlapping between the repayments to the several *consortia*. It is unlikely that, as a rule, loans were made earlier than in the twelve months preceding repayment, though it may well be that the dwindling repayments in 1178 and 1179 were in respect of loans contracted in 1176, that commenced to be paid off in 1177. The nearest analogy to these loans is the modern treasury bill. The king was anticipating his

[1] Ramsay, *Revenues of the Kings of England*, i. 113–37.

revenue and required only short credit. This may not be true of
the early years of his reign, when his Christian creditors were
granted a lien for several years on the revenues of the ports of
Dover and Southampton and the town of Northampton, an
expedient that points to very different conditions.[1] But, so far as
borrowings from Jewish moneylenders are concerned, there seems
to be no evidence that is inconsistent with the inference that the
loans were all for a short term and that repayments were usually
prompt. It seems evident also that lending to the king was not
a very profitable business and that there was a growing reluctance
to hazard in this fashion money that could be employed in the
ordinary way of business, by making private loans that carried
interest. For it is unlikely that the king paid interest or entered
into bonds with his own Jews. At most he paid back the borrowed
capital and looked favourably upon his creditors. But such favours
could be dearly bought, and as time went on pressure was necessary to extort a loan. It is significant that Isaac, the son of the
Rabbi, and Aaron of Lincoln, probably the two wealthiest of
English Jews, withdrew from the business, and that Le Brun and
Jurnet, who rivalled them in wealth and replaced them as the
king's agents for raising loans, paid heavily for their experience.
Once the alternative expedient of stiff taxation was adopted,
borrowings on the king's behalf from Jews were small and occasional, to meet some special emergency.[2] If, after Henry's death,
an English king wanted large loans, he obtained them from
Christians who, not being his subjects, were better able to make
favourable terms for themselves.

Jewish loans to the king, though of interest in the history of
finance, were but a transitory episode that had no permanent

---

[1] Above, p. 54.
[2] During Richard's absence on crusade money appears to have been borrowed
from Jews for the royal service by Geoffrey fitz Peter and others (*Pipe Roll
5 Richard I*, pp. 99, 132, 148). In 1203 John borrowed 800 *livres* from the Jews
of Rouen and Pont Audemer and undertook that repayment should be made at
the exchequer at Caen (*Rot. Litt. Pat.*, p. 25). There were some other borrowings
at this period of crisis, but the total amount does not seem to have been large
(below, p. 206).

consequence. There is no reason to suppose that the loans represented a large proportion of the king's revenue or were more than could be repaid in a short time, in months rather than in years. The figures for the king's revenue that have been calculated from the pipe rolls do not represent his true revenue, which was appreciably greater;[1] but it is nevertheless instructive to compare them with the repayments of loans also recorded in the pipe rolls. Both series of figures would need to be multiplied by unknown factors to give strictly comparable amounts, and it is quite unlikely that in any one year the same multiplier would apply to both sides of the account. But the revenue figures, which range from a minimum of £12,600 in 1174 to a maximum of £30,500 in 1177,[2] are so much greater than the repayments in any year between 1166 and 1179[3] that we are justified in concluding that no multiplier is conceivable that would convert the king's borrowings from the Jews into a serious burden of debt. In truth, although there was plenty of borrowing in anticipation of revenue throughout the Middle Ages, borrowing was never a real instrument of finance and there was never much system behind it. The device of a funded debt lay in an unimaginable future: loans were incurred to be repaid. Prudent finance meant the amassing of treasure, an aim that Henry II pursued with remarkable success.[4] Such a policy left no place for systematic borrowing.

[1] Failure to appreciate this fact, at least adequately, vitiates all the elaborate calculations of Sir James Ramsay.

[2] See the table in Ramsay, *Revenues of the Kings of England*, i. 191.

[3] Above, pp. 61–3.

[4] The wealth of Henry II and his sons was notorious and was ascribed to their illicit exactions (Giraldus Cambrensis, 'De Principis Instructione', *Opera*, viii. 316). Henry left 43,000 (silver) marks to charity in his will (*Foedera*, i. 47; Gervase of Canterbury, *Historical Works*, i. 298–9): we can safely deduce that his accumulations were several times this amount.

# IV

# THE JEWISH MONEY MARKET

THE NUMBER OF JEWS able to accommodate the king was very restricted and to accumulate the necessary capital quickly they had only one means, lending money to all and sundry at interest. Whatever profits they might derive from trade could have gone but a little way towards amassing a fortune. To the poorer Jews trading was presumably of more importance, for their gains from moneylending must have been small. Doubtless there were some of middling condition, like Vives and Comtesse of Cambridge and Jacob and Mirabelle of Newport who accommodated Richard of Anstey with small sums,[1] but it was the wealthy Jews who made loans to bishops and high-ranking barons. A list of the bonds of any leading Jew would be very much like the surviving list of Cade bonds, for much the same clients went to a Jewish as went to the Flemish moneylender. It would contain such names as Bishop Alfred of Worcester,[2] Bishop Nigel of Ely,[3] the Countess Bertha of Brittany,[4] all of whom, as we learn incidentally from the early pipe rolls, had resort to the Jews. At the other end of the scale there would be very humble folk, though their only representatives on the pipe rolls are the sick poor of Canterbury, whose pledges were redeemed

[1] Palgrave, *English Commonwealth* (1922), ii. 117–18. Richard borrowed from nine Jews in all, but the only one from whom he had substantial sums is an unidentified Hakelot, though this may be Isaac, the son of the Rabbi, who was so well known as to need no other description (*ibid.*, pp. 117–19).

[2] *Pipe Roll 8 Henry II*, p. 61.

[3] *Pipe Roll 14 Henry II*, p. 222.

[4] *Pipe Roll 21 Henry II*, p. 3. This is a late reference to a transaction which occurred not later than August 1167 when the Countess was dead (Clay, *Early Yorkshire Charters*, iv. 91, 110).

by the king out of the revenues of the see while Becket was in exile.[1] The borrowers were, however, the inmates of the Hospitals of Saint Nicholas and Saint John the Baptist, which had been founded by Lanfranc and which were maintained by the archbishop's alms.[2] The bonds of Aaron of Lincoln for Rutland give us the best idea of the scope of a rich Jew's transactions. Rutland is the smallest of English counties, and after Aaron's death inquiry yielded no more than eleven bonds from there, but the sample is the only one available.[3] The borrowers range from Count Aubrey of Dammartin, who gave a bond for £115, to a lady named True, who was in debt for a mark only. Among the noble debtors was William Mauduit, one of the king's chamberlains, who had previously borrowed from William Cade. The local clergy were well represented: the prior and convent of Brooke and the parsons of Luffenham, Morcott and Whissendine. The parson of Whissendine was indebted not only directly to Aaron for 140 marks but also for 92 marks borrowed under a bond to Deulesalt of Stamford that had been transferred to Aaron. The other sums covered by these bonds range from 20 shillings to £32, but one bond is for a debt, not in money but in kind, and covers two debtors who were due to deliver 125 and 40 seams of oats. In one respect the bonds from Rutland are not representative, for none of the debtors owed any very large sums, as was the case elsewhere. The county was not a rich one and there were no large towns. Brooke Priory, the only religious house among the borrowers, was insignificant and owed only £13. By way of contrast nine Cistercian abbeys between them owed Aaron 6,400 marks, while a single landowner in Yorkshire had a debt of 1,800 marks.[4] Again, there are no Jews among the Rutland debtors, for there seems to have been no Jewish settlement in the county; but there is ample

---

[1] *Pipe Roll 13 Henry II*, p. 201.

[2] For the foundation see Eadmer, *Historia Novorum*, p. 15. The identification of the *infirmi* with the inmates of the hospital does not admit of doubt, since they were maintained by a charge upon the manors of Reculver and Boughton under Blean, to which the entry on the pipe roll refers: cf. *Bibliotheca Topographica Britannica*, i. 173, 191.

[3] Below, pp. 247–53.          [4] Below, pp. 89–71.

evidence that Jews as well as Christians were among Aaron's clients.[1]

While, then, the Rutland bonds do not fully represent the scope of Aaron's business, they are representative in the sense that they provide the text of a good many variant instruments and enable us to appreciate how the form of bond was adapted to the circumstances of the debtor and the nature of the transaction. Particularly instructive is the bond of Count Aubrey of Dammartin, for this states, without disguise, that the capital sum which the borrower undertook to pay included interest. If the stipulated term was exceeded, then the interest for which provision was made began to accrue.[2] No doubt we have here the explanation of bonds which do not provide for interest at all. The loan was, in fact, less than the amount to be repaid and to ensure his profit the creditor counted upon payment by the due date. It was not unusual to stipulate that the creditor's consent was necessary to any delay in payment, and the implication is that, without this consent, any sanction there might be would be enforced. The obvious sanction, although this is not expressed in any of Aaron's bonds, would be the forfeiture of any valuable pledge that might be deposited with the creditor, but it is noteworthy that in not one of the bonds is there mention of any kind of pledge, except land or tithes.[3] Where tithes were pledged the intention of the parties appears to have been that they should be accepted in place of the periodical payments due under the bond.[4] Where land was pledged, the intention appears to have been that, if the borrower defaulted in his payment, the income from the land would come into the creditor's hands until the debt was discharged.[5] As a rule the borrower pledged his faith to abide by the bond, but it was usual for him to find sureties who would become liable in the

[1] *Pipe Roll 3 Richard I*, pp. 23–4, 51, 60, 90; *5 Richard I*, p. 69; *10 Richard I*, pp. 57, 58; *1 John*, pp. 6, 41, 42, 62, 107; *3 John*, p. 183; *Rot. Oblat.*, pp. 121–2.

[2] Below, pp. 250–1.

[3] Chattels are, however, mentioned in a bond of Jurnet of Norwich printed below, pp. 257–8. Deeds were sometimes accepted as security, though the land was not mortgaged (Cole, *Documents*, p. 312; below, p. 152).

[4] Below, pp. 252–3 (no. 11).          [5] Below, pp. 248–9, 250–1(nos. 2, 8).

event of his default: normally there was a single surety or two sureties, but in one case there were as many as twenty.[1] Where the rate of interest is stated, it is sometimes a penny in the pound a week or twenty-two per cent. per annum;[2] sometimes the rate is twopence and exceptionally threepence,[3] reflecting doubtless the credit of the borrower. These terms are similar to those in other Jewish bonds of the period, though twopence in the pound seems to be the usual rate of interest, while the exceptional rate of sixpence in the pound may be found in a case where the borrower appears to have been obviously insolvent.[4]

A comparison with the bonds of William Cade[5] shows a general similarity to the Jewish bonds of some twenty years later, though the forms are not on the same model. If the surviving specimens are a fair guide, specific provision was rarely made for the payment of interest:[6] for the most part interest must be included in the periodical payments stipulated in the bond. Where land was pledged, interest was provided by the whole income or a specified charge upon the land, *sine adquietacione*, that is without reducing the capital: the transaction was in fact a mortgage in the contemporary sense of the term.[7] As in the Jewish bonds, the debtor pledged his faith to William Cade and also found sureties.[8] There

---

[1] Below, pp. 248–52 (nos. 1, 3, 5–10). The twenty sureties are given by the parson of Whissendine (no. 10). A surety might obtain an indemnity from the borrower, as the prior of Dunstable did from St Bartholomew's Priory (*Bedfordshire Historical Record Soc.*, vol. x, p. 84): this, of course, was no protection from the creditor, though it might assist the surety to recover from a defaulting borrower any loss he sustained.

[2] Below, pp. 249–51 (nos. 4–6, 8).

[3] Below, pp. 248–9, 251–3 (nos. 2, 3, 9, 11).

[4] In the bonds printed below (pp. 242–69) the only exception is the loan made by Benedict *parvus* to Michael de Wanchy where the rate is 6*d.* a week (p. 246). The rates paid by Richard of Anesty were variously 2*d.*, 3*d.*, 4*d.* and 4½*d.* in the £. a week (Palgrave, *English Commonwealth*, ii. xxiv–xxvii).

[5] Printed by Sir Hilary Jenkinson in *Essays in History presented to R. L. Poole*, pp. 205–10.

[6] *Ibid.*, p. 206 (no. ii).        [7] *Ibid.*, pp. 205–9 (nos. i, iii, vi, vii).

[8] One minor difference may be noted. In the Cade bonds others, besides the borrower, might join in pledging their faith, presumably in order to give jurisdiction to an ecclesiastical court. This device ceased to be effective when the king asserted the jurisdiction of his courts in pleas of debt, whether there had been

was nothing clandestine about Cade's moneylending. It was as open, and as openly usurious, as any Jewish moneylending, and it seems to have been not unusual for the bond to be executed before the barons of the exchequer.[1] Such differences as there are between Cade's bonds and Jewish bonds, which are not more than verbal, arise from the circumstances of the Flemish moneylender's business: the fact that it was a firm, with William's son Ernulf and his brother Eustace as partners, and the fact that the seat of the business was at Saint Omer, though it had a branch house at London.[2] In essentials Flemish—and, we may guess, all Christian —moneylending and Jewish moneylending were identical and, as we have seen, the Jews replaced the Fleming and other Christians when their business with the king of England ceased. Jewish bonds were negotiable instruments, but apparently in the twelfth century they remained in the hands of some member of the Jewish community. That does not mean that Christians did not become parties to transactions arising out of the bonds: as we shall see, mortgages were a very effective means of promoting the transfer of land.[3]

As time went on, Christians became more directly involved and trafficked freely in Jewish bonds, not only with the intention of acquiring a title to gaged land but for the purpose of enjoying the fruits of usury. Since the later history of the financial relations between Christians and Jews has been misunderstood, it may be well, though it means some deviation from the immediate theme, to explain what really was happening under Henry III and Edward I. Accident has given undeserved prominence to the name of Adam of Stratton, the accident that, at a late stage in his career, he became notorious for his criminal practices. But there was

a pledge of faith or not (cf. *Constitutions of Clarendon*, c. xv). It was, in any case, not a device likely to commend itself to a Jewish moneylender. Whatever the form in which third parties guaranteed a debt, they seem all to have been treated by the exchequer as sureties (*ibid.*, p. 200). That is, no distinction would be made between *fideiussor* or *plegius* and the debt would be enforced against either on the failure of the principal debtor.

[1] Jenkinson, *op. cit.*, pp. 206 (no. i), 208 (no. vi).
[2] *Ibid.*, pp. 208 (no. vi), 209 (no. vii): cf. p. 195.     [3] Below, pp. 86-103.

nothing reprehensible, and certainly nothing exceptional, in his dealings in Jewish bonds. He did, indeed, have fairly extensive dealings and by this means acquired a number of usurious debts[1] and a certain amount of landed property.[2] And though his operations cannot be singled out as an evil example, they can be used as a convenient illustration of the relations between Jewish moneylenders and Christians associated with the king's court in the second half of the thirteenth century. One of Adam's transactions is fortunately abundantly documented: that by which he acquired a number of bonds from Hagin, the son of Master Moses, who was at the time archpriest and high in the royal favour.[3] One of the bonds that Hagin transferred to Adam he had, in fact, purchased from the king (that is, through the Justices of the Jews) and all of the bonds that Adam purchased were regularly deposited in the *archa* in London. The transaction was quite above board and was as straightforward a piece of business as one could find. The purchaser naturally wished to get value for money and Hagin, as vendor, undertook to have the transaction confirmed, at his expense, by royal charter, with a clause providing that the king would not, without the assent of Adam, pardon the debts due under the bonds or permit the debtors to pay by instalments. This undertaking was duly performed and Adam obtained his charter.[4] Now, doubtless both parties were men of official standing and thoroughly conversant with the niceties of procedure in such matters; but there is no reason to suppose that what was done was anything but a matter of everyday business, provided the appropriate fees were paid. Nor is there anything to suggest that the debtors were in any worse case when they had Adam for creditor than when they had some Jewish moneylender or the Crown. All this is worth emphasizing, because the truth of the

[1] *Cal. Plea Rolls*, i. 193, 206, 275–6; ii. 100, 164, 181, 239, 245; iii. 86, 90, 126.

[2] Several deeds have survived relating to his acquisition of land by discharging mortgage debts (P.R.O. Ancient Deeds, A. 6876, 6920, 13421–2).

[3] The key document is the agreement between Hagin and Adam (Nero C. iii), printed in *Starrs and Jewish Charters*, i. 12–20. The deeds mentioned in the preceding note are cited *ibid.*, ii. 81–102.

[4] *Cal. Charter Rolls, 1266–1272*, p. 180 (12 January, 1268).

matter has not been grasped and the commonplace has been made
to appear extraordinary and sinister.[1] In fact Adam's transactions
seem to have been insignificant in extent compared with those
of Robert and Henry Braybrooke earlier in the century.[2] Fellow
servants of the Crown did as Adam did: for example, Walter of
Merton, chancellor and future bishop,[3] Robert Walerand, for a
time steward of the household and an intimate counsellor of the
king and Prince Edward,[4] as also Roger Leyburn, a later steward
of the household and Prince Edward's lieutenant in Gascony.[5]
And not only men such as these, but barons of the highest rank,
William of Valence and Gilbert of Clare, made their profit in
the same way.[6] And when there was a fresh development in the
practice of Jewish moneylenders, who, instead of taking gages of
land in return for repayable advances, provided capital sums in
return for annual rentcharges, created for life[7] or in perpetuity,
in their favour, ministers and barons did not hesitate to acquire
them when they came upon the market or fell into the king's
hands. William of Valence trafficked in rentcharges as he did in
other debts due to Jews,[8] and among the ministers and future
bishops who did so were Robert Burnell[9] and Godfrey Giffard.[10]

After the Barons' War, and certainly from 1269, the climate of
opinion began to change and restrictions were placed upon both

---

[1] The editors of *Starrs and Jewish Charters* did not fully appreciate the nature
of the transaction. There is a lamentable and largely irrelevant excursus by
W. Page on Adam of Stratton, *ibid.*, ii. lxxv–lxxx; but this represents the state
of knowledge when he wrote.

[2] Below, pp. 100–2.

[3] Cecil Roth, 'Oxford Starrs', *Oxoniensia*, xxii. 63–77.

[4] *Cal. Charter Rolls, 1257–1300*, p. 39; *Close Rolls, 1261–1264*, pp. 127–8.

[5] *Cal. Plea Rolls*, i. 138. Both Walerand and Leyburn acquired rentcharges
from Jewish moneylenders. A rentcharge disguised the usurious nature of the
transaction: see below, pp. 104–6.

[6] For Gilbert of Clare, see *ibid.*, i. 137, 158–9, 199, 200; ii. 117. For William of
Valence, see *Cal. Patent Rolls, 1247–1258*, pp. 543–4; *Close Rolls, 1256–1259*, p. 446.

[7] P.R.O. Ancient Deeds D.6 is a deed of 46 Henry III creating a rentcharge
for life of one mark and one seam of wheat in favour of Isaac, son of Diai of
Worcester: this is in form a gage of land. Most rentcharges seem to have been
granted in perpetuity.

[8] Rigg, *Select Pleas*, pp. 56–60; *Cal. Plea Rolls*, i. 228.

[9] *Ibid.*, i. 162.          [10] *Ibid.*, i. 194–5.

the scope of Jewish financial transactions and the participation of Christians in them. But, whatever may have been the views of a restricted number of ecclesiastics,[1] there is no reason for supposing that, before the spate of anti-Jewish legislation that began late in Henry III's reign and ended in the Expulsion, any stigma attached in public opinion to financial dealings with the Jews.

Until well into the thirteenth century, Christians do not seem to have discounted or purchased Jewish bonds. As between Jew and Jew, however, the transfer of bonds must have been the commonest of transactions. They might be sold (that is discounted) or they might be pledged as security for a loan: in either way they might come into the hands of a third party.[2] Of the eleven Rutland bonds that were listed as Aaron's property no more than six were obligations contracted directly with him. One was with his son Vives, one with Benedict, the son of Isaac of Lincoln, one with Samuel, the son of Solomon of London, and two with Deulesaut of Stamford.[3] The bond with Samuel, the son of Solomon, is of interest since it was executed after mid-December 1185[4] and was transferred to Aaron before his death about 10 April 1186. Clearly it was almost immediately discounted. Since two other bonds that Aaron acquired were executed in 1184,[5] it is fair to infer that these, and others also, were discounted very soon after the loan was granted. On the other hand there must have been a trade in older bonds: this emerges

[1] See A. G. Little in *Collectanea Franciscana*, ii. 150–7, on the part played by the Franciscan friar, Henry of Woodstone, and the brothers Giffard, archbishop of York and bishop of Worcester, who were Franciscan sympathisers. They appear to have been largely instrumental in obtaining the legislation of 1271. That Franciscan influence was directed against the Jews and transactions with them is suggested also by the correspondence of the Franciscan archbishop of Canterbury, John Pecham, notably that relating to synagogues in London (below, pp. 194–6) and the acquisition of landed estates by the queen (below, p. 107).

[2] For a clear statement of the current practice see the concluding portion of the writ to the Justices of the Jews of 22 March 1208: Vives, son of Aaron of Lincoln, is the moneylender concerned (*Rot. Litt. Claus.*, i. 112–13). A number of transactions in bonds or shares of bonds are recorded in Davis, *Shetaroth*, pp. 1–4, 14–17, 23–24 *et passim*.

[3] Below, pp. 249–53 (nos. 4, 8, 9, 10, 11).

[4] Below, p. 252.          [5] Nos. 4 and 8.

from the transactions in which the Crown was involved. When
Le Brun's bonds were handed over to Aaron of Lincoln and his
associates to realize, they could deal with them only in accordance
with current market practice.[1] Similarly, when a few years later
Jurnet's bonds were transferred to the Jewish community,[2] this
can have been only a stage in disposing of them in one of three
ways: to a Jew who would recover as much as he could of capital
or interest from the debtor; to the debtor himself for a cash
payment; or to a representative of the debtor's who would discharge the bond in consideration of some service or compensation
from the debtor. When, following upon the confiscation of
Aaron's estate, the officers of the exchequer had to realize his
bonds, they too could but follow the established practice. They
could arrange a 'fine 'with the debtor,[3] which meant that he paid
a smaller sum than the nominal amount of his debt or they could
sell bonds to Jews willing to buy them, in the expectation, of
course, of making a profit. To a limited extent the exchequer
officials could make a bargain with a representative of the debtor
by which a bond was cancelled and the debtor's land freed. Walter
of the Chamber, for example, who had married Hawise, the niece
and heiress of Roger Roselle, in this way got rid of Roger's debt
of more than 300 marks for a payment of 60 marks.[4] These were
exceptional terms; but Jewish moneylenders themselves were
willing to dispose of dubious securities at a handsome discount.[5]
Unless the exchequer could dispose of a bond to the debtor or
someone representing him or could sell it to a Jew, it was, at least
for the time being, valueless, for what the king's ministers could
not do was to retain the bond and require the payment of the
interest arising.[6] Usury ceased to run on Aaron's death. It follows
that a debtor who resisted the pressure of the exchequer to redeem
his bond was no worse off on that account: his indebtedness did
not increase. But the officers of the exchequer were tenacious of

[1] Above, p. 62.  [2] Above, p. 40.
[3] For such fines see below, pp. 143-5.
[4] *Pipe Roll 7 Richard I*, p. 87.  [5] Below, pp. 82, 89.
[6] Cf. Bracton, f. 60*b*: Et si debitum Iudei in manus domini regis devenerit, non
capiet rex nisi sortem, scilicet catallum in carta contentum.

the king's rights and did not despair of ultimately translating them into cash. It is not surprising therefore that the liquidation of Aaron's estate was a very protracted process; and some very old debts came into the hands of Jews to collect. Six years after Aaron's death, Benedict, son of Isaac, who had discounted bonds with Aaron during his lifetime, bought some of his bonds that the exchequer had not succeeded in realizing.[1] More striking still, twenty-two years after Aaron's death, one of his sons, Elias by name, agreed to pay 200 marks for bonds that were neither the best nor the worst of those remaining, to the face value of £400, an offer he increased by three marks of gold so that he might have a better selection.[2] In the same year the exchequer was itself pursuing a number of ancient debts.[3]

The broad consequences of Jewish moneylending are sufficiently clear. The one substantial result was to facilitate the transfer of land; but this complicated story must be told in a separate chapter. As in other ages, the result was the sequel to the pledging of land by improvident borrowers. The pledging of chattels had very different consequences. If the pledge was forfeited, as evidently it often was,[4] the chattel, not generally of very great value, passed into trade, at some loss to the borrower, at some gain to the lender. The volume of this traffic we have no means of estimating: it was not a form of business that led to permanent records, and incidental references are mostly concerned with the pledging of forbidden articles. When, however, we speak of forbidden articles, it must be remembered that few restrictions upon the Jews were consistently maintained and that a forbidden article is likely therefore to have been one which was commonly pledged. Henry II's charter had forbidden traffic in church ornaments,[5]

---

[1] *Pipe Roll 4 Richard I*, p. 231.

[2] *Rot. Oblat.*, pp. 420, 436. For bonds transferred to Elias, see *Pipe Roll 10 John*, pp. 4, 27, 80–1, 98.

[3] *Memoranda Roll 10 John*, pp. 28, 29, 34, 35, 43, 61, 62, 65, 67.

[4] This must be inferred from the clause of Henry II's charter (see below, p. 109) that secured to the Jews the right to sell pledges unredeemed after a year and a day.

[5] So we may infer from the clause in Richard's and John's charters: et liceat

but they must have been pawned not infrequently,[1] and though the offence was occasionally punished[2] it could hardly have been suppressed. We could scarcely have better evidence than the direction given to the sheriff of Northampton in 1246 that no Jew was *henceforward* to take in pawn books, chalices or other ecclesiastical ornaments.[3] Similarly, though the Assize of Arms of 1181 required Jews to dispose of armour that had come into their possession, so that it should remain in the king's service[4]—and, since Jews could not dispose of unredeemed pledges until a year and a day had elapsed, this was tantamount to prohibiting the pawning of armour[5]—nevertheless armour continued to be pawned.[6] Again, it seems evident, from the repeated prohibition of the traffic, that Jews continued to deal in blood-stained garments, that is clothing suspected of having been obtained by violence.[7] The interest of these prohibitions and their infraction lies chiefly in the indications they give that Jewish pawnbrokers dealt with all classes of society, from clergy and knights down to thieves. And this traffic, which we may describe as clandestine—though, probably, between the intervals of the spasmodic enforcement of prohibitions, it was well known—can have been but a fraction of a perfectly legitimate business of pawnbroking;[8] for it is only under the shadow of legitimate business that the trickle

---

Iudeis omnia que eis apportata fuerint sine occasione accipere et emere, exceptis illis que de ecclesia sunt . . . (*Rot. Chart.*, p. 93; *Foedera*, i. 51). There was the same prohibition under Henry II in Poitou and Gascony (*Rot. Litt. Claus.*, i. 397).

[1] *Gesta Henrici*, i. 106; Giraldus Cambrensis, *Opera*, vii. 36. The bishop of Ely pawned a cross and gospels under Stephen (Wharton, *Anglia Sacra*, i. 625).

[2] *Pipe Roll 16 Henry II*, p. 10; *29 Henry II*, p. 14.

[3] *Close Rolls, 1242–1247*, pp. 475–6.

[4] *Gesta Henrici*, i. 279: reprinted in Stubbs, *Select Charters*, s.a.

[5] *Pipe Roll 32 Henry II*, p. 78.      [6] *Curia Regis Rolls*, ix. 256.

[7] Forbidden by Henry II's charter, the trade was condemned in the legislation of 1233 (below, pp. 293–4). Such traffic was forbidden also by Henry II in his Continental dominions (*Rot. Litt. Claus.*, i. 397).

[8] Direct evidence of pawnbroking is rarely forthcoming, though notices occasionally occur, as when a surcoat (Cole, *Documents*, p. 312), a wife's dress (*Close Rolls, 1261–1266*, p. 19), rings (Rigg, *Select Pleas*, p. 107) and monastic linen (*Cal. Inquisitions Miscellaneous*, i. 92) are pawned. For further examples see Roth, *History of the Jews in England*, p. 275.

of reprehensible traffic flows. Apart from pawnbroking and the trade in precious and secondhand articles this implies, Jews must have traded extensively in corn. This took the form of advances of money on growing crops: if there were direct dealings in grain, the evidence does not seem to have been preserved. Though the evidence of credit dealings in corn in the twelfth century is scanty and is provided chiefly by the bonds of Aaron of Lincoln,[1] the evidence for Jewish trading in corn and also in wool, is abundant for the thirteenth century.[2] In trade of this sort Aaron, and doubtless other Jews, were not singular. They were doing what William Cade was doing in the early years of Henry II.[3]

Except for the gaging of land and pawnbroking, there could not have been many opportunities for lending money at interest, for there was little except land and chattels that a borrower could offer as security. One exception, however, is worth remarking. A religious house in need might raise money by selling corrodies, that is, in effect, the right to be a boarder for life at the convent and to be treated in this respect as one of the brethren. As a further step, a prebend might be created and sold: a prebend (in this sense) was much the same as a corrody, in that the monastery undertook to find so much food or drink or money annually, but the amount was not necessarily related to the monastic diet. This system was one of several, such as the creation of rentcharges, devised in the Middle Ages for the investment of capital in order to provide for the future and particularly for old age. Obviously there is a

[1] Below, pp. 248, 253. An action 'de bladis suis versus Asser Iudeum' can hardly arise out of anything but dealing in corn (*Pipe Roll 25 Henry II*, p. 49).

[2] *Cal. Plea Rolls*, i. 67–8, 95; Davis, *Shetaroth*, pp. 170–1, 219, 249; Stokes, *Studies in Anglo-Jewish History*, pp. 252–79; Jewish Hist. Soc., *Transactions*, vii. 79–89. The earliest perpetual rent of which particulars have come to light is a corn-rent of two loads of wheat and three loads of oats beginning in 1230: the document recording this is a list of Jewish bonds, prepared in 1262–3, many of which provide for payments in corn of various kinds (P.R.O., E. 101/249/10). Similar evidence is furnished by a list of bonds belonging to Abraham of Marlborough in 1250 (E. 101/249/6). A proportion of these transactions was doubtless fictitious (below, p. 106); but the volume of surviving documents is too great to permit us to suppose that Jews did not participate in the trade.

[3] *English Historical Review*, xxviii. 221, 223–5. All kinds of grain are concerned, wheat, barley, oats, peas. There are dealings also in wool and wool-fells.

general resemblance to modern annuities and, like annuities, corrodies and prebends might be pledged by the owners as security for loans. The moneylender thus acquired the right, while the loan was unpaid, to receive, or dispose of, the corrody or prebend. This is known to have happened at Dunstable Priory, and more than one Jew lent money on such security and was bought off by the canons.[1] This is not likely to have been an isolated case for, despite discouragement by authority, the practice of selling corrodies was widespread. It is cited, however, not as representative, but as an example of the wide range of Jewish moneylending, especially because it had its origins in the twelfth century.

Though men of all classes resorted to the Jews for accommodation, there are very necessary qualifications that must be added to such a statement. Credit transactions for the mutual benefit of lender and borrower, though not unknown, were exceptional in the Middle Ages. Without tangible assets in coin or gold or jewels, no medieval man was wealthy. To amass treasure was the policy of every prudent king and it was the policy of every prudent subject as well. A moneylender's clients were to be found, therefore, mostly among the necessitous and impoverished. There were, it is true, the temporarily embarrassed, the bishops and great lords and ladies, and there were quite exceptional borrowers who were associates rather than clients, but these were few.[2] The ordinary client was an extravagant or hard-pressed man.[3] Consequently moneylending was never fully respectable, and Jews, though they had no monopoly, were more open in their dealings, more willing to take risks, more accessible to high and

---

[1] Below, pp. 257–63.

[2] Such as the Cornhills and the sons of Peter fitz Alan, for whom see above, pp. 47–8.

[3] Two illustrations may be given. To make their peace with Earl William de Mandeville, the monks of Walden had to pay him 100 marks at short notice, 'pro quarum coactione tam cito soluendarum tanto usurarium astricti fuimus nodo ut Iudeis obligati essemus tempore longo' ( *Walden Abbey Chronicle*, lib. ii. c. 3: transcripts in Arundel MS. 29 and Vespasian E. vi). A parallel case is that of John Carun who gaged his land when he was made a knight immediately before leaving for Gascony in the king's service (*Cal. Inquisitions Misc.*, i. 25).

low, and so were regarded as the universal pawnbrokers and mortgagees.

It was, of course, the debts which ran on for years or which were never paid off that occasioned resentment. It is of these that monastic chroniclers have to tell. Of the eleven bonds included in the Rutland roll, two, it was discovered, had been discharged, while a third bond seems to have been discharged, although this was not discovered when the roll was annotated in the exchequer.[1] It may be that the unfamiliarity of the exchequer officers with Aaron's methods led to some confusion between debts that had been discharged and debts that were still current at his death. The intricacy of some of the transactions, which involved several parties and the transfer of debts, will explain some of the confusion. But incidental notices in the pipe rolls make it clear that debtors, or their representatives, at times had a good deal of difficulty in proving that they held a valid discharge.[2] When, however, we have made ample allowance for all such cases, it is evident that the bulk of Aaron's bonds confiscated by the king had not been discharged and, but for his death, were likely to run on for a long time, accumulating interest meanwhile: and apparently interest unpaid at the end of a year was capitalized. The impression is perhaps a false one that in most cases loans ran on beyond the term specified in the bond, for naturally enough we do not hear of loans promptly repaid, which may have been the greater number: it was not these that called for comment. Of some transactions between the sacristan of Saint Edmund's Abbey and Benedict, the brother of Jurnet of Norwich, we are given details by Jocelin of Brakelonde.[3] The sacristan borrowed 40 marks and the debt ran on until it had accumulated to £100. At this point the creditor took steps to enforce payment in the king's court. The issue of the writ brought the matter to the notice of the abbot, with the result that a fresh bond was entered into with

---

[1] Below, p. 138.

[2] The case of William Fossard is a striking example (below, p. 90). For references to other cases see below, pp. 105, 151.

[3] *Chronica Jocelini de Brakelonda* (Camden Soc.), pp. 2–3.

Benedict. Under this bond, the debt of £100 was renewed and a further sum of £100 was advanced on an undertaking that at the end of four years £400 would be repaid. At the due date the money could not be found and another bond was made for £880 repayable by instalments of £80 a year. Benedict had also a number of other bonds for smaller sums, one of which was fourteen years old, doubtless accumulating interest. The total of the abbey's indebtedness to this one creditor was £1200. It needed no very exceptional rate of interest to bring about a result of this kind: even the low rate of a penny in the pound a week would convert £100 into £1,000 in less than twelve years, and twopence in the pound was more usual, at which rate the capital debt doubled every second year. Even when interest was paid in part, the total debt continued to rise. The same chronicler of Saint Edmund's tells of a debt incurred by the cellarer to Jurnet of Norwich that had accumulated to a total of £60: the original capital is not stated. After payment of sums amounting to £50, the debt still stood at £26 and the initial debt had apparently not been reduced.[1] A layman, Roger de Wanchy, had a similar experience. He had mortgaged a manor to Le Brun of London, which meant that the creditor received the profits by way of interest. In 1170, the total debt was 210 marks. Roger, however, continued to borrow on the same security, and his entire resources were inadequate to keep the debt down. When he died in 1180 or 1181, his indebtedness had doubled: he owed more than 420 marks.[2]

It is highly probable that in such cases as these, the borrower had little idea of what would happen if he failed to pay his capital debt promptly. Monastic writers, who might be supposed to have an advantage over laymen, seem to have had no conception of what were the mathematical consequences if interest was allowed to accumulate and if interest was then charged upon the accumulation. Medieval arithmetic was hardly equal to the computation of compound interest. By experience the members of a monastic house might know that borrowing at interest, from Jew or

[1] *Ibid.*, pp. 4–5; above, p. 43.    [2] Below, pp. 87–8.

Gentile, might be disastrous, and laymen would not be ignorant of what happened to their neighbours. But no matter what was written in the bond, the outcome was unexpected and outrageous. Told from the lender's standpoint, the story might be different. There is evidence that, as men of business, lenders were willing to make a heavy reduction for a cash settlement of a long-standing debt. Jurnet accepted 32 marks in settlement from the prior of Hatfield Peverel, who had stood surety for a third party in a bond for £40: this represents a discount of nearly fifty per cent.[1] Nor can such a settlement have been altogether unusual, for Aaron of Lincoln was prepared to make similar concessions.[2] Doubtless, even with such discounts, the transactions would yield substantial profits, but the points are worth making that a bond cannot be taken at its face value and that the profits of Jewish moneylending cannot be estimated from the fragmentary evidence that has come down to us. Loans running on for years and accumulating interest the whole time are not likely to have been the most profitable. In all probability the most desirable client was one who repaid a loan promptly and who was not charged interest at an excessive rate, excessive by twelfth-century standards. We rarely hear of such clients—Richard of Anstey is one of the few who have left a memorial[3]—but they may have represented the chief part of the moneylending business.

[1] *Feet of Fines 7 & 8 Richard I* (Pipe Roll Soc.), p. 130.
[2] Below, pp. 89–90.
[3] He borrowed twenty-one separate amounts from nine Jews. When he made up his accounts all but two debts were discharged with interest, usually at the rate of 3*d.* or 4*d.* in the £. a week (Palgrave, *English Commonwealth* (1922), ii. 117–19).

# V

# JEWS AND THE LAND

THE JEW WAS A town-dweller. Whatever his occupation, he was not an agriculturist and, except as a source of profit, agricultural land had no interest for him. Under whatever title the Jews held the houses in which they were first settled in London, this carried no obligations which were not borne by the citizens around them. Indeed the Jews' obligations were less than the citizens', for they were not at scot and lot with them. A Jew was not, and could not be, a member of the London *commune*: he was a member of the *commune* of London Jews and of the wider *commune* of the English Jewry.[1] The few conveyances to Jews that have survived from the twelfth century mention nothing, however, of those things which differenced the Jew from other landowners.[2] They are concerned solely with the relations between vendor and purchaser. The plot of land is described and the amount of the quit rent to be paid at stated terms of the year. The grant—for all conveyances are in the form of a grant—is in fee and inheritance. Unless there was some special covenant to the contrary, the purchaser was free to dispose of the land as he wished. If for greater security the conveyance took the form of a fine, this too did not differ in its terms whether the purchaser was Jew or Christian.[3]

[1] For the 'commune Iudeorum Anglie' see *Memorandum Roll 1 John*, p. 72. For the local Jewish *communes* and their status see below, p. 134.

[2] See below, pp. 239–40, for an example. Two other examples (*c.* 1152) are printed by Adler, *Jews of Medieval England*, pp. 255–60, and another (*c.* 1197) at p. 261: in the case of this last deed a Jew succeeds a Jew; in the case of the others Jews succeed Christians.

[3] See the fine in favour of Jurnet of Norwich of 1189 (*Feet of Fines, 1182–1196* (Pipe Roll Soc.), no. 3) and the later fines in favour of Jacob, the son of Samuel, of Northampton and Isaac of Colchester (*Feet of Fines, 9 Richard I*, no. 167, *10 Richard I*, no. 291).

But outside the towns other conditions and considerations obtained. It may be that in the twelfth century manors or agricultural land had been granted to Jews on terms which did not differ from those in grants to Christians. Very few instances, however, are known of grants which may have been in fee. Isaac, the son of the Rabbi, acquired 'Hame' by grant from Henry II 'pro servicio suo' and he also acquired Thurrock by purchase from Earl Ferrers.[1] These he held during his lifetime and transmitted to his son, Josce, who sold Thurrock early in the reign of Richard I to Henry de Gray.[2] What became of Ham, which has not been identified, is uncertain, but there is nothing to suggest that Isaac's family long retained it. How Isaac and his son fitted into the network of feudal obligations is a problem for which no easy solution can be suggested, though it was not, in truth, an isolated problem, for the Crown was continually faced with the not dissimilar problems of heirs under age, heiresses, widows and ecclesiastics. But since Jews held manors in fee simple so rarely,[3] no rule was established, as it was in the case of other tenants in chief who lay under a disability.

While Jews can rarely have held land, other than their own houses, in fee simple, nevertheless they were frequently given seisin of land, but this seisin was *ut de vadio*, as of a gage. This was not a form of tenure peculiar to Jews, for Christians might hold land in the same way in like circumstances. A great deal of land must have been held *ut de vadio* in the twelfth and thirteenth centuries, and the earliest discussion of the gage of land, that in *Glanville*, does not refer to Jews at all.[4] A gage of land or, as we should say, a beneficial lease was one of the more usual ways of investing money. It assumed a different aspect, however, when the land was pledged to a Jewish moneylender as security for a loan,

---

[1] *Foedera*, I. i. 51 (Richard I's charter of 22 March 1190).

[2] Richard I's confirmation to Henry de Gray is dated 11 June 1195 (Morant, *History of Essex*, i. 95; Landon, *Itinerary of Richard I*, no. 451).

[3] This is clear from the proceedings and legislation of 1271, which turned upon the question whether Jews should be permitted to hold in fee and in consequence to have wardships, marriages and advowsons (*Liber de Antiquis Legibus* (Camden Soc.), pp. 234–6).　　　[4] *Glanville*, lib. xiii, cc. 26–30.

since the Jew does not seem to have occupied the land,[1] whereas the Christian commonly did so. The Jew would either leave the owner in occupation or sub-let the land to a Christian. An alternative arrangement was possible. A landowner who had bound himself to Jewish creditors might enter into an agreement with a fellow Christian—it might be a religious house—who discharged his debts or undertook his liabilities and received in return a gage of the land for a term of years or until the money had been repaid.[2] Where the gage of land took this course, the pattern of landownership was unaltered. The owner of the fee simple might be temporarily out of possession, but when the capital had been repaid or the term had expired, the land reverted free of the encumbrance to the owner or his heirs. But we must distinguish. While the gage might be the equivalent of a beneficial lease purchased for a capital sum, where land was pledged as security for a debt, the agreement between the debtor and the creditor might not provide for the capital to be reduced by the profits from the land. Such an agreement, says *Glanville*, is unjust and dishonest, though it is not forbidden: it is a kind of usury and it is called a mortgage.[3] To all seeming, the author of *Glanville* has not in mind Jewish bonds, which usually stipulated for a given rate of interest and were more akin to a modern mortgage, but agreements into which Christian moneylenders might enter without openly infringing the ecclesiastical law against usury. However, whether it was a Jewish or a Christian mortgage and the debtor could not pay, the inevitable consequence was that he lost his land. The legal and practical consequences of a Christian mortgage we need not seek to follow: but what of the Jewish mortgage and the Jewish mortgagee who had no interest in retaining possession of the land?

---

[1] For a case where a Jew held land 'ad firmam et ut vadium suum' see *Close Rolls, 1242–1247*, p. 139. He does not seem, however, to have occupied it, for the debtor obtained seisin of the land and sold it, thus defrauding the Jew of his debt.

[2] See the agreement between the abbey of Beddlesden and William fitz Gregory (*Starrs and Jewish Charters*, i. 128, 130). For similar transactions between laymen, see *Curia Regis Rolls*, i. 104–5, 212; ix. 294–5; x. 144–5.

[3] *Glanville*, lib. x, c. 8.

When a Jew obtained seisin of a gage, the sheriff or one of his officers accompanied him to the place, gave him the keys and required the villeins to do fealty to him. If the Jew were indebted to the Crown, any chattels found there—the corn in the barns, the oxen and horses—might be sold by the sheriff, who would account for them at the Exchequer of the Jews.[1] These, however, were but preliminaries. What became of the land? It is plain that, when land was pledged to a Jew and he received seisin of the gage, he experienced no difficulty in finding Christian sub-lessees.[2] Their title depended upon his and if their right to the land was challenged they vouched the moneylender to warranty.[3] If the borrower was unable ultimately to pay off his debt, the Jewish creditor did not obtain seisin 'as of fee',[4] but he arranged for the conveyance of the property to a purchaser who was willing to pay the Jew his price. There can be no doubt that in course of time a regular market developed in encumbered estates. Our fullest information regarding transactions of this kind comes from religious houses, but there is no reason to suppose that laymen did not purchase such property as freely as ecclesiastics, although not many details appear to be available except in the case of only one family.

It is perhaps desirable to state at the outset that a large number of

[1] The fullest account of the procedure will be found in *Curia Regis Rolls*, v. 169, a case arising out of a complaint by Moses, the son of Le Brun, that Matthew Mantel, sheriff of Hertfordshire (1204–1208), would not give him full seisin of his gage at Standon. Light on the procedure for valuing and selling the live- and dead-stock, is provided by a case in 1199 where Isaac of Colchester was concerned (*Curia Regis Rolls*, i. 110) and a Braybrooke deed of 1209 (below, p. 273 (no. 3)). In the latter case the sheriff was the purchaser. For some further details of the procedure see Cole, *Documents*, p. 294. At a later date chattels seem to have been sold to discharge a debt secured on land although the debtor was not in debt to the Crown (*Cal. Plea Rolls*, ii. 255–6; below, p. 158).

[2] It has to be borne in mind that at this period land was commonly leased fully stocked: this is the rule with the St Paul's leases (*Domesday of St. Paul's* (Camden Soc.), pp. 122–39; see also *Law Quarterly Review*, lvii, 327–8). For an illustration of a Christian seeking out a Jew who has obtained seisin of his gage and persuading him to lease the land see *Curia Regis Rolls*, ix. 261.

[3] *Ibid.*, viii. 307; ix. 23–4, 153–4.

[4] Cf. *ibid.*, ix. 24: 'Et quia Isaac Iudeus est et non habet terram in feodo.' This is the case cited by Bracton, fo. 387, where he refers to 'Iudeus qui terram non tenuerit in feodo'.

the apparent benefactions to monasteries, the records of which so largely fill monastic cartularies, were in reality purchases for cash. It came, however, to be considered rather indecent to express the hard facts in the deeds which conveyed property to a religious house.[1] A pious motive is commonly ascribed, and it is only now and then that the full story is known; and we are told more in the deeds of the candid twelfth century than in those of the more sophisticated thirteenth century. By way of illustration, two stories may be related in some detail. They come from the reign of Henry II, when the Jewish community was at its most prosperous and when it was providing a large part, if not most, of the available credit in the country to everybody who could give security. The first story concerns Waltham Abbey, which was reformed and reconstituted by the king as part of his penance for the murder of Thomas Becket, and the second story concerns Meaux Abbey, in Yorkshire, in which the king figures only incidentally.

The Waltham story begins in 1170. In that year Roger de Wanchy owed to a Jew of London, called Le Brun (*Brunus*), the sum of 210 marks. This seems to be the balance on 8 July in that year of a long-standing account.[2] It included the small sum of £8. 6s. 4d. which had just been lent to Roger free of interest until Christmas, but all the rest seems to have represented old loans and interest. As security for the whole debt Roger mortgaged—or

---

[1] So, in drafting fines of land, the chirographer omitted any reference to the true consideration, but stated that the abbot and convent had accorded the vendor a share in any future (spiritual) benefits that might accrue to their church. This convention is explained on the ground that it was not consistent with the king's dignity to mention anything simoniacal (*Modus Cyrographandi* in Univ. Library Cambridge MS. Ll.4.18, fo. 184b). Again, when deeds were copied in a cartulary, they were often abbreviated and a clause stating the consideration might be omitted. Thus, of two independent copies of a deed of Healaugh Park, a house of Augustinian canons, one includes a clause to the effect that the canons have paid the grantor 120 marks with which he has acquitted all his lands of the Jewry (*Cal. Charter Rolls*, iii. 157), while the copy in the cartulary omits this clause (*Healaugh Park Chartulary*, Yorkshire Archaeological Soc., Record Series, xcii, 40).

[2] Roger, it may be remarked, was no stranger to moneylenders. He had been witness to one of Cade's bonds (*Essays in History presented to R. L. Poole*, p. 209), though there is no evidence that he was one of Cade's debtors.

rather extended the mortgage on—his manor of Stanstead. Roger was to have the opportunity of redeeming his mortgage at mid-summer in any year following, but meanwhile Le Brun was entitled to all the profits from the manor.[1] Roger did not repay his debt, and in 1172 he borrowed a further sum of £20. 11s. on the same security,[2] and evidently he continued to borrow, for, when he died in 1180 or 1181, his manor had been mortgaged for fifteen years and he owed £280. 17s. 3d.[3] His son, Michael, there-fore found his inheritance heavily burdened and he was hard pressed for money. This is made plain by his borrowing in 1185 from Benedict Le Petit of London, some years after he had been freed from his father's debt, the small sum of 40 shillings with interest at the onerous rate of 6d. in the £ a week.[4] Michael seems, immediately after his father's death, to have set about ridding himself of his *damnosa haereditas*. He entered into negotia-tions with the Hospitallers and the bishop of Ely with a view to the sale of his lands to the former,[5] but, before this transaction could be carried through, he was in touch with Walter of Ghent, a canon of Waltham who was a prominent minister of Henry II. Walter was the abbot-designate of the Abbey of Waltham, into which the king was transforming the priory, and he proposed that the king should discharge the debt on condition that Michael should grant half the manor to the abbey. The king further re-quested Michael to grant the other half to the abbey for a rent of £12. a year. Michael therefore surrendered the whole of the manor: as a consideration he and his brother secured small sums of ready money from the king (£10 and £5 respectively). On these terms the manor passed from the mortgagee, Le Brun, to the

---

[1] Below, pp. 242–3.    [2] Below, pp. 243–4.
[3] Below, pp. 244–6.    [4] Below, p. 246.
[5] This is stated in a charter of Michael's son Roger who had presumably learnt the story from his father. His words are: 'Cumque fratres Hospitalis Ierosolime ex una parte et ex alia Galfridus episcopus Elyensis cum eo [*sc.* Michael] loquer-entur et iam pactum formauerunt de tota terra emenda, sicut michi relatum fuit, tandem pater meus utilius habuit consilium et fecit super hoc loqui per magistrum Walterum de Gant domino Henrico regi secundo qui eo tempore ceperat fundare abbatiam de Waltham' (Harl. MS. 391, fo. 85b–86b; Tiberius C. ix, fo. 86–86b).

abbey.[1] The transaction, however, cost the king practically nothing for, in circumstances of which we are ignorant, Le Brun, in association with Aaron of Lincoln, agreed some time later to pay a fine of 2,000 marks. Reckoned in this fine was the £280 that had been due from Roger de Wanchy.[2] Michael, it will be seen, saved very little from the wreck of his father's estate, but it should perhaps be added that the canons of Waltham discharged the small debt that he had borrowed from Benedict Le Petit.

While Roger de Wanchy was running into debt in Hertford-shire, William Fossard had been following the same path in York-shire. He had had transactions with a number of moneylenders, but all his debts seem to have been bought up by Aaron of Lincoln and ultimately they amounted to the formidable total of more than 1,800 marks. To free his mortgaged lands William proposed that the abbey of Meaux should acquire part of his estate and discharge his debt. This arrangement was evidently proposed with the assent of Aaron, and, it may be, at his instance, for he offered to forego over 500 marks of the total, if the abbot would pledge himself for the remainder. Ultimately an intricate agreement was come to, whereby the abbey was to pay 1,260 marks with interest at the rate of 60 marks a year until the capital sum was fully discharged. William for his part was to convey four and a half ploughlands to the monks and to gage to them for fifteen years without payment the lands that had been mortgaged, so that they might recoup themselves for their expenditure. The agreement between the monks and William was later modified, apparently to the disadvantage of the monks, but these modifications did not affect Aaron, who had given his acquittance of

[1] See pp. 244–6 below. There is a later charter by Michael (*c.* 1192) to the same effect, in which there occur the words 'locutus sum domino regi Henrico secundo per magistrum Walterum de Gant qui postea fuit abbas de Waltham'. (Harl. MS. 391, fo. 85–85b; Tiberius C. ix, fo. 85b–86). The facts are also set out in Henry II's charter of confirmation (dated October–December 1181 by Eyton, *Itinerary of Henry II*, p. 244), copies of which are in Harl. MS. 391, fo. 40–1, and P.R.O. Cartae Antiquae Roll M.

[2] *Pipe Roll 30 Henry II*, p. 138. Le Brun's share in the fine was assessed at £1,000.

William's debt at Michaelmas 1176. Before the monk's debt was discharged, Aaron died and the deeds concerning William Fossard's loans came, with the rest of his bonds, to the exchequer, which had the duty of administering Aaron's vast estate on behalf of the king. The barons of the exchequer proceeded to demand payment on the evidence of the bonds in their hands and left to the debtors the onus of proving that they had discharged their debts. The monks consequently were compelled to pay at short notice the full sum they owed and the exchequer further demanded from William Fossard the difference between his total debt and the amount the abbey had undertaken to find. (This difference, it is rather surprising to find, was £510. 14s., the equivalent of 766 marks, or nearly 40 per cent of the total debt.) William protested that the whole of his debts were a charge against the abbey, but it was only after much trouble and expense to the abbey that Aaron's acquittance of the whole debt could be found and the monks given a final quittance.[1]

It is in the light of this transaction that we should read the charter of Richard I which exonerated in 1189 nine other Cistercian abbeys from debts due to Aaron. Their total indebtedness amounted to over 6,400 marks, which the exchequer was endeavouring to recover. The king, who was gathering in all the money he could to defray the expenses of his crusades, released the debts for a cash payment of 1,000 marks.[2] The explanation has been offered and generally accepted that the debts had been incurred by the monks in borrowing from Aaron the funds necessary to meet the cost of building at the several abbeys,[3] but there is no evidence that they had raised money in this way for the purpose. In any case, if a charter had been given to monks to relieve them of usurious debts, we should expect that such a charter would be issued in general terms in favour of all religious houses, not that it would be confined to nine Cistercian abbeys. It is, moreover,

---

[1] *Chron. de Melsa*, i. 105, 173–8; *Pipe Roll 9 Richard I*, pp. 46, 61–2.

[2] *Memorials of Fountains*, ii. 18–19 n.

[3] Jacobs, *Jews of Angevin England*, p. 109; Roth, *History of the Jews in England*, p. 15; A. L. Poole, *Domesday Book to Magna Carta*, pp. 228, 422.

quite clear that these nine banded together and came to a bargain with the king to obtain relief from debts of common origin.[1] And, if we ask what was that common origin, we are likely to be at least as right in supposing that it was the acquisition through Aaron of encumbered estates as in supposing that the abbeys had borrowed money from him to extend their buildings. Moreover, it is certain that Roche Abbey, one of the nine, was in debt because it had acquired land through the intermediary of a Jewish moneylender, who can be none other than Aaron,[2] while Biddlesden, another of the nine, had obtained a gage of land through the intermediary of another Jewish moneylender.[3] And though the evidence for the twelfth century is meagre, there is evidence that in the thirteenth century Cistercian houses continued to acquire estates by transactions with Jewish moneylenders, and among those abbeys there are some of the nine of Richard I's charter.[4] The inference seems obvious that, besides Meaux Abbey, nine other Cistercian abbeys—Rievaulx, Newminster, Kirkstead, Louth Park, Revesby, Rufford, Kirkstall, Roche and Biddlesden —had in Henry II's reign engaged in transactions with Aaron of Lincoln for the acquisition of encumbered estates.

However that may be, the two cases which we know in detail justify certain deductions and merit comment before we proceed farther. If wealthy Jews were capitalists in the twelfth century, so also were wealthy religious communities. The intervention of Henry II in the transaction between Michael de Wanchy and Waltham Abbey was an unusual circumstance: it must not divert our attention from the preceding negotiations in which Michael

[1] *Pipe Roll 2 Richard I*, p. 89: 'Abbas de Rupe et abbas de Parco et socii eorum reddunt compotum de M. marcis pro fine facto cum rege de debitis Aaron Iudei Lincollie.'

[2] *Monasticon*, v. 505, no. xiv. Roche Abbey benefited by the remission of 1,300 marks, so that, assuming the total remission to have been distributed proportionately, its debt to Aaron had been 1540 marks, presumably the largest of the nine. The abbot in 1189 was Osmund, who had been cellarer of Fountains, and it is easy to see why he took the lead. The debt had been incurred by his predecessor, Hugh of Wadworth, who seems to have died in 1184.

[3] *Starrs and Jewish Charters*, i. 128.

[4] Below, p. 98.

had been engaged, seemingly of his own motion, with the Hospitallers, who were, it seems, quite ready purchasers.[1] He must have
been aware that there were religious houses who were prepared to
take over the debts of hard-pressed landowners in return for the
conveyance of part (at least) of the mortgaged land. And the story
of Meaux Abbey and William Fossard points unmistakably in the
same direction. Religious houses were—to use modern phraseology—in the market for encumbered estates. They must have
been clients equally welcome to debtor and creditor. If the debtor
rid himself of an ever-increasing debt and at the same time acquired a little ready money and perhaps some odour of piety into
the bargain, the creditor realised his capital and some part, at least,
of his interest which had hitherto been guaranteed to him on
rather poor security. For though we may speak of the gaging of
land as a mortgage, the transaction differed in important respects
from a modern mortgagee. The mortgagee could not, as a rule,
foreclose and enter into possession nor, as a rule, could he sell the
land.

Despite a wealth of surviving Jewish bonds, the manner in
which they were enforced remains obscure. All the accounts that
the creditors must have kept have long since perished. But it is
clear that, when a borrower offered a manor as security, what he
was offering to the lender was the income from the manor. Now
the manor consisted of the demesne—which might or might not
be cultivated by the owner—and a bundle of rights over the rest of
the estate, rights that were translated into a variety of payments
and that varied from year to year. The income was very largely in
kind, not money. Commonly the owner of the manor resided
there for some part of the year and had no need to turn much of
the income into cash. To do so meant trouble and expense, and
this trouble and expense would have been multiplied if the
marketing had been done by a creditor living in a distant town.
Doubtless we have here the explanation of the provision in bonds
not only for transferring the income of a manor to the creditor
but for the payment of interest. Income and interest, there seems

[1] Above, p. 88.

no reason to doubt, were alternatives: the creditor did not get both. And the fact that debts rapidly increased suggests that the income available did not suffice to cover the interest. But the bond gave no other security and seems usually to have provided no sanction if the interest were not met.[1] If occasionally the creditor reserved the right to dispose of the land[2] or if he obtained from the king's court the right to dispose of it, he still could not give a good title to a purchaser without the co-operation of the owner, whose seisin was protected by the common law; and resort to the king's court was likely to prove an expensive matter, for the king did not give his aid for nothing. We must, of course, draw a sharp line of distinction between loans secured on movables, which passed into the possession of the creditor and which he could sell, and loans secured on land, which he could not sell. It is with the latter that we are at present concerned. We have a good indication of the value of the security provided by land when Aaron of Lincoln reduced his claim by nearly 40 per cent. on the prospect of transferring the debt to a solvent religious house, and charged no more than 5 per cent. interest a year upon the capital sum, though part repayments of capital do not seem to have reduced the interest. It may perhaps seem remarkable that Jewish financiers continued to advance money to embarrassed landowners on the security of land. That they did so suggests that they had in view the prospect of the ultimate transfer of the debt to a religious house or other purchaser, who thereby acquired property that might not otherwise have come upon the market. In the calculation of risks, this was an important factor.

The situation was complicated by the relation of the Jews to the Crown. Not only was the Crown the universal heir to all Jewish property, but whenever the Jews were taxed or whenever a wealthy Jew was compelled to submit to a heavy fine, inevitably pressure was applied to borrowers to pay off their debts.[3] Thus

---

[1] See the examples printed in the Appendix, pp. 242–67.

[2] See below, pp. 254–6.

[3] This is implied when the bonds of Jurnet and Le Brun are confiscated and realized (above, pp. 40–1, 62).

93

the transfer of debts and lands to religious houses was accelerated.[1] And if Jewish financiers followed their calling in full knowledge of the burdens and hazards that confronted them and their families, so also we must assume that landowners borrowed and entered into obligations with at least some inkling of the prospects before them if they let their debts run on. With each party independently pursuing his own ends, this complex system provided, accidentally but surely, the solvent which broke down the apparent rigidity of the structure of feudal land tenure and facilitated the transfer of estates to a new capitalist class, the religious communities, or to new men who were making their fortune in the service of the Crown. This generalization must be justified by further instances. Rarely do we get examples so detailed as the two already reviewed. The indication that apparent benefactions to monasteries are in reality the transfer of property in return for the acquittance of debts may be no more than the entry in a cartulary of a bond binding a landowner to repay a loan with interest or of an acquittance given by a moneylender to a landowner or to a religious house. It seems to have been the exception, and not the rule, to copy documents of this kind. If the deeds were copied that conveyed the property from the original owner to the religious house, it might seem a superfluous precaution to copy documents that were, after all, incidental. A mass of ephemeral documents had to be excluded from cartularies if they were not to become unwieldy. What has come down to us is, then, but a fraction of the evidence, but the surviving evidence is adequate to show that there was a steady, unceasing stream of transactions of this kind throughout the thirteenth century. The process may have been slowed down, but it was certainly not brought to an end, by the Statute of the Jewry of 1275.[2]

We may begin by tracing some further transactions in which

---

[1] So the Meaux chronicler, commenting on the case of Thomas of Etton (below, p. 95), writes: 'cum omnes qui erga Iudeos qualicunque debito obligati erant regi de ipso debito satisfacere compellerentur, predictus Thomas pro ccxl. marcis per xii. annos reddendis, quolibet scilicet anno xx. marcis, finem pacificum cum rege composuit' (*Chron. de Melsa*, i. 375).

[2] *Statutes of the Realm*, i. 220–1.

Meaux Abbey was involved. Shortly after the monks had cleared themselves of the burden of William Fossard's debts, they found 50 marks to acquit another borrower from the Jews and in exchange acquired the whole of the mortgaged property.[1] Late in John's reign or early in Henry III's they assisted Thomas of Etton to discharge his debts to the Jews, the greater part of which was demanded by the king, who had taken the debts over.[2] In return Thomas gaged certain lands for twenty years and gave the monastery certain other lands outright. Under Henry III the abbey continued its policy of acquisition. The term *policy* is fitting, for it cannot be merely by accident that a series of like transactions affecting different landowners occurred in the same villages, all of them involving the acquittance of debts to Jewish moneylenders and the transfer of the pledged lands to the monks.[3] Meaux is in the East Riding of Yorkshire. Fountains Abbey in the West Riding was pursuing the same policy, which is evidenced by a like series of documents.[4] That there was nothing fortuitous in the transactions and that there was active co-operation with the Jewish creditors is strikingly illustrated by the existence of two quitclaims from Aaron, the son of Josce, of York, executed on the same occasion before the mayor of York in respect of lands in different parishes transferred to the monks by different borrowers.[5] In the North Riding of Yorkshire lies Malton Priory, and the canons of this house were treading the same path under Henry III as the Cistercians of Meaux and Fountains. We learn this from a series of acquittances which were not originally intended to be entered in the priory's cartulary but which some cautious person transcribed in the margins of the book.[6] They all come from the forties of the thirteenth century; but that this should be so is probably mere accident: they were the only ones which the

---

[1] *Chron. de Melsa*, i. 315.      [2] *Ibid.*, i. 374–7.

[3] *Ibid.*, ii. 9–12, 109. For another series of transactions in which Meaux Abbey was involved see below, p. 105.

[4] *Chartulary of Fountains Abbey* (ed. W. T. Lancaster), pp. 234, 311, 340–1, 384–5.

[5] *Ibid.*, pp. 528, 609. The parishes are Long Marston and Goldsborough, eight miles or so apart.      [6] Printed below, pp. 281–4.

annotator had conveniently to hand. A number of Jews of York and Lincoln are concerned: Aaron of York; Josce, his nephew; Jacob, the son of Léon, of Lincoln; Léon, the bishop of the Jews of York; Benedict of Nantes, now of Lincoln. The priory is in relations with them all. Two borrowers are principally concerned, William of Richborough and William of Redburn, but a third is incidentally mentioned, Geoffrey of Grimston. It is significant that, in the acquittance in which the last-named is mentioned, William of Redburn also appears. Here are its terms:

> To all who shall see or hear this letter Léon, bishop of the Jews of York, sends greeting. Know that I have received quittance in full for all debts which Geoffrey of Gimston, clerk, owed to me or my heirs from the beginning of the world to the end of time and likewise in regard to William of Redburn for all debts which he owed to me from the beginning of the world until Easter in the year of Grace 1243. Wherefore I have granted to the prior and convent of Malton complete immunity in respect of the lands which they hold, both by grant of the said Geoffrey and by grant of the said William.[1]

Just as in the case of the quitclaims which Fountains Abbey obtained on one and the same occasion from different borrowers, so in the case of this quitclaim, which covers the borrowings of two landowners, we have evidence of a well-organized business for marketing encumbered estates.

Another of the Malton Priory acquittances sheds welcome light upon some of the details of the business. The instrument reads:

> To all who shall see or hear this letter Josce the Jew, nephew of Aaron the Jew of York, sends greeting. Know that I have granted and committed to the prior and convent of Malton six bovates of land in Little Edstone, long ago mortgaged to me by William son of William of Redburn and at last passing to me by the king's authority, to have and to hold, with all its appurtenances, peacefully and without disturbance from me and my

---

[1] Below, p. 284.

heirs for ever, quit of any debt contracted between me and the said William from the beginning of the world to the end of time. I give, moreover, the same undertaking in respect of all debts contracted with any Jew whomsoever up to the making of this instrument, excepting only Sir Léon, the bishop of the Jews of York; but the instrument of no other Jew shall be valid if henceforth it shall be produced against them by anyone whomsoever. If, moreover, the said William or any one of his family shall in any way disturb the aforesaid prior and convent in the possession of the aforesaid six bovates of land, I will refund to them forthwith the whole of the money I have received from them, without argument and with no dissimulation, when they shall have restored to me the chirographs of the preliminary agreements between me and the said William which were committed to them in trust, and I will restore the deeds of the Jews to whom the said William was bound, so that their immunity may be fully safeguarded. And of all these engagements I have appointed my uncle Aaron to be surety and he, as well as I, has inscribed this deed in Hebrew as evidence of the security he has given.[1]

Some points in this deed should perhaps be emphasized. The creditor did not obtain the right to dispose of the land until he had the king's authority—exercised, doubtless, through the medium of the Justices of the Jews. He also found it necessary to enter into an agreement with the landowner for the conveyance of the property to the monastery. Thus safeguarded, the monastery was prepared to buy out the creditor's claims for an agreed sum. Until, however, there was a formal grant by the landowner to the monastery and until the monastery was put in seisin of the land, the monastery was not yet secure, and so this elaborate agreement was required between the prior and convent and the mortgagee to safeguard them in case the landowner should not fulfil his obligations. It will be noticed that the mortgagee gave an indemnity against any claims from any other Jewish moneylenders,

---

[1] Below, pp. 281–2.

except one, namely Léon, the bishop of the Jews of York. With him the monastery had to conduct separate negotiations so that it might obtain, two years later, an acquittance from him in the terms stated above.

If this procedure appears to be very complicated, we may reflect that conveyancing in the Middle Ages was apt to be a very complicated business and that infinite precautions were thought necessary to defeat any possible adverse claims. There was much buying off of possible claimants—a cheaper alternative to litigation. A Jewish moneylender, although he had acquired the right to dispose of land, could not himself convey it and could not give the purchaser a good title. In the end the land was conveyed and the purchaser put in seisin, and those used to the business doubtless took the multiplication of documents very much as a matter of course. And if dealings in mortgaged land were more difficult than dealings in land that was unencumbered in this way, the complications were not very much greater.

It would be wearisome to go in detail into other examples of these transactions, but something must be said of them because we have no other material for answering the question: how extensive were dealings in land that had been mortgaged to Jewish moneylenders? The religious houses which have so far provided our examples have been houses of Cistercian monks and Augustinian canons. We can find a good deal of evidence for dealings by houses of these two orders. Waltham Abbey, for example, not only profited by the transaction between Le Brun and Henry II, but is found, not very long after, engaged in dealings on its own account.[1] Other houses of Augustinian canons to acquire land in this fashion in the thirteenth century were Holy Trinity, Aldgate,[2] and Healaugh Park.[3] Further examples of Cistercian dealings are provided by Kirkstead[4] and Biddlesden.[5] The Premonstratensian

---

[1] Below, p. 268; Waltham Abbey was still trafficking in Jewish debts in 1268 (*Cal. Plea Rolls*, i. 211).

[2] *Starrs and Jewish Charters*, i. 47; Davis, *Shetaroth*, p. 351 (no. 194: before 1250).

[3] *Cal. Charter Rolls*, iii. 157. For a somewhat similar transaction by Dunstable Priory, another house of Augustinian canons, see below, pp. 259–63.

[4] *Starrs and Jewish Charters*, i. 34–6.          [5] *Ibid.*, pp. 128–30.

canons are represented by Newhouse Abbey,[1] the Gilbertines by Bullington Priory,[2] the Cluniacs by Lenton Priory.[3] The Benedictines are represented by Christ Church, Canterbury,[4] Hyde Abbey,[5] Durham Priory[6] and St. Neot's Priory;[7] and there can be no doubt that St Albans was also in the business.[8] Nunneries, as well as monasteries, took the opportunity to acquire mortgaged lands, as we know from the cases of Greenfield Priory (Cistercian)[9] and Flixton Priory (Augustinian)[10]. And while the majority of examples come from Yorkshire and Lincolnshire, there are examples also from Buckinghamshire, Durham, Hampshire, Hertfordshire, Kent, Northumberland, Nottinghamshire, Suffolk and London. Since the evidence is fragmentary and fortuitous, it cannot be without significance that the examples cover so wide a geographical range and so many religious orders. It is obviously impossible to say how much land was acquired by religious houses by means of transactions in encumbered estates, but it is safe to infer that the practice was widespread and general.[11] There was land available on the market, waiting for purchasers, and whether it was acquired by a religious house or not must have depended primarily upon the financial resources that house commanded at

---

[1] *Ibid.*, pp. 2–4, 36–52, 56–68.   [2] *Ibid.*, pp. 30–2.

[3] Davis, *Shetaroth*, pp. 277–8 (no. 136: *c.* 1230).

[4] *Starrs and Jewish Charters*, i. 122–4; ii. 305–19.   [5] *Archaeologia*, lix. 263.

[6] Davis, *Shetaroth*, pp. 360–4 (nos. 196–200); Adler, *Jews of Medieval England*, pp. 169–73.   [7] Fowler, *Cartulary of Old Warden*, p. 364.

[8] In the St Albans cartulary, Otho D. iii, fo. 29*b*, col. 1, there is an acquittance by Elias l'Eveske, of 24 Henry III, in respect of land pledged by Colmer of Oxhey. What lies behind such an acquittance is made clear by what Matthew Paris tells us of another transaction with Elias. The abbey was bound to him in respect of a debt of Richard of Oxhey. The debt was paid off; the counterparts of the deeds were surrendered by Elias and the keepers of the *archa* and the abbey received a starr of acquittance (*Chronica Majora*, v. 398–9). The abbey had later dealings with Cok Hagin, the results of which are shown in deeds of 1271 in *Cal. Patent Rolls, 1266–1271*, pp. 511–12. Walsingham's picturesque account of the transactions in *Gesta Abbatum*, i. 401, is quite unreliable.

[9] *Starrs and Jewish Charters*, i. 78–80.   [10] *Ibid.*, pp. 124–7.

[11] Particulars of some later transactions of Meaux Abbey are given below, p. 105. The religious houses under Edward I, to which references are given at p. 107, n. 4, are Guisborough and Drax (Augustinian), Beaulieu (Cistercian) and Glastonbury (Benedictine).

any particular time. A house financially embarrassed could not go upon the market: a house with funds for investment is not likely to have had to look long for suitable property.

We catch a glimpse of transactions in which laymen might be involved in the history of the manor of Tottenham. This was pledged by William of Tottenham to Avigai of London and her son Abraham. The bond is an elaborate one and it contains an express provision under which the creditors had the right to dispossess the mortgagor and to lease the manor if he failed to keep up his payments. He seems to have got into difficulties, for he appears to have conveyed the manor to Earl David of Scotland, who presumably settled with the mortgagees. The earl, in turn, appears to have found it necessary to mortgage the manor, but he was fortunate in being able to arrange with King John to get free from his debts on easy terms.[1] We have here but an indication of the way in which through the intermediary of Jewish money-lenders property passed from layman to layman in the twelfth century. It is, however, in line with our much more extensive knowledge of the way in which father and son, Robert and Henry of Braybrooke, built up extensive estates in the reigns of John and Henry III. The Braybrookes were 'new men'. The father was sub-sheriff of Bedfordshire and Buckinghamshire from 1197. He became sheriff of these counties in 1204, of Northampton in 1208, and of Rutland in 1209. On his death in 1211, Henry of Bray-brooke succeeded him and held the four counties until the eve of the Barons' War.[2] It was he who figured in the well-known incident which led to the fall of Fawkes de Bréauté in 1224: offended at a decision that Henry had given as justice of assize,

---

[1] Below, pp. 254–6.

[2] For particulars see Public Record Office *List of Sheriffs*. The Braybrookes did not farm the counties they held, but had their custody: for the significance of this see S. Painter, *The Reign of King John*, pp. 118–22. As steward of William of Aubigny, Robert appears to have acted for him when he was sheriff of Leicestershire and Warwickshire in 1197–1198 (*Memoranda Roll 1 John*, pp. 52–3). Henry was of some consequence among the rebellious barons. His opposition to King John led to the loss of his shrievalties, Bedfordshire and Buckinghamshire at Michaelmas, 1214, Rutland at Easter, 1215, Northampton in June, 1215, while the king seized his lands (Painter, *op. cit.*, pp. 287, 302, 307, 329).

Fawkes' brother imprisoned him in Bedford Castle.[1] The Bray-brookes were, then, men of the ministerial class who, without attaining high office, were responsible for much of the day-to-day administration of the country. Their official position put them in touch with both landowners and moneylenders and they would seem to have used their official connexions to their personal advantage. So effectually, indeed, did Robert Braybrooke take advantage of these connexions that the family from which he seems chiefly to have profited, Wischard Leydet and Margery Foliot his wife, not only parted with their lands but with their only daughter and heiress, Christiane, who became Henry Bray-brooke's wife and so brought to him what remained of her inheritance.[2]

The surviving deeds display various aspects of the Braybrookes' transactions and they relate to the lands they acquired not only in their native Northamptonshire and in Bedfordshire and Bucking-hamshire but also in Essex and Leicestershire and as far afield as Somerset.[3] Rarely have all the deeds connected with any one transaction come down to us, and a good many of the survivors are too sparing of details to give any indication of the land to which they relate, but the inference from every one of them must be that they represent stages in the acquisition of property. Sometimes a landowner may have approached one of the Braybrookes for the money to release him from his debts to the Jews and agreed to

---

[1] K. Norgate, *Minority of Henry III*, pp. 230–3: corrections in Richardson and Sayles, *Select Cases of Procedure without Writ*, pp. xxx–xxxii.

[2] *Excerpta e Rotulis Finium*, i. 80. For Wischard Leydet and his wife see below, pp. 272–5. There is an elaborate fine of 27 April 1214, by which Wischard and Margery convey land to Earl David (himself a heavy borrower from Jewish moneylenders) who, in turn, conveys to Henry Braybrooke (Hunter, *Fines*, i. 88).

[3] The deeds printed below (pp. 271–80) represent but part of their transactions. The grant to Robert of Braybrooke of land in Horsington, Somerset, in consideration of 60 marks which Robert has provided to acquit the vendor against the king for debts to Jews, is printed in *Pipe Roll 12 John*, p. 16. An action arising out of the conveyance of Kinwick (in Sandy, Beds.) to Robert 'pro debito Iudeorum', apparently in 1209, is in *Curia Regis Rolls*, vi. 361. For an action arising out of another transaction of Robert's, whereby he acquired land at Evenley, Northants, see *ibid.*, viii. 376: the grant to Robert by the embarrassed landowner, Maud of Combe, is in Sloane MS. 986, fo. 14.

convey land in exchange. In other cases there seems to have been a
preliminary agreement between the creditor and one of the Braybrookes to which the debtors were induced to conform. The
necessity for a conveyance from the mortgagor to the acquirer of
the encumbered estate gave the former some scope for bargaining,
but his position must in most cases have been nearly desperate. The
Braybrookes, however, are but a type. Of the same type, though
he operated on a humbler scale, was master Philip Galle, rector of
St Clement's, Saltfleetby, who, for a good many years in the
latter part of Henry III's reign, was steadily building up a modest
estate in his corner of Lincolnshire by the acquisition of small
parcels of land. He, too, had no scruple in availing himself of the
opportunities offered by Jewish moneylenders, as surviving starrs
in his favour testify.[1] In any case, the surviving plea rolls of the
Exchequer of the Jews contain many indications that laymen, as
well as ecclesiastics, were acquiring property in the same way.[2]
The transfer of land by the intermediary of a Jewish moneylender
became so general and was thought so prejudicial to the king that
tenants on ancient demesne holding in socage or villeinage were
forbidden to borrow on the security of their lands.[3] The prohibition is eloquent testimony to the widespread use of the facilities
offered by Jewish moneylenders and the frequency with which a
change of ownership resulted. There is no reason, however, to
suppose that these restrictions extended beyond the ancient
demesne of the Crown[4] or that the movement was sensibly

[1] P.R.O., D.L. 36/2, nos. 8, 130, 213: three separate Jewish moneylenders are
concerned, including Hagin, the son of master Moses, who had dealings with
Adam of Stratton (above, p. 72). Philip Galle is described as rector of St
Clement's in D.L. 25/2705: no other deed seems to mention his ecclesiastical office,
and the episcopal registers, which are defective, throw no light on the period of
his incumbency. The earliest deed of his, dated 1250, appears to be D.L. 25/3057:
he was certainly dead by 1280 (*Cal. Inq. Post Mortem*, ii. 219). He has left behind
him a mass of deeds (mostly between D.L. 25/2350 and D.L. 25/3000) which
invite investigation for the light they throw on the extensive traffic in small
parcels of land in the thirteenth century.

[2] *Cal. Plea Rolls*, i. 87, 155–6, 200, 207–8, *et passim*.

[3] *Close Rolls, 1231–1234*, p. 592.

[4] On this point I cannot follow Mr Roth at p. 52 of his *History of the Jews in
England*: his references do not seem to bear him out.

retarded until the legislation of Edward I restricted the forms that
Jewish moneylending could take.[1]

The fortunate survival of the Braybrooke muniments enables
us to prove that laymen, as well as religious houses, were in the
market for encumbered estates on an extensive scale. There is less
evidence in the case of laymen because far fewer records have been
preserved to throw light upon their transactions in land in the
twelfth and thirteenth centuries. However, we know enough to
be certain of the essential facts. The transaction might be in the
nature of a family arrangement for paying off imprudently
incurred debts or there might be a series of transactions whereby
a prudent landowner profited by the misfortunes of others to
extend his boundaries. One truth it is important to stress, namely,
that the market in encumbered estates was open to all with money.
If religious houses figure prominently in the story it is principally because they have left more records behind them. It may also
be emphasized that these transactions took the form they assumed
because of the legal status of the Jews. A Jew, says Bracton, can
have no property in land because whatsoever he acquires is
acquired not for himself but for the king. Bracton is theorizing
here, for he is finding a reason for one practical consequence of
Jewish transactions in land, that the law of distress would not
touch a Jew because he would not be in occupation of agricultural
land. Again it was supposed that, because a Jew did not hold in
fee, the land could not be seized into the king's hand. These explanations might serve to give plausibility to rules of procedure, but
Bracton never seriously considers the anomalous title by which
Jews held land.[2] Elsewhere in his treatise he contemplates the conveyance of land to Jews.[3] The inconsistency is perhaps more

---

[1] The twenty-fifth article of the Petition of the Barons (Stubbs, *Select Charters*,
p. 385) shows that in 1258 the mortgaging of land to Jews continued on a substantial scale. This is not in itself considered an abuse. Objection is taken to the
transfer to magnates of land gaged to Jews and the refusal of these Christians to
treat with the representatives of an heir under age for the repayment of the loan
and accumulated interest. For the position under Edward I see below, pp. 106–7.

[2] Bracton, fo. 386*b*, 387. He is seemingly influenced by the *Leges Edwardi
Confessoris* (below, p. 109).      [3] Bracton, fo. 13, 47*b*.

apparent than real. It would seem that the deeds which bound a landowner to a Jewish moneylender might, in Bracton's time, take the form of a grant in fee.[1] But whatever form a bond might take, Jews seem never to have had more than a limited and transitory interest in the land, though the fear that they might so extend their interest as to give them the right of wardship and marriage and presentation to churches led to restrictive legislation at the end of Henry III's reign.[2] Still, whatever fear may have inspired the legislation, the incident in itself shows how far the Jews were from acquiring an estate in land of the same kind as Christians enjoyed.

Reference has already been made to one development of Jewish financial practice[3] that calls for some brief notice here. About the middle of the thirteenth century the device appears to have become common of accommodating landowners with capital sums in return for the creation of an annual rentcharge upon his land.[4] The instrument by which this was effected appears to have been a gage of land. Such rentcharges, if granted in perpetuity, found a ready market among Christians, and they might lead eventually to the transfer of the land upon which the rent-charge was secured. The further creation of such rentcharges was forbidden in January 1269 and those created that had not been sold to Christians were annulled.[5] But for a number of years there appears to have been a brisk traffic in rentcharges of this

---

[1] The legislation of 1271 (see following note) prohibited the acquisition by Jews of freeholds 'per cartam, donum, feofamentum . . .' For an actual convey-ance by way of grant in 1270 see *Cal. Charter Rolls, 1257–1333*, p. 160.

[2] *Liber de Antiquis Legibus*, pp. 234–6; *Foedera*, i. 489.     [3] Above, p. 73.

[4] The practice had begun earlier. A perpetual corn-rent, commencing in 1230, is recorded (P.R.O., E. 101/249/10), and there is a reference to a render of corn as a 'fee' under a chirograph of 1237 (*Close Rolls, 1234–1237*, p. 500).

[5] The legislation of 1269 is in *Cal. Patent Rolls, 1266–1272*, p. 376, and *Red Book of the Exchequer*, iii. 978 (whence Rigg, *Select Pleas*, pp. xlviii–li). This is in French. In Latin form it appears as directions to the exchequer dated 14 May 1270 (*Close Rolls, 1268–1272*, p. 268). The 'dettes a Gyus ke sunt fees' or in Latin 'debita Iudeorum que sunt feodi' are more precisely defined in the confirming legislation of 1271 (above, n. 2) as 'redditus de terris et tenementis Christianorum tanquam perpetuos'. Their nature is shown quite clearly in a starr of Adam of Stratton's of 1267–8, which speaks of 'une dette de vint livres de fe' (*Starrs and Jewish Charters*, i. 12–20).

kind.[1] An actual example will explain the circumstances in which they were likely to be created and suggest the reason why they came to be regarded with disfavour, though ministers and the highest in the land had not scrupled to buy and sell them. Once more the example is provided by Meaux Abbey. John of Skerne was a distant neighbour of the abbey, who, when a youngish man, had got into financial difficulties and had sold part of his land to the monks to quit himself of his debts to the Jews.[2] But before very long he must have begun borrowing again and at last found himself indebted to Benedict, the son of Josce of York, to the extent of 250 marks or so. In the hope of freeing himself from this debt, he granted a perpetual rentcharge of £10 to Gamaliel of Oxford, who transferred it to Prince Edward. What John realized by this transaction does not appear, but it is plain that he did not free himself from his debt to Benedict, and he was now faced with the problem of finding £10 a year payable to a creditor who was not likely to be lenient. Once more, then, John turned to the monks of Meaux and gaged his land to them for a term of years. The monks proceeded to buy up John's debts to Benedict and the rentcharge that had passed to Prince Edward. Meanwhile, however, Benedict seems to have sold such rights as he had in the land to William d'Aubigny, who ejected the monks, but finally an agreement was reached with him, and the monks possessed themselves of the land, leaving John apparently with nothing. From first to last, the transaction cost the monks a little over £100, despite the expense to which they were put in making their claim good, and though we cannot put a precise figure on the total of John's liabilities, it is evident that the abbey had to pay a good deal less than that, and the impression remains that the business was a profitable one for the abbey.[3]

[1] *Cal. Plea Rolls*, i. 138, 152, 161, 162, *et passim*; *Close Rolls, 1259–1261*, p. 344; *1261–1264*, pp. 127–8; *1264–1268*, pp. 57, 404–5, 428.

[2] *Chronica Mon. de Melsa*, ii. 55. Skerne is a little more than 20 miles north of Meaux.

[3] The story is told in *Chronica Mon. de Melsa*, ii. 115, and *Cal. Plea Rolls*, i. 152, 161, 173. The details are not easy to harmonize, but the general outline is clear enough.

Although the creation of perpetual rentcharges was forbidden in 1269 and this legislation was confirmed in 1271,[1] it is by no means certain that it was effective, except in a narrow, formal sense. The legislation was directed against the form that money-lending took. To prevent the creation of perpetual rentcharges or the conveyance of land in fee simple, however, was one thing: other forms of bond could be devised without difficulty, even when to existing restrictions there was added in 1275 the prohibition of usury.[2] A deed of Henry of Berkeley may provide our first illustration. In return for a payment of £120 from Aaron, the son of Vives, of London, he granted an annual rent of £40 for ten years from Candlemas 1276. This was no clandestine transaction, for it was acknowledged before the Justices of the Jews and entered on their roll. The deed is in the form of a gage. There is no provision for the payment of usury should Henry default in his payments, but he submits to a penalty to be paid to the king and to distraint by the sheriff.[3] A parallel transaction, which illustrates another form of evasion (if evasion it should be called)[4] is a bond of 1286 between Henry le Palmer of Costock and Hagin, the son of Bateman, of Nottingham. In this case there is a purported sale to the moneylender of forty quarters of wheat, for which payment is acknowledged, though no sum is stated. The debtor agrees to deliver the wheat twelve weeks later or alternatively to pay cash at the rate of five shillings a quarter. If the debtor should default, he submits to distraint by the sheriff or the constable of Northampton Castle or any other bailiff until the debt has been

[1] Above, p. 104, n. 5.

[2] *Statutes of the Realm*, i. 220–1. The prohibition could not have affected more than certain overt forms of usury. Pawnbroking, which might be thought to be impossible under the prohibition, certainly continued: see the case of 1280 in Rigg, *Select Pleas*, p. 107.

[3] *Cal. Plea Rolls*, iii. 53. For further dealings in the gaged land see *ibid.*, pp. 283–4. The limitation of ten years shows that the instrument was framed in the light of the statute of 1275 which provided 'k'il pussent prendre e acheter fermes à terme de dyz ans' (*Statutes of the Realm*, i. 221a: the text as printed is not satisfactory).

[4] The practice was perfectly well known to the authorities, so much so that it was proposed to abandon the formal prohibition of usury and instead to regulate the rate of interest (Rigg, *Select Pleas*, pp. xl, xli).

paid, together with the losses and expenses incurred by the creditor.[1] In such ways, so long as there was no overt usury, the requirements of the law were satisfied, and the ordinary machinery of the law was employed to secure payment. The details we have of the bonds that passed to the Crown at the Expulsion suggest that the bond between Henry le Palmer and Hagin may be typical of many executed after the prohibition of usury.[2] Very much more needs to be known before we can assess the effect of the legislation of 1269–75, but a *caveat* must be entered against the inference that it put an end to profitable moneylending.[3]

The discussion of these late developments in Jewish finance is in the nature of an aside. Nothing of the kind can be traced in the twelfth century or under John. But it may be well to be reminded that, under changing forms, the relations of the Jewish moneylenders to landowners, the official class, the monasteries, remained essentially the same, multiplying indeed as the technique of finance was developed. Under Edward I as under his predecessors, abbots and priors[4] and laymen[5] are acquiring encumbered estates and the greatest acquirer of them all is Edward's consort, Queen Eleanor.[6] This tangled story, however, must be left to another hand to write.

[1] P.R.O. Ancient Deeds C. 1360. This bond has points of similarity to the forms used by contemporary Italian moneylenders, especially the final clause providing for distraint 'quousque tam de dampnis et expensis suis quam de principali debito dicto Iudeo vel suo attornato, prius et pre omnibus aliis debitis nostris [i.e. the debtor's] plene et integre fuerit satisfactum, renunciando omni iuris remedio'. The unstated sum received by a debtor was, of course, substantially less than the £10 he was required to pay; but he could not plead this if, in any way, the case came into court.

[2] Jewish Hist. Soc., *Transactions*, vii. 79–89.

[3] Mr Roth's interpretation of the legislation (*History of the Jews in England*, pp. 70–1) certainly needs qualification. But much investigation is necessary before a more exact picture can be drawn of the conditions in the period 1275–1290. This is hardly possible until all the plea rolls of the Exchequer of the Jews have been calendared.     [4] *Cal. Plea Rolls*, iii. 61, 76–7, 140–1, 273.

[5] *Ibid.*, pp. 72, 75, 77, 78, *et passim*.

[6] As late as December 1286 Archbishop Pecham was remonstrating with the queen, through her treasurer, at the accumulation of properties encumbered by usurious debts that she had acquired and was continuing to acquire (*Registrum Epistolarum Iohannis Peckham*, iii. 927). For some account of these see Tout, *Chapters in Medieval Administrative History*, v. 270–1, and references there given.

Living largely, as he did, beyond the frontiers of the common law and living largely by transactions forbidden by ecclesiastical law, the Jewish moneylender played an anomalous but necessary part in the economy of a Christian state. Moneylending at interest was at no time confined to Jews nor did it cease with their expulsion. But creditors of no other class were incapable of acquiring a freehold interest in land while acquiring the right to dispose of land. This circumstance, and their predominance for a time as private moneylenders, caused the Jews to become the vehicle—though not, of course, by any means the sole vehicle—for the transfer of land. Before the Expulsion of the Jews, repeated attempts were made to curb their dealings in land or to mitigate the consequences, and with their disappearance from England transactions in the form they took when a Jew was the intermediary necessarily ceased; but the market in land continued to be as active as ever. It cannot, however, be too strongly emphasized that the Jews did not act in the least like modern bankers, as the Templars did, nor were they international financiers as the Flemings had been and as, at the time of the Expulsion, the Italians were. Though the activities of the Jews and the Italians may have occasionally overlapped and both were, as contemporaries called them, usurers, their functions lay mainly in different fields and any comparison between them, though it may have contemporary warrant, is, at best, superficial. To suggest that in England the Jews were replaced by Italians[1] is to misconceive the course of history.

[1] P. Elman in *Economic History Review*, 1st Ser., vii. 151.

# VI

# THE JEWRY AND THE STATE

Two documents, which both reflect the position under Henry I, inform us of the juridical status of a Jew in England. The one document is a chapter of the Laws of Edward the Confessor; the other is the charter granted to the Jews of England and Normandy by Henry II. The Laws of the Confessor are of no authority, but they set down what the compiler, writing probably in the last years of Henry I or the first years of Stephen's reign, understood to be the law. As regards the Jews he said that they and all their possessions belonged to the king and that, without his licence, they might not put themselves under the protection of a magnate. The king had the right to demand their return as well as the return of their money. Wherever there were Jews in the kingdom the king's lieges were under an obligation to guard and protect them.[1] These broad principles were observed until the Expulsion in 1290. The text of the charter granted by Henry II has not survived, but its terms can be recovered from charters of Richard I[2] and John.[3] There was confirmed to the Jews of England and Normandy the right of residence, with all the customs and privileges they had exercised under Henry I. Jewish heirs were to be entitled to succeed to their fathers' estates.[4] Jews might trade freely in all things, except church ornaments and blood-stained garments. Pledges unredeemed for a year and a day might be lawfully sold by them. They might take their chattels with them freely

[1] For the text (chapter 25) see F. Liebermann, *Gesetze der Angelsachsen*, i. 650; for date, *ibid.*, iii. 341.
[2] *Foedera*, i. i. 51: in favour of Isaac, the son of Rabbi Josce.
[3] *Rot. Chart.*, p. 93: to Jews of England and Normandy.
[4] For the limitations on this right see below, pp. 115–16.

wherever they went and they were to be exempt from customs and tolls. Jews could sue and be sued only in the king's court and in courts held by the keepers of the castles within whose bailiwick they resided. Provision was made for proof in litigation between Jews and Christians, for the evidence of witnesses of both religions and for oaths to be taken according to the Jewish fashion.

Very much, of course, depended upon the way in which the rights accorded to the Jews were interpreted, and we must always remember that the charter had to be construed within the context of feudal custom[1] and that much was understood that was not expressed in writing. It is evident that although, in a sense, a Jew, or at least his property, might belong to the king, yet the Jew was a free man and the charter guaranteed him freedom from arbitrary treatment. As against all other men, except the king, he was protected. He was protected physically because he dwelt within the shadow of a royal castle, the keeper of which would incur the king's displeasure if any harm should happen to Jews within his jurisdiction. A further measure of protection was afforded because the king's lieges were also bound to protect the Jews, and this meant that the town authorities would be held responsible for any harm that might happen through mob violence to the Jewish community in their midst. The responsibility of keepers of royal castles (usually the sheriff) and of town authorities for protecting the Jews was maintained throughout the twelfth and thirteenth centuries,[2] but, as soon as we begin to get

[1] The word 'feudal' is used here as a convenient and conventional term; but, in its strict sense, the term is not a very apt one to apply to England in the twelfth century.

[2] The earliest reference is to the sheriff of Norfolk, John de Chesnay, who protects the Jews of Norwich under Stephen (Jessopp and James, *Life of St. William of Norwich*, pp. 29, 95, 111). The accounts of the massacres of 1190 refer to the protection due from the sheriff and town authorities and the sheltering of Jews in the king's castles (R. de Diceto, *Historical Works*, ii. 75–6; W. of Newburgh, *Historia* (ed. Howlett), ii. 312–24). In the thirteenth century the evidence is abundant (*Rot. Litt. Pat.*, p. 33; *Rot. Litt. Claus.*, i. 354b, 357, 359b; Cole, *Documents*, p. 301; *Patent Rolls, 1216–1225*, p. 157). A particularly detailed and instructive case is that of the Jews of Norwich which came before the king in 1235 (Richardson and Sayles, *Select Cases of Procedure without Writ*, pp. 21–3). See also below, p. 182.

references to litigation in which Jews were engaged, it is clear that they no longer commonly resorted to the courts held by castellans. The inference is that Henry II's charter was granted in the early years of his reign, before the reorganization of the judicature led to the supersession of much of the hitherto prevailing local administration of justice.

It may be said, in passing, that there is no reason to suppose, as has been sometimes suggested,[1] that Henry I had himself granted a charter to the Jews. If he had done so, we should have expected that a reference to it would have been preserved in later confirmations, whereas the only previous charter these confirmations mention is that of Henry II.[2] Yet that charter does reflect the conditions under Henry I, when justice was normally rendered in England in the county court, over which the local justice and the sheriff presided.[3] And it has to be remembered that the charter applied to Normandy as well as to England, where also justice was administered locally, though not on English lines.[4] Common, however, to both countries were the duke-king's courts and royal castellanies, which the king could strictly control, as he could not control local justice. We can hardly be wrong in inferring that the charter does not reflect specific English conditions at all and that what Henry I did was to extend to England the conditions governing the Jewish community that had gradually grown up in Normandy. Of medieval castle courts at any period little is known, and no document seems to have survived that tells of any case in which a Jew was involved elsewhere than in the court of the constable of the Tower of London.[5] Probably the English Jewry,

---

[1] Jacobs, *Jews of Angevin England*, p. 330; Roth, *History of the Jews in England*, p. 6; S. Painter, *The Reign of King John*, p. 143.

[2] This is true both of Richard I's charter to Isaac, the son of Rabbi Josce (*Foedera*, i. 51) and John's charter to the Jews of England and Normandy (*Rot. Chart.*, p. 93). Again John's charter to Deusaie of Bernay mentions only the 'libertates et liberas consuetudines per quas ipse et alii Iudei nostri solebant tractari tempore Henrici regis patris nostri et regis Ricardi fratris nostri' (*ibid.*, p. 27).

[3] Sayles, *Select Cases in the Court of King's Bench*, i. xix.

[4] C. H. Haskins, *Norman Institutions*, pp. 99–104, 148–52, 167–9.

[5] The jurisdiction claimed by the constable in the matter of pledges of the value of forty shillings and under is presumably a relic of his ancient jurisdiction,

concentrated as it was in London under Henry I, knew little of them, though it may be that, as Jewish settlement gradually extended under Stephen, Jews did at times resort to them. The important fact is that they need not seek justice in the London husting court or in any shire court. Presumably at Bungay and Thetford the Jewish communities were under the protection of the earl of Norfolk and resorted to a court held in his name. It is, however, only of the king's court that we can make positive statements.

The king's court was not necessarily held *coram ipso rege*. Since twelfth-century kings had to divide their time between Normandy and England, it was necessary for them to devise a form of administration in both countries that would provide adequately for effective and uniform government. This was secured by constituting the justiciar the principal minister in the king's presence and his viceroy in his absence. The justiciar presided over a permanent sedentary tribunal, the exchequer, and was responsible for the conduct of the normal business of administration. Not only did he preside over a central court but he controlled the itinerant justices, who brought uniform royal justice to all parts of the kingdom. Although this system can be seen operating under Henry I, it was not fully developed until the reign of Henry II.[1] Into this system the king's jurisdiction over the Jews necessarily fitted, and it is for this reason that we find them suing and being sued before the justices in eyre as well as in the exchequer and sometimes before the king himself. The entries in the pipe rolls, which are our sole source of information, give few details, but it is clear that most of the actions in which Jews were plaintiffs were for the recovery of money lent[2] or for the possession of land that had been mortgaged

---

though nothing seems to be known of it before 1261 (*Close Rolls, 1259–1261*, p. 385). For the criminal jurisdiction of the constable's court, see below, p. 155.

[1] Sayles, *op. cit.*, pp. xix–xxi, xxix; *Memoranda Roll 1 John*, pp. xi–xvi, lxxxii–lxxxiii.

[2] *Pipe Roll 16 Henry II*, p. 39; *19 Henry II*, pp. 18–19; *22 Henry II*, p. 85; *25 Henry II*, p. 41; *29 Henry II*, pp. 102, 128; *31 Henry II*, pp. 40, 222; *et passim*. See also *Three Rolls of the King's Court* (Pipe Roll Soc.), p. 30; a bond is alleged to be forged (1194).

to them.[1] Occasionally there are glimpses of actions where Jews sue Jews, arising out of financial transactions between them,[2] despite the practice, which was confirmed by King John, of settling disputes between Jews by Jewish law.[3] Civil actions by Christians against Jews are comparatively rare,[4] doubtless because Christians were creditors but rarely. The number of criminal actions or serious offences against the Crown involving Jews is not large. The most serious offence is rape,[5] and another serious offence, by the standards of the time, is surreptitiously dealing in treasure trove.[6] Other offences, to which there are many references, do not appear to have been very grave: seeking to recover a debt twice;[7] perjury;[8] assaulting a knight;[9] waste and hunting in the forest;[10] conspiracy;[11] association with outlaws;[12] infraction of the assize of wine.[13] There is nothing in all this that marks a distinction between Jew and Christian in the eye of the law. The clipping of silver coin,[14] accepting forbidden articles in pledge[15] and building a house despite the king's prohibition[16] are more specifically Jewish crimes. But Jews, it is significant to note, are like Christians in the use they make of the appeal of felony in the county courts.[17] What

---

[1] *Pipe Roll 22 Henry II*, p. 192; *1 Richard I*, p. 230; *6 John*, p. 78.

[2] *Pipe Roll 26 Henry II*, p. 32; *28 Henry II*, p. 162; *31 Henry II*, pp. 94–5, 198; *32 Henry II*, p. 78; *8 John*, p. 102.      [3] *Rot. Chart.*, p. 93*b*.

[4] *Pipe Roll 16 Henry II*, p. 150; *25 Henry II*, p. 49; *28 Henry II*, p. 162; *30 Henry II*, pp. 84, 121; *31 Henry II*, pp. 40–1, 222. Cf. *Rotuli Curiae Regis*, i. 289.

[5] *Pipe Roll 25 Henry II*, p. 35. The woman is a Christian. For a Jew suspected of being an accessory to the murder and robbery of a Jew by Christians see *Curia Regis Rolls*, iii. 146.

[6] *Pipe Roll 1 Richard I*, p. 110; *5 Richard I*, p. 29.

[7] *Pipe Roll 29 Henry II*, p. 159.

[8] *Ibid.*      [9] *Pipe Roll 31 Henry II*, p. 222.

[10] *Pipe Roll 34 Henry II*, p. 38; *2 Richard I*, p. 36; *1 John*, p. 207.

[11] *Pipe Roll 5 Richard I*, p. 92.      [12] *Ibid.*, p. 121.

[13] *Pipe Roll 23 Henry II*, p. 176; *7 Richard I*, p. 76; *5 John*, p. 193.

[14] *Pipe Roll 7 John*, pp. 213–14: cf. *Rot. Litt. Pat.*, p. 47*b*.

[15] *Pipe Roll 16 Henry II*, p. 10; *29 Henry II*, p. 14; *32 Henry II*, p. 78.

[16] *Pipe Roll 14 Henry II*, p. 5.

[17] *Pipe Roll 28 Henry II*, p. 161; *9 Richard I*, p. 114; *1 John*, p. 32; *7 John*, pp. 213–14; *Rot. Oblat.*, p. 391. See also *Rotuli Curiae Regis*, i. 79, for a duel between Jews at Tothill in 1194; this, however, was not necessarily in an appeal of felony.

is important is that the evidence for the access by Jews to the ordinary royal courts is continuous from 1170 onwards. In 1188 Jews were engaged in litigation before the justices in eyre in at least seven counties as wide apart as Devon is to Kent and Essex to Northumberland,[1] and at this period they were constantly engaged in litigation before the bench at Westminster.[2] There was, let it be emphasized, no special tribunal to try cases in which Jews were involved. In the actual trial, there were, it must be presumed, though direct evidence is wanting, exceptional modes of proof. A plaint, whether by or against a Jew, had to be supported by men of both religions,[3] and if a case went to a jury, the jury must include Jews.[4] If the action were about borrowed money, it was for the Jewish lender to prove the amount of the capital and for the borrower to prove the amount of the interest due.[5] But in a society which set up special courts for merchants where there were peculiar forms of process and proof,[6] there was nothing particularly strange in prescribing rules that secured indifferent justice to Jews.

It seems to have been by an accident, through an expedient devised to deal with a particularly difficult task, that this uniform system of justice, common to Jews and Christians alike, was overturned and a special tribunal erected to deal with Jewish affairs. It

---

[1] *Pipe Roll 34 Henry II*, pp. 37, 38, 100, 168, 177, 199, 207.

[2] A good example is furnished by *Pipe Roll 31 Henry II*, pp. 40–1, 94–5, 222. See also the remarkable case in 1200 where the Jews of Norwich sued the burgesses for breaking into their cemetery (*Rotuli Curiae Regis*, ii. 155).

[3] *Et si querela orta fuerit . . . ille qui alium appellaverit ad querelam suam diracionandam habeat testes, scilicet legitimum Christianum et legitimum Iudeum* (*Foedera*, i. 51; *Rot. Chart.*, p. 93).

[4] *Et si Christianus habuerit querelam versus Iudeum sit iudicata per pares Iudei* (*ut supra*). For the way in which this provision was interpreted see Cole, *Documents*, pp. 288, 293, 297–8, 301.

[5] *Iudeus probabit catallum suum et Christianus lucrum* (*ut supra*). This was done before a mixed jury, as in the case of Simon of Kyme who offered the king 20 marks 'pro habenda iurata legalium Christianorum et Iudeorum' to determine what his father's debts were (*Pipe Roll 5 John*, p. 99).

[6] Holdsworth, *History of English Law*, v. 104–8. The use of mixed juries suggests the recognition of a common principle in the administration of justice between natives and strangers.

has already been explained that the pipe rolls record the results of the audit of the accounts of sheriffs and others by the barons of the exchequer and that these accounts did not by any means cover all of the king's revenue.[1] Special receipts were liable to be specially treated. The precise arrangements for enforcing control are unknown, but it is clear that the tallage imposed upon the Jews by Henry II at Christmas 1186 and other taxes imposed later were managed as a separate branch of the revenue. This is doubtless true also of taxes earlier than 1186, which have left little or no trace at all upon the pipe rolls.[2]

The system whereby Jewish taxes were separately collected and recorded was capable of extension or adaptation to other branches of the revenue. An occasion arose on the death in 1186 of Aaron of Lincoln, the wealthiest Jew of his time.[3] As we have seen, the charter which guaranteed the liberties of the Jews contained a clause assuring the right of succession to the heirs of the dead; but the king was wont to demand a price before the heir was admitted,[4] just as he demanded a relief from the heir of a landowner before his homage was accepted. We know that Aaron left two sons, Vives[5] and Elias,[6] and also a nephew, Benedict,[7] all of whom seem to have been associated with him in business. Elias ultimately purchased some of his bonds,[8] but none of his relatives succeeded, as heir, to Aaron's estate. It was perhaps because of the immensity of the estate that the heirs did not, or were not permitted to, succeed. The price the king was likely to demand would

[1] Above, p. 51–2.  [2] Below, pp. 161–2.
[3] The date of his death, in the week before Easter 1186, appears to be recorded only in a Cluniac chronicle, extracts from which have been published in the *English Historical Review*, vol. xliv, 94–104. The entry, *s.a.* 1186, runs: 'In ebdomada ante Pascha obiit Aaron Iudeus Londoniis morte subita' (*ibid.*, p. 95). He held property in London of the earl of Gloucester at a rent of 44s. (*Pipe Roll 33 Henry II*, p. 15; *Rot. Chart.*, p. 115). For the Gloucester soke, and for the site of Aaron's house, see above, pp. 7–8, 47.
[4] The king normally took a third of the deceased Jew's estate (Cole, *Documents*, p. 319; *Rot. Oblat.*, pp. 391, 420).
[5] *Pipe Roll 31 Henry II*, p. 95; *1 John*, p. 152; below, p. 249 (no. 4).
[6] *Rot. Oblat.*, pp. 420, 436.
[7] *Pipe Roll 31 Henry II*, p. 95; *3 Richard I*, p. 159.
[8] Above, p. 76.

have been correspondingly immense, and some of the assets were doubtful. Whatever the circumstances, Aaron's possessions were seized into the king's hand and the exchequer proceeded to realize upon them.[1] Aaron's bonds presented a special problem: not all were in his own name, some represented very complicated transactions, and it was not always certain whether or not loans had been repaid. The bonds were classified, county by county, and entered on special rolls. The roll for only the smallest of English counties, Rutland, has survived, but there is no doubt that it is typical of all.[2] The debtors were summoned to account with the king, apparently at different times at different centres— Nottingham, Northampton and Oxford are named.[3] Some borrowers were able to show that their debts had been discharged:[4] others compounded or, as it was said, 'made a fine' for their debts. The abbot of Peterborough settled for £100[5]: nine Cistercian abbots who were involved treated with Richard I as a body and were quit of a debt of 6,400 marks on payment of 1,000 marks.[6] There were a good many loans to Jews: whether these bore interest or not does not appear, but they seem to have been made largely to people in poor circumstances, who certainly, in many cases, were unable to repay what they had borrowed.[7]

We need not, however, go into many details of this kind. For our present purpose the importance of Aaron's bonds is that the method adopted by the exchequer for dealing with them illustrates a practice that was capable of development and generalization until it covered nearly all the relations between the Jewish community and the Crown. In the first instance the receipts from

---

[1] The rule, as stated later, was that 'it is the custom of the Jewry that the king can dispose of the chattels of a dead Jew unless the said Jew's relatives have made a fine for them' (*Cal. Inquisitions Misc.*, i. 201). 'Chattels' included real property and bonds.

[2] Below, p. 247.

[3] *Pipe Roll 32 Henry II*, p. 102; *33 Henry II*, p. 45. For the writ of summons see *ibid.*, pp. 39, 40.

[4] Below, pp. 247–8.

[5] *Pipe Roll 2 Richard I*, p. 29.

[6] *Ibid.*, p. 89. For this transaction, see above, pp. 90–1.

[7] For references see above, p. 69, n. 1.

Aaron's estate were kept separate from other revenue.[1] They appear to have been in the charge of Richard le Breton, archdeacon of Coventry, and Robert of Inglesham, archdeacon of Gloucester, who were doubtless engaged also in the arrangements for tracing and collecting the debts.[2] These men presumably were in charge of the *Scaccarium Aaron*, as it was called.[3] Their main work must have been completed by 1191, five years after Aaron's death, when the residue of debts outstanding was transferred for collection to the ordinary machinery of the exchequer.[4] Evidently the *Scaccarium Aaron*, like the arrangements for collecting tallages, was regarded as a temporary expedient. But very soon after 1191 there must have come into existence a permanent organization for collecting taxes levied upon the Jewry and for dealing with other matters relating to the Jews. In 1197 the title of the ministers in charge of this organization is given: they are the keepers of the Jews.[5] Their full title became 'the king's justices at London assigned to have custody of the Jews',[6] and in John's reign they are termed indifferently 'keepers' or 'justices'. Evidently fresh duties were from time to time placed upon them. One such step can be traced in the pipe rolls of 1198 and 1199, which record the gradual removal of debts owing by Jews from those rolls to a special account.[7] This means that the debts were removed from the normal process by which the main exchequer account was audited in the

---

[1] This is clear from the pipe roll of 1186, made up at the Michaelmas following Aaron's death. His deeds are taken to Northampton; his cash, lying at Nottingham, is given by the king to his son John for use in Ireland (*Pipe Roll 32 Henry II*, p. 102). In the following year there is mention of the 'recepta pecunie Aaron', which was at Oxford when the session of the exchequer was held there at Easter, and of the transport of the money paid in there from Oxford to Winchester (*Pipe Roll 33 Henry II*, p. 45).

[2] *Pipe Roll 2 Richard I*, p. 8.

[3] *Pipe Roll 3 Richard I*, p. 135. This entry gives the names of the two clerks of the *Scaccarium Aaron*, Joseph [Aaron] and Roger, upon whom the bulk of the work doubtless fell. For a later reference to the *Scaccarium Aaron* see *Pipe Roll 2 John*, p. 68.

[4] *Pipe Roll 3 Richard I*, 17, 22–4, et passim.

[5] *Pipe Roll 10 Richard I*, p. 165.          [6] *Rot. Litt. Claus.*, i. 11b.

[7] The 'roll' or 'account' of Benedict of Talmont: see the indices, s.v. Talemunt, to *Pipe Rolls 8 & 9 Richard I*.

Michaelmas term. Though we do not possess the special account, there has come down to us a document that is probably much more informative, namely a record of the queries that arose out of that account, contained on a membrane of the Memoranda Roll for the Michaelmas term 1199.[1] From this document, coupled with another of 1194 that Roger of Howden incorporated in his chronicle,[2] we derive most of our detailed knowledge of the organization for dealing with Jewish financial affairs.

First let something be said of Howden's document.[3] This is an ordinance closely connected with the chapters of the eyre of 1194 and evidently designed to be put into effect by the itinerant justices. We may detect in both the hand of Hubert Walter, who had been appointed justiciar at the close of 1193. The scheme of the ordinance was to set up a number of *archae Iudeorum*, or registries of deeds, as we should now term them, at six or seven centres. Each of these registries was under the joint control of Christians and Jews and they were all under the general supervision of two royal clerks, William of Sainte-Mère-Église and William of Chimillé. In the first place, there was to be registered all the property of each individual Jew, including his bonds, and, in the second place, any bonds made in future were to be executed in duplicate and also enrolled. The duplicate and the enrolment were to be preserved in the registry. Any modifications in the terms of any bond were to be recorded, and a record was also to be kept of debts and payments. There were certain minor transitory provisions for the detection of crime, but these need not detain us. To the main provisions of the ordinance we will return, but here let it be noted that one of the royal clerks in charge of the organization was William of Sainte-Mère-Église. This clerk is named also in a receipt roll of Jewish taxation for the Easter term 1194, and it appears that he was specially engaged in collecting

[1] *Memoranda Roll 1 John*, pp. 69–72.
[2] R. de Hovedene, *Chronica*, iii. 266–7.
[3] Mention should be made of a brief article by Miss A. C. Cramer, who was perhaps the first to stress the importance of this document: 'The origins and functions of the Jewish Exchequer' in *Speculum*, xvi. 226–9. Her views are, however, rather different from those expressed in the following pages.

the gold besants which the Jews were contributing, apparently as a poll-tax.[1] In this task he has a companion, Hugh Bardolf, a layman, who is specially concerned with Lincolnshire.[2] Now in the Memoranda Roll of 1199 a certain amount of history is told and we learn that William of Sainte-Mère-Église and Hugh Bardolf had had the bailiwick and custody of the Jews: again Hugh's name is mentioned with particular reference to Lincolnshire.[3] Since the keepers or justices of the Jews who were appointed by King John in April 1200 are said to be bailiffs,[4] it is quite clear that we must recognize in William of Sainte-Mère-Église and Hugh Bardolf keepers or justices of the Jews who were in office as early as 1194.[5] The Memoranda Roll tells us also of another Hugh, Hugh Peverel, who had had the bailiwick of the Jews, with special reference to Norwich and St Edmunds,[6] and he seems to be the third of the keepers who were holding office in 1194. And then, as we have seen, William of Chimillé, a clerk and archdeacon of Richmond, was associated in 1194 with William of Sainte-Mère-Église, and we seem to have a fourth keeper. It would, of course, be a typical medieval arrangement to have two clerks and two laymen associated, and we can assume with little hesitation that these four were in office in 1194. That they had recently been appointed may probably be deduced from another little piece of history told in the Memoranda Roll, namely that Hugh of Nonant, bishop of Coventry, had been the predecessor of William of Sainte-Mère-Église in keeping a record of certain Jewish debts.[7] This Hugh had fallen out of favour with Richard I in 1193 or early in 1194[8] and had presumably then

---

[1] Jewish Hist. Soc., *Miscellanies*, i. lxvi, lxx. Despite its title the roll is not solely concerned with the Northampton *donum* and it contains a few items other than contribution to taxes.    [2] *Ibid.*, p. lxx.

[3] *Memoranda Roll 1 John*, p. 72.    [4] *Rot. Chart.*, p. 61.

[5] It is to be noted that these two were acting as escheators in this year (*Pipe Roll 6 Richard I*, pp. 1–27) and that in Normandy responsibility for the Jews and for escheats devolved on the same ministers (below, p. 210).

[6] *Memoranda Roll 1 John*, p. 72.    [7] *Loc. cit.*

[8] He had conspired with John against Richard I and had been deprived of the shrievalties of Stafford, Leicester and Warwick between Michaelmas 1193 and Easter 1194 (R. de Hovedene, *Chronica*, iii. 241–2; *Pipe Roll 6 Richard I*, pp. xviii–xix).

vacated office. It is the mention of Hugh of Nonant in this connexion which enables us to take the history of the keepers of the Jews back beyond the year 1194, though to the identity of Hugh's companions, if he had them, the information at present available gives no clue and we are told little of the functions of the keepers at this period. From 1194 onwards, their duties were, however, increasing and were to continue to increase: before that date their duties must have been restricted, and it seems improbable that they could have been in existence when it was decided to set up the *Scaccarium Aaron*, which appears to have functioned from 1186 to 1191.[1] It would seem therefore likely that the keepers of the Jews were first appointed in this latter year or soon after, and indeed we may be justified in seeing them as the successors of the ministers who were in charge of the *Scaccarium Aaron*. Certainly the clerk of the keepers of the Jews in 1198 was Joseph Aaron,[2] who had previously been employed in the *Scaccarium Aaron*,[3] and this is evidence of the continuity of administration. Whether the *Scaccarium Iudeorum*[4] is merely a continuation of the *Scaccarium Aaron* or is a new creation is not a question of great moment. The appointment of keepers of the Jews in the early 1190's cannot have been a matter of much significance, being merely a rearrangement of the business of the exchequer, and it could not have been foreseen at the time how great a part they would play in Jewish affairs.

That the institution of the keepers of the Jews was of little significance will be apparent when we view the relations of the Jewry to the Crown from the point of view of the Jews. Like other medieval communities—the English clergy, for example, or English cities and boroughs—the Jewry was largely self-govern-ing.[5] In the closing years of the twelfth century its representative

---

[1] Above, pp. 115–17.     [2] *Pipe Roll 10 Richard I*, pp. 210, 214.

[3] Above, p. 117, n. 3.

[4] The first known mention of the *Scaccarium Iudeorum* is in 1209 (*Pipe Roll 11 John*, p. 27): it was never a common phrase.

[5] The point was made about the middle of Henry II's reign, perhaps with reference to his charter to the Jews (*Materials for the history of Thomas Becket*, iv. 148).

in its financial dealings with the Crown was the priest of the Jews. When, in 1199, Jacob the priest describes his functions,[1] he states that he is answerable for the great debts of the English Jewry—'the *commune* of the Jews of England'—from the time of Henry II and Richard I. By the great debts he evidently means taxes, fines payable for charters and other common responsibilities, such, for example, as the amercement of Jurnet of Norwich. For the small debts—individual fines and amercements—Jacob disclaims responsibility, though he admits that his clerk, Abraham by name, has written the roll which recorded them, subject to the control of the steward of William of Saint-Mère-Église.[2] A similar arrangement was in force, it would seem, in the time of Hugh of Nonant, William's predecessor, and there are good grounds for believing that the system at work under Richard I goes back well into the reign of Henry II, since Jacob admitted responsibility for the great debts of Henry II and since he already held the office of priest in 1183.[3] It would seem clear too that in 1185 Abraham, the son of Rabbi Josce, was responsible for the small debts, so that there appears to have been then the same arrangement and the same division of responsibility as existed in 1199.[4] But backwards beyond the 1180's the evidence fails us. Now about the year 1180 there was a change in Henry II's policy towards the Jews: he ceased to borrow from them and resorted instead to taxation. Is it not likely that it was at this point of time that the office of priest of the Jews was instituted and also a minor office, to which no name was given, but which was charged with responsibility for small debts?

Why the senior office carried with it the title of *presbyter Iudeorum* or *archipresbyter Iudeorum*, as it is alternatively rendered, has never been satisfactorily explained. Perhaps a full explanation may for ever elude us, but, in any case, a necessary preliminary

[1] *Memoranda Roll 1 John*, p. 72.
[2] For whom see above, p. 118.
[3] *Pipe Roll 29 Henry II*, p. 15.
[4] *Pipe Roll 31 Henry II*, pp. 41, 149, 198. Abraham takes sureties for the payment of these debts. It is unlikely that this Abraham is to be identified with the clerk Abraham of 1199.

is to ascertain the facts, not only the facts that relate to the arch-priest, but also those that relate to other Jewish 'priests' and to Jews who bore other ecclesiastical titles, 'bishop' and even 'archbishop'.

Though the title of archpriest would seem to connote some religious function, it is only in connexion with secular duties that the title is used in the documents that have come down to us. The title was, moreover, conferred by a royal appointment. At the time, the title of archpriest was most commonly applied among Christians to the ecclesiastic who was alternatively called a rural dean, the president of the local ecclesiastical court or rural chapter. Though another explanation will be tentatively suggested, there is perhaps the possibility that the archpriest of the Jews presided over the *capitulum Iudeorum* and, as such, was the channel through which negotiations between the English Jewry and the Crown were conducted.[1] That this was broadly the function of the arch-priest and that he was responsible, in some measure, for seeing that the communal obligations of the Jewry were duly honoured are facts that hardly admit of doubt. It is clear from references in records of the thirteenth century that he was in attendance at the exchequer, that he kept rolls and was able to inform the Justices of the Jews of the facts regarding inquests by mixed juries of Jews and Christians.[2] It is worth noting also that, before the appoint-ment, on 28 December 1236, of Aaron of York to supersede Josce, the son of Isaac (who had succeeded Jacob), he 'resided' at the exchequer in order to advise the Justices of the Jews.[3] If this were all the evidence, the picture might be clear, the explanation of the functions of the *presbyter Iudeorum* reasonably certain. But there is other evidence which makes it difficult to assume that these civil functions and these only were exercised by the officially appointed priests or archpriests. For not only were there priests of the Jews resident at the exchequer, but there were 'priests' who seem un-

[1] This involves the assumption that a chapter would deal with questions other than legal, for which there seems to be no direct evidence.

[2] Cole, *Documents*, pp. 297–8; *Close Rolls, 1234–1237*, p. 408; *1247–1251*, pp. 163, 165, 179–80.     [3] *Close Roll, 1234–1237*, p. 243.

doubtedly to be serving local communities. There were, for example, Samuel *le prestre* of Norwich, who is mentioned in 1194,[1] Peter *presbiter Iudeorum* at Northampton, who is mentioned in 1213,[2] Moses *presbyter* at Canterbury in 1221,[3] Meir *presbyter* or *le prestre* at Stamford in 1223 and 1226[4] and Aaron *le prestre* at Hereford in 1226.[5] A long list of later 'priests' could be given.[6] Under Edward I the alternative description of 'chaplain' tends to be substituted: thus, at York Sampson *le prestre* of 1274[7] becomes Sampson *le chapeleyn* of 1276.[8] Since 'chaplain' seems to be the nearest equivalent that French could provide for hazzan,[9] it would appear that 'priest' must have this meaning also: a Christian chaplain was necessarily a priest. There is nothing to suggest that these 'priests' held, as such, any office outside the synagogue, and certainly nothing to indicate that they had the social status which, as we shall see, Jewish 'bishops' not uncommonly possessed and which recommended them for civil office. 'Priests' indeed, seem to be sharply distinguished from 'bishops', save in one single instance, which is really no exception, when Elias l'Eveske became archpriest.[10] And if 'priests' were in fact, hazzanim and were

---

[1] Jewish Hist. Soc., *Miscellanies*, i. lxvii.

[2] P.R.O., E. 401/1564, m. 3*d*.

[3] Jewish Hist. Soc., *Transactions*, xi. 110.

[4] E. 401/6, m. 12; E. 401/8, tallage membrane, dorse.

[5] *Ibid.*, recto.

[6] E.g. *Close Rolls, 1237–1248*, p. 28; E. 401/43: 1568: 1571: 1572; E. 101/249/16: 22; *Cal. Plea Rolls*, i, ii, iii, indexes *s.v.* Le Prestre, Prestre.

[7] E. 401/1568.

[8] E. 401/1572. For other instances see Stokes, *Studies*, p. 22. The *capellani de Iudaismo* cited by Canon Stokes, *ibid.*, p. 21, were, however, the Christian chaplains of the London Jewry who claimed their parochial dues from the Jewish residents in their parishes.

[9] Neither the Latin *cantor* nor the French *chantre* appears to be employed as an equivalent in English documents of the period. In any case *chantre* does not seem to have acquired its specialized, ecclesiastical, meaning until the fifteenth century. The surname *le Chantur* is found in the later thirteenth century (*Cal. Plea Rolls*, i. 145, 258; ii. 11, 49, 57, 213; iii. 276, 291); but this word has no specialized meaning. It may be applied to a professional singer, a minstrel.

[10] The suggestion that *le prestre* 'may be supposed to be an alternative' to *le eveske* (Stokes, *op. cit.*, p. 21) receives no support from the mass of evidence provided by the records.

elected, as they were elsewhere, largely for their good looks and good voices, by the congregations they served, this would explain their relatively lowly status: in lowliness they did not differ from Christian chaplains, poorly paid and ill-regarded. Yet unless 'priests' acted for some purposes as the representatives of the local communities, it is difficult to understand how the title of arch-priest came to be given to the 'priest' who was appointed to reside at the Exchequer of the Jews: conversely, it is difficult to understand how this 'priest' received his title unless, in addition to his secular functions, he had some liturgical functions as well. These seem to be the best guesses we can make in our present state of knowledge: they are indeed questions rather than guesses. They are no final answer to the awkward problem why an ecclesiastical title was given to a functionary who, so far as the records show, had no religious duties.[1]

The problem is made no easier by the little we know of the office of *episcopus Iudeorum*, another religious title which is associated with secular duties. There is no doubt that the appellation—to use a neutral word—of *episcopus* or (as it is familiarly rendered) *l'Eveske* was used as an alternative to Cohen,[2] though it does not follow that all Cohens were 'bishops'; and there are unmistakable indications that some 'bishops' were men of authority in secular matters, though none that Cohens were. Thus Deulacresse l'Eveske of Exeter[3] is described in 1219 as the king's bailiff there and the sheriff and constable are instructed to consult him when Jews are attached by gage and safe pledges to appear before the Justices of the Jews.[4] It is not to be inferred, however, that he was the king's bailiff because he was the 'bishop' of the Exeter Jewry.

---

[1] Neither Canon Stokes (*op. cit.*, pp. 23–43) nor Michael Adler (*Jews of Medieval England*, pp. 137–9) was able to find that any religious functions were attached to the office of priest or archpriest. In certain circumstances the archpriest passed sentence of excommunication (*Curia Regis Rolls*, xiv. 209); but among the Jews this is not an ecclesiastical function.

[2] Stokes, *op. cit.*, pp. 18–22.

[3] He occurs as early as 1205 (*Rot. Oblat.*, p. 315).

[4] Cole, *Documents*, p. 301. The Jewish bailiffs in other towns do not seem to have had the same status: see the letters of 19 June 1218, in *Patent Rolls, 1216–1225*, p. 157, and *Foedera*, I. i. 157.

Every recognized Jewish community had its Jewish bailiffs,[1] but there is no evidence that 'bishops' were invariably or usually chosen to fill the office. Still, it would seem obvious that the dignitary who is described in 1241 as 'dominus Leo Iudeorum Eboraci episcopus'[2] was holding a public office. We certainly cannot suppose the title to be Latin for plain Léon l'Eveske and that here *episcopus* is just a surname and does not imply a function. And it is noteworthy that, in this same year, 1241, he was constituted one of the king's bailiffs for the purpose of collecting the Jewish tallage of that year. Nor was he singular in this respect, for we find other 'bishops', at Exeter, Hereford and London, appointed to a like office.[3] It occasions no surprise that the 'bishop' so appointed at Exeter should be Deulacresse, who was the king's bailiff nineteen years before, nor does it seem hazardous to infer that Jewish 'bishops' were men performing some public function in their community, who were not infrequently regarded as suitable to act as royal bailiffs.[4]

Before we proceed farther it may, however, be as well to adduce more evidence for the conclusion that usually, though not invariably, the addition of *episcopus* or *l'Eveske* to a man's name signified that he held public office in his community. Evidence is scant for the twelfth century; but in the pipe rolls of 1187 and 1188 there are two independent entries mentioning 'Deodatus episcopus Iudeorum', words that must be drawn from a royal writ and cannot be a vagary of an exchequer scribe.[5] Dieudonné was a leading member of the *consortium* formed in 1177 to provide the king with funds and appears to have belonged to the London

---

[1] Below, pp. 285–92.

[2] Below, p. 281: see also p. 284 for a similar description.

[3] *Close Rolls, 1237–1242*, pp. 353–5. In all four cases the title is in the French form 'le Eveske'.

[4] It seems to follow that a royal bailiff is to be distinguished from, and not identified with, the parnas, as Mr Roth seems to suggest (*History of the Jews in England*, p. 118). Of the medieval parnas very little is known and the surname 'Pernaz' is infrequent: it does not appear to be given to men in authority.

[5] *Pipe Roll 23 Henry II*, p. 80; *24 Henry II*, p. 73. Canon Stokes (*op. cit.*, p. 19 n.) suggested that *Iudeorum* might be an error for *Iudeus*; but there is no likelihood of this.

Jewry.[1] Again, in 1230, there is mention of Solomon, the son of Benedict, who is described as *episcopus de conventibus Iudeorum*, 'bishop of Jewish congregations', and who evidently belongs to London.[2] Evidence of another sort is provided by an entry on the receipt roll of 5 Henry III: 'De Milone et Ysaac episcopis x. solidos pro habenda domo que fuit Sapphire matris eorum'.[3] Here the plural *episcopi* cannot be rendered otherwise than 'bishops': the brothers did not necessarily bear the same surname, but they followed the same calling. Similar evidence is provided by an entry on the close roll of 20 Henry III, which mentions Manasser 'fiz le Esveske' as one of the Jews of Hereford who have lent money to Henry de Brayboef:[4] he is doubtless so distinguished because his father, also Manasser, was 'bishop' at Hereford.[5] Nevertheless 'l'Eveske' was unquestionably sometimes given as a surname, pure and simple, for, as Canon Stokes pointed out, it might be borne by a woman.[6] As so often happened, an occupation gave rise to a surname, and it may not always be easy to distinguish a surname from a title of office, though usually the context makes the meaning reasonably plain.

For the year 1221 we possess unusually full information regarding the English Jewry and we find 'bishops' in eight of the seventeen recognized communities then existing.[7] With the exception of York, and, apparently by accident, at Gloucester, in each case only one 'bishop' is mentioned. At York, at the time the richest

[1] See above, p. 63. For another reference to 'Deodatus episcopus Iudeorum' see *Pipe Roll 5 John*, p. 99: that the entry is under Lincolnshire does not signify a connexion with Lincoln, for he is associated with Isaac and Abraham, sons of the Rabbi, as well as with Jacob of Lincoln.

[2] *Memoranda Roll 14 Henry III*, p. 64.

[3] P.R.O., E. 401/4, m. 5: for further comment on this entry see below, p. 127.

[4] *Close Rolls, 1234–1237*, p. 307.

[5] Manasser is *episcopus* in 1221 (P.R.O., E. 401/4, m. 4(2)*d*) and in 1240 is entitled 'le Eveske' (*Close Rolls, 1237–1242*, p. 353).

[6] Stokes, *op. cit.*, p. 19. For another example, 'Florie la Veske', in 1274, see P.R.O., E. 401/1568 (Kent).

[7] Receipt Roll 5 Henry III (P.R.O., E. 401/4, mm. 4(2)*d*, 5), partly printed in Jewish Hist. Soc., *Transactions*, xi. 99–111. The eight communities are Bristol, Exeter, Gloucester, Hereford, Lincoln, London, Worcester, York: for particulars of the recognized communities see above, pp. 14–16.

and perhaps the most numerous community,[1] there are two.[2] Gloucester presents a problem: we find there not only Samuel *le Arceveske* but also Meir (Milo) and Isaac, the 'bishops', who have succeeded to the house formerly belonging to their mother Sapphira. It is, however, practically certain that the two 'bishops' were not resident in Gloucester, though they succeeded to property there: in other rolls they are located at Bristol, where, moreover, there were two 'bishops' in 1226.[3] We must remember that in the thirteenth century there was much movement from one centre to another and that men described as of one place, and presumably owning property there, are found permanently resident in another. Samuel *le Arceveske*, the third bishop mentioned under Gloucester, bears an unusual title, which seems to imply that there were other 'bishops' subordinate to him: otherwise the explanation of the higher status the title implies is not obvious. There seems no reason to doubt that Samuel was the 'bishop' at Gloucester and, so far as the evidence goes, the sole bishop. Taking the evidence as a whole, it appears legitimate to conclude that each of the recognized communities had at least one 'bishop' and might have two or more; but there seems no reason why any considerable settlement of Jews outside these centres might not have its own 'bishop', and in 1219 we have mention of 'Salamon

[1] This is evident from the payments recorded in respect of the aid for marrying the king's sister. York contributes £164. 10s. 0d., London £80. 10s. 4d. Canterbury and Lincoln are the only two other communities that contribute (just over) £50 (Jewish Hist. Soc., *Transactions*, xi. 111). These are not final figures, but they are significant.

[2] The same two 'bishops', Léon and Benedict, are found at York again in 1223 (E. 401/6, m. 11).

[3] In the receipt roll for 1222 the brothers are again found under Gloucester: the entry runs 'De Milone le eveske et Isaac fratre suo . . .' (E. 401/5, m. 11*d*). In the roll for 1223 (E. 401/6), they are found both under Gloucester, 'De Milone et Isaac episcopis . . .' (m. 9*d*) and under Bristol as Isaac *episcopus* and Milo *episcopus* (m. 12). In the roll for 1226 there are three successive entries under Bristol, giving the names of Michael *l'evesque*, Milo *episcopus* and Isaac *frater suus* (E. 401/8, tallage membrane). On this evidence it seems safe to identify Milo *episcopus* entered under Bristol in 1221 (Jewish Hist. Soc., *Transactions*, xi. 109) with Milo *episcopus* entered (with his brother) under Gloucester (E. 401/4, m. 5). The status of Isaac seems to have been equivocal, and in 1226 he may no longer have been 'bishop'.

episcopus de Dorcestria Iudeus'.[1] But Dorchester was evidently a place of growing importance for Jewish business, and by 1241 there was a recognized community in the town.[2] 'Bishops' outside the recognized communities have, however, left little mark on the records and it is probable that they were appointed only occasionally.

The evidence for the use of *episcopus* as a title of office comes mainly from the thirteenth century, but some light upon the twelfth century is cast by the receipt roll for the Easter term 1194, in which nine 'bishops' are named in Latin, French and English.[3] Isaac, at Bristol, is termed both *episcopus* and *evesqe*;[4] Samson and Josce at Lincoln are termed both *episcopus* and *bissop*;[5] there are three *evesqes* in London—Abraham, Deulesaut and Vives.[6] Solomon, *episcopus* in Hampshire,[7] we may perhaps allot to Winchester, and Samuel, *episcopus* in Nottinghamshire,[8] to the county town. Jude, *episcopus* in Lincolnshire,[9] may perhaps belong to Stamford, which is not mentioned specifically in the roll. Had we the roll for the Michaelmas term 1194, we might find bishops elsewhere. But we can say, with some confidence, that the evidence of the roll for the Easter term is strongly in favour of the inference that the qualification *episcopus* denoted an office in one of the larger Jewish settlements and was not normally a Latin rendering of a French surname. How else can we account for English *bissop* as an alternative to the Latin?

In seeking for the meaning of the titles of 'priest' and 'bishop' it is pertinent to ask how they originated. It seems altogether unlikely that these titles were in the first place bestowed by Christians. On the contrary it would seem probable, if not quite certain, that by the description of *le prestre* or *le eveske* Jews sought to convey to Gentiles the nature of the functions the Jewish 'priests' and 'bishops' performed. Certainly the title of 'bishop' was not confined to England. At Cologne there was an *episcopus*,

---

[1] Cole, *Documents*, p. 317.  [2] Above, p. 16.

[3] Jewish Hist. Soc., *Miscellanies*, i. lxii–lxxiv: for this roll see above, p. 15.

[4] *Ibid.*, pp. lxvi, lxix.

[5] *Ibid.*, pp. lxvii (Lincoln), lxx (Lincolnshire). cf. *Close Rolls 1234–1237*, p. 37n.

[6] *Ibid.*, p. lxxii.  [7] *Ibid.*, p. lxix.  [8] *Ibid.*, p. lxx.  [9] *Ibid.*, p. lxix.

whose further description, *magistratus Iudeorum*,[1] suggests a close parallel with the English 'bishops' who were the king's bailiffs. In England the medium of communication between Jew and Gentile was French, and since many of the names by which Jews were known are translations from the Hebrew into French, it is clear that these names, at least, were not bestowed by Christians but by bilingual Jews, who alone had knowledge enough for the purpose.[2] The Latin forms *presbyter* and *episcopus* are thus, it would seem, mere renderings from the French, of which any Christian clerk would be capable. It is reasonable to conclude, therefore, that when a Jew was called *le prestre* or *le eveske*, this was done, in the first place, by his fellow Jews to indicate to Christians that, in some way, his functions corresponded to those of Christian priests and Christian bishops. The comparison was doubtless inexact and to Christians misleading: but it could not have been altogether inapt. The question is, what were the functions of a priest or a bishop that would, in the twelfth century, arrest the attention of a French-speaking Jew who viewed the Christian Church from without and perhaps with little comprehension? To this question no very satisfactory answer has yet been given.

If uncertainty surrounds the offices of *presbyter* and *episcopus*, the organization and functions of 'chapters' of the Jews are equally obscure.[3] The chapter is rarely noticed in the records. It is mentioned in 1191, when its decision was sought on the question whether a Jew might take usury from another Jew.[4] A payment in 1226 for delaying a chapter (*pro respectu capituli*) shows that it was, in some measure, under royal control,[5] and, in fact, the

---

[1] Stokes, *op. cit.*, p. 20. The Rabbi Moses, whose daughter became a convert at the end of the fourteenth century, is described as *l'evesque des Jues de France et d'Almaigne*: whatever this description may mean, it is clearly implied that he held a public office somewhere on the Continent (Adler, *Jews of Medieval England*, pp. 323, 368–9).

[2] Many examples are given by Jacobs, *Jews of Angevin England*, pp. 345–71: see also Roth, *History of the Jews in England*, pp. 93–5.

[3] The suggestion was made by Joseph Jacobs that the chapter was the *bet din* (*op. cit.*, p. 155) and this is accepted by Canon Stokes, *op. cit.*, p. 50.

[4] *Pipe Roll 3 Richard I*, p. 98.

[5] P.R.O., E. 401/8, *rotulus Iudeorum*, dorse (Gloucester).

holding of chapters was, for a time, forbidden by the Crown some years later.[1] At this period, as in 1191, the purpose of a chapter seems clearly to have been to decide questions of Jewish law. We get a further indication that a chapter was a court of law when, in 1275, there is agreement between two Jews that resort might be had there to enforce a covenant between them as an alternative to resorting to the Exchequer of the Jews.[2] Not that chapters and the Exchequer of the Jews were necessarily mutually exclusive, for a case is recorded in 1267 where the masters of the law failed to agree upon the validity of an alleged marriage until they had been summoned before the Justices of the Jews, when they declared against it.[3] And, just as the Justices might assume jurisdiction when the masters of the law failed to reach a decision, so the highest secular tribunal of all might supersede allegedly vexatious proceedings in chapters. For when, in 1279, Aaron, the son of Vives, was in bad odour with his fellow Jews of London and they proposed to harass him by calling him before 'chapters of the Jewry', the king intervened to stay proceedings until the next parliament, where Vives was prepared to stand his trial.[4] The picture we form of Jewish chapters is one of a tribunal which, although it administers Jewish law, is, like other subordinate tribunals, subject to the control of the king's courts. The nature of such little evidence as we possess perhaps distorts the picture. For while there is no doubt that at a chapter the masters of the law were the predominant element,[5] a reference in 1277 to what appears to be a chapter suggests that not only were the masters of the law present but that 'the entire community of the Jews' was represented.[6] That there were gatherings at which the whole

---

[1] *Close Rolls, 1237–1242*, p. 464.    [2] *Cal. Plea Rolls*, ii. 237.

[3] *Ibid.*, i. 152. It is not without significance that one of the parties was himself a master of the law.

[4] Close Roll 7 Edward I (C. 54/96), m. 4*d*. The calendar (pp. 570–1) hardly elucidates the Latin, which runs: 'ipsum ad capitula Iudaismi vocando aut summas aliquas in ipsum Aaron promulgando.' The letter to the chancellor, printed in Jewish Hist. Soc., *Transactions*, iii. 211, appears to be connected with the proceedings: Aaron seems to have been thought too free in communicating with the king's ministers on matters affecting the Jewry.

[5] See especially Rigg, *Select Pleas*, p. 66.    [6] *Ibid.*, p. 96.

of the English Jewry was in some fashion represented cannot be doubted.[1] Tallages or other obligations assumed by the community seem to have been more often negotiated than imposed. A striking example occurs in 1262, when the Jews objected to being tallaged on the assumed value of their bonds and gave a large number to the king 'to make a clearance of their chattels' or, in other words, to obtain a discharge.[2] Similar negotiations must have taken place before the Jews obtained their charters[3] or when they bought the life of Moses, the son of Le Brun.[4] Doubtless the relatively few wealthy Jews, upon whom the financial burden would fall, could speak in the name of all. Perhaps a specially afforced 'chapter' was the means whereby a representative body could be assembled for conducting negotiations. We can but speculate.

Almost the whole of our evidence regarding 'priests', 'bishops' and chapters comes from a date after 1189, and it casts an uncertain light upon the manner in which the Jewry was organized under Henry II or earlier still. But it is unquestionable that, soon after his death, there were 'priests', 'bishops' and chapters, presumably with functions similar to those of later times, and it follows that in his reign the English Jewry was organized internally much as it was in the thirteenth century. There were therefore 'priests' and 'bishops' among the Jews and Jewish chapters before ever the civil power thought to make use of them. It was of pre-existing offices and pre-existing organizations that the ministers of Henry II and his successors took account, and these they employed or adapted as best suited their own ends. Thus, the synagogue was employed for controlling, in some measure, the financial relations between Jews and Christians:[5] this is the outstanding example of

---

[1] The summoning of representative Jews to Worcester in 1241 by means of writs addressed to the sheriffs (*Close Rolls, 1237–1241*, pp. 346–7) appears to be unparalleled.

[2] P.R.O., E. 101/249/10: 'in puramento facto de catallis eorum'.

[3] Cf. *Rot. Oblat.*, p. 133: Iudei de Anglia dant domino regi quatuor milia marcarum pro cartis suis confirmandis. The charters are to be delivered to them (*eis*) before the bishops of London and Norwich on certain terms.

[4] Below, p. 287.          [5] Above, p. 7, n. 4.

the adaptation of a Jewish institution to serve the purposes of the Christian state, but it is symptomatic. For the rest, however, the extent and manner in which Jewish institutions were utilized remain obscure. It seems noteworthy that, so far as surviving records show, Jewish priests appear to have been rarely employed by the State,[1] if we except the highest civil office (that of arch-priest) to which a Jew could attain; and while 'bishops' were extensively employed, it was not by reason of their communal functions, but because they had the qualities and status that recommended them for appointment as royal bailiffs. These bailiffs were not domestic officers of the Jewish communities, but were chosen, in ways of which we are ignorant, to act as intermediaries between the Crown and the local Jewries: if a 'bishop' was chosen to be a bailiff, this was on personal grounds and not *ex officio*. The outstanding feature of Henry II's organization was the appointment by the Crown of a 'priest' resident at the exchequer. This preceded, and must have been one of the main factors that determined, the evolution of the Exchequer of the Jews. There can be no doubt that the organization of the Jewry for the purposes of royal administration was a necessary preliminary to the regular appointment of Justices of the Jews and not, as has been supposed, the other way about.[2]

We must not leave the problem of the relation of the Jewry to the State without saying a few more words on its local organization. The Jews were self-governing at two levels: as a community co-extensive with the kingdom and in their local communities. Of the local communities little is known, though some light is shed by documents coming from the early years of Henry III's reign, which presumably reflect the conditions of the twelfth century. In their relations with the Crown these communities, which, as we have seen, attained more definite shape towards the end of the century, were represented by bailiffs chosen—in what way we are ignorant—from among themselves, who acted for the king very much as the bailiffs of a town would act: these

[1] Isaac le Prestre was, for a time, chirographer at Bristol (*Cal. Plea Rolls*, ii. 138, 198).     [2] Roth, *op. cit.*, p. 31.

were the king's Jewish bailiffs, of which something has already been said in passing. Thus, when a Jew of Colchester was to be summoned before the Justices of the Jews, it was the bailiff of the Jews of that town who was ordered to attach him by gage and safe pledges.[1] Similarly, if the sheriff of Devon or the constable of Exeter castle wished to attach a Jew against whom a charge was laid, this was to be done in the presence (*per visum*) of the king's Jewish bailiff in those parts.[2] At the same period we find these Jewish bailiffs acting for the Crown in ascertaining what debts of a date prior to the 'general arrest' in 1210 had not been liquidated. Writs are addressed to them to which they make returns, like any other public officers; they hold inquests and they take evidence on oath from members of the local community.[3] It seems clear that in 1219 some of the communities are grouped under the same bailiffs: Lincoln, Stamford and Nottingham constitute one group and Hereford and Worcester another.[4] This, however, may be no more than a temporary arrangement made necessary by the decline in the Jewish population after 1210, as the result of the king's savage treatment of them and the hazards of the Barons' War. With more settled times and the return of exiles from abroad, the Jewish communities seem to have grown. But, after the early years of Henry III, evidence for the forms of self-government still existing at that time fades away: the local communities appear to be ruled directly by sheriffs and constables of castles. In any case we must not exaggerate the independence of these local communities, even in the golden age of Henry II. They were too much at the mercy of hostile Christians, too vulnerable to attack, to do without the protection of the local castellan or the urban authority. Since they could not stand by themselves, as prejudice against them grew and as the attitude of the king turned to indifference or hostility, the Crown no longer found it convenient to treat with the local communities through Jewish bailiffs. It is true that we hear of such bailiffs in 1241, but in terms that make it clear that they had been appointed *ad hoc* to assess and collect

---

[1] Cole, *Documents*, p. 312.   [2] *Ibid.*, p. 301.
[3] Below, pp. 285-92.   [4] Below, pp. 285-6, 288, 291.

the tallage of that year.[1] This responsibility they shared with the sheriff, but there was nothing new in such an arrangement. Twenty years previously the Jewish bailiffs of the older type had been required to act with the sheriffs in collecting taxes.[2]

Centring as it did upon the synagogue, the local community was more than a convenient organization for fiscal purposes, though in the eyes of royal officials this might be its obvious purpose and for this it was used. And though the king's Jewish bailiffs disappeared, as they seem to have done, not many years after Henry III had come to the throne, the local community, the *commune* of the Jews, survived. It was, if we may express the position in modern terms, a juridical person with a capacity for holding property and incurring common burdens.[3] There was, indeed, nothing very exceptional in that: a *commune* of this kind was not dissimilar to an urban *commune*. What was remarkable about a Jewish *commune* was that it existed within, and yet apart from, an urban *commune*: in the words of a royal letter of 1218, the Jews were accustomed to have *communam inter Christianos*[4] or, as it is elsewhere expressed, *communam cum eis*.[5]

---

[1] *Close Rolls, 1237–1242*, pp. 353–5; Madox, *History of the Exchequer* (1769), i. 224 n.

[2] Below, p. 291.

[3] The conveyance of a messuage to the *commune* of the Jews of London for the construction of a synagogue is the best possible evidence (*Cal. Charter Rolls*, ii. 245, 253). Such deeds have survived only exceptionally; but there is much other evidence that implies their existence. Thus the same *commune* owned property in Wood Street (P.R.O., C. 67/4). At Northampton the *commune* owned a tenement, a cemetery and a rent for its maintenance (P.R.O., E. 101/249/30, m. 2); at Bristol the *commune* took a lease for twenty years (*ibid.*, m. 4*d*). In the account of the sheriff of Kent for receipts from the Jews of Canterbury in 37–38 Henry III there are frequent entries of payments 'del commun' on varying occasions (P.R.O., E. 101/249/8) and there are similar entries in the accounts of the underconstable and serjeant of the Tower of London in 1275–1278 (E. 101/249/22).

[4] *Patent Rolls, 1216–1225*, p. 157; *Foedera*, I. i. 151.

[5] *Rot. Litt. Claus.*, i. 567.

# VII

# THE EXCHEQUER OF THE JEWS

THE FULL WORKING OF the Exchequer of the Jews is disclosed by the rolls of the Justices of the Jews; but no such rolls have survived from a period earlier than the Michaelmas term 1218,[1] although a regular series of *rotuli Iudeorum* certainly existed from the first year of John.[2] There is, moreover, sufficient information to show that the organization and functions of the Justices of the Jews were already fully developed when John was on the throne.[3] Before, however, describing that organization and its working, it will be well to say something of the men who administered it.

The four keepers of the Jews who appear to have been in office in 1194 had, by 1198, been superseded by Simon of Pattishall, Henry of Whiston and Benedict of Talmont.[4] Simon of Pattishall was a prominent royal justice who sat regularly on the Bench.[5]

[1] The first surviving roll was printed by Cole, *Documents*, pp. 285–332: calendared by Rigg, *Cal. Plea Rolls*, i. 1–55.

[2] *Pipe Roll 9 John*, pp. 20, 95: for references to later rolls see *ibid.*, p. 36; *Pipe Roll 11 John*, p. 27; *12 John*, p. 12; *13 John*, pp. 64, 114. To judge from the scanty particulars in the pipe rolls, the *rotuli Iudeorum* of John's reign seem to have been in the nature of memoranda rolls, as the later plea rolls also are. There appears to have been a separate series of receipt rolls, of which some specimens have survived: that for the Easter term 1194, printed in Jewish Hist. Soc., *Miscellanies*, i. lix–lxxiv, and another for the Easter and Michaelmas terms 1213 (P.R.O., E. 401/1564). The latter is entitled *rotulus Iudeorum*, as are also the membranes of the general receipt rolls of the early years of Henry III devoted to Jewish items.

[3] The conclusions reached in this chapter are in harmony with the views expressed by Miss A. C. Cramer in her article 'The Jewish Exchequer' in the *American Historical Review*, xlv. 327–37. Her purpose was to challenge the interpretation placed by Sir Hilary Jenkinson on the evidence from the reigns of Henry III and Edward I.     [4] *Pipe Roll 10 Richard I*, pp. 210, 214.

[5] He continued to do so under John: cf. Foss, *Judges of England*, ii. 160–2; S. Painter, *Reign of King John*, p. 82.

Less is known of Henry of Whiston, but incidental references to him indicate that he was employed upon general financial business,[1] and he acted on occasion as a justice itinerant.[2] It was upon Benedict, a Jew from Poitou, with apparently no other administrative responsibilities, that the burden of business in the Exchequer of the Jews seems to have devolved.[3] These three were in turn superseded in April 1200 by William d'Aubigny, William de Warenne, Thomas de Neville and Geoffrey of Norwich—two barons and two clerks.[4] The first-named seems never to have acted as a justice of the Jews, but the other three are frequently mentioned in this capacity until November 1208, when (or soon after) William de Warenne died.[5] Geoffrey of Norwich is not mentioned in the records after June 1212[6] and Thomas de Neville (now archdeacon of Salop) had become sole justice or keeper by October 1213[7] and so continued until August 1215,[8] when the organization of the exchequer as a whole disintegrated in the war between King John and his barons.

The Justices of the Jews, as we see them functioning under Richard and John, were covering all aspects of the relations of the Jewry to the Crown, though they had no strictly exclusive jurisdiction. With few exceptions—a notable one being the tallage of 1210—they collected the revenue accruing from the Jewry, retained it in a separate treasury and disbursed it on the king's instructions. Though their accounts were subject to audit by the

---

[1] *Pipe Roll 3 Richard I*, p. 164; *4 Richard I*, p. 297; *6 Richard I*, p. 48; *7 Richard I*, pp. 27–8.

[2] *Pipe Roll 5 Richard I*, p. xxiv; *7 Richard I*, pp. xix–xx; *Curia Regis Rolls*, i. 22. He appears to have sat regularly on the Bench in the first three years of John's reign (Hunter, *Fines*, i. lxiv).

[3] *Memoranda Roll 1 John*, pp. xc, xcii. For further evidence of Benedict's activities see *Pipe Roll 1 John*, p. 263; *2 John*, p. 69.

[4] *Rot. Chart.*, p. 61.

[5] He was certainly dead well before Easter 1209 (*Pipe Roll 11 John*, pp. 50, 201). The last mention of him as Justice of the Jews is in *Rot. Oblat.*, p. 425, the date of which is indicated by entries on the dorse of the membrane (pp. 501–3). The three rendered their account as 'custodes Iudeorum' at Michaelmas 1208 (*Memoranda Roll 10 John*, p. 64).

[6] *Rot. Chart.*, p. 187.  [7] *Rot. Litt. Claus.*, i. 152b.

[8] *Ibid.*, p. 223b. He died in 1217 (*ibid.*, pp. 323, 346).

barons of the exchequer,[1] they were in other respects independent. A writ of *liberate* of 1208 is conclusive: the keepers of the Jews are instructed to pay 370 marks from *recepta vestra* into the treasury at the king's exchequer.[2] This is consistent with earlier payments, or instructions to pay, from the issues of the bailiwick of the Jews.[3] On the other hand, the keepers might be ordered to hand bonds over to the barons of the exchequer for the latter to put *in summonicione*.[4] Such an instruction was presumably necessary because the keepers had no effective sanctions at their command whereby they could compel Christian debtors to pay: resort therefore must be had to the machinery of the exchequer. But, though the powers of the keepers of the Jews needed to be supplemented in this way, nevertheless they were not the subordinates of the barons of the exchequer, though they, like every other minister not attached to the royal household, were subordinate to the justiciar. The keepers appointed in 1200 were, in fact, nominated by the justiciar,[5] and on occasion the keepers are found sitting as a tribunal with the justiciar or other barons of the exchequer.[6] As so often at the period, there seems to be no clear-cut distinction between the functions of one organ of government and another. Indeed the conception of an organ of government cannot be pressed too far: what appear to be specialized tribunals are, in fact, delegacies, and the king, who possesses the original jurisdiction, may resume the delegated power or remit it to others.[7] Hence, though it is not incorrect to see in the appointment of keepers of the Jews the creation of a special organ of government to deal with Jewish affairs, we must bear in mind that such a phrase is a modern one with a modern connotation, and that,

---

[1] *Ibid.*, p. 95.

[2] *Ibid.*, p. 103. For similar payments to royal ministers in 1208 and 1212 see *Memoranda Roll 10 John*, p. 65; *Pipe Roll 14 John*, p. 75.

[3] For this and similar phrases, see *Rot. Litt. Claus.* i. 29*b*, 68*b*, 75–6, 87. Such payments had been made under Richard I (*Memoranda Roll 1 John*, pp. xcii, 75).

[4] *Rot. Litt. Claus.*, i. 95.

[5] *Rot. Chart.*, p. 61: per consilium G. filii Petri iusticiarii nostri.

[6] *Pipe Roll 10 Richard I*, pp. 165–6; Cole, *Documents*, p. 328.

[7] See Bracton's discussion, *De Legibus*, fo. 108–108*b*. Here Bracton is following Tancred (*Traditio*, vi. 66–9).

in the twelfth and thirteenth centuries, the erection of this special tribunal was not incompatible with the handling of particular Jewish cases by other tribunals. This administrative heterogeneity was not confined to financial affairs, but, as we shall see, extended to judicial matters. Still, the great bulk of business, whether financial or judicial, in which Jews were directly concerned came before the Justices of the Jews, and even matters which could not affect any Jewish interest might come before them. This wide extension of their jurisdiction is well illustrated by the instructive story of Richard of Bisbrooke.

In 1179 Richard had pledged his land to Aaron of Lincoln, and his bond is in the roll prepared for the exchequer on Aaron's death.[1] Although the debt is not noted in the roll as discharged, we can infer that Richard had, in fact, paid off his debt to Aaron. This he appears to have done by mortgaging the land to Samuel of Stamford for 50 marks,[2] although the original loan from Aaron had been 15 marks only. It would seem that this second loan was made on conditions similar to the first: the creditor was entitled to interest and was to recoup both capital and interest from the issues of the land. However, before there was time for the loan to be repaid in this way Samuel in turn died, very soon after Aaron, for he was dead before Michaelmas 1186, and his chattels and gaged land escheated to the king.[3] Richard's land at Bisbrooke was among the latter and was treated like any other escheat. It was farmed for 10 marks a year and so continued until 1197, when Richard applied to the keepers of the Jews for an audit of his account, for which he had to pay a fine of 15 marks. The audit showed, of course, that more than the capital of 50 marks had been received from the land since it had escheated and Richard was thereupon reinstated, though, so far as appears, no part of the losses he had suffered in the past was recouped to him.[4] If he paid dearly for his loan, the fault, it would seem, was his. He had delayed taking the necessary steps to recover his land and,

---

[1] Below, p. 248 (no. 2).

[2] For Samuel's mortgage and its consequences see *Pipe Roll 10 Richard I*, pp. 124–5.    [3] *Pipe Roll 32 Henry II*, p. 80.    [4] *Pipe Roll 10 Richard I, loc. cit.*

though the king claimed no more than the capital of the bond, a mortgagor must suffer for his own negligence. But our immediate concern is not with the position of mortgagors who had entered into bonds that came into the king's hands, but with the jurisdiction of the Justices of the Jews. Why should Richard arrange for the audit, as he did, with Benedict of Talmont, and why should the Justices of the Jews be concerned with the matter at all? The reply must be that all escheats of Jewish property, whether these had fallen in before or after the appointment of keepers of the Jews, were regarded as coming within their jurisdiction. The further inference seems justified that before there was any thought of such a specialized tribunal, the receipts from Jewish sources had been in some way kept apart in the exchequer and were identifiable: there are, as we have seen, other indications that this must have been the case.

A new factor was introduced into the relations of Jewish moneylenders and their clients when the pope assumed the power of dispensing crusaders from the obligation to pay usury on money they had borrowed. Usury had long been condemned as immoral by Christian doctrine, but neither ecclesiastical courts nor royal courts afforded any effective control. In principle the Church dealt with Christian usurers in their lifetime, leaving the king to confiscate their ill-gotten gains on their death: but very little was effected except gradually to disguise the open taking of interest.[1] Jewish usury was regulated, if at all, by the king, and since Jews were not expected to conform to Christian standards in this matter, there was no need for disguise, although, in point of fact, by no means all Jewish bonds provided expressly for interest payments. The terms upon which money was borrowed, whether the lender was Christian or Jew, were the result of a bargain and the forms of bond varied widely.

---

[1] The form of the bonds used by Italian merchants was greatly influenced by the canonists, especially by Raymond of Peñafort: see his *Summa*, lib. ii, tit. vii, § iv.: 'Si vero pena sit conventionalis, id est de communi consensu partium in ipso contractu apposita, ut saltem metu pene debitum certa die solvatur, usura non committitur, dum tamen sit intentio recta.' A wrong intention was practically impossible to prove.

The earliest papal legislation was that of Clement III at the beginning of the Third Crusade. It was based upon the current practice of borrowing money at interest on the security of income from landed property.[1] Many crusaders, lay and clerical, had already gaged some part of their lands and they were to be assisted, in the first place, by being allowed to retain the current year's income, which otherwise would accrue to the creditor, and further by reducing subsequent payments, for the duration of the crusade, by the amount of any usury that might be included. This relief would not, of course, provide a capital sum, and a further provision authorized crusaders to gage their rents for three years.[2] No restriction was placed upon the terms the moneylender might exact, although the transaction the pope intended to authorize was presumably the gage of land which *Glanville* regards as lawful[3] but which there was no means of ensuring. Clement's legislation relieving crusaders of usury was reinforced in 1198 by Innocent III, who released debtors from their oaths to pay usury to Christian creditors and required the latter to repay any usury already exacted. At the same time the pope called upon secular princes to compel Jews to remit usury: until they did so, they were to be cut off from all commerce with Christians.[4] That portion of the decretal touching Jewish moneylending passed into the *corpus* of canon law without any limitation to crusaders, first in the *Compilatio Tertia* (1210) and, in due course, in the Gregorian Decretals (1234).[5]

It is not to be supposed that legislation of this kind would be directly effective, for money is not commonly lent without

---

[1] So Geoffrey of Vigeois writes: Feneratores olim publici obnoxii principibus erant, nunc tam crebro reperiuntur ut aliqui usuras vocerent census, quasi redditus agrorum (Labbe, *Nova Bibliotheca*, ii. 328). The chronicler doubtless had Poitou in mind, but his words would apply to Western Europe generally towards the end of the twelfth century.

[2] *Gesta Henrici*, ii. 32; R. de Hovedene, *Chronica*, ii. 337; Gervase of Canterbury, *Opera*, i. 410; William of Newburgh (ed. Howlett), *Chronica*, i. 273–4; above, p. 38, n. 3.

[3] Above, p. 85; below, p. 265.

[4] Migne, *Patrologia Latina*, ccxiv. 311–12; R. de Hovedene, *Chronica*, iv. 70–5; Potthast, no. 347; above, p. 38, n. 3.      [5] X.5.19.12.

inducement, but it may have helped a crusader to come to terms with a creditor, especially if the creditor sought to recover his debt by legal process. The practical outcome of papal legislation is illustrated by a later letter of Innocent's in October 1208, issued on the occasion of another crusade, that against the Albigeois. If, he says, any of the nobles, clerks or laymen who are proceeding against these heretics have bound themselves by oath to pay usury, their creditors are to desist, under pain of excommunication, from demanding it, the oath notwithstanding, and payment is to be suspended until the borrower has returned from the crusade; usury already exacted is to be repaid.[1] The pope at the same time wrote to Philip Augustus asking him to ensure that the Jews remitted usury on their loans to crusaders and postponed the date for the repayment of the capital.[2] These are papal pronounce-ments, but there were many lesser voices repeating much the same message. We may mention the statutes of Cardinal Robert de Courçon when legate in France in 1214, for these affected the dominions of King John and were sent to him under the cardinal's seal with an intimation that they were not to the prejudice of himself or his heirs. These statutes are noteworthy because they indicate how ineffective papal pronouncements had been. Barons and all those who 'keep' Jews[3] are to compel them to remit usury to crusaders. If they fail to do this, all merchants are to be com-pelled by ecclesiastical censure to refrain from any association with the Jews, whether in contracts or merchandizing or any other way. Barons who fail to act are threatened with excommunica-tion, the release of their subjects from their fealty, interdict and forfeiture.[4] The violence of the threats suggests the unlikelihood of compliance.

The position, then, at the end of the twelfth century was that moneylending at interest was practised generally by Christians and Jews, and that, while the Church affected to condemn it,

[1] Migne, *Patrologia Latina*, ccxv. 1170; repeated in November 1209 (*ibid.*, ccxvi. 159).

[2] *Ibid.*, ccxv. 1171.     [3] The cardinal's words are 'qui tenent Iudeos'.

[4] *Rot. Litt. Pat.*, pp. 139b–140.

so authoritarian a pope as Innocent III was compelled to recognize it and to seek to mitigate its consequences. Action, such as it was, could be taken by ecclesiastical authorities only against Christians, but pressure could be brought upon secular rulers to control Jewish moneylenders. What was of greater consequence in England, a principle was established that was capable of wide application. If usury could be suspended while crusaders were engaged in the wars of the Church, it was not unreasonable to suspend usury while vassals were engaged in the king's wars.[1] Nor were these the only circumstances that called for consideration. The king might feel justified in relieving any favoured subject.[2] And there were other objects of benevolence. Though they seem to have been pushing at an open door, the articles the barons presented to King John demanded, and Magna Carta conceded, that usury should not run against heirs during their minority.[3] Nor was it a simple matter of suspending or cancelling the payment of usury, for unpaid interest was itself capitalized. There was no half-way house between enforcing a bond on the one hand and, on the other, reviewing the whole circumstances of the debt and enforcing a settlement against a possibly unwilling creditor. This was recognized in the Articles of the Barons and Magna Carta. The widow's dower must be protected (a reassertion of a rule already established in the courts)[4] and provision must be made for the upbringing of orphan children.[5] These were prior charges, and only the reduced income was available for the reduction of the debt.

We must, of course, distinguish between the position that arose when bonds came into the king's hands on the death of a moneylender and the position when the moneylender was himself

---

[1] *Rot. Litt. Claus.*, i. 33*b*–34*b*, 36*b*, 89, 89*b*, 107*b*; *Rot. Oblat.*, p. 519. For similar action in Normandy see below, p. 205.

[2] Cf. *Rot. Chart.*, p. 165 (11 November 1206); *Rot. Oblat.*, p. 227.

[3] Articles of the Barons, c. 34; Magna Carta, c. 10 (Stubbs, *Select Charters*, pp. 293, 298).

[4] The earliest case surviving appears to be one of 1198 (*Curia Regis Rolls*, vii. 339): for later cases, see *ibid.*, i. 4, 17; vii. 70–1.

[5] Articles of the Barons, c. 35; Magna Carta, c. 11.

required to give terms. As we have already remarked, when there were escheated bonds for disposal, the officers of the exchequer realized them as best they could, giving perhaps special terms to favoured debtors.[1] In any case the king could not exact usury on the bonds that fell into his hands; the barons thought that he should be content with the original capital advanced and Magna Carta endeavoured to enforce this principle.[2] Quite different considerations obtained when a living creditor was concerned. Much as the king might be moved to relieve the debtor, it was not to the king's interest to deprive a Jewish moneylender either of his capital or of his livelihood. There is no reason to suppose, however, that the king's interest and the interest of the moneylender were necessarily in conflict. We have seen that, if there was a prospect of obtaining cash, Jewish moneylenders were prepared to settle for a much smaller sum than the nominal amount of the debt due to them. What the terms of the settlement should be was a matter of private bargaining that normally involved a third party with money at his command.[3] With the appointment of Justices of the Jews, a tribunal was set up that could arbitrate in such matters. Early in John's reign a debtor is found asking that his Jewish creditors may be summoned to the exchequer to come to a reasonable settlement of the debt due to them,[4] and there is no doubt that this procedure had been available for some years. The normal outcome was that the debtor was formally acquitted of his debts to Jews. Instances of this can be found as early as 1195,[5] and it may well be that we have here an outcome of the reorganization of the Justices of the Jews in the previous year. Under John notices of such acquittances are numerous.[6] They were not, of course, granted except for a substantial consideration. The debtor had to pay a fine to the king or, alternatively, to

[1] Above, p. 75.
[2] Articles of the Barons, c. 34; Magna Carta, c. 10.
[3] Above, pp. 82, 85.
[4] *Pipe Roll 2 John*, p. 253. Cf. *Rot. Oblat.*, p. 40 (Geoffrey de Neville).
[5] *Pipe Roll 7 Richard I*, pp. 8, 203.
[6] *Rot. Litt. Pat.*, pp. 15b, 16, 30, 30b, 85b; *Rot. Lib.*, pp. 24, 38, 71, 73, 84; *Rot. Oblat.*, pp. 263, 280.

maintain so many knights and serjeants-at-arms in the king's service.[1] A corollary was a suitable payment or allowance to the creditor:[2] there was no arbitrary confiscation of Jewish assets, though doubtless the king sometimes made concessions to debtors without too nice a regard for the consequences to other parties. Both the complications that might ensue and the principles that guided the king's courts may be best illustrated by an actual example. Ralf of Thiville had gaged his manor of Intwood to Isaac of Norwich for a term of years, and Isaac had in turn gaged it to Roger of St Denis and Sarah his wife, against whom Maud, Ralf's daughter-in-law, brought an action, since the manor had been given to her as her dower. This was in 1220. Roger and Sarah vouched Isaac to warranty, and he defended the action, relying upon his gage which, he said, was entered on the king's rolls (in the *archa*). While the action was in progress Ralf intervened and claimed that he had fined with King John for £120 to have seisin of the manor, and this allegation the Justices of the Jews confirmed. Not all the complications of the case need to be told: suffice it to say that Ralf was given seisin of the manor, that Roger and Sarah were relieved of any obligation towards Isaac, who was, in turn, told to sue before the Justices of the Jews for compensation.[3] Perhaps the commotions of the later years of John and the early years of Henry III prevented the smooth working of the system and, for that reason, the case cannot be regarded as typical; but the underlying principles would be unaffected. A debtor had the right to redeem his lands over the head of the creditor (who was also the gagee) and the sub-tenants: on the other hand the creditor was entitled to an equitable settlement of his claims.

Jewish moneylenders were themselves willing to negotiate settlements of this kind, without the king's intervention, though doubtless they had to have regard to any sub-lease they may have

[1] *Rot. Lib.*, pp. 42, 44, 48.

[2] *Ibid.*, pp. 86–7; *Rot. Litt. Claus.*, i. 107b.

[3] *Curia Regis Rolls*, ix. 23–4, 153–4. Maud had to proceed against her father-in-law to recover her dower, but this is a separate issue (*ibid.*, p. 371; x. 154).

granted. These settlements were also called 'fines', just as the settlements effected with the king were called, and they involved a payment to the Justices of the Jews.[1] Since bonds were treated as negotiable instruments and as such were discounted and might then be marketed to a Christian who desired to acquire the land upon which the loan was secured, the transactions might be complicated. An actual case will again be the best form of illustration. Two Jews of York, Poitevin and Isaac, the son of Isaac, had acquired from other Jews two bonds of £30 and £60, of which they were prepared to dispose. They began negotiations with one John of Harpham, who appears to have offered 30 marks for them, to be paid, not by himself, but by Thomas fitz Herbert, though he would stand surety for Thomas. While the negotiations were in progress in the chamber of the archbishop of York, the sheriff, at the instigation of John, arrested Poitevin and Isaac on the ground that they were seeking to dispose of the bonds clandestinely, though they asserted that they were acting in the king's interest.[2] The final outcome is unknown, but it is clear that John of Harpham was endeavouring to trap the Jews, and it seems incredible that so improbable a bargain as he proposed could have been seriously entertained. Whether the charge against the Jews was true or false, the story does illustrate how the market in bonds was conducted. Especially does it show that Jews with bonds to sell acted not only on their own behalf, but the king's. The result may be seen in one of the documents that Robert of Braybrooke has left behind him. This shows him reaching agreement with a moneylender whereby the debtor was relieved of his debt on the payment of 50 marks by Robert: of this sum 20 marks were for the use of the king and 30 for the creditor.[3]

With the appointment of Justices of the Jews and the institution of *archae cyrographorum* in 1194, there was set up, in all appearance,

---

[1] For the use of 'fine' in this sense, see *Curia Regis Rolls*, iv. 86; vi. 125; *Close Rolls, 1227–1231*, pp. 305–6. The receipt roll of 1194 records the receipt of 50 marks from Jacob, the son of Samuel, 'de fine abbatis de Pipewell' (Jewish Hist. Soc., *Miscellanies*, i. lxxi). For a similar case, see below, p. 272 (no. 2).

[2] *Curia Regis Rolls*, i. 389–91, 424.

[3] Below, pp. 271–2.

an articulated organization for controlling the credit transactions of the Jews. Yet one of the remarkable aspects of the history of the English Jewry in the thirteenth century is that the rolls of the chancery are as important a source of information as the rolls of the Exchequer of the Jews. This is not merely because, until the reign of Edward I, the latter records are fragmentary, but because action is being continually taken at a higher level than that of the Justices. In other than routine matters we come to expect that writs to the sheriffs will issue, not from the exchequer, but from the chancery. Ultimately this is doubtless because so many important people were interested in the transactions of Jewish moneylenders, because the moneylenders themselves had the ear of important people and because the revenue that could be squeezed from the Jewry was at times of great consequence to a needy king. A system, therefore, which on paper might look self-contained, was not allowed to function without frequent interference from above, and this interference justified further interference. For without doubt the constant by-passing of the Justices affected their status, and it is evident that their standing and quality declined from the high level set in the reigns of Richard and John, and that, under Henry III and Edward I, they were not of great account in the official hierarchy.[1] Yet, if their quality had been of the highest, the system was perhaps too elaborate, by the standards of the thirteenth century, to work efficiently, even if it had not afforded a constant temptation to an unscrupulous king to divert it from its purpose in order that he might prey upon the Jews and their clients. How then did the system work?

There is no reason to suppose that, when the *archae* were instituted, they were contrived as a device for protecting the king's revenue; but, once established, they were essential for maintaining an open market in bonds and so securing that the king took his share of the profits. From the beginning, however, it seems to have been not unduly difficult to evade the requirements of the system, either with the connivance of the chirographers or by

---

[1] See the biographical details in 'Justices of the Jews, 1218–1268' by C. A. F. Meekings (*Bulletin Inst. Historical Research*, xxviii. 173–88).

negotiating loans clandestinely,[1] and it would appear that by 1210 evasion was widespread. Otherwise there could have been no purpose in requiring all Jews to produce their charters and chirographs so that they might be enrolled.[2] When articles of value were pawned there was no risk to the moneylender if the transaction was surreptitious, while the borrower would have good reason for avoiding the light of day if the articles had been acquired dishonestly. When loans were made upon the security of rents, it was possible to avoid the use of an official chirograph by employing a tally. This practice had been forbidden as early as 1220, though the prohibition had not, in practice, been enforced.[3] The prohibition was renewed in the earliest legislation governing the Jewry of which a record has been preserved, that of 1233. This not only prohibits the use of tallies for the purpose, but, what appears to be novel, requires a tripartite chirograph in the case of all loans. The third part (or foot, *pes*) was to be kept in the *archa* and was essential to prove the bond: any chirograph of which the foot was not to be found was held to be invalid.[4] After a few years' experience this regulation proved to be ineffective against fraud, and in November 1239 there was a clean sweep of the keepers of the *archae* and the clerks, while new and elaborate regulations were enacted governing the preparation and custody of bonds.[5] It would seem clear that the scheme for the registration of Jewish bonds worked with difficulty. The king's ministers spoke of the malice and falsity of the Jews,[6] but the

[1] *Curia Regis Rolls*, v. 182, 246. It was clearly possible to confect a bond for a sum greater than the amount actually lent, though this was *contra assisam domini regis* (Cole, *Documents*, p. 301).

[2] *Ibid.*, p. 302: quando omnes Iudei Anglie capti fuerunt, preceptum fuit quod omnes Iudei proferrent cartas et cyrographa sua et quod irrotulata essent.

[3] Below, p. 193.

[4] Below, p. 294. These regulations did not institute the tripartite chirograph which was in use at the beginning of Henry III's reign, though apparently not compulsory (Cole, *Documents*, p. 301). For a still earlier tripartite chirograph, of 1205, see below, pp. 264–7

[5] *Liber de Antiquis Legibus*, p. 237. In the form here given these regulations apply to London, but there can be no doubt that they were general.

[6] *Ibid.*: 'ad malitiam et falsitatem Iudeorum reprimendam'.

connivance of many people—lenders, borrowers and officials—was necessary to make clandestine transactions easy and safe. Yet the incentive to avoid the requirements of the system must have been great. The mulct the king imposed when the debtor compounded with his creditor was inevitably reflected in the terms that moneylenders could offer to borrowers. So long as good faith was maintained between the parties to a clandestine transaction all would be well; but if the creditor was driven to resort to the courts, the debt had, in principle, to be proved by the production of the enrolment or of the counterpart of the bond deposited in the *archa*. However, evasion cannot have been infrequent,[1] and for a time it seems to have become a matter almost of routine to allow a moneylender, for a consideration, to sue before the Justices of the Jews on bonds that had not been registered.[2] It was stipulated that usury was not to be demanded, but if the creditor recovered his original capital, even though the king took his share, he probably had little ground for complaint. It is plain that the penalties threatened against evasion in 1239—amercement of the Christian, forfeiture of the Jew—could not be enforced. On the other hand, the system had its advantages for the creditor, for his counterpart of the bond might go astray and he might have to rely upon that in the *archa*.[3] In a nice balancing of risks, it might well have seemed the better course to keep within the law. The system certainly continued to work until the eve of the Expulsion, for, despite all legislative hindrances, moneylending was still active under forms that did not offend the law.[4] How much clandestine lending there was must be, for all time, a matter of conjecture.

Let us now turn from the administrative aspect of the jurisdiction of the Justices of the Jews to its judicial aspect, from the Exchequer of the Jews as a financial department to the Exchequer

[1] See the cases collected by Madox, *History of the Exchequer* (1769), i. 245–6.

[2] *Close Rolls, 1247–1252*, p. 382; *1251–1253*, pp. 63, 140, 319; *1259–1261*, p. 344. Four moneylenders are involved, including Aaron of York, the most prominent Jew of his time.

[3] Davis, *Shetaroth*, pp. 99, 101, 103, 148, 191, 243, 249, 280.

[4] Above, pp. 106–7.

of the Jews as a court of law. These functions are not strictly separable, for the forms of procedure adopted by the Justices are throughout judicial. But though it would be hard to say where the one function ended and the other began, yet the rolls of the Exchequer of the Jews—call them plea rolls or memoranda rolls,[1] as we will—contain many records of activities which we should regard as appropriate only to a court of law, extending to the punishment of crime. So wide a jurisdiction does not seem to have belonged to the Justices of the Jews in their early days, but by John's reign it appears to have been well established. This we deduce from the earliest surviving plea roll of the reign of Henry III, beginning in the Michaelmas term 1218;[2] for there can have been no new departure at that time, when the king's government was slowly recovering from the dislocation of prolonged civil war and picking up, as best it could, the threads of administration. But though this wide jurisdiction was well established by the beginning of John's reign, nevertheless cases concerning Jews continued to come before the Bench and before the king. Why this was so requires explanation, and as a preliminary it will be as well to explain the difference between the two supreme tribunals or, as it might be better to express the position, between the two divisions of the high court.[3] For there were not, until 1234, two distinct courts of King's Bench and Common Bench, each with its own staff of judges. Under John, as under his father, the court held before the king and the court held before the justiciar were staffed by the same corps of judges. Whether two courts (or two divisions of the same court) were maintained when the king was in England was no more than a matter of administrative convenience. If the king stayed for some time at Westminster it would be unnecessary to divide the corps of judges into two, and so the two divisions of the court would coalesce.[4] In the

---

[1] Cf. Jenkinson, *Cal. Plea Rolls*, iii. l–li, where he begins 'Our rolls are essentially *Memoranda Rolls* . . .'    [2] Above, p. 135.

[3] This is Maitland's phrase (*Select Pleas of the Crown*, p. xvii).

[4] For a summary statement see *Law Quarterly Review*, lxx. 568–70. For details see *Memoranda Roll 1 John*, pp. xi–xv; D. M. Stenton, *Pleas before the King or his Justices* (Selden Soc.), i. 49–149.

latter years of John's reign, when the king became permanently resident in England, the justiciar's separate court was suppressed, to the inconvenience of his subjects, who had become used to a resident tribunal at Westminster.[1] After John's death no court *coram rege* was held during Henry III's minority, but a single central court was established at Westminster.[2] This satisfied the requirement of Magna Carta that common pleas should be held in some fixed place.[3] When, however, the judiciary was re-organized on the suppression of the justiciarship in 1234, three courts of common law emerged: the ambulatory King's Bench, the sedentary Common Bench and the Exchequer, with a re-stricted competence. These courts were more than different divisions of the same central court; there was, in fact, now a hierarchy of courts, for the King's Bench had superior status, being the court held technically before the king himself.[4]

The purpose of this explanation is to remove any ambiguity there might be in saying that in John's reign cases concerning the Jews came before the Bench and before the king. These are but two aspects of the same tribunal, although it might happen that, for some special reason, a case was adjourned until the king could be present. This did not, however, mean that the jurisdiction of the justiciar was ousted, for both he and the king might be present at the same session of the court. Nor need the business taken when the king presided be of great importance: on one occasion Jews were summoned to appear before the justiciar and the king when it was a question of the terms upon which a debt was to be remitted.[5] The reason why the high court was preferred was doubtless because the Justices of the Jews were of lowly rank in the official hierarchy. Consequently those who could afford the expense would, if the issue were of sufficient importance to them, pay for the transfer of an action to the Bench or the court held

---

[1] Articles of the Barons, c. 8.

[2] Richardson and Sayles, *Select Cases of Procedure without Writ*, pp. xv–xvi.

[3] Magna Carta 1215, c. 17; in later issues, c. 12.

[4] Sayles, *Select Cases in the Court of King's Bench under Edward I*, i. xxxiv–xxxviii; ii. xliv–li.; iv. xxvii–xxxii; Richardson and Sayles, *op. cit.*, pp. xv, clxvi–clxvii.          [5] *Rot. Litt. Claus.*, i. 107*b*.

*coram rege.* Even if a case had been decided by the Justices, it might be reheard 'before the king'.[1] A case of some interest is one of a loan by Aaron of Lincoln which the Justices of the Jews were endeavouring to recover from the widow and heirs of the borrower (a Jew named Dieudonné) as late as the year 1201, although the defendants had (so they said) written evidence that they were quit of the debt. Indeed they were prepared to pay 10 marks to be allowed to produce their bonds and acquittances in the court *coram rege*, where evidently they expected a judgement in their favour.[2] The result is not known; but it looks as though the Exchequer of the Jews was inclined to be excessively cautious in protecting the king's interest. This case helps to explain why there were tried in the higher court, from time to time, cases of the same types as were tried before the Justices, though very little of the administrative work that largely occupied their attention came before the justiciar or the king. The number of actions to come before the higher court was never large—a few cases of debt[3] and dower,[4] a few criminal cases[5]—although there were other cases which arose incidentally from transactions with Jewish moneylenders[6] and some which involved them because they were vouched to warranty when they sub-let gaged land.[7] These exceptions, which it is not difficult to explain, left the Justices of the Jews with jurisdiction over the everyday affairs of the Jewry. But there were other exceptions to this generalization which do not admit of any easy explanation.

In the first place let us notice that, as in the twelfth century,[8] so in the early years of the thirteenth, cases in which Jews were

---

[1] *Curia Regis Rolls*, v. 169–70.

[2] *Rot. Oblat.*, pp. 121–2.

[3] *Curia Regis Rolls*, i. 110, 114, 184, 422, 427; iii. 159; iv. 86; *Pipe Roll 1 John*, p. 224.

[4] *Curia Regis Rolls*, i. 417; vii. 70–1, 339.

[5] *Ibid.*, i. 359; a case of rape; *Pipe Roll 7 John*, pp. 213–14: coin-clipping. An accusation of forgery goes to a mixed jury, but the finding does not, apparently, come before the Justices of the Jews (*Pipe Roll 5 John*, p. 99).

[6] *Curia Regis Rolls*, i. 104–5, 212, 390; v. 169; ix. 294–5, 387–9; x. 56, 144–5, 252.

[7] *Ibid.*, viii. 307; ix. 23–4, 153–4.　　　　[8] Above, pp. 112–14.

the defendants continued to come before justices in eyre. Thus, in the Bedford eyre of 1202, a Jew named Bonenfant defended an appeal of felony. He did not, however, fight a judicial duel, but he paid the king a mark for an inquest, with, doubtless, a mixed jury, which found him innocent.[1] This is a remarkable case, for it implies that some time, perhaps several years, previously, there had been an appeal before the coroners and in the county court. It may well be that these preliminaries had happened before the Justices of the Jews had established their jurisdiction and that the case reflects the conditions of the twelfth century: in any case the justices in eyre determined the issue finally. We may contrast this case with one that came before the justices in eyre in Gloucestershire in the early years of Henry III. A Jew of Bristol who bore, rather surprisingly, the name of Adrian, was accused of the murder of a Christian, but already, before the eyre began, he had been sent up to London for trial before the Justices of the Jews. Still there were left a number of matters connected with the case that required the attention of the itinerant justices. At an early stage the case had come before the coroners and bailiffs of the town and, according to their story, Adrian's wife, who bore the equally remarkable name of Richolda, had been mainprised by five Jews, who had also undertaken to produce Adrian's chattels. This story the Jews denied. The justices did not come to any decision, but remitted this aspect of the case too to London.[2] The complications did not, however, end here. A Jewess, named Douce Furmagère, was alleged to be an accessory, for the obscure reason that she had pledged a charter (presumably belonging to the dead man) with 'a little old woman' (*cuidam vetule*). She denied everything, but submitted to a fine of twenty shillings imposed by the justices for her trespass.[3] The justices also accepted the offer of a mark from Isaac of Gloucester that he might find

---

[1] Maitland, *Select Pleas of the Crown* (Selden Soc.), p. 26; Bedfordshire Historical Record Soc., *Publications*, i. 230–1.

[2] Maitland, *Pleas of the Crown for the County of Gloucester in 1221*, p. 115.

[3] *Ibid.*, pp. 115, 134. Douce's surname is obscured by the spelling. She doubtless belonged to a well-known Bristol family with the surname *Furmager*, i.e. Cheesemonger (above, p. 26).

sureties, doubtless for his appearance to stand his trial, but on what charge or where is not stated, though we may suppose that he, too, was to appear before the Justices of the Jews.[1]

Vague and unsatisfying as these brief notes of cases are, they are useful for the indications they give of the transition from the conditions under Henry II to the conditions under Henry III. They strengthen the view that there was no abrupt change of procedure, that the jurisdiction of the Justices of the Jews was gradually evolving under Richard I and John and was not deliberately conferred at one stroke. One expedient led to another and, in turn, became a precedent, but never a precedent to be rigorously followed. Apparently, when some measure affecting the Jewry generally was of exceptional importance or presented some exceptional difficulty,[2] there was a tendency to set up a special agency. Thus, the assessment and collection of the Bristol tallage of 1210, which was of unprecedented severity, was put into the hands of ministers appointed *ad hoc*. These same ministers were charged with the disposal of the property of prominent Jews condemned in consequence of the general *captio Iudeorum* earlier in that year.[3] In like manner, when sweeping charges of coin-clipping were made against the Jews in Edward I's reign, special commissions of justices were appointed for the purpose of trying them and special agents were appointed to dispose of the property that had fallen as escheats into the king's hand.[4] Inevitably the suspicion arises that the Justices of the Jews were not employed because they were in daily touch with the Jewry and were advised by some of its prominent members: by their habitual intercourse they were well informed and were as likely as any Christians could be to prove unprejudiced. That there were circumstances in which the Jews felt more confident of fair treatment

---

[1] *Ibid.*, p. 163.

[2] This does not seem to be the explanation in such a case as the employment of Stephen Seagrave in 1230 to deal with Jews accused of larceny and coin-clipping and to arrange a settlement between a landowner and his Jewish creditors. But the king seems to have been personally interested in both matters (*Close Rolls, 1227–1231*, pp. 304–6).

[3] Below, pp. 168–70.          [4] Below, pp. 217–20.

in the Exchequer of the Jews than before other tribunals is well illustrated by an incident before the justices who were sitting in Northamptonshire in 1268 to try charges arising out of the disseisins and acts of violence that had accompanied the baronial rebellion. A certain Osbert of Crowthorpe had been charged with depredations in the Jewry at Northampton, but when the Jews of that town were asked by the justices whether they wished to prosecute Osbert and other depredators of the Jewry, they replied with one accord that they would not prosecute 'except before their justice assigned to the Jewry'.[1] There can be no doubt that they had in mind the archpriest, Hagin, the son of master Moses, 'who had taken oath to the king faithfully to advise his justices in the Exchequer of the Jews'.[2] Yet there may well have been reasons, other than the bias of the Justices of the Jews, for preferring a different agency on extraordinary occasions. Not only were they men of relatively lowly standing among the king's ministers, but the Exchequer of the Jews does not seem to have been staffed for more than the routine functions of the office. The Justices might, however, be entrusted with clearing up a special piece of work that had already been largely accomplished, and so we find them in the early years of Henry III's reign gathering in overdue instalments of the Bristol tallage.[3] The untidiness of these expedients, the confusion into which administration must inevitably have been thrown, was somewhat mitigated by the accountability of all concerned to the exchequer, for, in the normal course, all accounts, whether of the Justices of the Jews or of ministers with a special mission, came up for audit and thus enabled the barons of the exchequer to exercise control over the financial aspect of Jewish affairs, even though they had little or no concern with policy and were only exceptionally concerned with the administration of justice.[4] And it was the financial aspect of Jewish affairs

---

[1] Hunter, *Rotuli Selecti*, p. 210: dicunt se nolle prosequi nisi coram iusticiario suo ad Iudaismum assignato.

[2] Rigg, *Select Pleas*, p. 73. This is five years later.

[3] See pp. 172, 285–6, below.

[4] Under Henry III financial control over the Justices of the Jews must have been very close, for the membranes recording their receipts seem normally to have

that had become the predominant interest of the king's government.

If the jurisdiction of the Justices of the Jews was limited in the sense that they were not entrusted with business out of the ordinary to which the king's government attached special importance, so it seems that they might be excluded, for another reason, from the cognisance of petty affairs. The establishment of the Exchequer of the Jews, which, as we have seen, was a gradual process, does not seem to have been accompanied by any measure designed to oust the jurisdiction of keepers of royal castles. However, the superiority of the justice to be expected in the central courts, in this as in other fields, led litigants to prefer it, with the consequence that the jurisdiction of local courts diminished or decayed. There is, at least, one exception to this rule. The constable of the Tower of London retained a certain measure of both criminal and civil jurisdiction.[1] In the London Jewry the authority of the mayor and sheriffs was ousted and the constable of the Tower maintained order by means of a serjeant of the Jewry.[2] Offences committed there, whether by Jews or Christians, came before the constable's court.[3] If the constables of other castles within whose liberties Jews dwelt—Bristol, Devizes, Marlborough, Stamford—exercised a like jurisdiction, as they may well have done, no record appears to have survived. In so far as they were responsible for the local Jewry, they exercised, as the constable of the Tower did, certain of the powers and duties of a sheriff; but that was because the sheriff was excluded from the liberty, and what they did was on the instructions of the Justices

formed part of the exchequer receipt roll (Jewish Hist. Soc., *Transactions*, xviii. 291–2). The memoranda rolls also indicate that the Justices of the Jews became subordinate to the barons of the exchequer: see the extracts printed in Madox, *History of the Exchequer* (1769), i. 221–61.

[1] *Close Rolls, 1259–1261*, p. 385.

[2] *Cal. Plea Rolls*, iii. 290. A number of references to the serjeant, as well as an account of his, will be found in P.R.O., E. 101/249/22, as to which see below, pp. 156, n. 3, 159, n. 2, 160, n. 1.

[3] For the court and its clerk see *Cal. Plea Rolls*, iii. 100. The serjeant of the court, who acts with the clerk, may be identical with the serjeant of the Jewry. Other references to the court will be found in E. 101/249/22.

of the Jews.[1] Besides his police jurisdiction, the constable of the Tower successfully maintained, in face of the opposition of the Justices, his claim to try in his court actions between Christians and Jews where the pledge taken in pawn did not exceed the value of forty shillings.[2] There is no trace of a parallel jurisdiction elsewhere. Though such knowledge as we have of these matters is fragmentary and comes from the last thirty years before the Expulsion,[3] it is reasonable to suppose that the jurisdiction of the constable of the Tower, which he claimed always to have exercised,[4] is a survival from ancient times.

We have said that constables exercised within the liberties of their castles certain of the powers and duties of a sheriff. What then were the powers and duties of sheriffs in regard to Jews? They were, of course, responsible for their protection, a duty that flowed from the charter of Henry II which guaranteed their liberties; but the Jews did not ordinarily fall within the jurisdiction which a sheriff exercised in the county court. If a Jew chose to sue there voluntarily, that was his affair, and we find evidence from an early date of Jews making use of the normal procedure of the appeal of felony.[5] But though a Jew might elect this course, it does not follow that it was practicable to employ the same procedure against a Jew, who would have the best of reasons for avoiding it. If then an aggrieved party desired to charge a Jew with felony and to proceed by way of appeal, he must do so before the Justices of the Jews.[6] In the end the legal consequences were the same, a trial before the king's justices; and the plaintiff was not disadvantaged, though the accused Jew might well believe

---

[1] For Bristol see *Cal. Plea Rolls*, ii. 122–3, 139, 153, 161, 183, 198; iii. 133, 196, 202, 221, 227: for Devizes, *ibid.*, iii. 43, 204; for Marlborough, *ibid.*, ii. 161; iii. 51, 102, 119: for Stamford, *ibid.*, ii. 33, 98; 131–2. For the frequent references to the constable of the Tower see *Cal. Plea Rolls, passim*.

[2] *Close Rolls, 1259–1261*, p. 385.

[3] The rolls of accounts of the under-constable and serjeant in E. 101/249/22 cover the years 1275–1278.

[4] 'Quia custodes et constabularii . . . semper habere consueuerunt . . .' (*Close Rolls, ut supra*).          [5] Above, p. 113.

[6] *Cal. Plea Rolls*, iii. 185–6, 288–9. The first reference is to three cases of an appeal by an approver, but the principle is the same.

that he stood a better chance of proving his innocence in the Exchequer of the Jews. However, the important principle here is that Jews were not suitors of the county court and that, at least in the thirteenth century, the procedure of that court was not normally available against them. It seems, therefore, anomalous that, at the direction of the Justices, Jews were outlawed in the county court. This procedure involved the 'exaction' of the defendant four times at successive courts and, on his failure to answer, his formal outlawry. Since there was no assumption in law that a Jew would be present or represented in court, it follows that the procedure was purely formal: the decision had, in fact, already been taken by the Justices and the remission of the matter to the sheriff was merely to secure outward compliance with the law. Though the consequences of outlawry might be serious, it is not to be supposed that an outlawed Jew was necessarily in danger of his life or of bodily harm: the outlawry was what Bracton called a minor outlawry[1] and its purpose was to compel appearance in court. It might proceed from evasion of taxation[2] or misconduct in the office of chirographer[3] or failure to answer to a criminal charge.[4] If, as seems to have been usual, the accused fled, he suffered forfeiture,[5] and the sheriff might be responsible for ensuring that his chattels were seized on behalf of the king; but the machinery of the county court was employed solely for the formality of outlawry. Though our evidence comes mainly from the late thirteenth century, the clumsy and long-drawn-out procedure has an archaic air which suggests that it was traditional and remounts to the earlier days of the Jews' settlement in England.[6] This strict adherence by the Justices to the formal processes

---

[1] Bracton, fo. 441.  [2] Rigg, *Select Pleas*, p. 95.

[3] *Cal. Plea Rolls*, iii. 42–3.

[4] *Ibid.*, pp. 162–3.  [5] *Ibid.*, p. 211.

[6] The earliest case that has come to light occurred in 1230, when the procedure seems evidently well established. Seynuret, a Jew of Norwich, was accused of circumcising a Christian boy. He fled, was outlawed and suffered forfeiture (*Cal. Inquisitions Miscellaneous*, i. 171 (no. 522): for later proceedings see *ibid.*, p. 141 (no. 428)). This case probably originated in an appeal of felony, as in the earlier case of Bonenfant of Bedford, where the charge of 'ementulation' may mean circumcision (Maitland, *Select Pleas of the Crown*, p. 26; above, p. 152).

of the law contrasts starkly with the arbitrary power of arrest which the king exercised from time to time in the thirteenth century[1] and suggests why on such occasions other agents were employed by the government.

In the normal course sheriffs and, when Jews resided in liberties, constables were called upon by the Justices of the Jews, as they were by other courts and departments of government, to perform administrative acts for which no other agent was available locally: to compel appearance in court, to summon juries, to hold inquests into facts alleged before the court, to collect taxes, to recover money due to the Crown or to some private party and so forth. These were purely ministerial acts and were not performed in consequence of any right of jurisdiction. This is true even when, as might occasionally happen, there were formal proceedings in the county court. A specific case will illustrate the point. Josce, the son of Benedict, had lent money on the security of his land to one Simon de Grainville, who lived at Newton in Norfolk. Simon defaulted and Josce thereupon obtained an order of the court putting him in seisin of Simon's land and chattels until the amount due was recovered. To execute the order Josce appointed Abraham of Norwich as his agent, and Abraham, accompanied by the sheriff's bailiff, came, in accordance with the customary procedure, to take possession.[2] Actually the chattels they seized were of greater value than the debt, and on these facts Simon brought an action of trespass against Abraham. Instead of summoning a jury to Westminster, the Justices ordered the sheriff newly in office to ascertain the facts in the county court in the presence of his predecessor and the coroners. A mixed jury was empanelled whose findings were returned to the Justices and judgement was given in court accordingly.[3] The procedure in this case was exceptional and was doubtless devised because the conduct, not only of the creditor's agent, but of the sheriff's officer, was impugned. A Jew might himself prefer to have an inquisition taken in the county court rather than in the Exchequer of the

[1] Below, pp. 169–70, 214, 218, 225.  [2] Above, p. 86.
[3] *Cal. Plea Rolls*, ii. 255–6.

Jews, as when Aaron, the son of Hake, of Worcester offered half a mark for this alternative. Doubtless he did so to save delay and expense, for the jury would be composed in the same way and probably of the same men, whether it was summoned to Westminster or delivered its findings locally.[1] There is no suggestion that the county court, as such, had any jurisdiction in these matters.

There is a postscript it may be well to add on the relations between the Jews on the one hand and sheriffs and constables on the other. If they were the protectors of the Jews and responsible to the Crown for their safety, the helplessness of those they protected gave them power which it was easy to abuse. Of the constable of the Tower is this specially true, for not only had he wide powers of arrest and imprisonment over both resident and visiting Jews, but he was by prescriptive right the sole gaoler to whom might be committed such Jews as the Justices or higher authorities decided to keep in custody.[2] He and his subordinates were therefore in a position to exact protection money and to show favour for a consideration;[3] and this is true, if the possibilities were fewer, of other constables and of sheriffs. The medieval official was notoriously venal, especially gaolers, as sheriffs and constables, directly or through their subordinates, perforce became. The threat of arbitrary imprisonment was constantly hanging over the Jews, and their anxieties were the greater because the relations of sheriffs and constables with them were far more intimate than they were with any other class or community, extending over much of the Jews' daily life.[4] Some few Jews had

---

[1] *Cal. Inquisitions Miscellaneous*, i. 133 (no. 396). The issue was whether Aaron had acquired his house or had inherited it from his father, in which case it might have been claimed by the Crown as an escheat.

[2] *Close Rolls, 1259–1261*, p. 385.

[3] The accounts of the under-constable are full of such entries as: De uxore Cok Hagin pro respectu prisone dum Cok fugitiuus erat; pro libera prisona; ut possint esse ad largum; ut possint esse in villa quia grosse (E. 101/249/22).

[4] The items in the account of the sheriff of Kent, Reginald of Cobham, for 37–8 Henry III are particularly instructive. The following are examples: pur la norice Dame Avigae et pur nos doner congé à manger nostre aignel à Paschez; de Dame Avigae la fame Sale pur lui aider; de cele meime Jiue quant son baron

friends of such exalted rank that perhaps they could show a bold
face to any man, but to the majority, sheriffs and constables, their
serjeants and their bailiffs, were potential oppressors to be placated
with gifts. It was a matter of course that sheriffs and constables
should take advantage of their opportunities; and their gains,
which were, in their eyes, legitimate and by no means illicit, set
down without concealment in their accounts, were scarcely
inferior to those drawn from the Jewry by the king.[1]

fu outre mer et eie jut en gisine; de Salle le Juif pur venir à unes noces à Londres;
del commun pur ce qe Mosse et de Samekin et Florie ne jeteissent pas lor taillage
sor le commun; del commun de menues prises qe nos ne savom mie uncore
(E. 101/249/8).

[1] The total of the account of the under-constable of the Tower, covering four
years, is £426. 3s. 9d., though some part of this was apparently passed on to the
exchequer; the total of the account of the serjeant, covering one-and-a-half years,
is £564. 10s. 11d., but again some part was apparently not retained (E.101/249/22).

# VIII

# THE TAXATION OF THE JEWS

SOME INCIDENTAL REFERENCE HAS already been made to taxes levied upon the English Jewry, but it is desirable to bring together such evidence as is available for the reigns of Henry II, Richard I and John. The evidence is fragmentary and, for the period as a whole, inferences are hazardous. It has already been suggested that about the year 1180 the king abandoned the policy of exacting loans from the Jews and relied upon taxation to give him the revenue he needed. The facts, so far as they are known, are consistent with this hypothesis. The absence of borrowing in 1168 may be related to the tax imposed in that year, just as the cessation of borrowing after 1179 may explain the exceptionally heavy taxation of 1186. But the danger of arguing from silence is here particularly obvious, and the details of taxation between 1168 and 1186, could they be recovered, might cause us to modify or abandon a hypothesis which, in the light of available knowledge, is plausible and attractive. The early pipe rolls of Henry II's reign mention a few payments by Jews,[1] one of which is specifically called a *donum*,[2] but there is no conclusive evidence of any general tax until 1159, when the sheriffs of nine counties account for a little under 550 marks.[3] Since the sheriffs of neither Essex[4] nor Kent[5] account for any part of the tax, it may be that the pipe roll

---

[1] *Pipe Roll 2 Henry II*, pp. 8, 15, 36; *3 Henry II*, p. 96; *4 Henry II*, p. 127: the total is less than 100 marks.

[2] *Pipe Roll 2 Henry II*, p. 36: de dono Iudeorum [Oxford].

[3] *Pipe Roll 4 Henry II*, pp. 3, 12, 17, 24, 28, 35, 46, 53, 65.

[4] For a settlement at Newport in Essex, see above, p. 10.

[5] The evidence for the early settlement of Jews at Canterbury is examined by Michael Adler, *Jews of Medieval England*, pp. 49–51. For the beginning of Henry II's reign it is not conclusive, though a settlement is highly probable.

does not give complete particulars and that payments were made by Jews in these counties in some other way than through the sheriffs. This is an important point, because it suggests that the few odd payments recorded in the earlier years may indicate, not exceptional payments by Jewish communities in individual towns, but taxes imposed generally on all Jewish communities in England. Indeed it would be strange if, when landowners and churchmen, burgesses and moneyers, were taxed, the Jews should escape. And though the pipe rolls for the rest of Henry II's reign contain no trace of any tallage on the English Jewry, yet it is certain that tallages were imposed and presumably fairly frequently imposed. A chronicler, Gervase of Canterbury, refers to an exaction of 5,000 marks in 1168 and apparently other, extraordinary, payments by the wealthier Jews,[1] and, while these details may be inexact, the silence of the pipe rolls does not indicate that the story is ill-founded. Since this department of the revenue was separately managed, it was only when, as a matter of administrative convenience, a sheriff was required to collect any part of a tax on the Jews that a reference to the tax would appear on a pipe roll. A good illustration is afforded by the Guildford tallage, which was imposed by Henry II at Christmas 1186.[2] Gervase of Canterbury said that the amount collected was £60,000;[3] but though this figure is no more than a symbol for a very large sum, we may be sure that the tallage was heavy and that it was imposed upon the whole of the Jewry. Yet when, in 1190, the justiciar, William Longchamp, directed that the balances due should be accounted for on the pipe roll, this direction applied to four counties only,

[1] *Opera Historica*, i. 205: 'fecit rex ditiores ex Anglia Iudaeos transfretare et reliquos in quinque milibus marcis describere.'

[2] The king held a council at Guildford on the occasion of this feast. No other occasion than this therefore seems likely: see *Gesta Henrici*, ii. 3, and Eyton, *Itinerary of Henry II*, pp. 275, 284–9. A difficulty is created by the statement in *Pipe Roll 1 Richard I*, p. 230, that this was the tallage 'quod rex Henricus pater fecit apud Geldeforde post susceptionem crucis', and Henry II is said to have taken the cross at a colloquy with Philip Augustus near Gisors on 21 January 1188 (*Gesta*, ii. 30, 58–9). There seems to be no evidence for Henry's presence at Guildford between February and 10 July 1188 when he was last in England.

[3] *Opera Historica*, i. 422.

London, Essex, Kent and Sussex, and the names of the debtors number only seventy odd.[1] We cannot account for the omission of other counties in which Jews dwelt by supposing that all debts had been paid or by referring to the massacres of 1190 in Norfolk, Suffolk, Northamptonshire and Yorkshire:[2] Hampshire, where there were no disturbances, is equally missing, as well as other counties where, so far as we know, the Jews were left in peace. This is not the only difficulty in the way of interpreting the evidence relating to the Guildford tallage. By one usually well-informed chronicler the Guildford tallage appears to be confused with the Saladin tithe. The basis of assessment may very well have been, as he asserts, the same, namely one-tenth of rents and movables, and this, in the case of the Jews, would have yielded the *inestimabilis pecunia* of which he speaks.[3] But the Saladin tithe was announced at a council at Geddington in February 1188, more than a year after the probable date of the Guildford tallage. What may well have happened is that the king took the occasion of general taxation for the crusade to make a further demand upon the Jews, a demand limited, however, to 10,000 marks. Certainly a tax of this amount was levied in the closing years of Henry II's reign and, it would seem, after the Guildford tallage,[4] that is at some date between Christmas 1186 and the king's death in July 1189, and 1188 seems to be the most likely year. The London Jews were separately tallaged, apparently in 1187, when the king demanded a quarter of their chattels.[5]

[1] *Pipe Roll 1 Richard I*, p. 230; *2 Richard I*, p. 159; *3 Richard I*, pp. 32, 60–1, 139–40, 148.

[2] As Joseph Jacobs explained some apparent omissions from the receipt roll of 1194 (*Jews of Angevin England*, p. 163).

[3] *Gesta Henrici*, ii. 33; R. de Hovedene, *Chronica*, ii. 338. The obvious difficulty here is that the tallage was certainly determined upon at Guildford and not at Geddington, as the chronicler implies.

[4] *Pipe Roll 3 Richard I*, pp. 50, 139. Cf. *Pipe Roll 4 Richard I*, p. 305, where an entry on *Pipe Roll 3 Richard I* is elucidated. The arrears shown amount to just under £700, about a tenth of the total. See also *Memoranda Roll 1 John*, p. 70.

[5] There seems no good reason for assuming that a tax assessed at one-fourth was imposed elsewhere than in London. The only entry mentioning this basis occurs under London and Middlesex in *Pipe Roll 33 Henry II*, p. 44: 'De predictis debitis Iudeorum sustinemus ad presens quia dominus rex capit quartum de

In the early years of Richard I there can have been little scope for fresh taxation of the Jews. On the pipe roll of 1191 there is a reference to the second 1,000 marks that the Jews of England had promised to Richard I,[1] so it is clear that the new king had obtained two *promissa* of 1,000 marks each, which later were regarded as a single tallage of 2,000 marks.[2] After Richard's return from Germany a further levy of 5,000 marks was made upon the Jews. This levy goes by more than one name. Since it is called the *promissum* made at Northampton[3] and since the king held a council there at Easter 1194, details were presumably settled on that occasion,[4] but elsewhere this 'tallage' is said to have been 'made' at London.[5] Meanwhile negotiations must have been on foot to determine the amount of the contribution to be paid by the English Jews towards Richard's ransom. Finally they agreed to contribute 3,000 marks, and we are specifically told that they fined for this amount at Laigle, where Richard was on more than one occasion in May 1194.[6] The king insisted upon prompt payment at stated terms, failure to be visited with an increase of the 'tallage' to 5,000 marks.[7] Fortunately there has survived the receipt roll for the Easter term 1194 which gives details of the receipts for a single term from these two taxes and from some other Jewish contributions.[8] Payments in respect of the tax of 5,000 marks came to rather more than a half of the entire amount. It should perhaps be remarked that there is no ground for supposing that no more was collected, for many of the payments

catallis suis'. A similar note occurs in *Pipe Roll 34 Henry II*, p. 22, but for the words following 'ad presens', there is substituted 'propter tallagium quod dominus rex capit ab eis'. On the same roll (p. 16), the reeves of Bosham account for £40 'quas receperunt a Ricardo de Windresores et aliis receptoribus de tallagio Iudeorum Londoniarum', and this tallage must evidently be that on the one-fourth basis.

[1] *Pipe Roll 3 Richard I*, p. 98. It is possible that payments of half a mark and 16s. at p. 49 'de dono' are in respect of the same contribution.

[2] *Memoranda Roll 1 John*, p. 69.

[3] In the title to the receipt roll mentioned below.

[4] Landon, *Itinerary of Richard I*, p. 87.     [5] *Memoranda Roll 1 John*, p. 69.

[6] Richard is recorded there on 12 and 31 May (Landon, *op. cit.*, pp. 93–4).

[7] *Memoranda Roll 1 John*, p. 71. Possibly the penalty for failure was 5,000 marks, not 2,000; but in any case the penalty was not exacted.

[8] Jewish Hist. Soc., *Miscellanies*, i. lix–lxxiv.

recorded on the roll were made in instalments, and it must be presumed that similar instalments continued to be paid and were recorded on later receipt rolls.[1] While the great bulk of the payments in this term are in respect of the Northampton *promissum*, the roll records also payments in respect of another *promissum* of 3,000 marks, which would seem without doubt to be the contribution towards Richard's ransom,[2] and a trifling payment in respect of the 'old tallage',[3] which might mean the *promissa* of 2,000 marks or possibly the tallage of Guildford or the tallage of 10,000 marks. Various payments in respect of besants or gold are also entered on the receipt roll:[4] this was evidently another tax, perhaps a poll-tax.

Between Christmas 1186 and May 1194 there were then levied on the English Jews the following taxes. The Guildford tallage, of an unknown amount, though evidently large; the tallage on the London Jews of one-fourth of their personal property; a tallage of 10,000 marks; four contributions to Richard I, two of 1,000 marks, one of 5,000 and another of 3,000 making 10,000 marks in all, together with a payment of besants, the total of which cannot be estimated precisely but which cannot have been great. If this is a full list, as it seems to be, the remarkable fact is Richard's moderation. Of any taxes levied by Richard in the last years of his reign there appears to be no record, and when a review of Jewish debts is made at the beginning of John's reign, only the tallage of 2,000 marks, the tallage after Richard's return from Germany and the tallage for his ransom are mentioned.[5] Some small levies may have escaped particular mention, but it can hardly be the case that any major tax did not leave behind it debts substantial enough to occasion remark.[6]

---

[1] At Michaelmas 1199 Hugh Peverel had not yet accounted for £105 that he had received from Hakelin, the son of Jurnet of Norwich, in respect of this tax (*Memoranda Roll 1 John*, p. 72).

[2] *Miscellanies*, i. lxvii., lxxii., lxxiv.  [3] *Ibid.*, p. lxvii.

[4] *Ibid.*, pp. lxvi., lxx., lxxi.  [5] *Memoranda Roll 1 John*, pp. 69–72.

[6] There are substantial arrears of other taxes levied by Henry II and Richard I which occasion informative remarks. Nothing was likely to be let slip. Evidently the possibility was considered of demanding the penalty the Jews were alleged to

It is true that the disappearance of so many of the financial records of Henry II and Richard I means that we can never know the extent of the revenues derived from the Jews in those reigns, and even with the comparatively plentiful records of the reign of John, it is difficult to be certain of the full story of Jewish taxation, though we are in no doubt of the principal items. John exacted the high price of 4,000 marks for confirming their charters to the Jews.[1] He received a *promissum* of besants in 1205.[2] In 1207 he took a tallage of 4,000 marks[3] and in the same year he demanded from Jewish moneylenders a tenth of the value of their bonds.[4] There is an obscure reference in 1208 to a tallage *de tercio*, which must have been levied in the early years of the reign.[5] This is perhaps to be identified with a tax described in other terms elsewhere; but it may be a local levy. The parallel to the 'fourth' exacted by Henry II from the London Jewry suggests itself. The only Jew who, so far as the records show, was in arrear in his payments of the 'third' was Solomon of Milk Street in London, who owed 29 marks and had nothing on which a distress could be levied except his house. If this tallage is distinct from the other taxes known to have been levied before 1208 then, if it had been heavy or general, it would be odd that there should be no other trace of it, and we may assume that the mention of it does not imply a grievous burden on the Jews. In 1210, however, the king levied an extremely heavy tallage, said to have amounted to 60,000 or 66,000 marks, though, again, these figures are merely picturesque expressions for denoting a very large, an incalculable, sum of money.[6] This tax was extremely difficult to collect and was still in arrear when war broke out, in 1215, between the king and his barons. There were no regular revenues from Jews or others

have incurred because they had failed to keep the terms fixed for the payment of their contribution to Richard's ransom (*ibid.*, p. 71).

[1] *Rot. Oblat.*, p. 133.    [2] *Rot. Litt. Claus.*, i. 25b; *Pipe Roll 8 John*, p. 143.
[3] *Rot. Oblat.*, pp. 403, 418.
[4] *Rot. Litt. Claus.*, i. 113; *Rot. Litt. Pat.*, p. 81b.
[5] *Memoranda Roll 10 John*, pp. 64, 65.
[6] *Annales Monastici* (Waverley), ii. 264; *Liber de Antiquis Legibus*, p. 201; Cole, *Documents*, p. 287.

during the *tempus guerrae*, which did not end officially until Michaelmas 1217, after John had been dead nearly a year. This, in summary, is the story of Jewish taxation under John; but before entering into details some comment may be helpful in order to get the picture into perspective. The year 1210 marks a turning point in the history of the English Jewry: the eighty years then begun are a period of declining prosperity and mounting hardship. John, Henry III and Edward I were men of very different temperament, but John's savagery, Henry's piety and egotism, Edward's unscrupulousness, all alike worked to the destruction of the Jews. And it was their misfortune that the climate of Christian opinion, the growth of the spirit of intolerance and persecution, lent an air of justification to barbarities that would have shocked the better spirits of an earlier age, an Anselm, a Saint Bernard, even a Henry fitz Empress. One of the greatest Englishmen of that age lived on into the thirteenth century, Hubert Walter, justiciar from 1194 to 1198, and in a position of unusual authority as chancellor from 1199 until his death in 1205. To his wisdom and moderation, and that of other ministers who were formed in the same school, may be attributed the indulgence (if it may be so called) with which the Jews were treated in the second half of Richard's reign and the early years of John's. With Hubert Walter's disappearance the change came swiftly.

We need not discuss in detail any of the taxes levied by John except the second tallage of 1207 and the tallage of 1210. The former is remarkable for the means taken to obtain an accurate assessment. The basis of the tax was the estimated value of the debts due to Jewish moneylenders. Every one of them was required to furnish a list of debts, with the value he placed upon each, and, in order that the debts should not be undervalued, any debt might, at the king's discretion, be transferred to the exchequer at the value assigned to it, the Jew, of course, being credited with that amount.[1] How much was realized there is no means of telling, but the important point is that in this way the

---

[1] *Rot. Litt. Claus.*, i. 112b–113; *Rot. Litt. Pat.*, pp. 81b–82 (the date should be 22 April); *Pipe Roll 10 John*, pp. 112–13.

exchequer should have been well informed of the taxable capacity of the Jewry. For the purpose of this tax other forms of property, 'movables', do not seem to have been assessed. They had already been put under contribution a few months earlier when a tallage of 4,000 marks had been levied and they were presumably of relatively small importance. The two taxes of 1207, though doubtless burdensome in the aggregate, do not seem to have been beyond what the Jewry might be expected to find at a time when the king was making heavy demands on all his subjects. This was the year when a subsidy of a thirteenth on the laity and fines or *dona* from the clergy produced over £60,000.[1] Seemingly there was no further demand upon the Jews until 1210. The tallage of this year, the Bristol tallage as it was called, was preceded by the imprisonment of the Jews throughout England at some time before Easter, which fell on 18 April. From the phrases used to describe it—*captio Iudeorum*,[2] *communis captura Iudeorum*,[3] *generalis captio Iudeorum*[4]—there can be no doubt that it was indiscriminate and that, at least, all males of any substance, upon whom hands could be laid, were lodged in gaol.[5] Imprisonment was accompanied by the seizure of all the bonds, chirographs and tallies recording debts due to Jewish moneylenders,[6] which were then ordered to be enrolled.[7] Whether, at this stage, a tallage had been decided upon is uncertain, though later (and misleading) references to the 'general arrest of the Jews at Bristol'[8] implies that

[1] S. K. Mitchell, *Studies in Taxation under John and Henry III*, pp. 84–92. This is the English figure only. John had levied the thirteenth in Ireland also (Richardson and Sayles, *The Irish Parliament in the Middle Ages*, pp. 47–8).

[2] *Pipe Roll 13 John*, pp. 129, 233.

[3] Below, p. 288.  [4] *Excerpta e Rotulis Finium*, i. 104.

[5] Not, however, in Bristol, as some documents might seem to imply. Isaac of Norwich was certainly detained in the Tower of London (Cole, *Documents*, p. 304). Some may have been imprisoned in Bristol castle in 1213 for non-payment of the tallage (*Rot. Litt. Claus.* i. 139a; *Rot. Litt. Pat.*, p. 102b).

[6] This is implied by the writ printed below (p. 288): see also *Pipe Roll 13 John*, p. 129; Cole, *loc. cit.*; *Annales Monastici* (Dunstable), iii. 32.

[7] Cole, *op. cit.*, p. 302.

[8] *Excerpta e Rotulis Finium*, i. 104: 'occasione generalis captionis Iudeorum apud Bristolliam; Cole, *op. cit.*, p. 304: 'post capcionem Iudeorum Bristollie'; below, p. 291: 'communis capcio de Bristoe'.

the information thus obtained furnished the basis of the assessment. More ominously it afforded a means of testing the accuracy of the returns made in 1207.

To account for the events that followed, it must be supposed that wide discrepancies were discovered or imagined between the earlier returns and the evidence of the seized documents. It should perhaps be explained that the value of a debt was not disclosed on the face of the instrument securing it, and that any estimate of its value depended upon many factors, not least whether the king himself would grant special terms to the debtor. And while, in making his returns in 1207, a moneylender was not likely to over-value a debt, the Crown was protected from an undervaluation by reserving the right to take over any debt at the creditor's valuation. Still, an optimistic minister, then, as now, might put a much higher valuation upon a taxpayer's assets than the taxpayer would do. But there might be differences not only in valuation: the existence of certain debts, in particular debts not registered with the chirographers, might have been suppressed. In such a case a double offence might have been committed: to the fraudulent omission to register a debt there would have been added its fraudulent omission from the return of 1207. There might, of course, be good reason for an omission: it is evident that a bond might be still in the possession of a moneylender, although it had been discharged and although he (or the original creditor) had made out a starr of acquittance. It is plain from the many disputes on the point that it was not always easy to establish that a debt had been liquidated.[1] However that may be, the connexion between the general imprisonment of the Jews, the forfeitures and fines that followed and the Bristol tallage shows that the offences, with which those who suffered were charged, were revenue offences and it seems legitimate to infer that the evidence that came into the possession of the Crown convinced the king that he had been grievously wronged. The sequence of events is obscure, but it appears certain that the Jews were imprisoned early in the year,

[1] Above, pp. 80, 105, 138, 151. See also Gross, 'Exchequer of the Jews' in Anglo-Jewish Historical Exhibition, *Papers*, p. 208.

and the fate of those condemned settled by Easter.[1] Thereafter the king's mind was occupied by his expedition to Ireland and he was absent from the latter part of June until 25 August. The date when the tallage was 'made' is given precisely as the feast of All Saints (1 November),[2] so that it was not until well after John's return that the incidence of the tallage was settled. These dates might suggest that the events were unconnected, but there is much to prove a connexion and especially the account of one of the collectors, rendered at Michaelmas 1211, in which he groups together receipts from the tallage, sales of chattels of condemned Jews, the letting of their houses and the sale of the material of those houses that had been demolished.[3]

Let something be said, in the first place, of those who had been condemned. They included some of the most prominent of Jews, and we may presume that they were selected as condign examples. There were Isaac of Norwich, Abraham, the son of Avigai, of London and Isaac of Canterbury. Isaac of Norwich purchased the king's favour with a fine of 10,000 marks, to be paid at the rate of a mark a day, which was still being collected in 1220.[4] Evidently he was, for the time being at least, stripped of all his possessions, his house, his bonds[5] and his chattels: the latter realized a few shillings short of £140.[6] Isaac of Canterbury was hanged: his chattels fetched no more than £30, and in 1223 the king disposed of his houses to his sons for 20 marks.[7] Abraham's fate is uncertain,

---

[1] This must be so, since the proceeds arising from sales of the chattels etc. of condemned Jews are accounted for from this date (*Pipe Roll 13 John*, p. 105).

[2] *loc. cit.*: 'taillagium factum fuit in festo Omnium Sanctorum' at Bristol. The king, however, attests at Melksham on that day.

[3] *Ibid., loc. cit.* No houses are sold, but account is rendered 'de mairemio et aliis perquisitis in Iudaismo'. For the sale of stone and timber, apart from the site, of Jews' houses, see *Cal. Inquisitions Misc.*, i. 112 (no. 328). It does not appear whether the demolition in 1210 was by the mob or by judicial act (cf. Round, *Feudal England*, pp. 552–7; Petit-Dutaillis, *Studies supplementary to Stubbs' Constitutional History*, p. 86).

[4] *Patent Rolls, 1216–1225*, p. 180; *Rot. Litt. Claus.*, i. 459; Mitchell, *op. cit.*, p. 106.

[5] Cole, *Documents*, p. 304. Of some bonds, however, he must have regained possession (above, p. 144).

[6] *Pipe Roll 13 John*, p. 105.

[7] *Ibid.; Excerpta e Rotulis Finium*, i. 104.

but he seems to have been dead by 1218:[1] his chattels fetched 100 marks.[2] The names of the less notable Jews who were condemned have not been preserved. That later in the year there were negotiations with the Jews over the amount and assessment of the tallage is unlikely. The king's needs were great and he was avid for money and determined to exact the uttermost farthing. He had taken a scutage in respect of his Irish campaign, and this seems to have yielded some 10,000 marks. A tallage on cities, towns and royal demesne yielded over 12,000 marks.[3] According to the chroniclers enormous sums were levied upon religious houses, although no receipts from this source can be traced on the pipe rolls.[4] That the Jews should be heavily taxed was therefore to be expected, quite apart from the ill-favour into which they had fallen. Not only the wealthy but the poorest were required to contribute extravagantly, the minimum assessment being apparently 40 shillings.[5] Collection was evidently effected through some other agency than the Justices of the Jews, but of the special organization that was set up we have only glimpses.[6] The wealthier Jews, whose possessions had been seized, had no means of escape and could seek only to mitigate the exactions to which they were subjected. The poorer Jews, who had little to lose, seem in many cases to have fled the country; but this was of little moment to the king, who was not anxious to retain those who were unprofitable to him and was indeed prepared to expel them.[7] Enquiries were being

---

[1] When his son Aaron is prominent among the London Jews: he is not mentioned (Cole, *Documents*, p. 294).

[2] *Pipe Roll 13 John*, p. 105.

[3] Mitchell, *op. cit.*, pp. 96–101. Two aids were demanded in Ireland (Richardson and Sayles, *op. cit.*, pp. 48–9).

[4] Mitchell, *op. cit.*, p. 105.          [5] *Rot. Litt. Claus.*, i. 186b.

[6] The only surviving account is that of John fitz Hugh, who seems to have had no connexion with the Exchequer of the Jews and who was in charge also of the exchange of London and much else (*Pipe Roll 13 John*, pp. 104–6). The Jews of Canterbury made some payments to Hubert de Burgh, but the circumstances are obscure (L.T.R. Memoranda Roll 2 Henry III (E. 366/1), m. 2; *Rot. Litt. Claus.*, ii. 7b, 89). The local organization for realizing debts due to Jews was also exceptional (Cole, *Documents*, pp. 287–8).

[7] *Rot. Litt. Claus.*, i. 186b: instructions of 3 February 1215 to Thomas de Neville, the sole Justice of the Jews.

made in 1213 into the gaged land held by Jews and the houses and lands they held in fee or leased,[1] and later in the year instructions were issued for the imprisonment of Jews who had not paid their tallage.[2] While this is evidence that the Jews were being harassed, it is doubtful whether anything effective was accomplished. When the threads of administration were caught up after the *tempus guerrae*, there were large arrears and it seems evident that the assessment in many cases had had little relevance to the capacity of the taxpayer. There were still owing sums of 100 marks and more and intermediate sums down to 25 shillings—the last from a poor Jew who, as it turned out, had died penniless.[3] The debtors, as a whole, seem to have had few resources, and what little there was to recover came in driblets.[4]

Such is the general outline of the history of Jewish taxation under Henry II, Richard I and John. By themselves, the figures it is possible to give have little meaning. We cannot relate them to the revenue these kings enjoyed or the expenditure they incurred. We have no means of knowing how much these kings received nor how much they spent. Nor would anything be gained by adding to the naïve guesses that have served no better purpose than to mislead unwary historians. But still something may usefully be said to suggest how taxation affected the Jewish community.

It is sufficiently evident that, when large taxes were imposed upon the English Jewry, they were in practice borne chiefly by a few rich men. Le Brun's assessment to the Guildford tallage was seemingly 10,000 marks,[5] Jurnet's assessment 9,000 marks.[6] What the assessment was of Isaac, the son of the Rabbi, is not stated, but

---

[1] *Rot. Litt. Pat.*, p. 97.     [2] *Ibid.*, p. 102b; *Rot. Litt. Claus.*, i. 139a.

[3] P.R.O., E. 101/249/13: an incomplete file of writs and returns, described below, pp. 285–7. The highest figure is 107½ marks due from Dieudonné, the son of 'Annus', apparently of Bristol (no. 2): there is another balance of 99½ marks due from Ursel, the son of Pucelle, of Lincoln (no. 5). The poor Jew, 'mortuus sine catallis', came from Winchester (no. 8).

[4] These receipts are shown in the receipt rolls from 4 to 10 Henry III (E. 401/3B; 4; 5; 6; 7; 8). Some particulars from these and other sources are given by Adler, *Jews of Medieval England*, pp. 204–5: unfortunately he misread the documents on occasion.     [5] *Memoranda Roll 1 John*, p. 69.

[6] *Pipe Roll 9 Richard I*, p. 233; above, p. 41.

he seems to have owed more than £500 on Henry II's death.[1] Abraham, the son of Avigai, must also have been pretty heavily assessed, for at Michaelmas 1199 he still owed 260 marks for the Guildford tallage and 252 marks for the tallage of 10,000 marks.[2] To the Northampton *promissum* of 5,000 marks Jurnet appears to have been assessed at well over £400.[3] These large amounts were not always recovered. Le Brun certainly paid the greater part of his assessment to the Guildford tallage,[4] but Jurnet got his assessment reduced to £1,221.[5] Isaac, the son of the Rabbi, was able to arrange with Longchamp for the reduction of his debt from £526 odd to £200.[6] Under John, Isaac the Chirographer, together with his wife and sons, was charged with an assessment of 5,100 marks in respect of the tallage of 1210, of which he paid over 2,000 marks by Michaelmas 1211.[7] With figures such as these before us, a caveat is hardly necessary that the full amount of a tax was not likely to be realized, although we have quite inadequate material for estimating by how much the receipts fell short. The large assessments on a small number of wealthy moneylenders evidently could not be met at once, if ever. Their resources were not liquid and if the king's demands upon them for large sums were frequent, as at several periods they were, the wealthiest could not keep free from debt. They had to begin payments in respect of a fresh tax or fine before they were clear of the old. The state of Le Brun's account at Michaelmas 1199 may serve as an illustration. He was in the first place debited with arrears that had arisen under Henry II: £340, the balance of an amercement of 2,000 marks; a £10 deficiency in the sum of £400 realized on the sale (in 1182) of his chattels seized by the Crown;[8] and £1297. 1s.

[1] *Memoranda Roll 1 John*, p. 71.     [2] *Ibid.*, p. 70.

[3] *Ibid.*, p. 72. Jurnet's son Hakelin is charged, but he had succeeded to his father's estate (above, p. 42).

[4] *Ibid.*, p. 69.     [5] *Pipe Roll 9 Richard I*, p. 233.

[6] *Memoranda Roll 1 John*, p. 70.

[7] *Pipe Roll 13 John*, p. 105. He paid, or was credited with, further sums the following year (*Pipe Roll 14 John*, pp. 42, 50).

[8] The deficiency was caused because chattels were sold by his sureties to the value of £400 *in veteri moneta*, i.e. not of full weight, and therefore subject to a 10-per-cent. reduction on the face value (*Pipe Roll 28 Henry II*, p. 161).

2*d*. arrears of his assessment of 10,000 marks to the Guildford tallage. Against these items he was allowed credits amounting to £23. 6*s*. 8*d*. He was next debited with arrears accruing under Richard I: £22. 8*s*. 10*d*. from the tallage for the king's ransom; £21. 7*s*. from the tallage of of 5,000 marks; and £7 15*s*. 7*d*. from the tallage of 2,000 marks. His total indebtedness was therefore a little less than £1,652, towards which he was able to make a trifling payment, leaving him still £1,620 odd in debt.[1] While he was engaged on the one hand in satisfying the exchequer or at least keeping it at bay, Le Brun had of necessity to maintain a large capital earning the money necessary for the purpose. Le Brun's position was, broadly, that of every wealthy Jew. The situation was, of course, perfectly well known at the exchequer, where the best advice was available from the Jewish side, and in the twelfth century debtors seem never to have been unduly pressed to realize their assets.

It has already been said that, whenever Jews were taxed, pressure was applied to borrowers to force them to pay off their debts.[2] A good instance is afforded by some particulars that have survived regarding the Guildford tallage of 1186. Benedict of Chichester was assessed at 200 marks; but it is noted that he ought to be credited with 50 marks which had been paid to the justiciar, William Longchamp, by Peter le Blund to redeem the mortgage he had effected with Benedict on his lands at Paddington and Abinger.[3] Doubtless there were earlier instances of the same kind which the records do not reveal; and, quite obviously, should large sums be demanded, as in 1210, no more than a small part could be paid immediately from the cash or valuables in the hands of the wealthier members of the community, who bore the greater part of the burden. Their principal assets were their outstanding loans, which therefore had to be realized, mainly, it is to be presumed, by calling in those that had been left standing after the date of repayment provided in the bond had expired.[4] We are afforded

[1] *Memoranda Roll 1 John*, p. 69.    [2] Above, pp. 93–4.
[3] *Pipe Roll 3 Richard I*, p. 60. The entry has been paraphrased freely.
[4] For examples see below, pp. 247–69.

a glimpse of the procedure in 1210, when a Jew named Ursel (who seems otherwise to be unknown) travelled about Hampshire under instructions to distrain debtors (a term that included sureties as well as principals) to pay the collector of the tallage.[1] As the chronicler of Meaux Abbey puts it, 'all those who were bound to the Jews for any debt were compelled to satisfy the king in regard to that debt'.[2] In the absence of most of the memoranda and receipt rolls of this period, we cannot recover the details. Most of the borrowers would themselves have lacked ready money and they could not, for the time being, have looked to Jewish moneylenders for assistance. Consequently, in the best of circumstances, they might either have been compelled to raise money by the sale or lease of their land to some religious house or well-to-do Christian layman and so put the Jewish moneylender in funds or, alternatively, they might have made a composition, a 'fine', with the Crown (through the Justices of the Jews) which would be credited to the Jewish lender. If a borrower made default there was a third alternative: the sureties would become liable to the moneylender, though it was not every bond that provided for this form of security.[3] It was, of course, a matter of indifference to the Crown whether payment was made, directly, by the Jew who was assessed or, indirectly, by those who had borrowed money or by those who had guaranteed the loan. The result was the apparent anomaly that Christians figure prominently as contributors in the rolls recording receipts from tallages imposed upon the Jews.[4]

[1] Cole, *Documents*, pp. 287–8.  [2] *Chronica de Melsa*, i. 375.
[3] See above, pp. 43, 69–70.
[4] See the list of rolls in Jewish Hist. Soc., *Transactions*, vol. xviii. 291–3, where, however, payments by Christians are only occasionally noted. Apart from payments specifically in respect of tallage, it seems likely that many of the 'fines' paid by Christians arose through the calling-in of loans necessitated by taxation. For the procedure by which this was arranged see Rigg, *Select Pleas*, p. 28.

# IX

# THE ASSIZE OF THE JEWRY

To CONCLUDE, AN ELUCIDATION of the law under which the Jews lived may not be out of place, for on this matter there has been not a little misunderstanding. Their relations to the king were governed by custom. When Henry II granted his charter to the Jews of England and Normandy, it was assumed that the customs and privileges they had enjoyed under Henry I were known and were susceptible of proof, but they were not codified or formally reduced to writing. They might be modified or extended or elaborated, and Henry II's charter may have done all these three things. He certainly did not regard the customary law as immutable. It was during his reign that the office of arch-priest of the Jews was instituted and that the conduct of Jewish business in the exchequer was regulated; but our knowledge is derived from incidental references and no formal enactments, if any existed, have come down to us. The first formal enactment we know is the series of articles of 1194 preserved by Roger of Howden. Thereafter there is a wide gap of nearly forty years before the next surviving piece of legislation, that of April 1233. In the interval the chancery rolls include a number of important administrative acts, but nothing that we can call legislation. Though reference is sometimes made to an assize granted to the Jews,[1] it does not necessarily follow that there was any written

---

[1] Cf. *Liber de Antiquis Legibus*, p. 237: 'per assisam communiter Iudeis a nobis et antecessoribus nostris concessam'. Here all that is at issue is the lawful rate of interest (2*d.* in the £ a week) which had been fixed in 1233. For other references to an assize see Cole, *Documents*, pp. 301, 323; *Close Rolls, 1251–1253*, p. 319; *1264–1268*, pp. 404–5. Compare the parallel phrases: *consuetudo Iudeorum* (Cole, *Documents*, p. 301) or 'the custom of the Jewry' (*Cal. Patent Rolls, 1266–1272*,

document with this title, like the Assize of Clarendon and the Assize of Northampton or the other assizes of Henry II's reign, which have not come down to us, that regulated the principal forms of action at common law. Rather must we think of the Assize of the Jewry as that body of rules which, whether customary or prescribed on some occasion by authority, are to be deduced from the rolls of the central courts. Formal legislation, when it comes, is directed towards specific problems. That of 1233 is concerned with the registration of loans and limiting the rate of interest, with the expulsion of Jews who are not serviceable and loyal to the king and, finally, with prescribing those articles that might not be received in pawn, an elaboration of a long-established rule.[1] The legislation of 1239 does not refer to that of six years previously, but deals afresh with loans and interest, forbids the taking of interest for six months and orders all Jews to remain for a year in their existing place of residence, from which they were not to remove without the king's licence.[2] Later legislation deals more elaborately with the conduct expected of the Jews. That of 1253 enforces a good deal of ecclesiastical doctrine[3]—we can hardly call it ecclesiastical law—which, as we shall see, the Crown had hitherto refused to countenance. Otherwise legislation rarely makes any new departure from what had, in principle, been the rule, though it tends to impose greater and greater restrictions upon Jewish activities. Repetitive legislation, which seems to have been speedily lost to memory, except in so far as it was embodied in practice, was not confined to Jewish affairs. It is characteristic of the period before the conception of a statute-book had become established and given shape, and when enactments were translated into new forms of writ or rules of court or administrative acts and were not regarded as an abiding source of law to be preserved

p. 154; *Cal. Close Rolls, 1272–1279*, pp. 50, 261, 298, 371) or 'law and custom' (*ibid.*, pp. 386, 389, 547). See also the references to 'assize', 'statutes' and 'law and custom' collected in *Cal. Plea Rolls*, i. 339. The 'Assize of Jewry' in Jacobs, *Jews of Angevin England*, pp. 329–37, is explicitly a compilation from ecclesiastical and secular, including Jewish, sources: it is suggestive but must be used with caution.

[1] Below, pp. 293–4.     [2] *Liber de Antiquis Legibus*, p. 237.
[3] *Close Rolls, 1251–1253*, pp. 312–13; *Foedera*, I. i. 293 (without date).

for continual reference in the changing circumstances of everyday life. To *Glanville* and to Bracton, even to the author of *Fleta*, who completed his work after the Expulsion in full recognition of the importance of Edwardian legislation, the law of England is still 'unwritten', that is, there is no authoritative *corpus* of law such as Justinian and Gregory IX provided. Nor does any legal writer conceive it as within his province to summarize or expound the law relating to the Jews. Even Bracton gives them no more than a fleeting glance. In truth, written law would have afforded scant protection to a defenceless minority, for in the circumstances of the thirteenth century *quod principi placuit legis habet vigorem*. The prince could not change the law to the disadvantage of his Christian subjects, for the magnates were there to bridle him. There was no bridle, save his interest or his conscience, in the prince's dealings with the Jews.

Yet if the prince was capricious, his favour could, at times, be easily bought. If we were to take at its face value the order given on 30 March 1218 requiring English Jews to wear the *tabula*,[1] we might suppose that this 'badge of shame', as it has been called, henceforth distinguished them from Christians. But it was not a happily chosen moment for discriminatory legislation. As soon as settled conditions were restored after King John's death and the departure of Louis of France, the magnates who took over the government and acted in the boy king's name were anxious to protect the Jews[2] and indeed to placate them and to encourage those who had fled to return to England. Provided these returning Jews, and any others who desired to dwell in the kingdom, were prepared to register with the Justices of the Jews, they were free to come with their belongings. On the other hand, Jews resident in England were not allowed to go overseas without special licence.[3] This decision, taken in November 1218, was hardly consistent

[1] *Foedera*, I. i. 151; *Rot. Litt. Claus.*, i. 378*b*. Here the reference is to 'duas tabulas albas', but elsewhere *tabula* is usually in the singular.

[2] Below, p. 182.

[3] *Foedera*, I. i. 152; *Patent Rolls, 1216–1225*, pp. 180–1. It is to be assumed that Jews who had fled were chiefly envisaged (cf. *Rot. Litt. Claus.*, i. 186*b*), but the instructions issued to the keepers of the seaports were of general application.

with the order of March; but the obligations of Christian piety and common sense could be reconciled, and ways could be found to circumvent the order. Leave to dispense with the badge was freely given at a price related to the wealth of the applicant. This solution must have been devised by 1221 and probably well before, and there can have been few Jews who did not avail themselves of the opportunity to avoid the humiliation decreed by the Lateran Council.[1] The highest payment recorded is that by Moses, the son of Abraham (apparently of Norwich), who had to find £4; but many individual Jews and Jewesses[2] were charged no more than pence. For some reason many of those who were dispensed wished to have their licence in duplicate and for this they had to make an additional payment. The poorer members of the urban communities were covered by a general licence. Thus, the *commune* of Canterbury paid 8s. 4d. for a licence in duplicate, the *commune* of Hereford 12s. 5d., the *commune* of Stamford 18s. 10d. The *commune* of Oxford paid 5s. 6d. and 'the Jews of London' 13s.; but in neither case does the licence seem to have been duplicated. While some of the payments recorded may have been instalments of larger sums, the figures quoted will give a fair idea of the scale of charges and the manner in which it was graduated. The dispensations granted by 1221 had been so numerous and general that very few seem to have been required thereafter. Two payments for licences are recorded in 1225[3] and two in 1226,[4] one of the latter being apparently in respect of a communal licence for the Jews of Winchester.[5] Some Jews seem to have risked dispensing with the badge without troubling to obtain a licence and to

[1] P.R.O., Receipt Roll 5 Henry III (E. 401/4), m. 5.

[2] It has been inferred that the order of 1218 did not apply to women (Roth, *History of the Jews in England*, p. 71 n.). This cannot be the case, though the women who paid for a dispensation appear to have been heads of households. There is no indication in the receipt roll that the order applied to children.

[3] Receipt Roll 9 Henry III (E. 401/7), mm. 1, 12.

[4] Receipt Roll 10 Henry III (E. 401/8), *rotulus Iudeorum* (unnumbered), under Essex and Herts and Hampshire (see following note). This membrane is mutilated and many entries cannot be recovered in full.

[5] The Jews of Winchester make one payment for Moses, son of Le Brun (see below, p. 287) and 'pro tabula non portanda'.

have paid for their temerity; for in 1226 there are payments 'pro tabulis non portatis'[1] as well as 'pro tabula non portanda'. A gap in our sources of information[2] prevents us from continuing the story in detail; but it is safe to conclude that for a good many years, probably until 1253, no Jew, rich or poor, need unwillingly wear the badge. In 1253, as we shall see, there was a marked change in the attitude of the king towards the Jews, though it is by no means certain that, even thereafter, the badge was universally worn.

The order of 1218 was unquestionably an outcome of the discriminatory decrees against the Jews promulgated in the Lateran Council of 1215, one of which provided that in all Christian lands Jews (and Saracens) should wear a distinctive dress.[3] This order was, so far as is known, for many years the sole practical outcome of those decrees in England, and this order, it would appear beyond dispute, was effective only in bringing a little additional revenue into the exchequer. Conciliar decrees against the Jews were, in fact, not enforced because they were unenforceable. This is not the view which is commonly held.[4] It has been assumed that the pronouncement of popes and bishops, and notably the canons of the council of Oxford of 1222, which purported to give effect to what had been decreed against the Jews in the general council, had a force and validity which, in fact, they entirely lacked. If, indeed, we were to assume that Jewish affairs could be regulated by ecclesiastical authority, however exalted, we should grievously distort the picture we ought to draw of the conditions in which Jews lived in medieval English society, and we should misrepresent the nature of the authority that governed their conduct and of the law under which they fell. It will be well, therefore, to examine the facts and documents with some particularity.

The Fourth Lateran Council opened on 11 November 1215, and

---

[1] Receipt Roll 10 Henry III (E. 401/8), under Gloucester.

[2] No Jewish receipt roll is extant between 10 Henry III and 17 Henry III: the latter (E. 401/1565) has no references to the *tabula*: but it contains very few entries and appears to be incomplete.

[3] Canon 68 (69): statuimus ut tales utriusque sexus . . . qualitate habitus publice ab aliis populis distinguantur . . .          [4] Cf. Roth, *op. cit.*, p. 95.

was brought to a conclusion on the thirtieth. The principal outcome—apart from a decree for a new crusade, which does not
immediately concern us—was a body of seventy canons, which
must have been already prepared and which, with few exceptions,
passed, as pronouncements of Innocent III, into the body of canon
law, first into the *Compilatio Quarta* (1217)[1] and thence into the
Gregorian Decretals (1234). The last four of the seventy decrees
concern the Jews. The seventieth deals with converted Jews and is
intended to secure that they shall break entirely with the faith of
their fathers: this, of course, was a matter within the competence
of diocesan bishops. The efficacy of the sixty-seventh, sixty-eighth
and sixty-ninth depended, however, upon the lay power. Briefly,
these canons sought to restrict Jewish moneylending, to compel
Jews to pay tithes and ecclesiastical dues, to prevent miscegenation
between Jews (or Saracens) and Christians, to confine Jews to their
houses during Passion Sunday and Holy Week and, elaborating a
canon of the council of Toledo (589), to debar them from public
offices.[2] The papacy had never hitherto assumed direct jurisdiction in Jewish affairs, and had attempted, though with discretion,
to persuade secular rulers to act as the Church decreed.[3] Innocent III
adopted no new attitude: he 'enjoins' and 'orders' princes to
enforce the canons, but he acknowledges the limitations of
ecclesiastical authority.[4]

The text of the decrees must soon have reached England,
as it did all Western Europe, but it could not have arrived at a

[1] See the table in E. Friedberg, *Quinque Compilationes Antiquae*, p. xxxiii: here
the canons are divided into 71 and those affecting Jews are numbered 68–71. For
the date of the *Compilatio Quarta* see S. Kuttner, *Repertorium der Kanonistik*,
pp. 372–3.

[2] Hefele, *Histoire des Conciles*, v. 1385–8. It should be recalled that Sicily, with
its large 'Saracen' population, was much in Innocent's mind and that canon 68 is
most likely aimed at that target. For the canon of the Council of Toledo see
Hefele, *op. cit.*, iii. 227.          [3] Above, pp. 140–1.

[4] Principibus autem iniungimus (can. 67); precipimus . . . per principes secu-
lares (can. 68). No such words are inserted in canon 69, which was eminently a
matter for the lay power. A text in the Gregorian Decretals (X. 5.6.18), being a
letter of Gregory IX to the bishops of Astorga and Luga, shows, however, that
the Curia recognized this: the bishops were to prevail upon the king of Portugal
not to appoint Jews to public offices with authority over Christians.

more unpropitious time. The country was torn by civil war, which continued until the departure of Louis of France on 28 September 1217.[1] The *tempus guerrae*, during which ordered government was impossible, was reckoned officially to have lasted for two-and-a-half years, from Easter 1215 to Michaelmas 1217. Thereafter the threads of administration were taken up again: the exchequer re-opened in October and gradually the rhythm of government was restored.[2] It could not have been until late in 1217, if so soon, that the decrees of the Lateran Council were seriously considered. Then the king's council decided that the position of the Jews should remain undisturbed as it had stood under King John and that they should live as they had done hitherto in a community among the Christians. They were to be safeguarded by the local authorities, who were not to permit them to suffer harm or interference.[3] Further, on the personal initiative of William Marshal, the *rector regni*, a select body of twenty-four burgesses was set up in certain towns, charged with the duty of safeguarding the Jews, especially from the attacks of crusaders.[4] The sole concession in the way of complying with the decrees of the Lateran Council was the (evidently half-hearted) order issued on 30 March 1218.

It has to be remembered that, at the time, the archbishop of Canterbury, Stephen Langton, was still in exile and that the papal legate, Guala, was the effective ruler of the church in England and was all-powerful in the king's council. Langton returned to England

[1] For this date see Ramsay, *Dawn of the Constitution*, p. 14, and references cited.

[2] For the re-opening of the exchequer see the references in *Transactions R. Hist. Soc.*, 4th Ser., xv. 56, 58, and notes.

[3] It is specifically stated in the order of 19 June 1218, cited below, that the decision regarding the Jews had been taken 'de communi consilio nostro'.

[4] See the instructions of 10 and 30 March and 27 April 1218, to Gloucester, Lincoln, Bristol and Oxford: in the case of Gloucester and Oxford the instructions were given on the spot during a visit by the Marshal (*Rot. Litt. Claus.*, i. 354*b*, 357, 359*b*). The system of placing responsibility upon selected burgesses was extended to other towns: Norwich, where there were twenty-six, presents an instructive example (Richardson and Sayles, *Select Cases of Procedure without Writ*, p. 23). The reference to crusaders was doubtless inspired by the article in the decree for a new crusade, approved in the Lateran Council, which sought to protect those taking part from demands by Jewish moneylenders (Hefele, *op. cit.*, v. 1393).

from exile early in May 1218,[1] and shortly thereafter the English bishops, or many of them, not content with the action the king's council had taken, sought, of their own authority, to enforce the decrees against the Jews. Precise details of the bishops' action have not come down to us, but they had evidently issued some kind of 'prohibition' against the Jews and had endeavoured to draw actions arising out of debts owing to Jews into ecclesiastical courts where, of course, the issue of usury would be raised.[2] The council replied with an order of 19 June instructing the appropriate local authorities to proclaim throughout their bailiwicks that the Jews had been given the king's assured peace, notwithstanding any prohibition the bishop might have issued, 'because he has no business to meddle with our Jews'. Their relations with Christians were to remain unchanged and they were not to be impleaded in ecclesiastical courts in actions of debt.[3] There is no direct evidence to connect Langton with this concerted attempt to enforce the decrees of the Lateran Council, but since it cannot have originated with Guala, there is no other who can be suspected; and the suspicion becomes virtual certainty in view of the sequel.

Guala left England towards the end of November, 1218, and was succeeded by Pandulf, whose legation began formally on 3 December.[4] Very soon afterwards he must have raised with the justiciar, Hubert de Burgh, the question of enforcing the decrees in England;[5] but if he had expected any change in the attitude of the king's council, he was disappointed. However, an appeal to him in 1219 by the abbot of Westminster, who was being sued

[1] His presence in England is indicated by the series of instructions to sheriffs and others in his favour on 13 May (*Rot. Litt. Claus.*, i. 361*b*).

[2] These are the matters specifically mentioned in the order of 19 June, cited in the following note.

[3] *Patent Rolls, 1216–1225*, p. 157; *Foedera*, i. 151. As enrolled, the king's letter would appear to be limited to nine counties, presumably in those dioceses where the bishops had taken action. Similar instructions were given to the authorities at Exeter (Cole, *Documents*, p. 301), but there is no reference to action by the bishop.

[4] R. de Coggeshale, *Chronicon Anglicanum*, p. 186.

[5] So, on 7 July 1219, he writes to the justiciar, Hubert de Burgh, of Jewish extortions 'contra statuta Lateranensis concilii . . . super quo vobiscum meminimus nos habuisse tractatum' (*Royal Letters, Henry III*, i. 35, no. 28).

before the Justices of the Jews by Isaac of Norwich, moved him to action. He was too astute to threaten Isaac with harmless ecclesiastical censures. Instead, he endeavoured to enlist the support of the justiciar in interfering with the course of justice,[1] with what result is unknown. For more than two years and a half Pandulf was as influential in the king's council as he was in the English church, and the archbishop of Canterbury played a very subordinate part.[2] It was during the last year or so of Pandulf's legation that the decision was taken to dispense with the wearing of the *tabula*, and it is hard to suppose that the legate was not a party to the decision, presumably in Langton's absence. The archbishop had departed for Rome in the autumn of 1220 and did not return until August 1221. By then, however, the anomalous position he had hitherto occupied was righted, for Pandulf had resigned his legation in the previous month. Freed from restraint, Langton in the following year summoned a provincial council at Oxford at which there was promulgated, among much else that was strictly within the province of the Church, a series of canons directed against the Jews. These were plainly based upon the decrees of the Lateran Council, but in some respects drew upon earlier sources of canon law, notably in prohibiting the erection of new synagogues. The canon that affected to prescribe the form of *tabulae* to be borne by Jews of both sexes is of particular interest, because it appears to be a riposte to the dispensation recently granted by the civil authority.[3]

[1] *Loc. cit.*

[2] For Langton's position at this period see F. M. Powicke, *Stephen Langton*, pp. 143–8.

[3] The immediate source of canons 39 and 40 of the Oxford council must, however, be a collection of *Compilationes Antiquae*. Thus canon 39 opens with the words 'Quoniam absurdum est quod filii liberae ancillae filiis famulentur . . .', borrowed from Comp. IV, 'Quum sit nimis absurdum . . .', and Comp. III, 'ne filii liberae filiis famulentur ancillae . . .' The article against the construction of new synagogues is derived from Comp. I and II. The texts can be conveniently consulted in the Gregorian Decretals (X.5.6.3, 7, 13). It is to be noted that the form of *tabulae* prescribed differs from that in the order of 1218. Throughout there is no suggestion that the authority of the Church is to be used in aid of the civil power.

Fortified by the decisions of his provincial council and abetted by Hugh of Wells, the bishop of Lincoln, Langton now attempted —it would seem for the second time—to enforce the decrees of the Lateran Council against the Jews. Nothing, however, appears to have been effected except in the dioceses of Lincoln and, oddly enough, of Norwich.[1] Oddly enough, because the bishop, recently consecrated by the pope himself, was the former legate Pandulf. He was an absentee, continuously resident abroad, at Rome or in the king's service in France. He had not, of course, attended the Oxford council; he was at enmity with Langton; and he was not in the least likely to approve of action at variance with the policy of the government of which he had so lately been a prominent member. The absence of trouble in other dioceses is significant when we remember the clear warning given not long before to English bishops and the English people that the Crown did not lightly brook the interference of ecclesiastical authorities in Jewish affairs. Langton was not of the stuff to be moved by such a consideration; but most of the English bishops were prudent men and we can explain the exceptional conduct of Hugh of Wells by recalling the close ties that bound him to Langton, who had consecrated him and whose exile he had shared. In any case, the bishops could not act alone: if any action they took was to be effective, they must rely upon the co-operation of the authorities of the towns in which the Jews lived.

It should perhaps be explained that, while the canons might be enforced by the bishops so far as they involved the conduct of Christians in relation to Jews, they could take no direct action against the Jews themselves, who, unless constrained by the secular power, would not admit the authority of ecclesiastical tribunals. It was all very well to threaten Christian servants in Jewish households with ecclesiastical censures or to leave it to bishops to ensure that Jews did not enter churches or deposit their valuables there, but it was absurd to threaten Jewish householders with ecclesiastical censures or canonical penalties or, in the alter-

---

[1] Our sole source of information is the writ to the authorities of the three towns cited below.

185

native, extraordinary penalties to be devised by the diocesan.[1] Yet the Jews, might, it was thought, be coerced, if they were shut off from all communication with the Christians among whom they lived. The boycott, as we should call it, was a weapon repeatedly flourished. Though there is no reference to it in the canons of the Oxford council, its use is twice prescribed in the canons of the Lateran Council.[2] But any resort to the boycott by townsmen inevitably involved the urban authorities, who were responsible to the king for the welfare of the Jews and who were more likely to be in fear of the government than of ecclesiastical censures. And so, though Langton and Hugh of Wells gave orders that no one should sell food to the Jews or have any commerce with them, at only three centres does there seem to have been any real possibility that the necessaries of life would be denied them—Lincoln, Norwich and Oxford. Norwich had a long anti-Semitic tradition, and there was much feeling against the Jews in Lincoln, while Oxford, with its largely clerical population, dependent upon the bishop of Lincoln, was peculiarly susceptible to ecclesiastical pressure. The movement against the Jews does not seem to have extended any farther. As soon as the prospective victims notified the government of their fears, the urban authorities in the three towns were required to ensure that normal relations were resumed between the townsmen and the Jews and to take into custody anyone who refused to sell food and other necessaries to them.[3] And that, for all practical purposes, was the ignominious end of the attempt to enforce the decrees of the Lateran Council. The conflict, if it deserves so serious a name, was not of such importance as to cause a breach between the bishops and the king's council.

[1] Wilkins, *Concilia*, i. 591–2, canons 39 and 40. The prohibition of new synagogues and the injunction to pay tithes and parochial dues carried no specific sanction.

[2] Canons 67 and 69. The legate Robert de Courçon had, with papal authority, prescribed the same sanction in France (*Rot. Litt. Pat.*, p. 139*b*). Archbishop Boniface, in successive provincial councils, enacted that if a Jew did not recognize the authority of an ecclesiastical court, he was to be boycotted (Wilkins, *Concilia*, i. 736 n., 739, 751).

[3] *Rot. Litt. Claus.*, i. 567. The entry on the roll is blundered. It is possible that writs were sent to the sheriffs also.

Langton had made his protest in his characteristic manner and there the matter ended. It is hardly necessary to add that the Jews continued to be dispensed from any obligation to wear the badge imposed by the order of 1218.[1]

What has been already said will have made plain the impotence of ecclesiastical authorities to legislate for the Jewry in defiance of the civil power, and it is unnecessary to examine in any great detail the considerable body of subordinate legislation which affected to treat of Jewish affairs and regulate the conduct of English Jews. Some notice should, however, be taken of it, if only by way of illustrating the attitude of the Church. In the first place, though it means some retracing of our steps, mention should perhaps be made of the synodal statutes issued by the bishop of Worcester in 1219. At the time of the king's council's action against the bishops on 19 June 1218, William of Blois had been archdeacon of Buckingham: he had not been consecrated to the see of Worcester until 28 October following.[2] He held a diocesan synod within a year[3] and, while most of his statutes dealt, as was proper, with liturgical and administrative matters, a section dealing with the relations between Christians and Jews was interjected. The pawning of ecclesiastical books, vestments and ornaments with Jews is prohibited; Christians are forbidden to serve Jews as nurses or servants or to sleep in their houses; Christians are not to receive Jewish money for safe-deposit in churches nor are they to place money with Jews to be lent at usury.[4] The content of these anti-Jewish statutes is not drawn from the canons of the Lateran Council, and we should not know that the bishop had that council in mind but for a direct reference to the canon which excluded recalcitrant Jews from intercourse with Christians;[5] but whereas that canon was concerned with the restitution of immoderate usury, the statute is concerned with the restitution of

---

[1] Above, pp. 178–80.   [2] *Annales Monastici*, iv. 410.
[3] *Ibid.*, p. 411.
[4] Wilkins, *Concilia*, i. 571. The connexion between the statutes and the synod would seem obvious: cf. C. R. Cheney, *English Synodalia*, p. 91.
[5] The wording of the statute runs: subtrahatur eis participium Christianorum secundum tenorem concilii. This merely rearranges the words of canon 67.

pawned ecclesiastical property. The statute against the employment of Christian servants appears to be based upon a decretal in the *Compilatio Tertia*,[1] while that against the pawning of ecclesiastical property is, in substance, a repetition of a rule already laid down in the royal charters granted to the Jews and enforced in the king's courts.[2] The remaining statutes are of uncertain origin and in any case are hardly more than particular applications of the canon law against usury. There was nothing in these statutes to cause alarm to any secular authority, not even the threat to exclude recalcitrant Jews from intercourse with Christians, for the offence against which it was aimed was prohibited by the law of the land. If the statutes were ever remarked outside the diocese, they could well be regarded as domestic legislation affecting only the bishop's flock. One may conjecture that the good bishop, so lately promoted, was anxious to show himself no laggard in his zeal for the Church, while no less anxious to avoid embroiling himself with the lay power.

The synodal statutes of 1219 were embodied, with some changes of wording, in a more comprehensive series promulgated by the same bishop ten years later,[3] and again by his successor, who added that, in other matters, the statutes of the councils (of the Lateran and of Oxford) should be strictly observed.[4] Echoes of the Oxford canons are to be found in other diocesan statutes. Sometimes, as in the later Worcester statutes, there is little more than a general reference to the canons of the Lateran and Oxford councils.[5] One set of statutes, however, spoke of Jews who confessed to, or were convicted of, illicit intercourse with Christians, as though their appearance before ecclesiastical courts could be enforced; and, following canon 69 of the Lateran Council,

[1] Text in X. 5.6.11. Similar decretals are to be found in Comp. I and Comp. II: see X. 5.6.5, 8.

[2] Above, pp. 109, 113.

[3] Wilkins, *op. cit.*, i. 626.

[4] *Ibid.*, pp. 675–6: 1240 or later (cf. Cheney, *op. cit.*, pp. 90–6).

[5] Wilkins, *op .cit.*, i. 693: for the Chichester diocese, 1244–1253 (cf. Cheney, *op. cit.*, pp. 84–9). The specific references to new synagogues, the *tabulae* and miscegenation are drawn from the canons of 1222.

threatened them with exclusion from the society of Christians unless they made amends. The same statutes ordered that what had been prescribed at the two councils regarding distinctive dress should be observed.[1] Provisions of this kind cannot be taken seriously: they merely illustrate the truth that much of the content of diocesan statutes was never meant to be more than a pious gesture.

This is not to deny that endeavours may have been made to cite Jews before ecclesiastical courts. Indeed, a case is known where a Christian woman, having failed in an attempt to implead a Jewess on a charge of blasphemy before justices appointed to enquire into coin-clipping, thereupon impleaded her in the court of the archdeacon of Nottingham. The Jewess sought the protection of the Crown on the ground that proceedings in an ecclesiastical court were contrary to the law and custom of the Jewry, though she offered to stand her trial in the King's Bench or before the Justices of the Jews or any other justice the king might appoint. Her contention was upheld and the justice who had previously dismissed the charge (doubtless on the ground that he had no authority to deal with the matter) was appointed to conduct the trial.[2] The result is not known, but the Jewess seems to have been confident of acquittal. This is, however, an entirely exceptional case, and it is not to be supposed that Jews were frequently impleaded in courts christian or that, if perchance this might occasionally happen, they did not know how to discomfort their adversaries

---

[1] Wilkins, *op. cit.*, i. 719: Salisbury diocese, a composite collection, perhaps 1257–1262 (cf. Cheney, *op. cit.*, pp. 35, 49). The words of the statute 'omnis christiana communio . . . denegetur' are an unmistakable echo of 'christianorum communio in commerciis et aliis denegetur' of canon 69: the subject matter is quite different. The reference to Jewish midwives shows that the compiler had gone also to the Gregorian Decretals (X. 5.6.8) or to the source, the *Compilatio Secunda*.

[2] *Cal. Patent Rolls, 1272–1281*, p. 287. It is to be assumed that, in naming the justice appointed on 13 December 1276 to enquire into coin-clipping at Nottingham 'Henry' de Tybetot, a mistake has been made in his christian name (*ibid.*, p. 236). It is quite clear from the entry on p. 287 that it was Robert de Tybetot who had heard and dismissed the charge in the first instance. Robert was much employed upon judicial work, but 'Henry' is otherwise unknown.

and, if necessary, force them, as in this instance, to proceed, at their peril, before a secular tribunal. The same principle is illustrated by another case where, in highly unusual circumstances, a Jew had actually been sentenced by an ecclesiastical tribunal. The story is this—and it is well to remember that it is *ex parte*. A ribald Jew had assumed the habit of a Franciscan friar and, as such, had preached a sermon in which he had spoken contemptuously of the Christian faith and his pretended Order. Not without reason he had been brought before Archbishop Kilwardby who had sentenced him to public penance. At what stage the culprit disclosed that he was a Jew is not clear, but certainly before the sentence could be enforced. He claimed the protection of the sheriff, who first lodged him in Northampton castle and then released him on mainprise to stand his trial before the Justices of the Jews. Since no-one appeared against him, the Justices, in turn, released him on mainprise, but enquired of the sheriff what was alleged against him. The sheriff replied, giving an account of the proceedings in the ecclesiastical court and adding that he would not allow the sentence of that court to be carried out without a special order from the king. In the meantime the archbishop seems to have written to the king, on whose instructions a writ was issued commanding the sheriff to compel the Jew to undergo his penance. It is immaterial that, in the meantime, both the culprit and his mainpernors had departed out of the sheriff's jurisdiction and could not, therefore, be apprehended.[1] The point to emphasize is that, without a direct order from the king, the sheriff would not enforce the sentence of an ecclesiastical court, which, in any case, had no physical powers of compulsion. If the culprit had been a Christian, his contumacy would have been followed by excommunication and, in the last resort, by a writ *de excommunicato capiendo* addressed to the sheriff, who would have lodged him in gaol until he had reconciled himself to the Church. This pro-

[1] *Cal. Plea Rolls*, iii. 311–12. The record is long and confused and appears in parts to be self-contradictory. The nature of the penance is not material; but it may be added that the sentence was that the culprit should go naked through five towns (all, of course, with Jewries) carrying in his hands the entrails of a calf and with the carcase round his neck.

cedure was not applicable to a Jew, even to one who had masqueraded as a Christian.

The situation was very different when the king legislated, for he had the means of enforcement, and in January 1253 Henry III issued a series of statutes based largely upon ecclesiastical canons.[1] Of the twelve articles, six covered the same ground as the canons of the council of Oxford: these dealt with the construction of new synagogues, the payment of parochial dues, the employment of Jewish nurses and other Jewish servants by Christians, miscegenation, the *tabula* and the frequentation of churches. The draftsman may have consulted the Gregorian Decretals as well as the canons of the council of Oxford:[2] the brevity of the articles obscures their affiliations in canon law, for they are hardly more than notes for the guidance of the Justices of the Jews, who would presumably know where fuller texts were to be found. The all-important provision was the direction to the Justices to require the articles to be observed by the Jews under the threat of forfeiture. At long last the prince had taken the action that Innocent III had required of him in the Lateran Council. It is very doubtful whether the government of Henry III had previously done anything of the kind after issuing the dispensable order of 1218 prescribing the the wearing of the *tabula*. Though it may not be conclusive proof —since we cannot be sure that every piece of legislation has survived—it remains a fact that the earlier legislation of 1233 and 1239 is not at all on the lines of the canons.[3]

If we could treat diocesan statutes as evidence, we should be justified in construing them as an admission that the canons of the Lateran and Oxford councils had not hitherto been effectively applied: but there is good reason to doubt whether diocesan

[1] *Close Rolls, 1250–1253*, pp. 312–13.

[2] The latter is the more obvious source, though the wording of the statutes is carefully chosen to avoid the repetition of the same phraseology. The *tabula* was not prescribed in the canons of the Lateran Council and no particular form is laid down in 1253, neither that of the order of 1218 nor that of 1222: all that is prescribed is that the *tabula* must be *manifesta*.

[3] Above, p. 177. The statutes of 1253 do, in some measure, reflect earlier legislation, notably in regard to residence. Residence in England depends upon a Jew's usefulness to the king; residence locally is restricted by licence.

statutes reflected, in any way, local conditions or the special circumstances of the times, so imitative and perfunctory are they in
general. Doubtless these statutes served to keep the canons in
mind, but this was not inadequately done by the Gregorian
Decretals, which were in every canonist's hand. We must remember both diocesan statutes and decretals if we seek to recapture
the political climate of the time, to realize the implacable hostility
of the Church towards the Jews; but we must remember also
how ineffective it was without the active co-operation of the
State, a co-operation seemingly denied until 1253. In truth, as long
experience had shown, the Church was powerless to take direct
action against Jews. Its influence was exerted more subtly, by
appealing to the conscience of the king and his advisers or, with
questionable morality, by stirring up trouble. It is significant that
one of the enquiries which archdeacons were required to make in
the Lincoln diocese was whether any Jews were dwelling elsewhere than they were accustomed to dwell,[1] and this although no
Jew could dwell outside one of the recognized communities without royal licence.[2] If churchmen were denied authority over Jews,
they could still harass them. And although much that was said and
done by ecclesiastical authorities must have seemed at the time
merely vexatious, we should not underrate the influence of the
Church or, rather, the influence of ecclesiastics with pronounced
views. It can be seen, as the century progressed, in the growing
restrictions imposed by the Crown upon Jewish activities.

The immediate point to be made, however, is that, so far as the
evidence goes, it does not suggest that English Jews were required
to wear the *tabula* before 1253. Nor should we conclude, without
investigation, that the new order, when it came, was universally
effective or that dispensations could not, as before, be purchased
at a price.[3] Repetition is, in fact, a fair indication that the order of

---

[1] Wilkins, *Concilia*, i. 628, no. 42.          [2] Above, p. 20.

[3] It does not seem to have been difficult for Jews in France at the end of the
thirteenth century to obtain dispensation from wearing the *rota*; see the precedents
relating to the Jews in a formulary of the early fourteenth century in *Notices et
Extraits des Manuscrits*, xxxiv. 17–18. See also Ulysse Robert, *Les signes d'infamie
au moyen âge* (1891), pp. 35–8, 56–7.

1253 proved, like its predecessor of 1218, to be ineffective, at least in large measure.[1] And if the order of 1218, which had ecclesiastical as well as secular authority behind it, could be so easily waived, we must expect the same laxity in the enforcement of other orders. Apparently in 1220, or a little earlier, the Jews had been forbidden to secure loans by means of tallies (instead of written bonds). In this case dispensations appear to have been accorded to urban communities as a whole. The communities of Exeter, Hereford and Northampton each paid 20 shillings *pro licencia mutuandi per talliam*,[2] and there is no reason to suppose that other communities did not purchase licences on similar terms. Individual moneylenders do not appear to have obtained a dispensation; but there would seem to be no reason why they should, since a general direction addressed to the chirographers of the *archa* in any of the recognized communities would mean that loans secured by tallies would be registered by them without difficulty. The removal of the restriction presumably continued until it was ordered to be reimposed, as we know it was, in 1233,[3] although later it seems clearly to have been dropped.[4] The uncertainty surrounding this minor restriction on Jewish transactions is not an isolated example of the law governing the Jewry. It is paralleled by the uncertainty surrounding the restrictions on Jewish pawn-broking, of which something has already been said.[5] We can rarely know—and though Jews at the time had better knowledge than we have, they must often have been uncertain—what was permissible in law and what was permissible in practice.

The lesson is plain. We need to have before us not merely the text of a statute or a mandate, but we need to know how the

[1] For the repeated enactments see Roth, *History of the Jews in England*, pp. 70-1, 78, 95-6. To the references cited add *Foedera*, I. ii. 570, 599.

[2] P.R.O. *Receipt Roll 5 Henry III* (E. 401/4), m. 5.

[3] Below, p. 294.

[4] Otherwise the *archae* would not have contained a substantial proportion of tallies (Stokes, *Studies*, pp. 271-5; Adler, *Jews of Medieval England*, p. 245). Similar evidence is furnished by the list of Jewish debts surrendered to the king in 46 Henry III (P.R.O., E. 101/249/10).

[5] Above, pp. 76-7.

statute was administered, whether the mandate was enforced: for there might be a wide gap between precept and practice. An apt illustration, though a late one, is afforded by the Statute of the Jewry of 1275.[1] One article had required all Jews to reside only in those royal cities and boroughs where there were *archae*,[2] but it is certain that this was far from being strictly observed. The only practical way of enforcing a regulation of the kind was through the agency of the Justices of the Jews, who ought to have had particulars of all Jews resident in England. But in January 1284 these justices were ordered to cause all Jews, dwelling or staying (*habitantes seu morantes*) in cities, boroughs or towns where there was no *archae*, to be removed before the quinzaine of Easter. Now it is clear that the Jews were not at fault and that there was nothing clandestine or blameworthy about their residence elsewhere than in the recognized settlements, because care was to be taken to ensure that, on removal, they suffered no injury in their persons or their belongings. The obvious implication of the language of the order is that the Jews were where they were because they had received permission from the Justices themselves, who were required not to give such permission in future.[3]

It may not be amiss to give yet another late example of the way in which an apparent restriction was administered, for it may serve to correct a serious error. One of the articles of the statute of 1253 had provided that no synagogue should be permitted in any place except where one had existed in the reign of John.[4] This seems evidently to be reflecting the canon of the Oxford council of 1222, which affected to prohibit Jews from building synagogues

[1] *Statutes of the Realm*, i. 221–221a. For the date see Richardson and Sayles, *The Early Statutes*, p. 51, and references cited.

[2] E ke tus les Geus seit menauns en les citez e en les burgs propres le rey ou les huches cirograffes de Geuerie soleint estre.

[3] P.R.O., Close Roll 12 Edward I (C. 54/101), m. 8 *schedule*; *Cal. Close Rolls, 1279–1288*, p. 256. The text reads: Ita quod ipsi Iudei ab eisdem villis modis omnibus amoueantur citra quindenam Pasche proximo futuram, non permittentes ipsos in huiusmodi villis habitare decetero vel morari.

[4] *Close Rolls, 1251–1253*, p. 312: Et quod nulle ŝcole Iudeorum sint in Anglia nisi in locis illis in quibus huiusmodi scole fuerunt tempore domini Iohannis regis patris regis.

in future—*ne de cetero construant synagogas*[1]—but this canon was, in turn, based upon decretals which permitted Jews to retain or replace ancient synagogues, though not to enlarge or improve them or to erect new ones.[2] The Crown took a liberal view of the restriction. When in 1272 the synagogue in Coleman Street was closed by the king's order, on the ground that the Jews disturbed the Friars of the Sack next door (to whom the site of the synagogue was thereupon granted), this was done on the distinct understanding that the congregation should move to a new building in London.[3] It is not clear whether there was any delay in replacing the former synagogue, but, at all events, in 1280 a stone building in Catte (later Cateaton, now Gresham) Street was provided for a synagogue by Aaron, the son of Vives. The deed conveying the building to the community of Jews of London was executed before the mayor and was confirmed, in the first place, by Edmund, the king's brother (to whom Aaron had been granted)[4] and subsequently by the king.[5] Whether the building was in substitution for the synagogue in Coleman Street or one entirely independent, rumours of the construction of a new synagogue came to the ears of the archbishop of Canterbury, John Pecham, in the following year. Thereupon he instructed the bishop of London, Richard Gravesend, to prohibit the erection of the synagogue, enforcing his prohibition by excommunication and interdict.[6] It is hardly necessary to repeat that ecclesiastical censures could touch Christians only and, the synagogue being already built (though the archbishop did not appreciate this), could not prevent its use. A year later another (and most improbable) rumour reached the archbishop, namely that nearly all

[1] Wilkins, *Concilia*, i. 591.

[2] Text in X.5.6.3,7, from Comp. I and II: see above, p. 184, n. 3.

[3] *Close Rolls, 1268–1272*, p. 522. The location is indicated in *Rotuli Parliamentorum*, i. 162, and *Cal. Patent Rolls, 1301–1307*, pp. 316–17.

[4] *Cal. Patent Rolls, 1266–1272*, pp. 471, 515; *1281–1292*, p. 56.

[5] *Cal. Charter Rolls*, ii. 245, 253. The original charter is important because it gives precise measurements of the building. It was 7 ells 6 ins. in breadth and 9½ ells 8 ins. in width. Assuming the ell to have been 45 ins., this would mean a floor area of approximately 27′ × 36′. There was a courtyard of larger dimensions behind.       [6] *Registrum Epistolarum Iohannis Peckham*, i. 213.

the leading Jews of London had their private synagogues, and the bishop was again instructed to make inquiries to the intent that these Jews should be compelled by ecclesiastical censure to destroy their synagogues and content themselves with one synagogue in common. The bishop, prudent man, appears to have temporized and to have sought further instructions. He seems to have expressed some doubt on the archbishop's interpretation of the canons. In reply he was told that, in the archbishop's opinion, if the ancient (private) synagogues were destroyed, a new one might be built in their stead where those concerned might worship in common—'vex the air with their vain ceremonies', in his elegant phrase—unless, indeed, there was already a building sufficient for these profane uses. The bishop was therefore instructed to permit the Jews concerned to have one common synagogue in a place to be assigned by the king.[1] The Crown must have the last word, as the archbishop, rather belatedly, recognized.

There is no reason to suppose that the bishop did, or could, effect anything or that the archbishop's information was remotely correct. The whole episode is of a piece with the action of Stephen Langton in the council of Oxford or, one may add, of Innocent III in the Lateran Council. The Church, in principle, claimed the right to interfere in Jewish affairs and to enforce the ecclesiastical law which purported to affect the Jews. Bishops, however, knew full well that, if they trespassed upon the provinces which the Crown reserved for itself, they would be rebuffed. As churchmen, they would not surrender one iota of the Church's pretensions, but, for the most part, they—and Richard Gravesend among them—were men of the world. The constant sniping on the borderland between ecclesiastical and secular jurisdictions must not be taken for more than symbolical gestures of defiance. It is difficult, therefore, to suppose that the correspondence between archbishop and bishop was conducted with any serious intention,

---

[1] *Registrum Epistolarum Iohannis Peckham*, ii. 407, 410–11; also in Wilkins, *Concilia*, ii. 88–9. The archbishop's language might be clearer; but his intention does not seem to be, as has been supposed, to restrict the whole community in London to one synagogue.

though Pecham was a foolishly provocative man who might not have been sorry to see his suffragan embroiled with the civil authorities. Fortunately, perhaps, even if the bishop of London had the will to close synagogues, they knew that he had not the power. There is evidence enough to show that the Crown might do this,[1] but none to show that the power resided in any ecclesiastical authority. Later, Peter Quivil, the bishop of Exeter, is found promulgating synodal statutes purporting to enforce the canons against the Jews—prohibiting the erection of new synagogues, compelling them to wear the *tabula*, and so on.[2] But it is all, to adapt John Pecham's phrase, vexing the air with vanities.

Let it be repeated: only the Crown had power to impose disabilities and restrictions on the Jews. Now disabilities and restrictions imposed by authority, to be followed by dispensations granted for money, were a common feature of medieval life and were not a peculiar visitation upon the Jews. But there can be no doubt that, in the thirteenth century, the Jews were particularly afflicted. Nor should anything that has been said be construed as implying that legislation against them always remained a dead letter. That the law was not consistently enforced is unquestionable. But the Crown had a fickle memory. The Jews in thirteenth century England lay under the constant shadow of discriminatory orders and arbitrary prohibitions that might be let sleep or might at any time be revived and might entail heavy penalties for disobedience. Too often over their heads they must have feared a sword was suspended, hanging by a thread, to fall at a moment no man could foretell.

---

[1] Besides the synagogue in Coleman Street, another synagogue, apparently in Threadneedle Street, had been closed: thereafter it was converted into a chapel and then, in 1243, granted to St. Anthony's Hospital (*Close Roll, 1242–1247*, p. 142; *Stow's Survey* (ed. Kingsford), i. 183). Yet another synagogue in Basinghall Street, part of the site of the later Blackwell Hall, had been converted before 1256 into the chapel of St. Mary in the Jewry (*Close Rolls, 1254–1256*, pp. 369–70; *Rot. Hundredorum*, i. 403*b*, 431*b*).

[2] Wilkins, *Concilia*, ii. 115.

# *Supplementary Notes*

# THE NORMAN JEWRY

THE HISTORY OF THE Jews in medieval France remains to be written. It must be written region by region and province by province, and as yet comparatively little has been accomplished.[1] The story of the English Jews under the Angevin kings would, however, be incomplete without at least a brief account of the Norman Jews, with whom they formed, if not one community, two communities very closely allied. What there is to say will be based chiefly upon the few and fragmentary Norman pipe rolls and the chancery rolls of King John.

It has already been said that the English Jewry was an offshoot of the Norman Jewry, that the liberties of both were guaranteed by a common charter, and that family ties were maintained between London and Rouen until the eve of John's expulsion from Normandy.[2] By the end of Henry II's reign, and perhaps much earlier in the twelfth century, the Norman Jews appear to have spread widely over the duchy. Under Richard and John they are found in many towns and villages, especially in the present department of Seine-Inférieure.[3] For the most part they

---

[1] Bédarride's *Les Juifs en France* etc. is antiquated. There is a scholarly summary account by Israel Lévi in the *Jewish Encyclopaedia*, v. 442–66; but this has some regrettable omissions, notably the history of the Jews in the provinces belonging to the kings of England. *Les Juifs de France* by Robert Anchel (1946) does not pretend to be more than a collection of essays. There is a brief account of the Jews of Normandy in the twelfth century by Léopold Delisle in *Bibliothèque de l'École des Chartes*, xiii. 133–5. A rather fuller account of the Jews of Normandy after 1204 will be found in J. R. Strayer's *Administration of Normandy under Saint Louis* (1932), pp. 47–51.

[2] Above, p. 2.

[3] The evidence is chiefly provided by the Norman pipe rolls, edited by Thomas Stapleton for the Society of Antiquaries under the title *Magni Rotuli Scaccarii Normanniae* (1840–4) and also by Léchaudé d'Anisy for the Société des Antiquaires de Normandie under the title *Grand Rôles des echiquiers* (1840).

seem to have been directly dependent upon the duke-king, but, with his licence, they might be 'kept' by his barons. How extensive this practice was there is no means of knowing, but in the rest of France, in Aquitaine as elsewhere, it cannot have been by any means uncommon for Jews to be dependent, not upon the king or duke or count, but upon a vassal.[1] Migration within the whole of what is now France must have been very easy, and there was little to prevent a Jew from seeking a new master.[2] The majority of Jews in Normandy evidently belonged, however, to the duke, and when we learn something of their administration, as we do under John, it is plain that the organization was parallel, if not closely parallel, to that in England. If we guess that in this matter Normandy was the borrower, the grounds we have for such an inference are these: we are able to trace what appears to be the gradual evolution of the Exchequer of the Jews in England, without any abrupt imposition of a new order upon the Jewry; and since the English Jewry was of more importance than the Norman Jewry, it is natural to suppose that the greater influenced the less.

Of the relative importance of the two communities we have some fairly reliable indications. The comparative size of the duchy and the kingdom; the few important Norman towns as compared with the number of English towns of similar standing; and, in particular, the amount of the taxes levied upon the Jewish communities in the two countries. Under Richard the Norman pipe rolls record a fine levied upon the Jewry of 2,000 *livres* and two tallages of 1,000 marks; under John a tallage of 1,000 *livres*. It

---

[1] For France generally see the statutes of Cardinal Robert de Courçon (*Rot. Litt. Pat.*, pp. 139*b*-140; above, p. 141). For Normandy in particular see *Rot. Chart.*, p. 75*b*, the grant to William Marshal of a Jew at Chambay. William de Boelles seems to have been similarly privileged (below, p. 208). The same practice is found in England, apparently under Stephen and occasionally in the thirteenth century (above, pp. 9, 12–13, 16–17, 195).

[2] The Jew at Chambay had come there from *Francia*. It was feared that Dieudonné of Verneuil would leave the king's dominions and to prevent this his son was taken as hostage until he should find adequate security (*Rot. Oblat.*, p. 73). More extensive evidence is afforded by the presence in England of Jews from the Continent (above, pp. 2–3).

seems evident from the particulars in the pipe rolls that, in striking contrast to contemporary English practice, the whole of these taxes were at that period accounted for at normal sessions of the Norman exchequer and were not distinguished from the ordinary revenues of the duchy. Consequently, if the series of pipe rolls were complete, we should know the full extent of taxation in these two reigns.[1] As it is, the three surviving rolls, of 1195, 1198 and 1203, provide a fair sample for the reigns of Richard and John, and they furnish a certain amount of material for inferring what the missing rolls contained. The first tallage of 1,000 marks appears to have been levied in the twelve months ended Michaelmas 1195,[2] but the fine of 2,000 *livres* in some previous year, perhaps 1192–3.[3] There is no trace on the roll of 1195 of any payment in respect of an earlier tallage. In the roll of 1198, there are, however, small payments specifically in respect of the 'old' tallage, presumably that of 1195, while the payments in respect of the current tallage of 1,000 marks amount to just under a half of that sum and it may be inferred that it was imposed in 1197.[4] The roll of 1203 brings to account payments in respect of a tallage of 1,000 *livres* that had been received by the principal collector in the previous year[5] and a rather larger sum received by his successor in the current year.[6] Since only one tallage levied by King John is mentioned, it may be concluded that this was the first of his reign, that is, since 1199. We can hardly be wrong in deducing that the Jews of Normandy were taxed no more frequently than every two or three years and that in the fifteen years between Richard's accession and John's expulsion from the duchy[7] not more than six or seven taxes are likely to have been imposed, of which we have particulars of four. We may therefore, with some confidence, take these four as representative. If we seek to compare them with the parallel taxes on English Jews, we must, in

---

[1] Under Henry II receipts from the Norman Jewry may have been kept apart and separately accounted for (below, p. 210, n. 4).

[2] *Magni Rotuli*, pp. 134–5.     [3] *Ibid.*, pp. 135–6.

[4] *Ibid.*, p. 314.     [5] *Ibid.*, p. 543.     [6] *Ibid.*, p. 547.

[7] Richard was invested with the duchy on 29 July 1189. Rouen was surrendered on Midsummer Day 1204; this marked the end of John's rule.

the first place, convert the amounts into English values, for the *livres* and marks of the Norman exchequer were in Angevin currency and the *denier* was worth only a quarter of the English sterling. In English terms, therefore, 1,000 Norman *livres* means only £250 and 1,000 Norman marks only 250 English marks.[1] These are trifling sums compared with the levies of three, four and five thousand marks imposed by Richard and John on the English Jews, levies that were far below the high-water mark of taxation in England.[2]

There are other indications of the same relative scale of values. The highest mulcts inflicted upon individual members of the Norman community are much smaller than those sustained by prominent Jews in England, the 1,500 marks and 3,000 marks that Le Brun of London had to find, the 2,000 marks and 6,000 marks demanded of Jurnet of Norwich.[3] Apart from the 400 *livres* that Deulebenie of Laigle and Josce of Caen had each to pay to compromise an action that had proceeded to wager of battle,[4] there is singularly little evidence of amercements. The one Norman Jew famed for his wealth, Dieudonné of Verneuil, found sureties to the amount of 600 *livres* and was required to find sureties for 900 *livres* to ensure that he would not leave the king's dominions: it is noteworthy that the three sureties whose names are known were Christians.[5] Dieudonné remained in Normandy, so that the sureties were not running any great risk, but their liabilities by English standards were not high and do not suggest that Dieudonné was very rich in comparison with the wealthier English Jews. The highest personal liability recorded as falling on a Norman Jew is a fine of 500 *livres*, but this is the amount that Meir of Bernay agrees to find for the right to succeed to his brother's estate. He has, however, to find a further 20 *livres* to be allowed time in which to pay, hardly an indication of

---

[1] L. Delisle in *Bibliothèque de l'École des Chartes*, x. 187–96.
[2] Above, pp. 164–6.
[3] *Pipe Roll 30 Henry II*, p. 138; above, pp. 40–1, 62, 89.
[4] *Magni Rotuli*, pp. 315, 468.
[5] *Rot. Oblat.*, p. 73. It is evident that he soon regained the king's favour (*Rot. Chart.*, p. 96b). Something more is said of Dieudonné hereafter.

affluence.[1] Everything in Normandy appears to be on a smaller scale than in England. In 1195 seven Jews of Rouen are found bringing actions to recover debts from Christians, which, it is instructive to note, are nearly all still owing in 1203;[2] but apart from these, the only similar actions recorded on the pipe rolls appear to be two in 1198, by Deulebenie of Laigle and by a Jewess named Bonedame, and another in 1203 by Samuel, the son of Abraham.[3] Between these dates the Norman rolls record one fine by Josce, the son of Isaac, of Rouen, to bring an action of debt, but this seems to be the solitary entry of its kind.[4] To argue from the surviving pipe and chancery rolls may be dangerous, but the contrast with the English records, with their numerous references to corresponding actions, hardly leaves any doubt that, by English standards, few actions of debt were brought by Jewish moneylenders in Normandy—not because Norman debtors were better clients, but because loans were relatively few. It is true that King John remitted a good many debts owing to Jews in return for aid against Philip Augustus, but the whole number does not represent a very large capital;[5] and when the French king, after the conquest of Normandy, inquired into the amount of money owing to Jews in his dominions the total due to Norman Jews does not seem to have reached 30,000 *livres*.[6] The most prominent moneylender of Normandy, Dieudonné of Verneuil, had debts of less than 2,600 *livres*.[7] These figures should be compared with those

---

[1] *Magni Rotuli*, p. 333.  [2] *Ibid.*, pp. 168, 550.
[3] *Ibid.*, pp. 315, 387, 550.  [4] *Rot. Normanniae*, p. 42.

[5] *Ibid.*, pp. 73, 107. The consideration appears to be only exceptionally mentioned: compare *ibid.*, p. 100 (Ralf de Rupierre) with *Rot. Litt. Pat.*, p. 32b. Similar quittances were presumably given for a similar consideration (*Rot. Normanniae*, pp. 52–118 *passim*).

[6] *Historiens de la France*, xxiv, Préface, p. 277, no. 25. Apart from Dieudonné of Verneuil, who was owed 2,592 *livres*, the Norman Jews in the bailliage of Cadoc (i.e. of Pont Audemer) were owed 12,304 *livres* and those in Gournay, Longueville and Aumale 13,870 *livres*. No other Norman Jews appear to be included in the list.

[7] He is the only one separately listed among the Norman Jews. He was so well known as to be termed 'the Jew of Verneuil' (*Rot. Normanniae*, p. 45). Among his clients was the bishop of Lisieux (*ibid.*, p. 100); while the earl of Leicester stood surety for him in the sum of 300 *livres* (*Rot. Oblat.*, p. 73). He has some responsibility for collecting the tallage of 1197: see below, pp. 208–9.

for the Jews of Paris. Two brothers, in partnership, Dieudonné and Heliot, alone had bonds worth 30,000 *livres*, though the rest of the Parisian Jews seem to have had no more than 12,500 *livres* due to them. The Jews of the entire dominions of Philip Augustus —and this is a point worth making—were not, however, a very wealthy community: the whole of their bonds put together, those of the Jews of Normandy included, were worth only 250,000 *livres*.[1] The Norman Jewry had doubtless suffered severely in the war that gave the French king possession of the duchy. King John's remissions of debt were certainly intended, as in England, to carry with them a reciprocal allowance to the moneylenders concerned, but it is not likely that in the event the Jews benefited. Whether there had been a remission or not, it would have been difficult, if not quite impossible, after John's expulsion, to enforce debts against those who adhered to him and were deprived of their Norman lands. Forced loans to the English king, though these were not many,[2] would also be irrecoverable. But however reduced in circumstances the Norman Jewry might be, it had not fallen from a high pinnacle.

Small, and relatively poor, as the Norman Jewry was, its administration was, by the standards of the times, elaborate, as all Norman administration tended to be. To learn what is possible of the organization of the Norman Jewry under Angevin kings, we must start from the reign of John, when the records are comparatively plentiful, and work backwards. Let us begin with the appointment of Richard of Villequier, on 30 November 1203, to the custody of the Norman Jews, except those of Rouen and Caen.[3] This appointment did not mark a new departure, for Richard had been in office for some time,[4] and the reason for the fresh appointment is obscure. But formerly he had had a colleague in Henry de Gray,[5] and the purpose may have been to give

---

[1] *Historiens de la France*, xxiv., *loc. cit.*

[2] The only references to such loans appear to be in *Rot. Litt. Pat.*, p. 25, and *Rot. Normanniae*, pp. 72, 79.

[3] *Rot. Litt. Pat.*, p. 37a; *Rot. Normanniae*, p. 116. He had custody of escheats as well as the Jews.

[4] *Ibid.*, p. 45 (25 May 1202).          [5] *Ibid.*, pp. 52, 60; below, pp. 208–9.

Richard sole responsibility as keeper of the Jews.[1] The exception of Rouen and Caen does not denote a restriction of his authority, for Rouen (and presumably Caen) had previously been excepted from the jurisdiction of the keepers of the Jews. At Rouen there had been a local *bailli* of the Jews, clerks had been employed to engross Jewish deeds, and transactions concerning the Jews of the city had been conducted before the mayor.[2] We may perhaps assume a similar arrangement at Caen. Over the rest of the Norman Jewry, Richard of Villequier had full authority, subject to the control of the seneschal,[3] which might mean that his duties were, at times, shared with other ministers. The principal evidence for Richard's activities is the series of writs addressed to him from the royal chancery, the majority of those surviving being writs notifying him that the king had acquitted some borrower of the whole or part of his debt to the Jews. If a debt were remitted, and also if a surety were released from his obligation, Richard had to see that the bonds into which the debtors or their sureties had entered were returned to them.[4] It is clear from the phrasing of some of the writs that a system of registering Jewish bonds was in existence, that rolls for the purpose were kept at the exchequer and that when the debt was reduced this fact was recorded.[5] It must have been from such an enrolment that Richard could ascertain the amount of a borrower's indebtedness and could make the necessary adjustment when he was instructed to reduce the debt by one-third.[6]

Richard of Villequier's responsibilities extended beyond the control of Jewish debts. A Jew who had failed to pay the amount of tallage assessed upon him was to be arrested and Richard was

[1] It is difficult to explain the letters patent of 19 February 1204 addressed to the seneschal of Normandy and the 'keepers' of the Jews in Normandy (*Rot. Litt. Pat.*, p. 39b), for Richard seems to have been sole keeper.

[2] Léchaudé d'Anisy, *Grands Rôles*, p. 203; *Magni Rotuli*, p. 140; *Rot. Normanniae*, p. 118.

[3] *Rot. Litt. Pat.*, p. 39b.

[4] *Rot. Normanniae*, pp. 61, 72–5, 80, 87, 88, 90, 100, 107. Similar writs had previously been addressed to Henry de Gray (*ibid.*, pp. 52, 60).

[5] *Ibid.*, p. 68.

[6] *Ibid.*, p. 87.

to send him to Robert of Vieuxpont,[1] that is, to be imprisoned in the castle at Rouen.[2] Part, at least, of the contributions to the tallage passed through his hands, for he was directed to re-imburse the contribution paid by the Jews who resided on the fee of William de Boelles.[3] On another occasion he was directed to instruct Dieudonné of Verneuil to pay 50 marks to Robert of Vieuxpont instead of paying this sum direct to the exchequer.[4] Richard's responsibilities were therefore wide, but he was not solely responsible for Jewish affairs. The tallage—the first and only tallage, so far as we know, imposed by King John upon the Norman Jewry—had been assessed by Richard Silvain, apparently in 1201, and he had collected a large part of it.[5] He did not continue long in this employment, doubtless because he was called upon to discharge a great many other duties in the duchy,[6] and he handed over the collection of the tallage to the newly appointed *bailli* of Mortain, Richard of Fontenay, who accounted for it at Michaelmas 1203.[7] Obviously there must have been a working arrangement between these two men and Richard of Villequier: the solution to the problem doubtless is that they all acted under the direction of the seneschal, who presided over the Norman exchequer, just as his counterpart, the justiciar, presided over the English exchequer.

We cannot trace with certainty in Richard's reign any organization for the administration of Jewish affairs such as we find under John, but it would seem that in 1198, and apparently earlier, Henry de Gray, who was acting as keeper of the Jews in 1202, was already in office. Henry, who was the *bailli* of Verneuil, received from Dieudonné of Verneuil a substantial part (appar-

---

[1] *Rot. Normanniae*, p. 57. The Jew in question, named Jacob, had been assessed at 300 marks, or one fifth of the total tallage of 1,000 *livres* (above, p. 203): he had paid 60 marks only.

[2] Of which Robert was castellan: see F. M. Powicke, *Loss of Normandy*, p. 105.

[3] *Rot. Normanniae*, p. 79. This seems to have been at a place named Foillet, where he had a castle (*Magni Rotuli*, p. 315; and see Stapleton's note, *ibid.*, ii. li.).

[4] *Rot. Normanniae*, p. 45.     [5] *Magni Rotuli*, p. 543.

[6] *Ibid.*, pp. 356, 361; C. H. Haskins, *Norman Institutions*, p. 336; Powicke, *Loss of Normandy*, pp. 254, 279, 324, 355.

[7] *Magni Rotuli*, p. 547.

ently arrears) of the tallage of 1197 and various odd sums from other Jews in respect of the 'old tallage'.[1] Ralf Labbé, the *bailli* of Argentan and Alençon, accounted also for a substantial balance 'of his receipts from the Jews', which seems to mean the tallage of 1197.[2] If so, Henry and Ralf accounted between them in 1198 for little less than half of this tallage. There are no other receipts that can be identified with the tallage of 1197 and the inference must be that these two ministers shared the responsibility for Jewish taxes and presumably the other duties that fell upon keepers of the Jews.[3] The division of responsibilities may have been territorial, Henry taking the East and Ralf the West. The position of Dieudonné in the arrangements for collecting the tallage is uncertain. Obviously he was the intermediary for that part of the Norman Jewry for which Henry de Gray was responsible. Whether some other prominent Jew acted on behalf of the rest of the Jewry in regard to Ralf Labbé can be no more than a speculation, for the wording of the pipe roll at this point could not be more obscure. In any case, there is no trace of a similar expedient on other occasions, and evidently individual Jews accounted personally for their assessment to the tallage of 1195,[4] as they did again under John.[5]

In 1195 Gilbert de Marleiz appears to be acting as principal collector of Jewish taxes, both of the tallage of that year and of the fine of some previous year. Since the sums for which he accounts represent more than half the tallage of 1,000 marks[6] and nearly 300 *livres* of arrears of the fine of 2,000 *livres*,[7] it would seem obvious that he is responsible for more than the taxes in the Pays de Caux, with which his account is otherwise

---

[1] *Ibid.*, pp. 312, 314.    [2] *Ibid.*, p. 386.

[3] So far as Henry de Gray is concerned, this inference is consistent with the writs addressed to him in *Rot. Normanniae*, pp. 52, 60, and *Rot. Oblat.*, p. 73. Further evidence is supplied by *Memoranda Roll 1 John*, p. 70. Richard I, it is stated, had instructed Isaac, the son of the Rabbi, to pay 1,000 marks to Henry de Gray. Since this sum was not to be brought to account in the English pipe rolls, the inference is that it was to be paid in Normandy.

[4] *Magni Rotuli*, p. 386: see above.

[5] *Rot. Normanniae*, p. 57; above, pp. 207–8.

[6] *Magni Rotuli*, pp. 134–5.    [7] *Ibid.*, pp. 135–6.

principally concerned. Moreover, no one else appears to account for any items of Jewish taxation in this year. Again, it is to be noted that Gilbert does not account for the ordinary revenue of the *bailliage* of Caux but for the escheats, and that in this and some other matters his authority extends to the Roumois and beyond.[1] There seems to be some parallel here with Richard of Villequier, who had the custody not only of the Jews but of the escheats of Normandy:[2] there is a parallel also with the contemporary arrangement in England under which William of Sainte-Mère-Église and Hugh Bardolf were responsible both for the Jews and escheats.[3] It is to be inferred that, while Gilbert may not have been entitled keeper of the Jews, he was performing much the same functions as later keepers.

Beyond Richard's reign the story cannot be taken, for the one complete Norman pipe roll of Henry II's that has survived and the fragments of another contain no reference to the Jews.[4] If what has been said of the administration of the Norman Jewry gives the impression of complexity and fluidity, of expedients taken up and set aside in favour of other expedients just as transitory, that is the impression conveyed by the records of Norman financial arrangements as a whole. There was, of course, an underlying stability determined by custom, and over all there was the continuity on established principles of the Norman exchequer. But in the intermediate field administrators and accountants change offices, come and go, with bewildering rapidity and

---

[1] His accounts are scattered over *Magni Rotuli*, pp. 131–43, and include profits of justice and escheats in Rouen. See Stapleton's comments, *ibid.*, i. cxli, cxliii, cxliv.

[2] *Rot. Litt. Pat.*, p. 37a; *Rot. Normanniae*, pp. 54, 57, 58. He was also concerned with a tallage of 2 sous for the host, 'de hoc exercitu' (*ibid.*, p. 47). These entries are prior to his appointment, on 30 November 1203, to the custody of escheats and of the Jews (above, p. 206, n. 3).

[3] Above, p. 119, n. 5.

[4] *Magni Rotuli*, pp. 1–123. The complete roll is for the year 1180; the fragments are from a roll of 1184. Another fragment of the roll of 1184 is printed by Léopold Delisle, *Actes de Henri II*, Introduction, pp. 334–44. The silence of these rolls suggests that, as in England, there was a separate account for receipts from Jews in Normandy: see above, pp. 115, 139.

kaleidoscopic effect. Upon such a basis, it is impossible to construct a plain and simple story. In the administration of justice there seems to be no such complexity: justice resided throughout in the exchequer and does not appear to have been delegated to the keepers of the Jews, although, as in England, an action might occasionally, on the application of one of the parties, be reserved for hearing before the king himself.[1] Actions in the exchequer where Jews were plaintiffs were not only for the recovery of debts from Christians but were also against Jews. Isaac of Rouen sues his brothers to recover a house.[2] Deulebenie of Laigle loses his action against Meir of Bernay and compromises his action against Josce of Caen.[3] This is a short enough list of recorded actions, but it is all we have from which to generalize, and its brevity is to be explained not only by the paucity of the records but by the small numbers of the Norman Jewry. It may, of course, be also that the Jews settled their disputes in their own domestic courts, though King John's charter confirming this privilege was confined to the English Jewry.[4]

For lack of earlier records, the story of the Norman Jewry under Angevin kings must be the story of a very short period, between the accession of Richard I and the loss of Normandy by John. After its conquest by Philip Augustus the separate administration of Normany was maintained, with slightly restricted boundaries.[5] Thereupon, however, the history of the Jews in Normandy becomes part of the history of the Jews of France, that is, of the territories that depended directly upon the French Crown. That the Norman Jews lost their separate identity is plain from the reference in 1242 to a 'chapter' of the Jews of France, to which the English Jews had resort when they had been forbidden to hold chapters in England.[6] For the ties that bound the

---

[1] *Rot. Chart.*, p. 96b. The party in this instance is Dieudonné of Verneuil, whose right to retain escheated Jewish property which he had purchased was apparently being challenged.  [2] *Magni Rotuli*, pp. 168, 530.

[3] *Ibid.*, pp. 315, 468.  [4] *Rot. Chart.*, p. 93b.

[5] Strayer, *Administration of Normandy*, pp. 10, 39.

[6] *Close Rolls, 1237–1242*, p. 464. The purpose of a chapter on this occasion was to decide a point of matrimonial law.

English Jewry to the Continent were not severed when Normandy was lost to the king of England; and when he finally expelled them from his kingdom they sought refuge among their kin in France.[1]

[1] Roth, *History of the Jews in England*, pp. 86–7.

# THE EXPULSION

IF IN A BOOK concerned with the history of the English Jewry under Angevin kings a place is found for a discussion of the Expulsion, there is ample reason. The explanations that have hitherto been offered have been based upon assumptions for which no warrant can be found in historical facts. The falsification of the economic realities of the late thirteenth century has proceeded not only from ignorance but from a misunderstanding of the economic realities of the twelfth century. Indeed, the distortion of any part of the historical background of the medieval Jewry almost inevitably involves the distortion of the rest. The more serious distortions have, it is hoped, been corrected in the preceding chapters; but not merely has the economic basis of the medieval Jewry been misunderstood, the character of the principal actor in the Expulsion has been misconceived. The insularity of English historians led them to a conception of Edward I as an English hero: in truth, he was neither English nor heroic, and this truth is slowly being realized. What has apparently not begun to be realized is that the Jewish problem was not insular and that, if it existed in England, it existed also in Edward's continental dominions. It is inconceivable that his attitude towards the English Jewry should have been fundamentally different from his attitude towards the Gascon Jewry. His treatment of the Gascon Jews and his treatment of the English Jews are but two facets of the same story. If we explain the one, we explain the other: if we justify the one, we justify the other.

The initial difficulty in the way of advancing an explanation of the Expulsion which turns upon the personal character of the king is one that is common to other problems of Edward I's reign. Have we to do with a ministerial act performed in the king's name or with an action that was the result of his own decision?

To distinguish between administrative acts which were initiated or specifically authorized by the king and those for which his ministers assumed responsibility can, as a rule, be little more than a matter of conjecture. But we are able, in the case of the Jews, to point to unquestionable evidence of Edward's personal interest.

It will be well to begin by saying something of the financial contributions imposed upon the English Jewry in the earlier years of Edward's reign. Not long before Henry III's death a tallage of 5,000 marks had been assessed upon the Jews. This had been occasioned by Edward's crusade, which was largely financed by the revenues of the Jewry.[1] To accelerate collection it was thought necessary to imprison certain of the leading Jews in the Tower of London, from which they were released on undertaking to pay half the assessment on 8 July and the other half by the 25th of the month.[2] These terms were, in point of fact, impossible to realize. By Michaelmas 1272 less than 2,000 marks had been collected in cash: thereafter payments were made slowly and a substantial balance of arrears was therefore carried over into the new reign, which began on 20 November.[3] Edward did not return to England until 2 August 1274, but in the meantime, apparently late in 1273,[4] his ministers levied on the English Jews a tallage of extraordinary severity, unknown since 1241.[5] The

---

[1] *Close Rolls, 1268–1272*, pp. 498–9; *Cal. Patent Rolls, 1266–1272*, p. 671.

[2] *Ibid.*, pp. 660–1.

[3] P.R.O., E. 401/1567. See *Cal. Close Rolls, 1272–1279*, pp. 199–200, for a settlement of arrears in 1275.

[4] No reference to the tallage appears to be made in the records until February 1274 (*Cal. Patent Rolls, 1272–1281*, pp. 42–3); and it seems certainly to have been imposed in the second year of the reign, i.e. after 19 November 1273 (*ibid.*, p. 273). The scrutiny of the *archae* ordered in February 1273 (*ibid.*, p. 6) appears to have been a preliminary step.

[5] The complicated arrangements for the taxation of 1240–1241 are difficult to unravel, but it seems clear that the levy of one-third of chattels was commuted to a tallage of 20,000 marks. Payments in respect of the former were credited to the latter (*Close Rolls, 1237–1241*, pp. 281, 312). The summoning of representative Jews to Worcester early in 1241 and the elaborate arrangements for assessment of May of that year are in respect of this taxation (*ibid.*, pp. 346–7, 353–5). The document (E. 101/249/12) printed by Canon Stokes, *Studies*, pp. 250–1, and assigned to 1219, is connected with this tallage, as are also the tallies listed by

tallage was assessed at one-third of all the Jews' movable goods,[1] that is, their bonds and valuables, the bonds being the most important part. The effect was, of course, to throw the direct burden of the tallage largely upon the Christian debtors.[2] Some of these could pay only in instalments[3] and might even be driven to sacrificing their lands.[4] Substantial sums were found in cash within a few years,[5] but nothing like the total of 25,000 marks at which the exchequer appears to have estimated the proceeds.[6] As a necessary means of enforcement, all the possessions of the wealthier Jews were impounded and released only on the payment of the amount assessed or in consideration of an arrangement which secured the payment of this sum, an arrangement not infrequently preceded by imprisonment.[7] The realization of so many debts secured upon land led to an immense increase in the work of the Justices of the Jews, so much so that it was necessary to inaugurate a special series of memoranda rolls.[8] Nothing, however, could accelerate the process of extracting money from impoverished landowners sufficiently to meet the king's financial necessities, and while arrears of the 'great' tallage, as it was called,[9] were being collected, fresh tallages were levied in 1276, 1277 and 1278. The tallage of 1276 was nominally £1,000: unlike the tallage of 1272, it was paid almost entirely in cash by the Jews, and with remarkable

---

M. Adler in Jewish Hist. Soc., *Miscellanies*, ii. 11–19, 22. A series of misconceptions by various writers has multiplied and exaggerated the tallages imposed by Henry III, and the tallage of 60,000 marks ascribed to 1244 is mythical.

[1] P.R.O., E. 401/1568.

[2] Above, pp. 93–4, 174.

[3] *Cal. Close Rolls, 1272–1279*, pp. 105, 144–5, 157.

[4] *Ibid.*, p. 170.

[5] P.R.O., E. 101/249/16; E. 401/1568–1571.

[6] P.R.O., E. 401/1573: Rotulus recepte de tallagio Iudeorum viginti-quinque milium marcarum. On 16 February 1276, it was said that the largest part of the tallage was in arrear (*Cal. Plea Rolls*, iii. 103).

[7] *Cal. Close Rolls, 1272–1279*, pp. 100, 105, 140, 166, 168, 174, 180 *et passim*.

[8] Two have survived: a roll of nineteen membranes for the Hilary term 1275 (P.R.O., E. 101/249/19) and a roll of five membranes for the Michaelmas term 1275 (E. 101/249/20). The numerous entries on the chancery rolls bear witness also to the great volume of business.

[9] *Cal. Patent Rolls, 1272–1281*, p. 273; *Cal. Plea Rolls*, iii. 66.

promptitude.[1] The amount of the tallage of 1277 does not appear to be recorded;[2] that of 1278 was assessed at 3,000 marks.[3] The available information does not suffice to tell us the financial results of these two tallages; but it was anticipated that they would be difficult to collect. Defaulters were threatened with exile, which meant, of course, forfeiture.[4] This threat, however, could not have held out many terrors for the poorer members of the community, and there is good reason to believe that a fair number had already gone into hiding or escaped abroad to avoid the 'great' tallage or the consequences of failure to pay the tax assessed upon them.[5] In estimating the severity of the exactions of the 1270's, it must be borne in mind that the total population of all the Jewish communities in the country at the time can scarcely have reached 3,000 souls,[6] and that the great majority of them were poor, and, moreover, that the burden of taxation fell upon a small number of wealthy families, who were deprived of a large part of their working capital by the 'great' tallage and whose business was further restricted by the prohibition of overt usury by the statute of the Jewry of 1275.[7] It is significant that the tallage of 1278 was the last for nearly a decade.

[1] Payment was due on the quinzaine of Michaelmas 1276 (*Cal. Fine Rolls, 1272–1307*, p. 72): at the end of the term the amount outstanding was less than £27 (P.R.O., E. 401/1572).

[2] No receipt roll has survived and the amount is not stated in the chancery rolls.

[3] *Cal. Close Rolls, 1272–1279*, p. 484; *Cal. Patent Rolls, 1272–1281*, p. 282. See also P.R.O., E. 101/249/22, rot. 2: De communa Iudeorum Londoniarum pro porcione de tallagio iii M. marcarum . . .

[4] *Cal. Patent Rolls, 1272–1281*, pp. 215, 274; *Foedera*, I. ii. 560.

[5] *Cal. Plea Rolls*, iii. 103–4. The allegation in the writ of 16 February 1276 that a number have fled or are in hiding is borne out by the sheriffs' returns (*ibid.*, pp. 130–4).

[6] Georg Caro (*Sozial- und Wirtschaftsgeschichte der Juden*, ii. 63–4) was undoubtedly right in putting the Jewish population in 1290 at a figure no higher than 2,500–3,000, if we assume, as it seems we must, that the chevage (or poll tax) was paid by all above the age of twelve (*Statutes of the Realm*, i. 221a; *Cal. Patent Rolls, 1281–1292*, p. 398). The numbers of those paying in the years 1280–1283 are known and vary between 1,179 and 1,133 (Jewish Hist. Soc., *Transactions*, iv. 59–63): allowing for defaulters, it is difficult to suppose that the number liable exceeded 1,250 or the total of adults and children 2,500. By 1290 the total was probably smaller.          [7] Above, p. 106.

Another means of extracting revenue from the Jews was, however, discovered, almost perhaps by accident. The debasement of
the coinage was a very old story, in which the Jews had played
a part; but every class accustomed to handle money or to deal in
bullion was suspected, and with reason, of making illicit profits in
this way. The main offence was clipping coins in circulation, before
passing them on in the way of trade, and turning the clippings
into ingots or sheet silver; but associated with this practice was the
manufacture of sheets of base metal coated with silver, which
were then passed into trade as solid silver.[1] That the London
Jewry was a centre of this traffic, in which Christians actively
participated, there is no manner of doubt.[2] The traffic did not
escape the vigilance of the authorities and there seems to have
been no difficulty in bringing such cases before the courts;[3] but,
for reasons unknown to us, the ordinary processes of the common
law were considered inadequate and in December 1276 justices
were appointed, under special commissions of oyer and terminer
for London and Nottingham, to try accusations of coin-clipping
made against both Jews and Christians.[4] At this stage Christians
would appear to have been suspected as the principal offenders;
but the sessions of the justices came to be regarded as a means of
bringing Jews to trial and it seems clear that some very flimsy
evidence was adduced and that the justice meted out was not
impeccable.[5] Little is known of the result of the trials and perhaps
little did result: there was certainly no holocaust of suspected Jews
as there was alleged to have been two years later when similar
commissions were issued covering the whole country. Nevertheless, it might be thought that these proceedings would have been

[1] For the two types of plates see *Cal. Patent Rolls, 1281–1292*, pp. 56, 86, 128.

[2] All kinds of monetary offences are mentioned in the accounts of the under-
constable and serjeant of the Tower of London for 1275–1278 (P.R.O., E.
101/249/22).

[3] As well as the accounts noted above, the plea rolls of the Exchequer of the
Jews record a good many cases, see *Cal. Plea Rolls*, ii. 299; iii. 119, 124–5, 205, 209,
277, 290, 309, 318–19; Rigg, *Select Pleas*, pp. 91, 121, 125–7.

[4] *Cal. Patent Rolls, 1272–1281*, p. 236.

[5] *Ibid.*, pp. 285, 287. As to the Jewess accused before one of the justices of
blasphemy, see above, p. 189.

sufficient deterrent for a long time, had the Jews in the past been extensively engaged in offences against the currency. However, in 1278, the state of the coinage was arousing more serious concern and its deterioration was largely attributed, though perhaps erroneously,[1] to clipping. One outcome was the decision, taken at a council in January 1279, for a complete recoinage;[2] but already, in November 1278, many Jews, all over the country, had been thrown into prison on suspicion of coin-clipping,[3] and in December a further attempt to suppress illicit practices was made by prohibiting the export of silver plate, clipped coin and broken silver.[4] These measures were followed, at the same time that the recoinage was ordered, by fresh commissions of oyer and terminer for the trial of those who had been charged with coin-clipping;[5] and whereas hitherto the extreme penalty for the offence appears to have been banishment,[6] now those found guilty were liable to capital punishment. Later instructions to the justices made plain that the proceedings were unequivocally anti-Jewish,[7] and their jurisdiction was extended to the trial of charges of blasphemy laid against Jews.[8] Whether by design or carelessness on the part of the king's ministers, the position of the Jews was hopelessly prejudiced. The widespread arrests of Jews throughout the country had been a signal to the baser elements of the population. The houses of those committed to prison had been broken into and plundered.[9] Nor is this the only indication that the arrest of these suspects was the excuse for the molestation of the Jews by the populace. Late in 1279, after the king's ministers had had second thoughts, it was found necessary to order the sheriff of

---

[1] Oman, *The Coinage of England*, p. 158.

[2] *Cal. Patent Rolls, 1272–1281*, p. 338; *Red Book of the Exchequer*, iii. 980–3.

[3] *Annales Monastici*, ii. 390–1; iii. 279; iv. 278.

[4] *Foedera*, I. ii. 564.       [5] *Cal. Patent Rolls, 1272–1281*, p. 338.

[6] *Ibid., 1232–1247*, p. 228. For cases before 1279 see above, p. 217, nn. 2, 3: in none of these cases is there a suggestion that the offence is a capital one.

[7] *Cal. Close Rolls, 1272–1279*, pp. 529–30 (7 May 1279): text, in part, in *Foedera*, I. ii. 570.

[8] *Cal. Close Rolls, 1272–1279*, pp. 565–6; *Foedera*, ut supra. These instructions are undated: from their position on the close roll, they would seem to have been issued later in May, but before the 27th.       [9] *Cal. Patent Rolls, 1272–1281*, p. 338.

Yorkshire to proclaim in the city of York and in the county court that no one was to lay violent hands on the Jews or do them other mischiefs against the king's peace: they were to be allowed intercourse with Christians and to pursue their affairs as they had done in times past.[1]

The conditions, therefore, were hardly such as to ensure a fair trial and there is good reason to believe that convictions were obtained upon inadequate and perjured evidence. So plain did this become that the proceedings against the Jews were everywhere stayed. Those Jews against whom there was no certain evidence and who had not been indicted before 1 May were relieved of the charge of coin-clipping on the payment of a suitable fine. Those who had already been convicted and detained in prison were to be released on payment of a fine as an alternative to forfeiture, to which, in principle, they were condemned. Jewesses who were involved with their husbands were also mercifully dealt with.[2] These instructions, however, did not reach the justices before a good many Jews had been hanged. The estimates of the chroniclers —nearly three hundred in London alone,[3] an infinite number over the country[4]—are not to be taken seriously. We can, in part, test these stories by actual examples.[5] At Bedford three Jews were hanged; at Canterbury five. Four were hanged at Norwich, including a Jewess; but, in addition, Abraham, the son of Deulacresse, was burnt for blasphemy.[6] Here, however, two Jews suffered no worse fate than forfeiture, while one had fled. These

[1] *Cal. Close Rolls, 1272–1279*, p. 577.

[2] *Ibid.*, pp. 529–30: the text in *Foedera*, I. ii. 570, omits the supplementary instructions. Master Elias, the son of master Moses, one of the richest Jews of the time and a celebrated physician, was among the accused and was pardoned on payment of a fine of 1,000 marks (*Cal. Fine Rolls, 1272–1307*, p. 114; *Cal. Patent Rolls, 1272–1281*, p. 322).

[3] *Annales Monastici* (Dunstable), iii. 279; *Annales Londonienses* (Chronicles of Edward I and Edward II), i. 88. The 280 of the former and the 293 of the latter must both derive from the same rumour.

[4] *Annales Monastici* (Osney), iv. 279.

[5] These are taken from the account of sales of the houses of condemned Jews by Walter of Helyun and his fellows (P.R.O., C. 47/9/50).

[6] For Abraham see also *Cal. Patent Rolls, 1272–1281*, p. 377. This seems to be the only recorded case of burning for blasphemy.

figures relate solely to Jews who owned houses; but it is difficult to believe that poor Jews, those without property, would be thought to have much opportunity for coin-clipping. Doubtless the larger communities suffered more severely, though perhaps not more than proportionately to their numbers: the available information is inadequate to justify even a guess at the facts.[1] However that may be, the executions and forfeitures, with the consequent escheats, resulted in an embarrassingly large accumulation of property in the king's hands. With this unexpected windfall the normal administrative machinery could not easily cope, so that it was thought necessary to appoint special officers to deal with its disposal. The proceeds were largely used to finance the recoinage.[2] Some part was, however, paid into the wardrobe,[3] and the king did not forget his queen, who had her share of the profits from the goods of the unfortunates.[4] The total amount realized from forfeitures and fines is not known, but it was evidently substantial. This result being satisfactorily achieved, and the wealth of the Jewry having been largely drained at its source, there was no longer any necessity to continue the draconic penalties for coin-clipping that had been introduced in 1279. These were quietly dropped,[5] and the Jews had even a respite from tallage until 1287.

[1] In Walter of Helyun's account the properties of only five Jews in London are accounted for: three were hanged and two suffered forfeiture. It seems unlikely that all the escheated properties are included. The only other surviving account, that of William de Brayboef, for Winchester, Bristol and Devizes, is uninformative (Jewish Hist. Soc., *Miscellanies*, ii. 56–71). This gives no particulars of John Falconer's earlier account rendered with it. As regards Jews mentioned in Brayboef's own account, only one, Benedict of Winchester, was certainly hanged. Two—Belecote of Winchester and her son—had been fugitives since before Christmas 1274 (*Cal. Plea Rolls*, ii. 299: cf. *ibid.*, iii. 263). The fate of the rest is unknown, but the presumption is all against wholesale hanging.

[2] *Cal. Patent Rolls, 1272–1281*, p. 312; *Cal. Close Rolls, 1272–1279*, p. 527.

[3] *Cal. Patent Rolls, 1272–1281*, p. 305.

[4] *Cal. Patent Rolls, 1281–1292*, p. 62. This was but one of many gifts to the queen from Jewish sources. For example, she received the fine of £1,000 paid by the widow of master Elias for various favours (*ibid.*, p. 193) and all the debts of his brother Hagin, the son of master Moses, forfeited for trespass (P.R.O., C. 202/C. 2, no. 32).

[5] Certainly by 1283 coin-clipping was not a capital offence: see the case of

Before proceeding, we may ask what part the Jews actually played in the depreciation of the coinage through clipping. That they were the victims of prejudice, there is no gainsaying, though not all were guiltless.[1] If, however, any responsible person held at the time the sincere belief that Jews were a major factor in the circulation of clipped money, subsequent events should have disabused him. Despite, and perhaps partly in consequence of, the recoinage, the amount of clipped coin in circulation continued to cause alarm to the government. Clipping was one of the evils aimed at in the so-called Statute of Money of 1284,[2] but the alleged culprits were merchants and especially foreign merchants; and though vague allegations persisted that Jews were concerned with dealings in sheet silver made from clippings and in counterfeit plate,[3] there were no more special sessions for foredoomed Jewish suspects. After the Expulsion the Jews could no longer be the scapegoats and these were perforce sought, with perhaps equal

Aaron of Ireland in Rigg, *Select Pleas*, pp. 121, 127. The action was dropped in consideration of his payment of three besants and the surrender of a rent of eight shillings.

[1] In 1238 the leaders of the Jewry had sought an inquiry with a view to the expulsion of any guilty members of the community (*Cal. Patent Rolls, 1232–1247*, p. 228). In consequence Ursel of Exeter fled the country with his wife and children (*Cal. Inquisitions Misc.*, i. 25), and there may well have been other similar cases. Though the plea rolls record later cases of Jews caught *in flagrante delicto* (*Cal. Plea Rolls*, ii. 299; iii. 119, 124, 205), they suggest, too, how lightly suspicion could be aroused and how easy it was to manufacture evidence out of spite (*ibid.*, iii. 290, 309, 311, 318–19; Rigg, *Select Pleas*, p. 95). The surviving evidence for the court of the constable of the Tower of London, 1275–1278, is of the same nature (P.R.O., E. 101/249/22).

[2] The editors of the *Statutes of the Realm* have left the texts of the Statutes of Money (i. 219–220) in a state of confusion. The 'great' statute is a set of articles sent to the wardens of Boston fair and to commissioners in the city of London on 4 September 1284 (*Cal. Patent Rolls, 1281–1290*, pp. 129–30). A later commission for London and the parts adjacent was issued on 10 February 1289 (*ibid.*, p. 313), and this was extended to the whole realm on 1 March (*Cal. Close Rolls, 1288–1296*, p. 9). It is only at this stage that the articles became, in any sense, a general statute: they were ordered to be enforced in Ireland also (*ibid.*, pp. 9–10: not in Berry's *Early Statutes of Ireland*).

[3] *Cal. Patent Rolls, 1281–1292*, pp. 56, 128, 134, 187. Cf. Rigg, *Select Pleas*, pp. 125–7, for a case in 1283 where foreign merchants offered to buy plates, made from silver clippings, from Jews who were unable to supply them.

justification, elsewhere.[1] The 'little' Statute of Money, of September 1291, which superseded the articles of 1284, was directed primarily at foreign merchants.[2] As early as 1278 they had been under suspicion of trafficking in clipped silver[3] and by 1283 they were strongly suspected of introducing counterfeit coin also.[4] They were accused of secreting such false money in their bales and passing it off on the unsuspecting populace.[5] Searchers were posted at the ports;[6] the sheriffs were instructed to make proclamation of the penalties awaiting offenders;[7] agents were repeatedly appointed, with roving commissions, to seek out the hidden imports of base money.[8] These efforts were no more rewarding than hanging the Jews had been. The evil persisted and the government had no fresh solution. There was, it is true, a renewed outburst of activity for several years under Edward II, but the measures taken were a mere repetition of those devised in 1291.[9] To pursue the story would take us far from the history of the Jews; but one comment is permissible. The relative lenience of the penalties to be inflicted, in the unlikely event of the discovery of culprits, is a fair measure of the malevolence, and perhaps cupidity, that inspired the proceedings against the Jews

[1] For occasional instances of foreign merchants charged with the offence see *Cal. Close Rolls, 1272–1279*, p. 531; *Cal. Patent Rolls, 1281–1292*, pp. 79, 187.

[2] The *textus receptus* is a writ to the sheriff of Lincoln, issued by the exchequer in compliance with instructions of 23 September 1291 (*Cal. Close Rolls, 1288–1296*, p. 203). In the *Statutes of the Realm*, i. 220, a repetition of these instructions on 2 February 1319 is taken to be the originating instrument.

[3] *Cal. Close Rolls, 1272–1279*, p. 518.

[4] *Cal. Patent Rolls, 1281–1292*, p. 86: fuller summary in Ruding, *Annals of the Coinage* (1840), i. 196.

[5] In the articles of 1284 and in the commissions to roving agents noted below.

[6] Beginning in 1283 with the appointment of John of Bourne at the Cinque Ports (*Cal. Patent Rolls, 1281–1292*, p. 86) and continuing with the application of the articles of 1284 to all ports.

[7] So in the 'little' Statute of Money and its many repetitions.

[8] The barons of the exchequer appointed John of Basing and Richard of Eu (de Augo) on 13 June 1293 and renewed their commission on 10 March 1294 (P.R.O., L.T.R. Memoranda Roll 21 Edward I (E. 368/64), m. 25). They were superseded, or supplemented, by John of Gloucester and John of Lincoln on 20 May 1294 (E. 368/65, m. 44*d*.; Madox, *History of the Exchequer*, i. 293–4).

[9] *Foedera*, II. i. 269, 311, 386, 428.

in 1278-9: it was only on a third conviction that Christians were to be liable to the forfeiture of their bodies and their goods. Foreign merchants, to be sure, were not without remedies against injustice and few had extensive possessions in England from which, on their condemnation, the king could make his profit.

Let us now ask two questions. What evidence is there for Edward's personal concern with these proceedings against the Jews? What is the bearing of the proceedings upon the problem of the Expulsion? To the first question there is the obvious answer that a man, so pressed for money as Edward was in the 1270's and deriving so much from the Jewry, could not fail to take a lively interest in matters that touched his financial interest so nearly. But we can find a more direct answer in the rolls of the chancery. That the king was personally interested is indicated by the unusual terms of the commissions of oyer and terminer for the justices appointed in 1276 to try charges of coin-clipping in London and Nottingham: 'ad aures nostras' the writs begin—information has reached the king's ears.[1] Again, when the tallages of 1277 and 1278 were imposed upon the Jews and accompanied by threats of exile against defaulters, on each occasion the king gave verbal instructions to the assessors and collectors.[2] We have evidence also of Edward's personal concern about the realization of the forfeited property of Jews condemned in 1279. One of the officers appointed to deal with its disposal in the Jewries of Bristol, Devizes and Winchester was John Falconer, who died before he had completed his task. His place was taken by William de Bray-boef, one of the justices of oyer and terminer appointed in the

[1] The entries in the calendar are inadequate. After the address, the patents begin as follows: 'Ad aures regias noueritis peruenisse quod nonnulli Iudei et Christiani usualem regni nostri monetam passim et indistincte retondunt ac quidam Christiani consencientes bonam et integram monetam pro retonsa pecunia cambiunt et permutant (P.R.O., Patent Roll 5 Edward I (C. 66/96), m. 26d.).

[2] The commissions are in similar terms. That of 20 June 1277 is inadequately represented in the *Calendar* (p. 215): the commissioners are to proceed 'prout vobis iniunximus vobis oretenus' (Patent Roll 5 Edward I (C. 66/96), m. 11). The text of the commission of 15 July 1278 is in *Foedera*, I. ii. 560: *oretenus* has been replaced by *viua voce*.

previous January.[1] Before taking up his new duties Brayboef had an interview with the king, who gave him verbal instructions regarding the sale of houses, lands and rents of the condemned Jews.[2] Without multiplying examples of this kind,[3] one last instance may be noted because it happened not long before the king's departure for France and Gascony in May 1286: in the preceding February he had given verbal instructions (for what purpose is not clear) for the scrutiny of the *archae* in the city of London and in the exchequer at Westminster.[4] With this convincing evidence of Edward's continuous personal interest in the Jewry, we are justified in concluding that the elaborate instructions to the justices in May 1279, which stayed the proceedings against Jews charged with coin-clipping, substituted fines for imprisonment, permitted those not yet tried to pay for their release, and so forth, expressed the king's own decisions. When, therefore, we read that the king had been informed that some Jews did not fear to blaspheme the catholic faith and the sacraments of the Church, we must take these words literally and

---

[1] *Cal. Fine Rolls, 1272–1307*, pp. 111, 113; *Cal. Patent Rolls, 1272–1281*, p. 338

[2] P.R.O. Patent Roll 7 Edward I (C. 66/98), m. 11: writ of 1 August. The important words are 'prout vobis iniunximus viua voce': see preceding note. The writ is summarized in *Abbreviatio Rotulorum Originalium*, i. 34*a*; *Cal. Patent Rolls, 1272–1281*, p. 323; *Cal. Fine Rolls, 1272–1307*, p. 115.

[3] There are, of course, instances of another kind where the king was inevitably involved in Jewish problems. Two may be mentioned, which are taken by Mr. Roth (*History of the Jews in England*, pp. 78–9) as examples of 'unenlightened fanaticism'. In 1276, after considering what both the London Jews and the justices in eyre had to say, Edward decided to remit for consideration in parliament a revived charge of ritual murder (*Cal. Close Rolls, 1272–1279*, pp. 271–4). In 1280, at the king's instance and in compliance with the bull *Vineam Sorec* (*Bullarium Romanum*, iv. 45–7, 4 August 1278), instructions were issued compelling Jews to hear sermons aimed at their conversion from Dominicans (*Foedera*, I. ii. 576). A third instance may be added: in 1277, at the request of Archbishop Kilwardby, himself a Dominican, the king ordered that a ribald Jew, who had masqueraded as a Franciscan, should perform a particularly disgusting penance that had been imposed upon him by the archbishop (*Cal. Plea Rolls*, iii. 311–12). These instances are undoubtedly evidence of Edward's mentality; but he would have been a man of very different intellectual and moral stature if he had acted otherwise and, as we might think, more intelligently.

[4] *Cal. Patent Rolls, 1281–1292*, p. 227.

believe that, when such blasphemy was made a capital offence, this, too, was the will of the king acting 'as behoves a catholic prince'.[1] For Edward's piety was as that of Saint Louis and Henry III and the persecuting popes of the thirteenth century.

We may now turn to the second question and endeavour to demonstrate the bearing of the proceedings of 1278–9 upon the problem of the Expulsion. The two cardinal facts in this connexion are, firstly, that, as we have seen, a very substantial sum accrued to the king from Jewish forfeitures when he was in need of money for the entirely praiseworthy object of the recoinage and, secondly, that, as we have established, Edward took a personal interest in the operations that were to yield this extraordinary revenue. Next, in order to place the Expulsion in its contemporary setting, it is necessary to recall that in 1288 Edward had entered into heavy commitments to secure the release of his cousin, Charles of Salerno.[2] In due course this and other extravagances (if the term may be permitted)[3] were to lead to heavy taxation throughout his dominions,[4] but they had more immediate consequences. Early in 1289[5] Edward ordered the arrest of all Jews in Gascony and the seizure of their property. They were then expelled from the duchy and their assets realized for the benefit of the king. In the documents that have come down to us there is no pretence that this act of spoliation had any other motive than gain or that it was contrived for the benefit of the Gascons. As the king himself said, the Jews' debtors became his

---

[1] *Foedera*, I. ii. 570; *Cal. Close Rolls, 1272–1279*, pp. 529–30, 565–6.

[2] For a summary of these see Powicke, *The Thirteenth Century*, pp. 282–3.

[3] 'The lavish expenditure of the royal court . . . too great to be borne by the current revenue' (*ibid.*, p. 305).

[4] For this taxation in general see J. F. Willard, *Parliamentary Taxes on Personal Property*, pp. 26–8. The extension to Wales of the fifteenth granted by the laity was specifically 'to pay the debts which the king incurred . . . in effecting the liberation of Charles, king of Sicily, his kinsman' (*Cal. Patent Rolls, 1281–1292*, p. 419). The same reason was advanced in Ireland: see Richardson and Sayles, *Parliaments and Councils of Mediaeval Ireland*, pp. 193–9.

[5] The earliest surviving document appears to be that of 4 May 1289 (*Rôles Gascons*, ii. 457, no. 1473), which is evidently a good deal later than the original order. Those chroniclers who notice the event are of little help in fixing the date.

debtors;[1] and he was an exacting creditor who needed to realize his assets quickly. The resistance he encountered forced him to make concessions. It must be understood that, since there was in Gascony no organization resembling the English Exchequer of the Jews, it was necessary for the king's agents to rely for their information upon the Jews' own records, which they may have found difficult to understand. In any event, they appear to have demanded the full amount of the debt, however ancient, recorded in any bond that came into their hands,[2] without allowing for repayments. They also demanded the full amount of their liability from insolvent debtors. As a first sop, debts which were more than ten years old were written off; repayments, when proved, were allowed as a set-off; and 'of his special grace' the king expressed himself as content to rank with other creditors in cases where the debtor could not meet his liabilities in full. It was also conceded that creditors of the exiled Jews might be repaid from their assets, provided that a claim had been made when the Jews were arrested.[3] These concessions did not satisfy the unfortunate debtors who objected that the debts included accumulated interest, and the further protests were met by the reduction of the total debt to one half, which was taken as the amount of the bare principal. The debtors were given three months in which to pay the reduced amount.[4]

No special pleading can cloak Edward's action in Gascony with the garb of piety or justice. It is the reverse aspect of the 'comprehensive gesture by a great king on behalf of a friend', extolled by a recent panegyrist:[5] it is characteristic of a prince who, in his youth, had been base enough to raid the deposits entrusted to the Templars in London and to steal the great treasure he found there, amounting, it was said, to £10,000;[6] it is of a piece

---

[1] *Rôles Gascons*, ii. 358, no. 1128: 'debitoribus ipsorum Iudeorum vel pocius nostris'.

[2] It is interesting to note that the Jews in Gascony were already using paper 'per papyros ipsorum Iudeorum captorum cum ipsi Iudei capti fuerint' (*ibid.*, p. 457, no. 1473).  [3] *Loc. cit.*

[4] *Ibid.*, ii. 358, no. 1128 (27 June 1289).  [5] Powicke, *op. cit.*, p. 283.

[6] Annals of Dover, *s.a.*, in Gervase of Canterbury, *Historical Works*, ii. 222.

with what was to follow in England. By the spring of 1290, Edward would have been able to measure the outcome of his confiscation of the property of the Jews in Gascony.[1] There is no reason to doubt its financial success, but the proceeds could have gone but a little way to satisfy his needs. Nor could there have been the least hope of extracting, by normal methods, any appreciable amount of money from the English Jews. The for-feitures and fines of the earlier years of Edward's reign must have greatly reduced the resources of the Jewry. The day-to-day revenues collected from the Jews by the exchequer were derisory.[2] What of an extraordinary levy? Unfortunately, a heavy tallage had been imposed in 1287 and had produced a little over £4,000 by the Easter term of 1288, when collection seems to have been completed.[3] A further tallage, if it were substantial, would have been beyond the power of the Jewry—or its Christian debtors—to find with any promptitude; and the king's needs were pressing. The alternative was to extend to the English Jews the treatment he had meted out to those of Gascony. Varying explanations of Edward's action are given by the chroniclers.[4] One alleges that it was instigated by the queen mother;[5] another that it was decreed in response to complaints by magnates in the Easter parliament of 1290;[6] another conjectures that the decision was taken on the

---

[1] As shown by the instructions given in May for the disposal of part of the proceeds (*Rôles Gascons*, ii. 548, no. 1786, 549, no. 1792).

[2] The three terminal receipt rolls surviving for the years immediately before the Expulsion give the following totals: Michaelmas 17 Edward I, £60. 12s. 2½d.; Michaelmas 18 Edward I, £90. 2s. 10d.; Easter 18 Edward I, £163. 17s. 7½d. (P.R.O., E. 401/1586; 1587; 1588).

[3] E. 401/1584; 1585: the total, paid by the collectors in several sums, is £4,023. 8s. 9d. It is stated on 20 August 1287 that the tallage had been recently imposed (*Cal. Close Rolls, 1279–1288*, p. 456). This tallage appears to be identical with the levy of £12,000 alleged by two chroniclers to have been made in May 1287. They tell an improbable story of universal imprisonment as a means of extracting the grant. Mr. Roth accepts this story (*History of the Jews in England*, pp. 79, 273); but it derives no support from the records.

[4] Some not noticed here are mentioned by B. L. Abrahams, *The Expulsion of the Jews from England*, pp. 74–5.

[5] Annals of Waverley, *Annales Monastici*, ii. 409.

[6] *Chronicle of Walter of Guisborough* [=Hemingburgh] (ed. Rothwell), p. 226.

advice of the council.[1] All these explanations, though there is little authority behind them, might be half-truths and are not necessarily inconsistent; but Edward needed no encouragement to follow a course upon which he had already resolved.

The decision to expel the Jews from England and to confiscate their houses and their bonds must have been taken by the beginning of June 1290. Secret instructions were issued to the sheriffs on the eighteenth of that month to seal the *archae* on the twenty-eighth.[2] While this action was doubtless perturbing, it gave no hint to the Jews of what was to come, for within recent years there had been orders for the closing and reopening of the *archae*, as the policy of the king had shifted and veered.[3] But a month after the order had been given for the *archae* to be sealed, the sheriffs were notified of the forthcoming expulsion of the Jews and ordered to make proclamation that, in the meantime, no one was to injure or wrong them.[4] The comparative humanity with which the Expulsion was carried out we may perhaps ascribe to the king's counsellors. Yet though the Jews were not put under arrest and were allowed to take their personal property with them, the measure was nevertheless, like their expulsion from Gascony, one of spoliation. The victims were cast, for the most part without resources, upon the mercies of those who had been sedulously taught to hate them. The Gascon precedent was indeed repeated

---

[1] Annals of Osney, *Annales Monastici*, iv. 326.

[2] The writ is not enrolled, but four original writs and returns have survived, for Gloucestershire, Lincolnshire, Yorkshire (P.R.O., C. 202/C. 4, nos. 121, 122, 127) and Northamptonshire (C. 47/124/1, unnumbered). The sheriff was to be accompanied by two knights and all three were to affix their seals; but he was to act 'ita caute quod milites predicti seu quicumque alii citra diem predictum inde non premuniantur'.

[3] In consequence of the prohibition of overt usury by the Statute of the Jewry the *archae* were ordered to be sealed on 24 November 1275 (*Cal. Patent Rolls, 1272–1281*, pp. 126–7). This did not mean that the bonds were annulled, and business arising out of them continued, the *archae* being opened for the purpose. New *archae* were opened in 1283 for registering bonds that complied with the law: it was presumably these *archae* that were temporarily sealed in 1284 (*Cal. Close Rolls, 1277–1288*, p. 256).

[4] *Cal. Clase Roll, 1288–1296*, pp. 95–6. Instructions to the Cinque Ports followed on 27 July (*Foedera*, I. ii. 736).

in curious detail. At first, it would seem, the intention was to require the Jews' debtors to pay to the king the full amount of their debts, and it was only at a later stage, on 5 November 1290, that interest included in the bonds was remitted and the demand limited to the principal. This concession, the debtors were made to understand, was not of right but of the king's grace, moved, as he was, by pity.[1]

The occasion was taken to publish an elaborate defence of the king's action. Nothing was said of his pressing need of money, but the decree of expulsion was linked with the Statute of the Jewry of 1275, which had made usury illegal. In breach of the statute, it was said, the Jews had continued to take usury covertly under the name of *curialitas*.[2] The absurdity of the charge lies in the fact that the contents of the bonds were no secret from the king's own servants and that the forms employed, which, of course, omitted any overt provision for interest, were well known to the Justices of the Jews.[3] Nor was the iniquity of the Jews so heinous as to preclude the king from profiting by it. How much he profited it is hardly possible to estimate. It has to be remembered that all obligations arising out of Jewish moneylending were seized, whether they were in Jewish hands or had passed into Christian hands,[4] as the bulk of charges upon land seem to have done. The Crown itself had already a considerable holding of bonds in the treasury;[5] the accumulation of rent-charges in the hands of the queen was notorious; but many subjects had participated in the traffic in Jewish bonds.[6] So far as bonds had been

[1] Rigg, *Select Pleas*, pp. xl-xli.    [2] *Loc. cit.*
[3] Above, p. 106.

[4] This is made clear by the writ to the sheriffs of 18 June 1290 (above, p. 238, n. 2): Et quia volumus quod omnes carte et obligaciones quorumcumque Iudeorum regni nostri extra archam cyrographarum Iudeorum existentes ad scaccarium nostrum . . . deferantur . . . tibi precipimus quod per totam balliuam tuam publice proclamari facias quod omnes illi qui huiusmodi cartas et obligaciones habuerint extra archam predictam . . . eas habeant . . . ad idem scaccarium . . . ibidem liberandas.'

[5] A survey made on 16 July 1272 and verified on 5 December showed that the face value of the bonds in the treasury was £1,472, excluding rent-charges (P.R.O., E. 101/249/11).    [6] Above, pp. 73, 104–5, 107.

lawfully alienated by Jewish moneylenders, there could be no
intention of confiscating them.[1] The king, however, gave nothing
away willingly: it was, for example, for debtors to prove that
their bonds included interest which, therefore, should be excluded
from their indebtedness to the exchequer;[2] and a debtor who did
not pay might forfeit his land.[3] But whatever may have been the
king's expectations, no experienced minister would have anticipated any large immediate addition to the revenue from the
disposal of Jewish bonds.[4] The receipt rolls of the Exchequer of
the Jews, in fact, hardly change their aspect after the Expulsion,
except that the relatively few direct payments by Jews drop out:
payments by Christian debtors continue, but in diminishing
volume.[5] On the other hand, real property could be speedily
turned into money. The Jewish houses that escheated to him, the
king caused to be sold, without undue delay, for their market
value, and care was taken to make dilapidations good in order
to realize a better price. The total gain from this source was about
£2,000, a portion of which was applied, with filial devotion, to
completing Henry III's tomb and to inserting stained-glass
windows in Westminster Abbey.[6]

[1] The sheriffs were to proclaim 'quod omnes huiusmodi carte et obligaciones
quas . . . ad prefatum scaccarium non liberatas inueniri contigerit extunc pro
nullis penitus habebuntur'.

[2] See the writ of 16 November 1290 in *Cal. Close Rolls, 1288–1292*, p. 148: a
similar writ of 23 February 1293 is in P.R.O., L.T.R. Memoranda Roll 21
Edward I (E. 368/64), m. 20d.

[3] *Cal. Inquisitions Misc.*, i. 446 (no. 1584).

[4] We must be careful not to regard the face value of the bonds reaching the
exchequer as affording any basis for an estimate. This was, however, the basis of
the calculations of B. L. Abrahams, who put the amount of the bonds from eleven
towns at £9,100 and estimated that a figure of £15,000 might represent the total
for the country (Jewish Hist. Soc., *Transactions*, ii. 80–1).

[5] For the five years after the Expulsion the figures are: 19 Edward I, £195;
20 Edward I, £67; 21 Edward I, £41; 22 Edward I, £127; 23 Edward I, £118
(P.R.O., E. 401/1590; 1591; 1593; 1595; 1597; 1599; 1601; 1603; 1606; 1608).
Separate accounts then ceased to be kept.

[6] These details are from Hugh of Kendal's account, P.R.O., E. 101/250/1,
enrolled in Pipe Roll 22 Edward I (E. 372/139), m. 3. Hugh accounts for £1,850
odd; but all the houses in Bristol and some in other towns were yet to be sold.
For Hugh's appointment to sell Jewish houses, dated 20 December 1290, see *Cal.*

Edward's conscience had been stirred by his financial necessities. Hitherto, he and his ministers, before and after he had come to the throne, had been, if unsympathetic and occasionally cruel, on the whole tolerant towards the Jews—the judicial massacre of 1279 was probably not premeditated—nor had they been disinclined to share in the gains of moneylending. If Eleanor, the queen mother, refused to profit by Jewish activities,[1] Eleanor, the queen consort, had no such inhibition and had no scruple in enriching herself.[2] If in 1281 the archbishop of Canterbury disapproved of the new synagogue in London, this was after the king had approved it,[3] an approval which shows incidentally that the Expulsion had not been long premeditated. If in 1290 the king professed himself as averse from all usury, responsible advisers of his had inclined, not many years before, to the regulation of rates of interest[4]—the solution ultimately adopted to check the excesses of Christian moneylenders both in France and in England.

The tolerance of Jews, displayed in court circles, was not shared by the multitude or by the clamant among the clergy; but we must hesitate before accepting the chroniclers as the voices of the people. It is hard to believe with some of them that it was in gratitude to the king for the expulsion of the Jews that laity and clergy granted him subsidies.[5] We may well look askance at writers who make such an assertion and yet fail to record the ground upon which the king based his demands and of which no well-informed contemporary could be ignorant—the debts he had incurred in procuring the release of Charles of Salerno.[6] Even

*Patent Rolls, 1281–1292*, p. 410: it was evidently intended that he should have the best of advice in making his valuations.

[1] The Jewries at Cambridge, Gloucester, Marlborough and Worcester, in which she was financially interested, had been suppressed at her instance in 1275 (Rigg, *Select Pleas*, p. 85).   [2] Above, p. 107.   [3] Above, p. 195.

[4] Rigg, *Select Pleas*, p. lvi. The date is apparently 1285.

[5] Annals of Dunstable, *Annales Monastici*, iii. 361; *Chronicle of Walter of Guisborough*, p. 227. The Annals of Osney, on the contrary, complain of the burden of taxation, which is represented as a set-off to the loss of revenue caused by the Expulsion (*Annales Monastici*, iv. 327).

[6] See p. 225, n. 4, above.

E.J.A.K.—Q                231

if it could be supposed that those who granted the subsidies represented the debtors, these had little cause for gratitude. They had
merely exchanged one creditor for another, more exacting: and,
when the subsidies were granted, the king had yet to decide that
he would not exact usury as well as the principal debt.[1] Nor must
we believe that the departure of the Jews was universally welcomed.[2] As their memory faded from the minds of Englishmen,
they became an evil thing, unknown, dreaded and accursed. The
commons in parliament in 1376 could say nothing worse of the
Lombards than that many of them were Jews and Saracens and
secret spies.[3] But in Gascony, where there was actual knowledge
of the Jews and their activities, the story is very different. Both
Edward I and Edward II, or those who acted in their name, were
intent upon ridding the duchy of Jews. Not long, however, after
their formal expulsion in 1289 they had begun to reappear,[4]
perhaps from hiding, perhaps from over the border: and though
Edward I issued a further order for their expulsion in 1305[5] this
was ignored. At the beginning of Edward II's reign the Jews were
well established in Gascony[6] and an official organization had been
set up, of much the same kind as the English Exchequer of the
Jews.[7] But again, in 1310 or early in 1311, an order was given for
their expulsion and the confiscation of debts due to them.[8] This,

---

[1] The date of the grant of the lay subsidy is unknown, but the writs for its
collection are dated 22 September (*Parliamentary Writs*, i. 24). The clerical subsidy
was granted in the province of Canterbury on 2 October (Florence of Worcester,
*Continuatio Chronici* (English Hist. Soc.), ii. 243; Oxenedes, *Chronica*, p. 253). The
reduction in the amount of the debts was announced on 5 November (Rigg,
*Select Pleas*, pp. xl–xli).

[2] Some lords, at least, of towns in which Jews were living outside the recognized communities were loath that they should leave as had been ordered in 1275,
and their departure was therefore delayed (*Cal. Close Rolls, 1272–1279*, p. 260).

[3] *Rotuli Parliamentorum*, ii. 332, no. 58.

[4] *Rôles Gascons*, iii. 55, no. 2054 (14 July 1290).

[5] *Ibid.*, p. 461, no. 4786; Champollion-Figeac, *Lettres de rois*, ii. 12.

[6] For Edward II's reign, see the series of extracts from the Gascon Rolls printed
in Jewish Hist. Soc., *Transactions*, ii. 175–9.

[7] There was a *iudicatura Iudeorum* at Agen, and rolls and other records (*papiri*)
of Jewish debts were kept at Bordeaux (*ibid.*, p. 175, nos. 9, 10; *Foedera*, ii. 75).

[8] *Transactions*, ut supra, pp. 175–6, nos. 10, 11.

like the previous order, was ignored and several further orders for the expulsion of the Jews were issued, with no more effect, between 1313 and 1317,[1] for the Jews remained, some to suffer massacre at the hands of the Pastoureaux in 1320.[2] No more significance can be given to these massacres than to earlier massacres by crusaders, as the Pastoureaux, indeed, professed to be. Though there were occasional complaints against them by their debtors,[3] it is hardly possible to maintain that the Jews were universally unpopular in Gascony. There were evidently strong influences that encouraged and protected them[4] in despite of the English king. These influences, it may be remarked, were no less strong in the dominions of the king of France, to which the Jews were recalled in 1315 after their exile in 1306. But of all the provinces of France it was in Gascony that toleration was most marked. It is believed that at Bordeaux there has been a Jewish community since the Dark Ages. However that may be, the Bordeaux Jewry, tolerated by the rulers of Gascony under English kings and under the French kings who succeeded them, was one of the few European refuges for the persecuted in the later Middle Ages and the Modern Age.[5]

[1] *Ibid.*, pp. 176–9, nos. 13–16.

[2] A. de Murimuth, *Continuatio Chronicarum* (ed. Maunde Thompson), pp. 31–2; Guillaume de Nangis, *Chronique* (ed. Géraud), ii. 26–8. The worst excesses were apparently in Agen and Bordeaux: see the chronicle, *s.a.*, in the *Petit Thalamus de Montpellier* (1840), p. 345, and another vernacular chronicle of Montpellier cited in Ducange, *Glossarium*, *s.v.* Pastorelli. The picturesque stories told of the massacre by Solomon ibn Verga and often repeated (e.g. Depping, *Les Juifs dans le moyen âge*, pp. 258–9; Bédarride, *Les Juifs en France*, pp. 262–3; Malvezin, *Histoire des Juifs à Bordeaux*, p. 45; Gross, *Gallia Judaica*, pp. 44, 111, 545–6) have little or no historical value. When the news reached England, the concern of the king's ministers was to see that he profited by the seizure of the property of the victims (*Transactions*, ut supra, p. 179, no. 17: letter of 26 July 1320).

[3] *Ibid.*, pp. 177–8, nos. 12, 13.

[4] Partly, no doubt, because they were a source of revenue: cf. *ibid.*, p. 178, no. 14.

[5] A critical history of the Jews of Gascony in the Middle Ages is greatly to be desired. The accounts given in the older books may be true in outline, but they are inadequately documented and insufficiently detailed.

*Appendix of Documents*

# I. ABRAHAM, THE SON OF THE RABBI, AND THE GREAT SYNAGOGUE

T HE THREE CHARTERS PRINTED below help to establish the site of the Great Synagogue in the early years of the thirteenth century and probably in the latter part of the twelfth century. They must be read with two charters printed in *Starrs and Jewish Charters*. The area concerned lies between Cheapside and Gresham (then Catte) Street and was, as it still is, intersected by Iron-monger Lane. The plan prepared by Joseph Jacobs and reproduced in his paper on the London Jewry,[1] though its identifications may be questioned, gives a fair idea of the relation of the several prop-erties named in the charters. It should, however, be explained that, by the early thirteenth century, the northern part of the area was held of Hugh de Neville as chief lord of the fee and the southern part of Geoffrey fitz Peter and thereafter, from 1213, of his son, Geoffrey de Mandeville, earl of Essex.

The first charter is a conveyance by Gervase of Cornhill to Isaac, the son of Rabbi Josce. This is a very early example of a conveyance of land to a Jew. The vendor was justiciar of London under Stephen and sheriff of London in 1155: he was sheriff of Surrey from 1163 to 1183 and of Kent from 1168 to 1174, and he seems to have survived until 1185.[2] His uncle, the previous owner of the property, Ralf fitz Herlewin, was one of the sheriffs of London in 1130.[3] Since Ralf's father, Herlewin, is known to have had a house 'in foro',[4] there can be little doubt that the land conveyed by Gervase was somewhere 'in Cheap', nor can there be much doubt that this land included a house, for the site was

---

[1] Anglo-Jewish Historical Exhibition, *Publications*, no. 1, between pp. 20 and 21: the paper is reprinted in Jacobs' *Jewish Ideals*, where the map faces p. 162. The parish boundaries shown are certainly not those of the early thirteenth century and do not seem to be medieval.

[2] Round, *Geoffrey de Mandeville*, pp. 121, 310–12.

[3] *Pipe Roll 31 Henry I*, p. 149.   [4] *Essays presented to T. F. Tout*, p. 59.

237

evidently that of Isaac's intended residence. It is to be noted that, except with Gervase's licence, the property was not to pass to anyone but Isaac's heirs or his brother's. The brother's name is not mentioned, but it must have been Abraham, the son of the Rabbi, who was associated with Isaac in business.[1] The date of the conveyance is probably early in Henry II's reign, but the names of the witnesses are not informative.

The next charter to be considered is the second printed below, which comes from 1212–1213. Its interest lies in its reference to the land and Great Synagogue of the Jews which had belonged to Abraham, the son of the Rabbi. The land and the synagogue lay to the north of the land in the parish of St. Mary Colechurch which was the subject of the charter. To the south of it lay twelve shops with upper storeys: these shops must, it would seem, have fronted the street, now known as Cheapside, between Ironmonger Lane and Old Jewry, but to the west of the parish church, which stood at the corner of Old Jewry. The shops and the church are likely to have occupied the whole, or nearly the whole, of the site of the present Mercers' Hall.

Another charter of about two years later conveys to Geoffrey de Mandeville the house that had belonged to Abraham, the son of the Rabbi.[2] This also lay in the parish of St. Mary Colechurch, but is described as being in West Cheap and bounded by Ironmonger Lane. The house would seem to be identifiable with the property conveyed by Gervase of Cornhill to Isaac. It would appear to follow that Abraham's house (formerly Isaac's) was not adjacent to the synagogue, but lay on the west side of Ironmonger Lane. If this deduction is correct, the synagogue lay some distance up Ironmonger Lane on the east side.[3] It may be noted that Abraham's house was sold by Earl Geoffrey, soon after he had acquired it, to one Gilbert of Walton, who speedily disposed of it in turn: the charter which records these facts is of interest

---

[1] Above, pp. 2, 62.

[2] *Starrs and Jewish Charters*, i. 26–9.

[3] Joseph Jacobs, who was acquainted with part of the evidence, placed the synagogue in Gresham Street (*Jews of Angevin England*, pp. 235–6): see also his 'London Jewry', *ut supra*, p. 25 and map (*Jewish Ideals*, p. 167).

in the present connexion solely because it confirms the situation of the house and furnishes some information about the descendants of Abraham.[1]

The third charter, dated 4 September 1226, of which only a summary has survived, as printed below, is concerned with land to the north of the synagogue. This property lay in the parish of St. Lawrence Jewry and in the fee of Hugh de Neville. It extended in depth (southwards) from the king's highway (presumably the present Gresham Street) to the synagogue. To the east lay land that had belonged to Abraham, the son of Avigai, and to the west land belonging to Jude of Warwick. All three properties presumably lay between Ironmonger Lane and Old Jewry. The grantor was Samson, the son of Isaac: this Isaac may be identifiable with the son of the Rabbi. Samson, however, may not have succeeded immediately to the property on Isaac's death: in 1218 ten years' arrears of rent were demanded of him, but he asserted that only in that year had he come into possession.[2] The grantee was his son Abraham, and it is to be noted that this Abraham is described as the son both of his father and his mother (Melke), exactly as was Abraham, the son of Joseph and Miriam (or Muriel) the daughter of Isaac, who conveyed to Geoffrey de Mandeville the house of Abraham, the son of the Rabbi.[3] This suggests that Melke had an interest in the property, perhaps as the widow of a deceased brother of Samson's who had first succeeded to it. The property had certainly at one time belonged to Samson's father, Isaac,[4] and could not have descended to Melke by inheritance.

## 1. GRANT BY GERVASE OF CORNHILL TO ISAAC

P.R.O., D.L. 36/1, fo. 87, no. 3

Notum sit quod ego Geruasius de Cornhulle concessi Ysaac Iudeo terram illam que fuit Radulfi filii Herlewini auunculi mei, scilicet

---

[1] *Starrs and Jewish Charters*, i. 26–9.   [2] Cole, *Documents*, p. 293.

[3] *Starrs and Jewish Charters*, i. 26–9. To this deed one Abraham, the son of Samson, was a witness, but this can hardly be the same man as the grantee of 1226.

[4] Cole, *Documents*, p. 293. It would follow that the brother died early in the century, not very long after his father.

terram de qua ego emi feodum a Sewardo, in feodo et hereditate de me et de meis heredibus illi et heredibus suis tenendam pro ii. solidis per annum, scilicet ad festum sancti Michaelis. Pro hac concessione dedit mihi Ysaac xlix. solidos, eo pacto quod nullus ab eo illam abere[1] potest nisi mea licencia, nisi heredes sui vel fratris sui. Et ego debeo illam terram garantizare contra episcopum et contra canonicos sancti Pauli. Testes Radulfus de Chaineduit et Ricardus de Campaine et Tomas clericus et Simon clericus et Moises Iudeus.

## II. GRANT BY GEOFFREY FITZ PETER TO CHICKSAND PRIORY

P.R.O., E. 159/101 (K.R. Mem. Roll, 19 Edward II), m. 144
P.R.O., E. 368/97 (L.T.R. Mem. Roll, 19 Edward II), m. 44

Sciant presentes et futuri quod ego Galfridus filius Petri, comes Essexie, dedi et presenti carta mea confirmaui Deo et ecclesie beate Marie de Chikesand et canonicis et monialibus ibidem Deo seruientibus, pro salute anime mee et animarum regis Henrici et regis Ricardi et animarum patris et matris mee et antecessorum et successorum meorum et omnium fidelium defunctorum, in puram et perpetuam elemosinam, ad camisias predictis monialibus emendas, totam terram cum domibus et cum omnibus pertinenciis suis quam habui in parochia sancte Marie de Colcherche inter terram et magnam scolam Iudeorum que fuit Abrahe filii Raby versus aquilonem et duodecim soppas cum soliis quas dedi Deo et ecclesie beate Marie de Soldeham versus australem. Preterea dedi et presenti carta mea confirmaui predictis canonicis et monialibus vnam marcam redditus quam Ricardus filius Simonis Hakepetit et Iohanna vxor eius michi annuatim reddere solebant de terra cum domibus quam de me tenuerunt versus aquilonem capelle beate Marie de Cunehope[2] ad camisias predictis monialibus emendas, scilicet quicquid in predicta terra cum domibus et in predicto redditu habui in rebus cunctis cum omnibus pertinenciis suis integre habendum et tenendum prenominatis canonicis et monialibus et successoribus suis libere, quiete, bene et in pace et finabiliter, saluo seruicio capitalium dominorum quod facere debent quantum ad predictam terram cum domibus et redditu predicto pertinet. Hanc autem terram predictam cum domibus et cum predicto redditu ego Galfridus filius Petri, comes Essescie, et heredes mei predictis canonicis et monialibus et successoribus suis contra omnes gentes finabiliter debemus warantizare. Vt autem

---

[1] *Sic* for 'habere'.  [2] See above, p. 48, n. 1.

hec mea donacio et warantizacio et presentis carte mee confirmacio firma et stabilis perseueret in perpetuum presens scriptum sigillo meo confirmaui. Hiis testibus Galfrido de Bocl[ande] decano sancti Martini, Willelmo de Bocl[ande], Henrico de Gray, Iohanne de Chauz, Radulfo Chaenduit, Ricardo de Seyng[er], Hugone de Ryuesworthe, Iohanne de Math'a, Gilberto Croke, Rogero filio Alani tunc maiore Londoniarum,[1] Constantino filio Alulfi, [2] Radulfo Esswy aldermanno, Henrico de sancto Albano, Henrico de sancta Helena, Serlone Mercer, Ricardo de Stapilf[orde], Waltero filio Bernardi.

### III. GRANT BY SAMSON, THE SON OF ISAAC, TO HIS SON ABRAHAM

P.R.O., E. 372/73 (*Pipe Roll 13 Henry III*), m. 13 (London and Middlesex)

Sampson filius Ysaac . . . dimidiam marcam vt scribatur in magno rotulo regis quod ipse Sampson venit coram baronibus de scaccario et ibi recognouit quod quarta die Septembris anno regis xº [3] dederit et concesserit et carta sua confirmauerit Abrahe filio suo et filio Melke vxoris sue vnam terram quam habebat in parochia sancti Laurencii in Iudaismo Londoniarum de feudo Hugonis de Neuille cum omnibus ad eandem terram pertinentibus in edificiis ligneis et lapideis, que terra iacet inter terram que fuit Abrahe filii Auigaie versus orientem et terram Iude de Warewyc versus occidentem, que extendit in longitudine a regali via vsque ad sinagogam, habendam et tenendam sibi et heredibus suis libere, quiete et honorifice.

[1] 1212–1213.　　[2] Sheriff 1212–1213.　　[3] 4 September 1226.

## II. DEEDS OF ROGER AND MICHAEL DE WANCHY

THE DEEDS IN THIS series consist of bonds with Le Brun of London and other moneylenders (the earliest in date being of the year 1170) and documents connected with the conveyance of the manor of Stanstead to Waltham Abbey. The originals are no longer extant, but transcripts are available in the cartularies of the abbey. Only the first of the elaborate documents considered necessary for conveying the property to the abbey is reproduced. Among the documents in the series are a confirmatory charter of Henry II, a confirmatory charter of Michael de Wanchy in the time of Richard I and a charter by Michael's son Roger. They are lengthy and the additional information they contain does not justify their reproduction: the information has been used in the text.[1]

I

Tiberius C. ix., fo. 84*b*

Notum sit presentibus et futuris quod ego Rogerus de Waunci et ego Beatrix de Waunci, sua vxor, et ego Michaelis de Waunci, eorum filius, debemus Bruno Iudeo de Londonia ii.c. marcas argenti et decem. Et hec est summa totius[2] debiti nostri quod debuimus ei quindecim dies post festum sancti Iohannis Baptiste proximum postquam Henricus rex filius Henrici regis Anglie fuit coronatus,[3] et inter has ii.c. marcas argenti et decem habet octo libras argenti et dimidiam marcam quas accomodauit nobis vsque ad proximum Natale post festum sancti Iohannis Baptiste prenominati[4] sine lucro, et si vltra illas tenuerimus nos dabimus ei pro singula libra ii. denarios per septemanam[4] de lucro super eundem vadium nostri manerii quod ista carta diuisit vsque reddiderimus octo libras argenti et dimidiam marcam cum lucro. Et pro hiis ii.c. marcis argenti et decem inuadiauimus ei nostrum manerium

[1] Above, pp. 87–9.    [2] MS. toti.
[3] The young king was crowned on 14 June 1170: the date is therefore 8 July in that year.    [4] *Sic.*

242

de Ponte Tegule[1] et Stanstede,[2] in redditibus, in culturis, in nemore, in aqua, in pratis, in molendinis, in virgultis, in halla, in horreis, in domibus rusticorum. Et sic istud manerium inuadiauimus ei sicut nos habuimus, saluo tenemento hominum meorum, tali iure et talibus moribus sicuti nobis fecerunt et saluis nostris elemosinis, scilicet ecclesia de Stanstede quam dedimus ad ecclesiam sancte Marie de Mertune et xx. solidis redditus ad eandem ecclesiam, scilicet domus Ricardi filii Adam et vna mansura vastata, et ad Hospitalem Hierosolime mansuram Ricardi Lee. Et de nemore nostro habebit omnes exitus sicuti nos habuimus sine vendere et dare ad deuastandum. Et istud manerium predictum inuadiauimus ei cum omnibus pertinenciis sine omni retinencia ad nostrum opus. Et istud manerium predictum debet ipse habere de festiuitate sancti Iohannis Baptiste post coronacionem filii Henrici regis Anglie in vnum annum tali diuisione: si reddiderimus ei ad terminum predictum ii.c. marcas argenti et decem predictas, nostrum manerium erit quietum et ipse reddet nobis nostrum manerium ita restauratum sicut ei tribuimus, sicut cirographum inter nos testificabitur, et si magis super manerium imposuerit nos ei reddiderimus. Et si nos non reddiderimus ei debitum predictum ad terminum statutum, sicut predictum est, Brunus tenebit manerium predictum annuatim quousque plenarie reddiderimus ei debitum predictum, et quamdiu debebimus ei predictum debitum nichil capere possumus nec aliquis per nos quousque persoluerimus ei debitum predictum. Hanc conuencionem affidauimus legaliter tenendam [et] pro nobis et heredibus nostris warantizandam contra omnes homines illi et heredibus suis. Hiis testibus Rogero de Clare etc.

2

Tiberius C. ix., fo. 84–84*b*

Sciant presentes et futuri quod ego Rogerus de Waunci debeo Bruno Iudeo de Londonia xx. libras et xi. solidos sterlingorum reddendas ad proximum festum sancti Iohannis Baptiste postquam rex Henricus Anglie et regina sua, filia regis Francie, primum fuerunt coronati apud Wintoniam.[3] Et nisi tunc ei reddidero, quamdiu illas in antea tenuero dabo ei pro vnaquaque libra ii. denarios per ebdomadam de lucro. Et

---

[1] Pont de Thele, now Stanstead St Margaret.
[2] Stanstead Abbots.
[3] 27 August 1172: the date of payment is therefore 24 June 1173.

hoc catallum et hoc lucrum qui ascenderit ei grantam super eundem vadium quem habet de me, scilicet Pont de Thele et Standstede, super quos ei debeo ex altera parte septem viginti libras, vnde habet aliam cartam meam, et volo quod istud predictum vadium teneat donec ei redderam istud debitum cum alio debito suo. Et hoc pactum affidaui tenendum ei et vxori suo vel heredibus suis, ego Rogerus de Waunci et Rogerus de Waunci filius meus et Osbertus et Reinnerus filii mei, et sigillo meo et sigillo Beatrice vxoris mei defirmaui. Hiis testibus Hugone de Wind' etc.

3

Harleian MS. 391, fo. 77–8
Tiberius C. IX, fo. 85

Omnibus fidelibus et sancte matris ecclesie filiis Michael de Wanci salutem. Notum sit omnibus vobis quod Roger de Waunci pater meus debebat Bruno Iudeo de Londonia cc. et quater xx. libras et xvii. solidos et iii. denarios argenti super manerium suum de Stanstede et Pontis de Thiele quod iam per xv. annos predictus Iudeus in vadium tenuerat. Mortuo autem predicto patre meo ego Michael de Wanci heres eius, quia non valui predictum debitum adquietare, ne totum predictum manerium per vsuras cotidie crescentes perpetuo amitterem, requisiui dominum regem Anglie, scilicet Henricum secundum, per magistrum Walterum de Gant canonicum de Waltham,[1] quod pro amore Dei prescriptum debitum adquietaret et ego medictatem totius predicti manerii eo pacto illi darem quietam ab omni seruicio et omni calumpnia dandam cuiuellet domui relligiose. Ipse igitur ad peticionem meam predictum debitum totum adquietauit et dimidietatem totius prescripti manerii quam ei pro prenominata adquietacione dederam ecclesie sue de Waltham, quam tunc fundauerat, in perpetuam contulit elemosinam. Ego eciam pro predicta adquietacione et peticione domini regis prenominati aliam medietatem iam dicti manerii, que ad me debebat pertinere, cum omnibus suis pertinenciis, concessi et dedi eidem ecclesie sancte Cruicis de Waltham et canonicis regularibus Deo ibidem seruientibus in stabilem elemosinam perpetuo tenendam libere et quiete et sine omni grauamine de me et heredibus meis pro xii. libris argenti annuatim quas prefati canonici reddent michi et heredibus meis apud

---

[1] Walter of Ghent became abbot of Waltham before Michaelmas 1184 (*Pipe Roll 30 Henry II*, pp. 10, 53, 56, 70, 129; *Gesta Henrici*, i. 316–17).

Waltham, scilicet ad Pascha vi. libras et ad festum sancti Michaelis vi. libras, et qui ad predictos terminos pro isto redditu venerit erit ad Waltham ad custum canonicorum donec ei reddatur. Preterea ego Michael de Wanci et omnes heredes mei perpetuo debemus per has xii. libras defendere et adquietare totum predictum manerium et omnia eius pertinencia aduersus Gillebertum filium Ricardi de Strigoil[1] et aduersus heredes suos de omni seruicio et de omni iure quod ad prefatum Gillebertum vel ad heredes suos pertinebit exigendum de predicta terra et de predicto feudo vel de me vel de heredibus meis quocumque modo exigatur siue in pecunia siue in personali seruicio siue alio quocumque modo sicut si hic modus nominatus esset. Set quando ego Michael de Wanci vel aliquis heredum meorum releuium vel aliquid seruicium facere debebit Gilleberto de Strigoil[1] vel heredibus suis nichil omnino exigere poterimus a predictis canonicis vel predicto manerio nisi quod per manum canonicorum recipere debemus in auxilio de feudo Iohannis de Nouauilla quantum ad illud de iure pertinebit et iuste exigi debebit. Et ideo, quia totum predictum manerium de Stanstede et Pontis de Thiele predictis canonicis cum omnibus suis pertinenciis concessum est, sicut predictum est, tenendum, nichil omnino michi vel heredibus meis retineo in predicto manerio nisi tantummodo xii. libras quas michi et heredibus meis, sicut prescriptum est, canonici de Waltham annuatim soluent ad predictos terminos, nec eciam aliquid ius in ecclesia predicti manerii michi vel heredibus meis reseruo. Item certum sit omnibus quod ego Michael de Wanci et heredes mei debemus perpetuo warantizare per custum nostrum canonicis de Waltham totum manerium de Stanstede et Pontis de Thiele, cum omnibus pertinenciis suis, in bosco et plano, in pratis et pascuis, in aquis et molendinis et omnibus aliis rebus ad illud manerium pertinentibus, contra Gillebertum de Strigoil et omnes eius heredes et contra omnes homines et feminas et contra omnes calumpniatores et omnes calumpnias, quum certum est me tradidisse predictis canonicis totum predictum manerium liberum et quietum de omni querela et calumpnia. Et propter conuenciones suprascriptas predictus rex dedit michi x. libras et Osberto fratri meo c. solidos, per peticionem meam, preter supradictam manerii adquietationem. Hec omnia, sicut suprascripta et pacta sunt, ego Michael de Wanci, tactis sacrosanctis euangeliis, iuraui fideliter ex parte mea et meorum heredum esse custodienda. Istorum omnium supradictorum testes sunt: Ricardus Wintoniensis,

[1] Son of Richard earl of Pembroke, 'Strongbow'.

245

Galfridus Elyensis, Iohannes Norwicensis, episcopi, Rannulfus de Glanuilla, qui tunc fuit iusticiarius regis,[1] Ricardus thesaurarius regis, Willelmus de Ver, Hubertus cognomine Walterus, Rogerus filius Reinfredi, Gillebertus de Coleuilla, Rannulfus de Geddinges, Siluredus de Glanuilla, Henricus de Iclentona, Willelmus Reuel, Iohannes de Nouauilla, Willelmus Peregrinus, Symon de Stanstede, Ricardus filius Alcheri, Willelmus Napparius, Adam de Cyrecestre, Iohannes filius Ylgeri, Galfridus et Willelmus filii Roberti, Willelmus de Lindeseia, Ricardus marescallus Willelmi de Ver, Walterus filius Roberti, Edwardus Portarius.

## 4

Tiberius C. ix., fo. 84*b*–85

Notum sit omnibus tam presentibus quam futuris quod ego Michael de Waunci debeo Benedicto Iudeo de Londonia paruo xl. solidos sterlingorum reddendos ad festum sancti Michaelis proximum post primum aduentum Patriarche Ierosolime in Anglia,[2] et si illos vlterius tenuero per grantum suum, tenebo et dabo illi pro singulis libris omni septemana quamdiu illas tenuero vi. denarios de lucro ad terminos et respectus quos michi inde dare voluerit et infra xv. dies sue sumoni-cionis vel nuncii sui faciam grantum suum de catallo et lucro. Et de hoc debito recipiendo assignaui predictum Iudeum Benedictum paruum ad abbatem sancte Crucis de Waltham et ad canonicos eiusdem loci concessione et bona voluntate predicti abbatis et conuentus vt predicto Iudeo reddant predictum debitum de debito meo quod michi reddere debent ad predictum festum sancti Michaelis. Et quando predictus abbas et conuentus eidem Benedicto predictum debitum reddiderunt recipi-ent de illo hanc cartam meam in testimonium. Et si ita euenerit quod predictus abbas et conuentus predicto Benedicto predictum debitum ad terminum prenominatum non reddiderint, ego predictus Michael predicto Iudeo ad summonicionem suam reddam catallum et lucrum vel ei qui hanc cartam meam michi attulerit et tantum debeo illi facere de illo debito persoluendo quantum fecerim ipsi Benedicto Iudeo. Et hoc illi et heredibus suis tenendum pro me et heredibus meis legitime affidaui.

[1] Appointed in 1180, apparently in April (*Memoranda Roll 1 John*, p. lxxvii. and references). The charter may therefore be dated within the extreme limits of April 1180–September 1184.
[2] 1185.

## III. BONDS OF AARON OF LINCOLN

Upon the death of Aaron of Lincoln early in April 1186 his estate escheated to the king. One consequence was that his bonds were enrolled in the exchequer county by county.[1] The only surviving county roll appears to be that for Rutland. This consists of three membranes, of which the last is an addition in a different hand. On this membrane a bond (No. 11) is transcribed that must have been executed very shortly before Aaron's death. It was doubtless late in coming to notice, possibly because it was with an obscure Samuel, the son of Solomon of London, who had immediately discounted the bond with Aaron. All the other bonds enrolled are considerably earlier in date, none being later than 1184. Apart from marginal notes the only additions made to the roll in the exchequer are remarks in the case of two of the bonds to the effect that the obligations have been met and the deeds returned. Proof in these cases may have been exceptionally easy: it will be remarked that in one case (No. 4) the debtor is William Mauduit, a chamberlain of the treasury and himself a baron of the exchequer, while in the other case (No. 7) the amount involved was only a mark. The absence of a note to other bonds does not necessarily imply that they had not been discharged. There is hardly room for doubt that Richard of Bisbrooke had redeemed his bond (No. 2), for the land on which the loan was secured came into the king's hand, not as the result of the death of Aaron but as the result of the death of Samuel of Stamford, which occurred shortly afterwards, with the consequences that have been described above.[2] It is to be presumed,

[1] *Pipe Roll 3 Richard I*, p. 17, contains the heading: Rotulus de debitis Aaron Iudei in Lincollia et Euerwichesira. The details for these two counties extend to p. 24. Evidently similar rolls underlie the parallel items in other counties, e.g. Essex (p. 32), Norfolk and Suffolk (pp. 50–1).

[2] Pp. 138–9. Since no account is rendered for Aaron's debts in Rutland, the pipe rolls do not afford the means of verifying this inference.

however, that in this and other cases, where there is no annotation, any sums apparently due were put into collection and that if the debtor had paid the whole or part of the debt he disputed the claim. The pipe rolls afford a number of instances of successfully disputed claims.[1] The roll itself contains no indication of the subsequent processes.

This roll was known to Joseph Jacobs, who printed extracts from it, but he evidently had difficulty in reading it.[2]

P.R.O., Exchequer K.R. Accounts, E. 101/249/1

### ROTELANDE SIRE
#### [1] ROBERTUS PERSONA DE BITEBROC

Sciant presentes et futuri quod ego Robertus persona de Bitebroc debeo Aaron Iudeo Lincollie sexcies viginti summas et v. summas de auena ad mensura[m] de Stanford et pleuiaui eo quod ille due summe faciunt vnam magnam scutellam ad mensuram Lincollie et totum hoc bladum reddam ei infra xv. dies summonitionis sue et hoc affidaui tenendum. Et ego Ricardus de Bitebroc sum plegius de toto blado predicto et debeo eidem Aaron ex parte mea xl. summas de auena ad eandem mensuram redendas similiter infra xv. dies summonitionis sue et hoc affidaui tenendum.

#### [2] RICARDUS DE BITEBROK *ibidem*

Sciant presentes et futuri quod ego Ricardus de Bitebroc debeo Aaron Iudeo Lincollie decem libras de esterlingis quas accepi ab eo ad octabas sancti Michaelis proximi[3] post obitum Ricardi de Luci.[4] Et pro vnaquaque libra dabo ei vnaquaque ebdomeda duos denarios de lucro quamdiu hoc debitum per grantum suum tenuero. Et pro toto debito predicto, scilicet catallo et lucro, inuadiaui ei totam terram meam de Bitebroc donec ipse habuerit totum debitum predictum, scilicet catallum et lucrum, et si hanc terram non possum ei warantizare dabo ei

---

[1] *Pipe Roll 9 Richard I*, pp. 11, 61–2; *10 Richard I*, pp. 43, 64, 98–9; *1 John*, pp. 140, 152; *3 John*, pp. 4, 183; *4 John*, p. 223. Cf. *Pipe Roll 8 Richard I*, p. 169, an instance of debts put in collection although the bonds were missing.

[2] *Jews of Angevin England*, pp. 66–7, 87–8.

[3] *Sic*.

[4] Richard de Lucy died in July 1179. The octave of the Michaelmas following was 6 October.

excambium ad valenciam huius ad grantum suum, et hoc affidaui tenendum. Et ego Robertus persona de Bitebroc sum plegius de toto debito predicto, scilicet catello et lucro, ad faciendum inde grantum predicti Aaron infra xv. dies summonicionis sue, nisi predictus Ricardus fecerit, et hoc affidaui tenendum.

### [3] HERBERTUS PERSONA DE WISSENDENE *ibidem*

Sciant presentes et futuri quod ego Herbertus persona de Wissendene debeo Aaron Iudeo Lincollie septies xx$^{ti}$ marcas argenti reddendas a secundo festo sancti Michaelis post obitum Ricardi de Luci[1] in vi. annos, scilicet vnoquoque anno reddam ei xx. marcas ad duos terminos in anno, ad Rogaciones[2] x. marcas et ad Vincula sancti Petri[3] x. marcas, et sic de anno in annum quousque totum debitum persoluatur. Primus terminus recipiendi est ad secundas Rogaciones[4] post obitum Ricardi de Luci. Et si forte aliquis istorum terminorum preteriret dabo ei vnaquaque ebdomada ii. denarios de lucro pro qualibet libra quamdiu debitum per grantum suum tenebo, et hoc affidaui tenendum et sigillo meo confirmaui.

### [4] WILLELMUS MAUDUIT *ibidem*

Sciant tam presentes quam futuri quod ego Willelmus Mauduit camerarius domini regis debeo Viues filio Aaron xxx. et duas libras esterlingorum ii. solidos minus reddendas ad festum sancti Andree[5] proximum post obitum Ricardi Cantuariensis archiepiscopi.[6] Et nisi tunc reddidero dabo ei de lucro i. denarium pro libra in ebdomada quamdiu debitum tenuero per grantum suum, et hoc ei affidaui.

*Carta ista de xxxii. libris quieta est per quitanciam et reddita.*

### [5] RADULFUS PRIOR DE BROC *ibidem*

Sciant presentes et futuri quod ego Radulfus prior de Broc et canonici eiusdem loci debemus Aaron Iudeo Lincollie tresdecim libras quas recepimus ab eo ad festum sancti Luce[7] proximum postquam

---

[1] The second Michaelmas after Richard de Luci's death was 29 September 1180.
[2] Rogations: the three days preceding Ascension Day.
[3] 1 August.
[4] Not the second day of the Rogations, but the second series of Rogation days after July 1179, i.e. 11–13 May 1181.
[5] 30 November.     [6] 17 February 1184.     [7] 18 October.

Walterus de Constanciis fuit sacratus in episcopum Lincolniensem.[1]
Et hoc debitum debemus ei pro negocio domus nostre. Et debemus ei
reddere de lucro in vnaquaque ebdomoda pro vnaquaque libra vnum
denarium quamdiu hoc debitum per grantum eius tenebimus et hoc
pacti sumus ei in verbo veritatis. Et ego Herbertus de Wissendene et
ego Robertus de Brante[stona] sumus plegii de toto catallo et lucro et
vterque nostrum de toto ad faciendum grantum eius infra xl. dies sue
summonicionis, si idem prior et canonici non reddiderint. Quod si
reddiderint omnes quieti erunt. Et hoc affidamus ei tenendum nos et
heredes nostri ei et heredibus suis.

## [6] SYMON FILIUS PAGANI *ibidem*

Scient presentes et futuri quod ego Simon filius Pagani de Rihale
debeo Aaron Iudeo Lincollie xx. solidos de esterlingis[2] quos accepi ab
eo xv. diebus ante Purificacionem sancte Marie[3] proximam post obitum
magistri Petri de Melide, pro quibus dabo ei vnaquaque ebdomada i.
denarium de lucro quamdiu eos per grantum suum tenuero, et hoc
affidaui tenendum. Et ego Aluredus de Rihale sum plegius de toto
debito predicto, scilicet catallo et lucro, per fidem meam.

## [7] TRUUE *ibidem*

Sciant presentes et futuri quod ego Truue debeo Aaron Iudeo Lincollie vnam marcam argenti reddendam ad Pascha proximum postquam comes Galfridus Brutannie[4], filius regis Anglie, factus fuit miles,[5]
et si vlterius illam teneam reddam eam ei ad summonicionem suam,
et hoc affidaui tenendum.
*Carta ista de i. marca quieta est et reddita*

## [8] COMES ALBERICUS *ibidem*

Sciant presentes et futuri quod ego comes Albericus de Dammartin
debeo Benedicto filio Ysaac Iudeo Lincollie centum libras et quindecim
libras de esterlingis de quibus debeo ei reddere viginti libras ad Natale
Domini anno regni regis Henrici secundi xxx⁰ primo[6] et alias viginti

---

[1] 3 July 1183.    [2] MS. esterlingorum.
[3] 2 February. But the year of the death of Peter of Melide is unknown.
[4] *Sic.*
[5] Count Geoffrey was knighted on 6 August 1178. Easter 1179 fell on 1 April.
[6] 25 December 1184.

libras ad Pascha proximum sequens et alias viginti libras ad festum sancti Michaelis primum sequens et alias viginti libras ad Natale Domini primum sequens et alias viginti libras ad Pascha primum sequens et quindecim libras ad festum sancti Michaelis primum sequens. Et sciendum est quod ante hos terminos nullum lucrum ei debeo de hoc debito, nam totum lucrum ante hos terminos computatum est in hac prefata summa, set si ad hos terminos non soluam ei hos denarios, vel saltem infra xv. dies post vnumquemque terminum, a xv. diebus post vnumquemque terminum in antea dabo ei de lucro pro vnaquaque libra que deficiet ad terminum vnum denarium in ebdomada quamdiu hoc debitum tenebo per grantum suum. Et pro hoc catallo et lucro inuadiaui ei totam terram meam de Rihale et de Nortone et de Wake-lingewurde ad accipiendum inde predictum catallum et lucrum et hec vadia debeo ei warantizare. Et hec omnia ei affidaui ei tenenda.

## [9] HUGO PERSONA ECCLESIE DE LUFFENHAM

Sciant presentes et futuri quod ego Hugo [persona] ecclesie de Luffenam debeo x. marcas argenti Deulesaut Iudeo de Stanford reddendas ad Pascha proximum postquam rex Francie orandi gracia venit Cantuariam,[1] et si forte tunc ei non reddidero dabo singulis ebdomadis iii. denarios in ebdomada pro libra de lucro quamdiu eas assensu eius tenuero. Hanc conuencionem affidaui tenendam ego vel heredes mei Iudeo vel heredibus suis et hii prefati debiti sumus fideiussores, ego Henricus persona de Morcot et ego Robertus persona de Bitlisbroc, et hoc tenendum affidauimus et iurauimus et sigillis nostris confirmauimus.

(m. 1d)  *Summa cc et li. libri et xi. solidi et iiii. denarii.*

### ROTELANDE

(m. 2)              ROTELANDE SIRE

## [10] HERBERTUS PERSONA DE WISSENDENA

Sciant tam futuri quam presentes quod ego Herbertus clericus persona ecclesie de Wissendena debeo Deulesalt Iudeo de Stamfort lxxx. marcas argenti et xii. marcas reddendum in viiito annis scilicet vnoquoque anno xi. marcas et dimidiam marcam argenti duobus terminis per annum. Primus terminus reddendi est ad octabas sancti

[1] Louis VII visited the shrine of St Thomas on 23 August 1179. Easter 1180 fell on 20 April.

Andree,[1] alter terminus ad octabas Clause Pentecostes,[2] ad vtrumque terminum v. marcas argenti et x. solidos. Primus terminus reddendi incepit ad proximum festum sancti Andree postquam Henricus rex Anglie filius Matillidis imperatricis recepit hominia Scottorum et liganciam Scocie apud Eboracum.[3] Et inde sunt plegii Willelmus decanus de Saitona, Symon Basset, Ricardus de Freneto, Willelmus de Fredneto, Willelmus filius Akardi, Robertus filius Ricardi de Brantestona, Adam de Brantestona, Henricus filius Grimbaldi, Gilebertus de Berch, Symon de Ocham, Willelmus de Westona, Hernisius sacerdos de Wissendena Willelmus persona de Cottes Mora, Ricardus persona de Thy, Nicolaus de Thinincwella, Robertus sacerdos de Horna, Adam de Hayuilla, Odo pincerna, Hugo de Berch, Martinus de Hegeluestona. Et hanc conuencionem affidaui tenere, et si Herbertus deficeret vnusquisque plegiorum reddet ad terminos prelocutos quantum ad eum pertineret sicut Herbertus debet.

(m. 2d)          *ROTULUS DE ROTELANDE*

(m. 3)                    ROTELONDE

### [11] HENRICUS PERSONA

Sciant tam presentes quam futuri quod ego Henricus persona ecclesie de Morcote debeo Samueli Iudeo filio Salomonis de Londoniis xl. et v^que marcas argenti quas reddam ei in vii. annos et dimidium annum, scilicet in vnoquoque anno vi. marcas ad festum sancti Michaelis et in octauo anno iii. marcas ad festum sancti Michaelis, et tunc sum quietus de predictis xl. et v. marcis. Primus terminus primi anni est ad festum sancti Michaelis proximum postquam Iohannes filius domini regis rediit primo de Hibernia cum excercitu suo[4] et tunc reddam ei vi. marcas et sic in singulis annis reddam ei ad festum sancti Michaelis vi. marcas. Et ego Ricardus Arbalester de Seitone sum plegius, reddens et debitor versus predictum Iudeum pro toto debito ad faciendum inde grantum suum ad predictos terminos si predictus Henricus non fecerit. Et ego

---

[1] 30 November.
[2] The octave of the Close of Pentecost is the second Sunday after Whit Sunday. In 1176 it fell on 6 June.
[3] 15 August 1175.
[4] According to R. de Diceto (*Historical Works*, ii. 39) John arrived in England on 17 December 1185. The news would become generally known towards the end of the month.

predictus Henricus tradidi Ricardo predicto, qui filius meus est, et Samueli predicto omnes decimas meas garbarum de Morcote habendas et tenendas in manibus suis in predictis vii. annis et dimidio pro predicto debito, excepta decima vnius bouate quam Hugo filius Oin tenet. Et in octauo anno habebo medietatem decimarum et illi aliam medietatem. Et ego predictus Ricardus qui sum plegius debiti predicti recepi medietatem decimarum contra Iudeum pro iii. marcis quas reddam eidem Iudeo ad duos terminos, ad festum sancti Andree xx. solidos et ad Pasca xx. solidos, et si preteriero aliquem predictorum terminorum dabo ei pro singulis xx. solidis in singulis ebdomadis duos denarios pro lucro quamdiu eos eius assensu tenuero. Et ego debeo warantizare predicto Iudeo predictas decimas de Morcote ita quod, si predictus Henricus eas difforciauerit vel aliquis alius, ego reddam ei in vnoquoque anno predictorum vii. annorum vi. marcas ad festum sancti Michaelis et in octauo anno iii. marcas ad festum sancti Michaelis, et si preteriero aliquem predictorum terminorum dabo ei pro singulis libris in singulis ebdomadis duos denarios pro lucro quamdiu eas eius assensu tenuero. Has conuentiones affidauimus ego Ricardus et predictos[1] Henricus et heredes nostri tenendas predicto Iudeo et heredibus sius, testibus sigillis nostris.

[1] *Sic.*

## IV. BOND OF AVIGAI OF LONDON

THIS BOND IS A further illustration of the variant forms used in the twelfth century. It has previously been printed, though not quite accurately and with contractions unextended, by J. H. Round, and it has been summarized by Joseph Jacobs, who suggested two possible interpretations, neither of which is, however, acceptable.[1]

The basis of the transaction is a loan to William of Tottenham of 80 marks, incurred at Martinmas (11 November) 1183, half of which had to be repaid by the following Christmas. To secure the loan the borrower entered into a bond for 100 marks, with a defeasance, which was embodied in the bond and was not, as later practice would require, endorsed upon the deed. If the terms of the defeasance had been observed, then the outcome would have been as follows. The borrower would have repaid 40 marks capital plus 45 shillings interest at Christmas. The loan would then have been reduced to 40 marks, upon which interest at the rate of $2\frac{1}{2}$ marks a quarter would have been due until the capital had been repaid. If the interest payments were not maintained any balance due was converted into capital bearing interest at the rate of 2d. in the £ a week. The manor of Tottenham was gaged as security for the debt, but the creditors were not to have possession unless the debtor failed to observe the terms of the bond, that is to keep up his payments of interest, whether under the defeasance or the original bond, whichever was effective. There was, however, to be no foreclosure in the ordinary sense, but the creditors would have the right to lease the manor until capital and interest were repaid.

What was the ultimate effect of the transaction is uncertain, but

---

[1] *Ancient Charters* (Pipe Roll Society), pp. 82–5; *Jews of Angevin England*, pp. 80, 423. Hubert Hall also gave an interpretation of the bond in *Court Life under the Plantagenets*, pp. 230–1.

not many years later the manor was in the possession of Earl David of Scotland, to whom it was confirmed by Richard I and subsequently by King John. Prior to the latter confirmation the manor seems to have been mortgaged to Abraham, the son of the Rabbi, but there is no reason for connecting this mortgage with the bond of 1183. What seems to have happened is that the earl acquired the namor (to which he had hereditary claims) from William of Tottenham in consideration of freeing him from his debt to the Jews and that the earl, in turn, mortgaged the manor. The earl seems, in any case, to have had extensive dealing with Jewish moneylenders, from which he freed himself by a series of arrangements with King John.[1]

P.R.O., D.L. 27/189

Sciant presentes et futuri quod ego Willelmus de Toteham debeo Auigaie iudee Londonie et Abrahe filio suo centum marcas argenti ad festum sancti Martini primum postquam Walterus de Custanz fuit consecratus in episcopum Lincolniensem[2] et pro centum marcis pre-nominatis dabo eis nouem libras per annum de lucro quamdiu has centum marcas prenominatas de catallo tenuero. Et pro his centum marcis prenominatis de catallo et pro nouem libris prenominatis de lucro inuadiaui eis manerium meum de Toteham cum omnibus per-tinenciis scilicet quicquid ibi habeo absque ullo retinemento et ex eodem manerio illum saisiui. Et has nouem libras prenominatas de lucro red-dam illis iiii. terminis anni, scilicet ad Natale primum post festum sancti Martini prenominatum reddam illis xlv. solidos et ad Pascha primum sequens xlv. solidos et ad festum sancti Iohannis Baptiste primum sequens xlv. solidos et ad festum sancti Michaelis primum sequens xlv. solidos et ita de anno in annum reddam eis nouem libras de lucro quamdiu has centum marcas prenominatas tenuero. Et hec est conuencio inter istos prenominatos quod si Willelmus prescriptus reddiderit Iudeis prescriptis xl. marcas ad Natale primum post festum sancti Martini prenominatum tunc quietus est Willelmus prenominatus ex toto debito

---

[1] *Rotuli Chartarum*, p. 29; *Rotuli Litterarum Patentium*, pp. 15b, 22b. Earl David still owed £300 in 1208 for old debts due to Aaron of Lincoln and he also took over the debts due by his brother, William the Lion: these were of the nominal value of £2,776 (*Memoranda Roll 10 John*, pp. 34, 65).
[2] 5 July 1183.

prenominato per alias xl. marcas ex catallo sine lucro. Et ego Willelmus
prescriptus reddam predictis Iudeis x. marcas de lucro pro xl. marcis
prenominatis per annum quamdiu illas tenuero, videlicet ad Natale
prenominatum ii. marcas et dimidiam et ad Pascha primum sequens
ii. marcas et dimidiam et ad festum sancti Iohannis Baptiste primum
sequens ii. marcas et dimidiam et ad festum sancti Michaelis primum
sequens ii. marcas et dimidiam et pro xl. marcis prenominatis de catallo
et pro x. marcis de lucro inuadiaui eis prescriptum manerium de
Toteham cum omnibus [pertinenciis][1] scilicet quicquid ibi habeo
absque vllo retinemento quousque habeant catallum suum et lucrum.
Et si ad terminos prescriptos hoc debitum predictum non reddidero
predictis Iudeis dabo eis ex hoc quod remanserit vnaquaque ebdomada
pro vnaquaque libra ii. denarios de lucro quamdiu illas tenemus. Et si
terminos predictos illis non tenuero ponent predicti Iudei manerium
predictum in manum cuiuscumque voluerint quousque habeant catallum
suum et lucrum. Et nisi ad Natale prescriptum xl. marcas prescriptas
illis reddidero debuero eis centum marcas vt prescriptum est. Et has
conuenciones affidaui ego Willelmus predictus tenendas predictis Iudeis
et heredibus illorum.[2]

גילמא דטוטהם מאה זקוקים למרטין
קמֹד בתשע ליט לשנה[3]

[1] MS. omits.

[2] The equestrian seal of William of Tottenham is affixed.

[3] I am indebted to Mr Cecil Roth for the translation: 'William of Totham
100 marks at Martin[mas] in the year 144(= 1183) at £9 a year.' This merely
puts into other words the first sentence of the bond.

# V. BOND OF JURNET OF NORWICH

This bond is another illustration of twelfth-century forms. It may be dated early in 1190, for John of Oxford, bishop of Norwich, who is mentioned as a crusader, was absolved by the pope from his vow to take the cross apparently in August–September 1190.[1] He must therefore have engaged himself to accompany Richard I's crusade, which was in preparation in the latter months of 1189. In form the bond is one for the repayment of a capital sum by instalments spread over two years. The loan was apparently negotiated at the feast of the Purification or Candlemas (2 February) and the first instalment was due at the following Midsummer (Nativity of St John the Baptist, 24 June), the second at Michaelmas (29 September), the third at Candlemas, and the rest at the same dates in the second twelve months. Interest was included in these instalments and the actual loan was, of course, much less than £6. If any sum remained due after the last payment date (2 February 1192), interest became payable at the rate of 2d. in the £ a week. The debtor pledged his land, houses and rents and all his chattels, but there is nothing to suggest that the creditors entered into possession.

Tiberius C. ix., fo. 120b

Notum sit omnibus quod ego Robertus Benne debeo reddere Iurneto Iudeo et Murieli vxori sue vi. libras argenti, ad proximum Natale sancti Iohannis postquam Iohannes Norwicensis episcopus crucem acceperit xx. solidos et ad festum sancti Michaelis sequens xx. solidos et ad Purificacionem sancte Marie [sequens][2] xx. solidos et ad Natale sancti Iohannis sequens xx. solidos et ad festum sancti Michaelis sequens xx. solidos et ad Purificacionem sancte Marie sequens xx. solidos. Et si vlterius tenuero, dabo eis singulis ebdomadis per annum pro quaqua

---

[1] *Gesta Ricardi*, ii. 115; R. de Hovedene, *Chronica*, iii. 42.
[2] MS. omits.

libra ii. denarios de lucro quamdiu tenuero per grantum illorum. Et pro isto debito et lucro inuadiaui eis totas terras meas et domos et redditus meos quos habeo infra willam Norwici et extra et omnia catalla mea. Hoc pactum affidaui tenendum eis ad grantum et summonicionem eorum.

# VI. DUNSTABLE PRIORY AND THE JEWS

THE THREE DOCUMENTS HERE printed are important for the light they throw upon otherwise obscure aspects of the English Jewry under John. They come from the early years of the priorate of Richard de Morins at Dunstable. Richard, who before entering religion had been a distinguished canonist and had taught at Bologna, had been elected prior in 1202,[1] on the resignation of his predecessor Thomas, under whom the affairs of the priory seem to have fallen into some disorder. It is clear from the second and third documents that the dubious practice of raising money by selling corrodies and prebends had been followed[2] and that part of the monastic property had been alienated. It is probable that Prior Thomas had had recourse to Jewish moneylenders,[3] and it is quite certain that he had stood surety for the prior of St Bartholomew's when he had borrowed from Aaron of Lincoln.[4] The extent to which the priory was involved is unknown but, at all events, Jews were very much on Prior Richard's mind: he himself relates how he saw in a vision two Jews who foretold the coming of Anti-Christ.[5] He seems to have determined from the outset to free his house from entanglements with the Jews, and it is ironical that he should have been the intended victim of Moses, the son of Le Brun, who endeavoured to plant upon him a spurious bond purporting to have been given by Prior Thomas:[6] Moses was certainly careless in selecting one of the ablest lawyers of the day upon whom to play his tricks.

The story the documents tell revolves round William of

---

[1] For Richard's career see *Annales Monastici*, iii. x–xii, and *Traditio*, vii. 329–39.

[2] For this practice see G. G. Coulton, *Five Centuries of Religion*, iii. 240–7.

[3] Otherwise it is unlikely that a spurious bond would have been confected in his name.

[4] *Dunstable Cartulary* (Bedfordshire Hist. Record Soc., *Publications*, vol. x), p. 84.

[5] *Annales Monastici*, iii. 33. He is the author of the Dunstable Annals.

[6] Cole, *Documents*, p. 312; below, p. 287.

'Husseburne', that is Husborne Crawley, not many miles away from the priory. He had purchased from the priory a 'prebend', in effect an annual rent to be paid to him partly in grain and partly in money,[1] and also some land in the township of Herne subject to a quit rent of 40 pence. On both prebend and land he had been forced to raise money by borrowing from a number of Jewish moneylenders. Evidently there were successive transactions: five Jews are named and William seems to have been uncertain whether he was entirely quit of others from whom he had borrowed. Perhaps it was *ex abundanti cautela* that Prior Richard required an indemnity against any lenders not named in the quitclaim, but other lenders there had evidently been. As William became more deeply involved, he had, in order to assure his subsistence, purchased a corrody from the priory—he is not likely to have done this while still a man of means—and this corrody he had had in due course to pledge to an unnamed Jew. Now a corrody normally implied residence in the monastery or at least the right to take meals there, and that this right should pass to a Jew was a scandal upon which the bishop of the diocese would certainly frown. It was then with the bishop's agreement that the Jew's claim was bought off for 13 marks. This money could be found only by selling the corrody once more, a course the bishop was willing to sanction to avoid the greater scandal. In some way or other from its own resources the priory found the 70 marks required to settle the claims of the moneylenders to whom William had gaged his prebend and his land. This transaction was not, however, different in principle from those in which other monastic houses were engaging at the time, except that the property the priory was acquiring had been previously alienated by the priory itself.

The first document below is not directly related to the story of William of Husborne. It is noteworthy as a surviving specimen of a licence given by the lord of a borough, in this case a monastic borough, permitting a Jew and his son to occupy premises for the

---

[1] *Prebenda* in this sense seems to be rarely used in English documents: Ducange, however, gives some pertinent examples *s.v.*

purpose of business. The terms upon which the licence was granted were not onerous: the render of a small silver spoon every six months. This was a minor item of expense, for doubtless licence had also to be obtained from the Crown and, of course, premises had to be bought or rented. There is no suggestion that the licensees, Fleming and Léon, who were members of the London Jewry, intended to take up permanent residence in the borough and, indeed, the contrary is implied. There had been Jews in Dunstable from the time of Henry II,[1] and it must be presumed that they and other Jews doing business there took out similar licences. It is quite likely that those others named in William of Husborne's quitclaim, Bendin, Aaron and Jacob, had done so, and also Moses, the son of Le Brun, who—whatever his dealings with Prior Thomas—had certainly lent a small sum to a tenant of the priory in Prior Richard's time:[2] for presumably such tenants would be expected to have recourse to the priory's licensees. The date of the licence must be put early in Richard's priorate: that is soon after 1202. For it can hardly be supposed that Fleming and Léon would do business with William of Husborne until after they had been licensed. But the date of document no. 3 and inferentially of document no. 2, William's quitclaim, must lie within the episcopate of William of Blois, bishop of Lincoln from August 1203 to May 1206, and the licence must have been granted not long after Richard became prior, for disaster did not overtake William of Husborne until after repeated recourse to money-lenders. The names of the witnesses are consistent with this date.

The substance of the three documents has been known since Thomas Hearne printed Humfrey Wanley's abstracts in 1733.[3] Slightly shortened versions of no. 1 and no. 3 were printed by G. H. Fowler in his abstract of the Dunstable Cartulary (pp. 101, 103). The three documents are now printed in full for the first

[1] *Pipe Roll 34 Henry II*, p. 127; *3 Richard I*, p. 111. No Jews appear in the receipt roll of 1194 as assessed in Dunstable and none was presumably permanently resident there.     [2] Cole, *Documents*, p. 312.

[3] *Chronicon . . . de Dunstaple*, i. xcv–xcvii. Again printed in the *Catalogue of the Harleian Manuscripts* (1808), ii. 310. Tovey reprinted in 1738 Wanley's abstract of no. 1 (*Anglia Judaica*, p. 84), presumably from Hearne.

time fom Harleian MS. 1885: as they stand there they have already been somewhat abbreviated.

I

Fo. 36*b*

Ricardus prior de Dunstaple et totus eiusdem loci conuentus . . .[1] presentibus et futuris salutem. Sciatis nos concessisse et hac carta nostra confirmasse Flemengo Iudeo de Londoniis et Leoni filio suo et suis et seruientibus eorum ire et venire et manere in villa de Dunstaple bene et in pace, quiete et honorifice. Concessimus etiam eisdem Flemengo et Leoni omnes libertates et liberas consuetudines ville de Dunstaple sicut aliquis de hominibus nostris de villa eas melius et plenius habet, nec nos nec nostri impedimentum faciamus predictis Iudeis quin lucrum suum fideliter faciant in villa nostra secundum consuetudinem Iudeorum. Et nos manutenebimus predictos Iudeos et suos et eorum seruientes et res suas in villa rationabiliter sicut faceremus si de nobis tenerent. Pro hac autem concessione nostra debet nobis predictus Flemengus quamdiu ipse moram fecerit in villa [de] Dunstaple singulis annis duo coclearia[2] argentea quorum vtrumque duodecim denarios ponderabit, vnum scilicet ad festum sancti Michaelis et alterum ad festum sancte Marie in Marcio. Si autem predictus Flemengus absens fuerit, predictus Leo filius eius eadem coclearia eisdem terminis persoluet. Hec autem concessio et conuencio tota vita predictorum Iudeorum durabit, ita quod, siue in predicta villa de Dunstaple siue alibi manserint, tota vita sua nobis predictum redditum fideliter persoluent quamdiu cartam istam retinebunt. Testes Iordanus filius Capmanni, Iohannes filius Aubree . . .

2

Fo. 43*b*

Willelmus de Husseburne . . . presentibus et futuris salutem. Sciatis me reddidisse et in perpetuum quietam clammasse priori et conuentui de Dunstaple totam prebendam meam quam idem michi concesserant et carta sua confirmauerant, scilicet quinque quartarios de frumento et quinque quartarios de auena et viii. solidos et viii. denarios,[3] que omnia singulis annis michi persoluere consueuerant. Dimisi etiam et concessi

---

[1] Supply *omnibus Christi fidelibus* or some similar phrase, and so in no. 2 and no. 3.
[2] MS., cloclearia.    [3] That is 2*d*. weekly, as in no. 3.

[et] in perpetuum quietam clammaui predictis priori et conuentui totam terram quam tenui de eisdem in villa de Hara[1] per seruitium quadraginta denariorum cum omnibus rebus ad eandem terram pertinentibus. Cartas etiam quas super predictis de predictis canonicis habui in manus eorum omnes resignaui et predictam quietam clammationem hac mea presenti carta confirmaui. Quare volo et concedo quod predicti canonici tam predictam prebendam quam predictam terram cum omnibus pertinenciis suis etc. Pro hac autem dimissione et quieta clammacione et presentis carte confirmacione predicti prior et conuentus adquietauerunt me erga Flemengum et Bendinum et Aaron et Iacobum et Leonem Iudeos de sexaginta et x. marcis. Et si quis Iudeus vel Iudea occasione alicuius inuadiationis per me facte de predictis prebenda vel terra predictos priorem et conuentum vexare voluerit, ego eos per omnia adquietabo. Testibus . . .

### 3

Fo. 36b–37a

Ricardus prior de Dunstaple et eiusdem loci conuentus . . . presentibus et futuris salutem. Sciatis nos de consensu tocius capituli nostri dedisse, concessisse et presenti carta confirmasse Iosep filio Rogeri Blundi vnius canonici conredium, scilicet vii. michas[2] et vii. galonas ceruisie et duos denarios pro campanagio per singulas[3] ebdomadas percipienda et singulis diebus vnum ferculum de potagio, si presens fuerit et illud suscipere voluerit, et hec omnia concessimus ei de domo nostra integre et plene quamdiu vixerit. Quare volumus et concedimus quod predictus Iosep predictum conredium in omnibus ita plene et sine disturbacione tota vita sua percipiat et habeat sicut Alardus capellanus vel aliquis alius conredium suum a domo nostra plenius et melius solet percipere. Pro hac autem concessione nostra dedit nobis predictus Iosep xiii. marcas argenti ad redimendum illud idem conredium de manu cuiusdam Iudei cui Willelmus de Husseburne illud impignorauerat et qui de nobis iure predicti Willelmi hoc ipsum conredium percipere solebat. Et hoc quidem fecimus consilio et assensu domini Willelmi Lincolniensis episcopi[4] vt sic bona ecclesie nostre, cum aliter non possemus, de manu Iudei liberaremus . . .

[1] Herne in Toddington, Beds.
[2] Fr. *miche*: according to Cotgrave synonymous with *pain de chapitre*.
[3] MS., singulos.
[4] William of Blois: consecrated 24 August 1203; died 10 May 1206.

## VII. GAGE BY ISAAC OF NORTHAMPTON

THIS IS AN EARLY example of the tripartite chirograph,[1] the part surviving being the left-hand top copy: a facsimile will be found in Hubert Hall's *Court Life under the Plantagenets*, facing page 36, and in the *Jewish Encyclopaedia*, v. 285. Some words of explanation are perhaps desirable. The bond (actually, in this case, a gage, *vadium*) was written three times on a rectangular piece of parchment, which was divided by a line parallel to the lower edge, while from the middle of that line another line at right angles divided the top portion into two. Along both these lines the word CYROGRAPHVM was written. In the three spaces thus formed the three copies of the bond were written: the left-hand copy began at the upper edge of the parchment below the vertical line; the right-hand copy began at the edge of the transverse line on the other side of the vertical line; and the bottom copy (or foot) began at the left-hand edge of the parchment below the transverse line. The two top copies were separated from the foot by a straight cut through the word *cyrographum* on the transverse line, and they were then separated from one another by an indented (wavy) line cutting through the word *cyrographum* on the vertical line. The left and right counter-parts, which were retained by the parties, were sealed; but the third copy (the foot), which was deposited in the *archa*, was not sealed.

The implications of the instrument need some explanation. The father of Roger of Hook (near Goole in the West Riding of Yorkshire) had borrowed from Isaac of Northampton on the security of his land. On the father's death, Roger's mother Avice was entitled to her dower of one-third of her husband's property. Half of this dower lay in Hook and the remainder in other property that had belonged to her husband and now descended to

---

[1] A chirograph of 1201 in two parts only is reproduced by Stokes and Loewe, *Starrs and Jewish Charters*, i. 24–5 (no. 1180): see also *ibid.*, pp. xiv–xv.

Roger. The dower was protected during Avice's lifetime, but on her death it would revert to Roger. However, on succeeding his father Roger found that half his inheritance (at least) was encumbered, and while he may have had the income from the rest, subject to his mother's dower, and from any land that his wife brought with her, he had no capital to pay off his father's debts. He therefore came to an arrangement (*finis*) with his creditor whereby the loan was to be paid off by annual instalments, very much as a building society's loan is today. But the total of these prospective payments, £83. 6s. 8d. or 125 marks, is regarded as the initial capital or the amount of Roger's debt to Isaac. This will be paid off at the rate of £5 a year, or £7. 10s. if Avice dies. The maximum term is therefore seventeen years, but this may be substantially reduced.

In form, this gage would seem to be what Glanville regards as a *conventio iusta*, since the annual payments reduce the principal. It is not a mortgage in the sense in which Glanville uses the word,[1] though there is, of course, no doubt that the annual payments must contain a substantial amount of interest on the original borrowing. What that original borrowing was there is no means of telling, but presumably a fraction of 125 marks. The remarkable feature of the instrument is that the gagor is Roger's wife, who was not *sui iuris*. If she had been ejected she could not have recovered the land unless her husband had been joined as plaintiff. As appears, however, on the face of this instrument, it is only one of a series of chirographs between Roger and Isaac and cannot be fully understood without them. Margery is plainly acting as Roger's agent, and presumably the reason for making her a party to the bond is to evade the difficulty that Roger held the land *ut de feodo* and Isaac *ut de vadio* and that Roger could not have a gage of his own fee, though it is difficult to see how Margery could have a gage of her husband's fee.[2]

---

[1] 'Mortuum vadium dicitur illud cuius fructus vel redditus interim percepti in nullo se acquietant' (lib. x., c. 6). The *conventio iusta* is one where 'ita convenit inter creditorem et debitorem quod exitus et redditus interim se acquietent' (lib. x, c. 8).

[2] Cf. Bracton, fo. 103*b*: Vxor autem sine viro suo stipulare non potest.

A translation of the bond was published by Hubert Hall and reproduced by Joseph Jacobs.[1] The text has not, however, hitherto been printed.

P.R.O., E. 326/11721

## CYROGRAPHUM

Sciant omnes presentes et futuri quod ego Ysaac Iudeus de Norhamton' dimisi ad firmam Margerie vxori Rogeri de Huc totam terram quam habeo in vadium de predicto Rogero viro suo pro quater xx[tl] libris et lxvi. solidis et viii. denariis argenti quos idem Rogerus michi debet de fine quem fecit michi de debito patris sui, sicud cyrographum inter nos factum testatur, tenendam et habendam predicte Margerie de me vel heredibus meis, reddendo inde annuatim michi et heredibus meis c. solidos sterlingorum, videlict quinquaginta solidos ad Pentecosten anni regni regis Iohannis vii[ml] [2] et quinquaginta solidos ad festum sancti Martini proximum sequens[3] et sic de anno in annum quamdiu predicta Margeria legitime annuatim ad statutos terminos firmam predictam michi reddiderit. Et si ita euenerit quod Auicia mater prenominati Rogeri viri sui decedat, tota medietas dotis sue in predicta villa de Huc, que me contingit secundum conuencionem alterius cyrographi inter nos facti, remanebit in manu predicte Margerie, reddendo inde annuatim michi et heredibus meis quinquaginta solidos, scilicet medietatem ad Pentecosten et medietatem ad festum sancti Martini, simul cum aliis c. solidis quos michi reddit pro terra prenominata quam ei commisi ad firmam. Et si ita contigerit quod predicta Margeria tenuerit predictum debitum xv. diebus vltra aliquem terminum vllius anni, tunc predicta Margeria michi dabit viginti solidos de pena extra firmam predictam et tota terra prenominata redibit in manu mea propria absque vlla contradictione, ita quod michi licebit terram predictam in manu mea propria retinere vel cuicumque voluero ad firmam committere, ita tamen quod commissio illa non sit ad exhereditacionem predicti Rogeri. Computando annuatim vniuersam firmam quam predicta Margeria michi reddere tenebatur in solucione principalis debiti Rogeri viri sui sicut cyrographum inter nos factum testatur. Et vt hec conuencio rata et inconcussa futuris temporibus

---

[1] *Court Life under the Plantagenets*, pp. 231–2; *Jews of Angevin England*, pp. 227–8. Jacobs' note is misleading.
[2] 29 May 1205.      [3] 11 November 1205.

permaneat sigillorum vtrorumque aposicione corroborata est et pes istius cyrographi in archa domini regis apud Eboracum remanet in testimonio.[1]

יצחק בר משה[2]

[1] The seal-tag only remains.
[2] Concealed by the fold for the seal-tag and not shown in the facsimiles. This is the signature in Hebrew of 'Isaac son of R. Moses'.

## VIII. BOND OF LÉON OF WARWICK

THIS BOND IS DATED by reference to the death of Hubert Walter, which occurred on 13 July 1205. The position it discloses is this. Miles of Bray, on succeeding his father, was in debt to Léon of Warwick under a bond for £31. 16s., apparently with accrued interest. He was endeavouring to negotiate a settlement (*finis*), but meanwhile he agreed to pay 4 marks a year interest in half-yearly instalments. If, however, he failed to keep these terms, he was to pay interest on the balance of interest due at the rate of 2d. in the mark a week. He agreed to make a further payment of a mark in consideration of this agreement, but he could not find even so small a sum in ready money and it was contemplated that this, too, would be added to the debt and would bear interest. It is not surprising, therefore, that he had to sacrifice part of his estate and within a short time he parted with one of the two mortgaged properties, Nettleswell, to Waltham Abbey.[1]

Tiberius C. ix., fo. 132b
Printed, *Cartulary of Old Wardon*, p. 363

Sciant presentes et futuri quod ego Milo de Bray debeo Leoni Iudeo de Warewic quatuor marcas argenti reddendas ei duobus terminis, scilicet ad Mediam Quadragesimam[2] proximum post obitum Huberti Walteri Cantuariensis archiepiscopi duas marcas et ad festum sancti Michaelis proximum post duas marcas, et sic de anno in annum reddam illi iiii. marcas argenti ad predictos terminos donec finem fecero de carta xxxi. librarum et xvi. solidorum que est sub nomine Rogeri patris mei et meo. Et si aliquem terminum preteriero dabo ei singulis septemanis pro singula marca duos denarios de lucro ad grantum suum. Et pro hoc debito, catallo et lucro, inuadiaui ei totam terram meam de Maudone[3] et de Nethleswelle[4] et omnes alias terras meas vbicumque sint cum

---

[1] Before 1210: see G. H. Fowler, *Cartulary of Old Warden*, p. 363.
[2] Mid-Lent 1206 fell on 12 March.
[3] Maulden, Beds.          [4] Nettleswell, Essex.

omnibus pertinenciis suis sine vllo retinemento ad recipiendum inde predictum debitum et lucrum. Et pro hac conuencione tenenda dabo ei infra xv. dies festi sancti Michaelis proximum post obitum predicti Huberti Walteri Cantuariensis archiepiscopi vnam marcam argenti in gersuma. Et si vlterius illam tenuero dabo ei singulis septemanis pro predicta marca ii. denarios de lucro ad grantum suum. Et quisquis michi hanc cartam portauerit ex parte predicti Iudei vel heredum suorum reddam illi predictum debitum et lucrum. Hoc affidaui ei fideliter tenendum et heredibus suis pro me et heredibus meis et sigillo meo confirmaui.[1]

[1] There is a marginal note: Ista queritur in pixide Iudaismi.

# IX. DEEDS OF ROBERT AND HENRY BRAYBROOKE

THE DEEDS IN THIS series are all concerned with the acquisition of land by Robert and Henry of Braybrooke in the reigns of John and Henry III as the result of borrowings by landowners from Jewish moneylenders. They are printed from Sloane MS. 986 in approximate order of date. In no case do all the deeds relating to a single transaction appear to have been preserved, and the series certainly does not represent all the transactions of this kind in which the Braybrookes were engaged.[1] A few of the deeds are conveyances from the borrowers to the Braybrookes; one is an indemnity; but for the most part they are acquittances (or starrs) in various forms given by the creditors, sometimes to the borrowers, sometimes to the Braybrookes. The originals are no longer extant. The scribe who transcribed them appears to have found the starrs difficult to decipher and in two cases he stopped short after copying the opening words.[2] The copies leave a good deal to be desired and appear sometimes to be abbreviated. Words necessary to complete the sense have been supplied within square brackets. The Hebrew inscriptions on the instruments were beyond the copyist's power to reproduce.

Although the starrs are obviously related to the deeds which conveyed property to the Braybrookes, it is only occasionally possible to match documents relating to the same transaction. Even where the documents can be matched, there may be discrepancies which it is difficult to explain. As a rule there is no mention in the conveyance of the true consideration for which the vendor transferred the property, though now and again it may be

[1] Above, p. 101, n. 3. There is reason to suppose that a number of starrs before the transcriber of Sloane 986 were not reproduced: see following note.

[2] At fo. 75 there is an unfinished entry: 'Ego qui inferius sum sigillatus recongnosco veram recongnicionem quod acquietaui Henricum de Braibroc . . .' Again at fo. 76b, the scribe has commenced transcribing a starr, 'Aaron filius Abraham recongnosco etc. pro se et Samuel' fratre . . .', and has got no farther.

stated that the grantee has acquitted the debts due to a Jewish moneylender; it is the exception therefore for the grant, or the fine that often confirmed the grant, to indicate the real nature of the transaction. One sequence of documents (no. 5) is sufficient illustration. A few of the documents bear a precise indication of date. As for the rest, those with which Robert is concerned are not later than 1211. The king's charters of confirmation of 25 July 1208[1] and 24 March 1211[2] assist in dating some documents more precisely. Robert was alive at the quinzaine of Easter (17 April)[3] but dead before Michaelmas of that year, when he was succeeded by his son Henry as sheriff of four counties, Bedford, Buckingham, Northampton and Rutland. Henry, as his heir, accounted in his place for the twelve months ended at Michaelmas 1211. The documents with which Henry is concerned are presumably for the most part subsequent to his father's death and some undoubtedly are, though there seems no reason why certain of them should not be earlier. He was dead by the spring of 1234 at latest.[4]

The folio references are to the Sloane MS.

I

Fo. 75b

Ego qui inferius sigillatus sum Ysaac filius Sampsonis recongnosco veram recongnicionem quod Ricardus filius Simonis de Foxton' et heredes [sui] quieti sunt de me et heredibus meis et de omnibus heredibus matris mee Ioie de omnibus debitis exactis, siue de plegiis siue de aliqua alia calumpnia, que venerit per matrem meam Ioie vel per me a creacione seculi vsque ad finem. Et si quis ex parte matris mee aliquod debitum exigerit, super me est acquietandum illum Ricardum filium Simonis et heredes suos. Et pro hac quietancia soluit idem Robertus[5]

---

[1] *Rot. Chart.*, pp. 180–1.
[2] Sloane 986, fo. 67b–71: not on existing Charter Rolls.
[3] When a fine was levied to which he was a party (below, p. 274, n. 1).
[4] *Excerpta e Rotulis Finium*, i. 258: his widow fines on 22 June 1234 for freedom to re-marry.
[5] Robert of Braybrooke, who had doubtless been previously mentioned in a clause that the transcriber has omitted. The grant of nine virgates and six tofts in Foxton by Richard fitz Simon to Robert Braybrooke, which will be found at fo. 32b–33, was confirmed by the king's charter of 25 July 1208 (*Rot. Chart.*, p. 180b).

predicto Ricardo filio Simonis l. marcas argenti, scilicet xx. marcas ad opus regis et xxx. marcas ad opus meum proprium.

2

Fo. 75. Printed, *Cartulary of Old Wardon*, p. 362

Ego Samuel filius Iacobi qui inferius sigilatus sum recongnosco veram recongnicionem quod Margeria Foliot et Ricardus Foliot et Elias Foliot et Wischardus Leydet et heredes sui sunt quieti de auo meo Samuel et de patre meo Iacobo et de heredibus suis de me et heredibus meis de omnibus calumpniis et plegiis a creacione seculi vsque ad Mediam Quadragesimam decimi anni rengni regis Iohannis[1] pro ccc. marcis argenti de fine facto inter me et Robertum de Braibroc. Et super me est warantizandum prescriptos et acquietandum de omnibus debitis, calumpniis et plegiis que scripta sunt nomine aui mei Samuel et patris mei Iacobi et versus omnes heredes patris mei per predictum finem.

3

Fo. 75b

Ego Ysaac filius Simonis cyrographarius recongnosco [veram recongnicionem] quod recepi de debito Roberti de Cortenay de carta xxxi. librarum, que quidem carta est sub nomine meo et Roberti de Cortenay, xii. libras et xviii. solidos de animalibus et bladis venditis de villa de Lenford[2] et item recepi vi. libras de animalibus et bladis venditis de villa de Rodeston',[3] et predictos denarios, scilicet xviii. libras et xviii. solidos, recepi de Roberto de Braibroc, qui michi liberauit animalia et blada inuenta in eisdem villis e precepto domini regis, et predictum receptum recepi vi⁰ die proximo post festum sancti Nicholai xi⁰ anno regni regis Iohannis.[4]

4

Fo. 75b
Printed, *Cartulary of Old Wardon*, p. 362

Ego Samuel filius Iacobi recongnosco [veram recongnicionem] quod Wischardus Leydet et Margeria vxor eius et heredes sui quieti sunt de

[1] Mid-Lent (8 March) 1209.     [2] Linford, Bucks.
[3] Radstone, Northants.     [4] 12 December 1209.

omnibus debitis que idem Wischardus, Ricardus Foliot, Elias Foliot et
Margeria mater ipsius Ricardi et Elie michi debuerunt et fratribus meis
et heredibus Iacobi filii Samuel de Norhanton' vel aliquibus parentibus
meis per cyrographum vel per talliam veterem siue sint de plegiis vel
aliis debitis. Similiter Robertus de Braibroc et heredes [sui quieti] sunt
de fine facto pro predictis debitoribus et super me [est] acquietandum
eos versus fratres meos et heredes patris mei, et similiter Robertus dictus
et heredes sui quieti sunt de me et heredibus meis de omnibus debitis a
creacione seculi vsque ad finem. Anno xi⁰.[1]

5A

Fo. 75*b*

Ego Samuel filius Iacobi qui [inferius sigillatus sum] recongnosco
[veram recongnicionem] quod Eustacius de Watford' quietus est versus
me et heredes meos de debito quod debuit super pratum de Sanford'
patri meo et heredibus suis, et acquietancia hac nullam ego vel heredes
mei habemus calumpniam in predicto prato quod dedit Roberto de
Braibroc, quia ei omnino dictum pratum quietum clamaui.

5B

Fo. 13

CARTA EUSTACII DE ARDENE

Sciant presentes et futuri quod ego Eustacius de Ardene dedi et
presenti carta mea confirmaui Roberto de Braibroc pro homagio suo
et seruicio et pro decem marcis argenti quas michi dedit totum pratum
meum in Watford' quod vocatur pratum de Sandford' cum omnibus
pertinenciis suis, habendum et tenendum predicto Roberto et heredibus
suis de me et heredibus meis libere et quiete, integre et hereditarie,
reddendo inde annuatim vnam bisanciam vel duos solidos ad festum
sancti Michaelis pro omni seruicio et exaccione seculari. Et ego Eustacius et heredes mei warantizabimus predicto Roberto et heredibus
suis totum predictum pratum cum pertinenciis contra omnes gentes.
Hiis testibus . . .[2]

---

[1] 11th year of John, 7 May 1209–26 May 1210.

[2] This grant is not mentioned in the king's confirmation of 25 July 1208, but
it is in the confirmation of 24 March 1211 (fo. 69): it must therefore have been
made between these dates. Henry Braybrooke subsequently granted this meadow
to Ralf of Thorpe (Torp) for a perpetual rent of eight marks a year (fo. 18).

5C

Fo. 13

### CONFIRMACIO EUSTACII FILII EIUSDEM

Sciant presentes et futuri quod ego Eustacius filius Eustacii de Ardene concessi et presenti carta mea confirmaui Roberto de Braibroc et heredibus suis donacionem quam Eustacius pater meus eidem Roberto fecit de toto prato de Sandford, habendum et tenendum predicto Roberto et heredibus suis libere et quiete, integre et hereditarie, sicut carta predicti Eustacii patris mei, quam idem Robertus inde habet, testatur. Hiis testibus . . .

6

Fo. 35*b*
Printed in part, *Cartulary of Old Wardon*, pp. 361–2

Sciant presentes et futuri quod ego Wischardus Leydet filius Cristiane et Margeria Foliot vxor eiusdem Wischardi, filia et heres Ricardi Foliot, dedimus et presenti carta nostra confirmauimus Roberto de Braibroc pro homagio suo et seruicio et pro quingentis marcis argenti quibus adquietauit nos versus Samuelem filium Iacobi Iudeum de Norhanton' et heredes predicti Iacobi pro debito predicti Ricardi Foliot totam villam de Sutton' in Bedefordesyre, que est de feodo regis Scocie, cum aduocacione ecclesie eiusdem ville et cum omnibus pertinenciis suis in dominicis et homagiis et seruiciis et redditibus et in omnibus aliis pertinenciis suis, in villa et extra villam, sine quolibet retenemento, exceptis seruiciis tenencium nostrorum in Holm' et in Straton', habendam et tenendam predicto Roberto et heredibus suis de nobis et heredibus nostris in perpetuum, bene et in pace, libere et quiete, integre et hereditarie, per seruicium feodi dimidii militis pro omnibus seruiciis. Et ego predictus Wyschardus et ego predicta Margeria et heredes nostri warantizabimus predicto Roberto et heredibus suis totam predictam villam de Sutton' cum aduocacione ecclesie eiusdem ville et cum omnibus aliis pertinenciis suis, sicut predictum est, contra omnes gentes. Hiis testibus . . . [1]

[1] The date is presumably late 1210 or early 1211. The charter was supplemented by a fine of 17 April 1211 (Hunter, *Fines*, i. 81–2). The property had already been included in the king's charter of confirmation of 24 March 1211.

7

Fo. 34
Printed in part, *Cartulary of Old Wardon*, p. 361

Sciant presentes et futuri quod ego Wichardus Leydet filius Cristiane dedi et presenti carta mea confirmaui Roberto de Braybroc pro homagio suo et seruicio et pro ducentis marcis argenti de quibus adquietauit me versus Samuelem filium Iacobi Iudeum de Norhanton' et heredes predicti Iacobi totam terram meam de Estrelangeton[1] cum aduocacione ecclesie eiusdem ville et cum omnibus pertinenciis suis in dominicis et homagiis et seruiciis et redditibus et cum omnibus aliis pertinenciis suis, in villa et extra villam, sine quolibet retenemento, et homagium Roberti de Westerelangeton' cum toto seruicio suo et cum pertinenciis, scilicet seruicium feodi vnius militis cum pertinenciis quod de me tenuit in Westerelangeton',[2] habenda et tenenda predicto Roberto de Braybroc et heredibus suis de me et heredibus meis in perpetuum, bene et in pace, libere et quiete, integre et hereditarie, per seruicium feodi duorum militum pro omnibus seruiciis. Et ego Wischardus et heredes mei warantizabimus predicto Roberto de Braybroc et heredibus suis totam predictam [terram] in Esterelangton' cum aduocacione ecclesie eiusdem ville et cum omnibus pertinenciis suis et totum seruicium predicti Roberti de Westerelangeton' cum omnibus pertinenciis suis, sicut predictum est, contra omnes gentes. Hiis testibus . . .[3]

8

Fo. 41–41*b*

Hugo de Bellocampo filius Oliueri[4] omnibus hominibus et amicis suis salutem. Sciatis me dedisse et presenti carta mea confirmasse Henrico de Braibroc pro homagio suo et seruicio et pro quadraginta marcis argenti quas michi dedit ad me adquietandum versus dominum

[1] East Langton, Leics.     [2] West Langton, Leics.

[3] The date is presumably about the same as that of no. 6. This property too had been included in the king's charter of confirmation of 24 March 1211 and it was the subject of a fine levied before the king and his justices at St Bride's, London, in 12 John, which is not more precisely dated but belongs presumably to the Michaelmas term 1210 or the Hilary or Easter term 1211 (P.R.O., C.P. 25(1)/126/6/153).

[4] For the grantor see the king's confirmation of 25 July 1208 (*Rot. Chart.*, p. 180*b*). Hugh died before 3 May 1217 when his brother Roger was granted seisin (*Rot. Litt. Claus.*, i. 308; *Excerpta e Rotulis Finium*, i. 2). The present charter must be dated after Robert's death in 1211 and in the later years of John's reign.

regem de fine quem cum eo feci pro debitis Iudeorum quadraginta
acras et decem perticatas terre in Eaton',[1] que iacent in Twedecroft,
scilicet triginta et septem acras terre et vnam rodam que iacent inter
terram Eudonis de Bellocampo et terram Radulfi filii Ailrici et duas
acras terre et tres rodas et decem perticatas que abutant super cheminum
de Huniden'[2] iuxta terram predicti Eudonis de Bellocampo cum toto
fossato, et preterea decem acras bosci et terre in Litelhay iuxta boscum
quem Robertus pater predicti Henrici de me tenuit in longitudinem
fossati quod abutat super croftam quam Willelmus Rungefer tenuit,
scilicet ab austro in aquilonem, habendas et tenendas predicto Henrico
et heredibus suis de me et heredibus meis libere et quiete, integre et
hereditarie, infra seruicia que michi facit pro aliis terris quas tenet de
me pro omnibus seruiciis et exaccionibus. Et ego Hugo et heredes mei
warantizabimus predicto Henrico et heredibus suis omnes predictas
terras et omnia predicta tenementa cum omnibus pertinenciis contra
omnes gentes. Hiis testibus . . .

## 9

Fo. 76

Ego Deulecresse Morel recongnosco [veram recongnicionem] quod
Henricus de Braibroc et heredes sui quieti sunt versus me et heredes
meos de omnibus debitis que Iohannes de Horsendon' michi debuit a
creacione seculi vsque ad finem et ego aquietabo versus omnes gentes
dictum Iohannem qui cartam vel tailliam nomine ipsius monstrabunt.[3]

## 10

Fo. 76

Ego Manasserus scriptor recongnosco [veram recongnicionem] quod
Henricus de Braibroc quietus est versus me et Deulecresse Morel de
debito Iohannis de Horsedon' et de omnibus debitis a creacione seculi
vsque ad Natale Domini proximum post coronacionem regis Henrici
filii regis Iohannis.[4]

[1] Eaton Socon, Beds.          [2] Honydon in Eaton Socon.
[3] Horsenden is in Buckinghamshire, where the property of the debtor presumably lay. The date of the starr is probably about the same as that of the
following document, which is concerned with the same debtor.
[4] Henry III was crowned at Westminster, which is presumably the occasion
meant, on 17 May 1220. The date of this starr is therefore 25 December following.

## 11

Fo. 76

[Ego] Ioseus presbiter recongnosco [veram recongnicionem] quod Henricus de Braibroc quietus est versus me de debitis Galfridi de Canceis a creacione seculi vsque [ad] Natale Domini proximum post coronacionem regis Henrici filii regis Iohannis apud Westmonasterium.[1]

## 12

Fo. 76

[Ego] Bonenfaunt filius Vrsel recongnosco [veram recongnicionem] quod Henricus de Braibroc et heredes sui quieti sunt de me et heredibus meis et de matre mea Henna de omnibus debitis et demandis a creacione seculi vsque ad Pentecosten proximum post consecracionem Eustachii de Faucunberg Londoniensis episcopi[2] et omnes illi qui taillias, cartas vel cyrographa monstrabunt nomine Iohannis de Horsendon et nomine matris mee Henne et mei sciant omnes quod quieti sunt.

## 13

Fo. 76

[Ego] Ioseus presbiter recongnosco [veram recongnicionem] quod Henricus de Braibroc et heredes sui quieti sunt versus me et heredes meos de omnibus debitis et demandis, sciant vniuersi, a creacione seculi vsque ad Pascha proximum post consecracionem Eustachii de Faucunberg Londoniensis episcopi[3] et quod[4] omnes carte et tallie et cyrographa que monstrabuntur facte infra dictum terminum false sunt.

## 14

Fo. 46

Sciant etc. quod ego Iohannes de Bello Campo quietum clamaui in perpetuum Henricum de Braibroc de tota parte que ad ipsum spectabat

John of Horsenden had previously conveyed to Robert Braybrooke all his land in Horsenden and this transaction was confirmed by a fine levied five weeks after Easter (8 May) 1211 (Hunter, *Fines*, i. 248–9).

[1] 25 December 1220. Two grants of land and other property in Bow Brickhill and Caldicott (Bucks) by Geoffrey le Canceis to Robert of Braybrooke are confirmed by the king's charter of 25 July 1208 (*Rot. Chart.*, p. 181).

[2] Whit Sunday fell on 30 May in 1221.

[3] Consecrated 25 April 1221. Easter fell on 3 April in 1222.　　[4] MS. per.

de debitis que Hugo de Bello Campo vel Oliuerus pater eius debuerunt domino regi de debitis Iudeorum racione terrarum quas idem Henricus tenet de terris que fuerint predictorum Hugonis et Oliueri, ita quod ego aut heredes mei nunquam versus dictum Henricum vel heredes suos aliquam mouere questionem pro aliquo debito quod debeam domino regi de debitis predictorum Hugonis et Oliueri occasione debiti Iudeorum. Et si forte contigerit quod occasione predictorum debitorum idem Henricus aut heredes sui in demandam vel in dampna inciderint, ego et heredes mei tenebimur illos de demanda illa omnino adquietare et eis de dampno illo respondere sine omni placito et contradiccione pro x. marcis quas recepi.[1]

### 15

Fo. 76b

[Ego] Samuel filius Aaron recongnosco [veram recongnicionem] quod Iohannes de Werewold et Richolda mater eius et heredes eorum quieti sunt de me et heredibus meis de omnibus debitis et demandis a creacione seculi vsque ad Natale Domini proximum post obitum regis Philippi Francie.[2]

### 16

Fo. 75b–76

Ego Benedictus de Cole[c]estr' recongnosco [veram recongnicionem] quod Gilbertus Foliot et Petrus filius eius et heredes eorum quieti sunt versus me et heredes meos de omnibus debitis et calumpniis et demandis a creacione seculi vsque ad festum sancti Michaelis anno regni regis Henrici xv°.[3]

---

[1] This indemnity follows upon the grant by Hugh de Beauchamp (no. 8). As stated in the notes to that document, Hugh was succeeded in 1217 by his brother Roger. Roger was succeeded, in turn, by his nephew John, who was granted seisin on 6 December 1221 (*Excerpta e Rotulis Finium*, i. 76). Presumably he gave this indemnity shortly afterwards and it may be dated c. 1222.

[2] Philip Augustus died 14 July 1223. The date of this starr is therefore 25 December following. Werewold may be Wherwell, Hants: cf. *Rot. de Oblatis*, p. 452, where the form is Werewulle.

[3] 29 September 1231. A grant, at fo. 50, by Peter Foliot to Henry Braybrooke of 82 acres in La Berewe (apparently Barrow in Great Wakering) must be related to this starr.

17

Fo. 76

Ego Samuel filius Aronis recongnosco [veram recongnicionem] quod quietaui et quietum clamaui Henricum de Braibroc et heredibus suis pro me et heredibus meis xlv. acras terre quas emit de Nicholao clerico de Wiggeberg'[1] quod ego nec heredes mei nichil exigere possimus in predictis xlv. acris terre occasione alicuius debiti quod predictus Nicholaus michi debuit a creacione seculi vsque ad finem.

18

Fo. 76

[Nos] Abraham filius magistri Salamonis et Messul' filius magistri Iosepi recognoscimus [veram recognicionem] quod quietum clamauimus Henrico de Braibroc vnam bouatam terre de terra quam Asserus Serut tenere soluit in Querinton'[2] et cum domo et pertinenciis et eciam cum omnibus accidentibus que accidere potuerit occasione illius bouate terre. Nec noc vel heredes nostri nichil exigere possumus super predictam terram cum pertinenciis a creacione seculi vsque ad finem, quia totum quietum clamauimus predicto Henrico et heredibus suis et nos acquietabimus versus omnes gentes totum debitum si quod exigitur per aliquem [hominem] vel feminam.

19

Fo. 76b

[Ego] Elias episcopus recongnosco [veram recongnicionem] quod quietum clamaui Henrico de Braibroc totam terram quam emit de Gilberto de Thotham[3] quam habuit in parochia de Toleshunt[4] et parochia de Saltcote[5], scilicet totam terram quam tenere soluit de Willelmo de Werewold et Roesia de Verly et de viro suo Philippo de

---

[1] Wigborough, Essex. A grant to Henry Braybrooke by Nicholas, son of William, of Wigborough is at fo. 50b-51: there is no indication of date.

[2] Quarrenden, Bucks.

[3] A grant to Henry Braybrooke by Gilbert of Totham and his wife Elicia of all their land in Salcot is at fo. 49b: it must be connected with this starr. There is no indication of date.

[4] Tolleshunt, Essex.      [5] Salcot, Essex.

Verly, ita quod ego vel heredes mei nullam exigere possumus demandam vel calumpniam in predicta terra occasione alicuius debiti quod
predictus Gilbertus debere solebat a creacione seculi vsque ad finem.

20

Fo. 76b

[Nos] Benedictus Crespin et Manasserus scriptor recongnoscimus
veram recongnicionem quod quietum clamauimus Henrico de Braibroc
et heredibus [suis] de tota terra de Toleshunt cum pertinenciis et totum
quod ei accidere posset vel euenire possit, scilicet illam terram quam
idem Henricus emit de Ricardo filio Roberti de Enefeld' in villa de
Toleshunt prenominata,[1] ita quod nos vel heredes nostri vel quis per
nos vel heredes nostros nullum predicto Henrico vel heredibus suis
debitum exigere possumus a creacione seculi vsque ad finem super
predictam terram vel pertinencia, et si quis homo vel femina per nos
vel heredes nostros veniat exigens aliquod debitum super terram predictam predicto Henrico vel heredibus suis nos et heredes nostri
predictum Henricum et heredes suos versus omnes acquietabimus.

21

Fo. 76b

[Nos] Leonus filius Ysaac et Aaron filius Abraham recongnoscimus
[veram recongnicionem] quod recepimus de domino Henrico de Braibroc duas marcas et dimidiam de vi. marcis et dimidia quas nobis debuit
pro Iohanne de Langedon'.[2]

---

[1] A grant to Henry Braybrooke by Richard, son of Robert, of Enfield, of all
his land at Tolleshunt is at fo. 47b: it must be connected with this starr. There is
no indication of date.

[2] A grant to Henry Braybrooke by John of Langdon of the service of 18d. a
year in Langdon at fo. 47b is doubtless connected with this starr: but there were
presumably other transactions. There is no indication of date. Langdon is probably
to be equated with Langdon Hills, Essex.

# X. DEEDS OF MALTON PRIORY

THE DEEDS IN THIS series are subsidiary to conveyances to Malton Priory of lands that had been mortgaged to Jewish moneylenders. With one exception (no. 5) they are starrs in favour of the priory, sometimes jointly with the original debtor, who is the nominal grantor of the land. With the same exception, they are entered in the margin of the cartulary of the priory (Cottonian MS. Claudius D.xi) against the conveyances to which they relate. The exception is a receipt by one of the debtors of payments by the priory in his name to the moneylender and to his mother in respect of her dower. The conveyances themselves, which are uninformative in the present connexion, have not been reproduced. None of the starrs has been preserved and the Hebrew inscriptions are therefore lost. All the deeds date from the 1240's.

The folio references are to Claudius D.xi.

I

Fo. 114 *in margine*

Omnibus has litteras visuris vel audituris Ioscy Iudeus nepos Aaron Iudei Eboraci salutem. Noueritis me concessisse et commisisse priori et conuentui Maltone sex bouatas terre in parua Edestona[1] michi pridem a Willelmo filio Willelmi de Redburn' inuadiatas et tandem potestate regia ad me deuolutas tenendas et habendas cum omnibus pertinentiis suis pacifice et absque inquietatione mei et heredum meorum in perpetuum quietas ab omni debito inter me et dictum Willelmum contracto ab initio mundi vsque in finem seculi. Hoc autem idem manucapio pro omnibus debitis a quibuscumque Iudeis contractis vsque ad huius instrumenti confeccionem, excepto tantummodo domino Leone Iudeorum Eboraci episcopo, nullius alterius valituro instrumento si que in posterum contra illos a quocumque alio proferatur. Si autem dictus

---

[1] Little Edstone, Yorks, N.R.

281

Willelmus vel quicumque suorum prefatos priorem et conuentum super predictis sex bouatis terre quomodolibet inquietauerit, totam pecuniam quam ab ipsis recepi eis protinus absque omni contradictione et quantulacumque dilatione refundam et ipsi michi cyrographos precedentium conuentionum inter me et dictum Willelmum fidei sue commissos restituent et ego scripta Iudeorum quibus dictus Willelmus obligatur ad ipsorum inmunitatem conseruandam plene restituam. Et horum omnium dictum Aaron auunculum meum plegium constitui qui vnamecum huic scripto litteram suam ebraycam in testimonium securitatis apposuit. Acta apud Eboracum in crastino Conuersionis sancti Pauli anno gracie M⁰CC⁰ quadragesimo primo.[1]

2

Fo. 114 *in margine*

Omnibus hoc scriptum visuris vel audituris Benedictus de Nantes Iudeus Lincolnie salutem. Sciatis quod ego nec heredes mei vel assignati mei nichil possumus exigere versus priorem et conuentum de Maltona de sex bouatis terre cum pertinentiis in parua Edestona[2] que fuerunt Willelmi de Redburne occasione alicuius debiti quod idem Willelmus vel heredes sui vel assignati sui michi vel meis debuit per scriptum vel per talliam ab initio seculi vsque ad finem mundi. In huius rei testimonium hoc scriptum pro me et heredibus meis et assignatis meis littera mea ebrayca signaui.[3]

3

Fo. 114 *in margine*

Omnibus hoc scriptum visuris vel audituris Iacobus filius Leonis Iudei Lincolnie salutem. Noueritis quod Willelmus de Raburne et omnes heredes sui sunt quieti de me et heredibus meis de omnibus debitis que michi debuit per cartam vel per talliam ab inicio mundi vsque ad Quadragesimam anno regni regis Henrici filii regis Iohannis vicesimo sexto,[4] et insimul prior et conuentus de Maltona sunt quieti de omnibus debitis que Willelmus predictus debuit super terram quam habent de eodem Willelmo ab inicio mundi vsque ad finem et similiter

[1] 26 January 1242.
[2] Little Edstone, Yorks., N.R.
[3] Since this starr refers to the same property as no. 1, it is presumably of about the same date.          [4] Lent 1242.

de omnibus Iudeis Lincolnie que debita sunt per cartam domini regis apud Lincolniam. In huius rei testimonium hoc scriptum littera mea ebraica signaui.

4

Fo. 64b *in margine*

Ego Iosceus nepos Aaron Iudeus Eboraci quietum clameo per presens starrum meum priori et conuentui de Maltona de me et omnibus heredibus meis totam terram, cum omnibus suis pertinenciis sine aliquo retenemento, quam idem prior et conuentus habent in Wellum[1] de Willelmo filio Thome de Richeburg' secundum tenorem cartarum et instrumentorum quas dicti prior et conuentus de ipso inde habent, ita quod nec ego prenominatus Iosceus Iudeus nec heredes mei nec aliquis alius Iudeus vncquam versus totam dictam terram de Wellum aliquid poterimus exigere occasione alicuius debiti vel demande in quibus predictus Willelmus de Richeburg' vncquam michi tenebatur vel teneri potuit vel poterit per cyrographum vel per talliam vel aliquo alio modo pro se vel pro plegiagio alterius ab initio seculi vsque ad finem seculi. In cuius rei testimonium presens scriptum littera mea ebraica signaui.[2]

5

Fo. 64b–65

Omnibus has literas visuris vel audituris Willelmus de Richeburg salutem in Domino. Noueritis me recepisse a priore et conuentu Maltone totam pecuniam quam michi debebant pro septem bouatis terre cum pertinenciis suis in Wellum quas habuit ex mea donacione, de qua pecunia soluerunt nomine meo domine Albrede matri mee tres marcas argenti pro quieta clamancia dotis sue de eadem terra de Wellum. Soluerunt eciam similiter nomine meo Ioscy Iudeo Eboraci nepoti Aaron triginta et sex marcas argenti et dimidiam pro alleuiacione partis debiti quo ei tenebar astrictus. In cuius rei testimonium etc. Hiis testibus etc.[3]

[1] Welham, Yorks., E.R.
[2] This starr appears to be earlier than no. 6 and is probably of much the same date as no. 1.
[3] This acknowledgement is evidently connected with no. 4 and is of about the same date.

6

Fo. 114 *in margine*

Omnibus has litteras visuris vel audituris Leo Iudeorum episcopus Eboraci salutem. Noueritis me plenam recepisse quietanciam de omnibus debitis que Galfridus de Grimstone clericus michi vel heredibus meis debebat a principio mundi vsque in finem seculi et similiter de Willelmo filio Wellelmi de Redburn et de omnibus debitis quecumque michi debebat ab inicio mundi vsque ad Pascha[1] anno gracie M°CC°xl°iii°, vnde concessi priori et conuentui Maltone omnem inmunitatem de terris quas habent tam de dono dicti Galfridi quam de dono dicti Willelmi. In cuius veritatis testimonium hanc litteram meam ebraicam scripsi etc.

[1] 12 April 1243.

# XI. THE KING'S JEWISH BAILIFFS, 1219–1221

In this appendix there are brought together two writs addressed to Jewish bailiffs in the early years of Henry III's reign, together with three returns to the first of them. The documents illustrate the degree of self-government enjoyed by Jewish communities in the early years of the thirteenth century and inferentially in the twelfth century.

The first writ and the returns to it come from an incomplete file of writs and returns concerning: (*a*) debts secured by deeds, tallies and chirographs incurred before the 'general arrest of the Jews' in 1210; (*b*) arrears of the Bristol tallage of the same year; and apparently some other outstanding matters. The file is too fragmentary to permit inferences to be drawn with much confidence; but it is to be observed that in the case of Oxford (no. 9) the opportunity was taken to press for the payment of a few miscellaneous debts including 'De communa Iudeorum v. solidos de nouo tallagio'. This item appears to be the sole evidence that has come to light for a tallage, apparently small in amount, imposed upon the Jews in the first three years of the reign. The documents remaining on the file number eleven, as follows:

(1) Writ to Exeter, 15 November.
(3) Return to (1).
(4) Writ to Northampton, 15 November.
(5) Writ to Lincoln, Stamford and Nottingham, 16 November.
(6) Return to (5).
(7) Writ to Winchester, 16 November.
(8) Postscript to (7), annotated and endorsed (in Hebrew).[1]
(9) Writ to Oxford, 20 November.
(10) Postscript to (9).

---

[1] Endorsement printed by M. D. Davis, *Shetaroth*, pp. 371-2.

(2) Postscript to a writ, apparently addressed to Bristol and
Gloucester.

(11) Return to a writ addressed to Hereford and Worcester.

Though the writ (no. 5) printed below brings together two different matters, it seems clear that, in the first instance, it was intended
that they should be dealt with separately: hence the postscripts
(2), (8) and (10). Of the eleven documents three returns (3), (6)
and (11) have been selected for printing as well as the writ. This
writ has already been published by Michael Adler,[1] but his text
deviated seriously from the original: moreover he did not print
the return to it (6) or either of the other surviving returns.

Though the year in which the writs were issued has hitherto
been in doubt, this can be established. It will be observed that the
Jews who were in default for the Bristol tallage were to be at
Westminster on the quinzaine of Hilary in order 'to give a
satisfactory reply' to the demand made upon them: in other
words, they were to make a proposal for paying off the arrears.
We should expect therefore that some at least of the defaulters
would make a payment in the course of the financial year. Since
eight of the thirty-one named in the writ here printed, and these
eight only, appear under Lincoln as paying instalments of the
Bristol tallage in the receipt roll of 4 Henry III, made up at
Michaelmas 1220,[2] the inference is that these eight, at least, had
appeared before the Justices in the previous Hilary term and that
the writ was issued in November 1219. This inference is confirmed by an entry on the plea roll of the Justices of the Jews for
the Easter term 1220.[3] Two of those, whose names are included
in the writ to the bailiffs of Lincoln, Stamford and Nottingham,
are Breton and Peitevin, the son of Serfdeu.[4] We can have no
hesitation in identifying them with Breton of Nottingham and
Peitevin of Stamford named in the plea roll. They have been
amerced by the Justices because they departed from court without
leave when they ought to have appeared to answer for the fines

[1] *Jews of Medieval England*, pp. 236-8.
[2] P.R.O., E. 401/3B, m. 4.  [3] Cole, *Documents*, p. 320.
[4] A full list of the names was printed by Adler, *loc. cit.*

they had made in respect of 'old deeds' and for other matters about which the Justices had written to them. They had doubtless appeared on the quinzaine of Hilary and fined for the deeds they held dating before the general arrest in 1210. A further inference is justified, namely, that separate returns (which are now lost) had been made to the writ in respect of Nottingham and Stamford.

The second writ printed below is entered on the Memoranda Rolls of 5 Henry III and, though not dated there (being transcribed from a draft), was certainly despatched in the Easter term 1221, presumably in April or May. The writ presses for the payment of contributions to a tallage of 1,000 marks, arranged with the English Jewry earlier in the year, and also of the contributions towards the ransom (as it may be called) of one of their number who was to be expelled from England. This was Moses, the son of Le Brun, who had recently been involved in an action before the Justices of the Jews arising out of a claim upon a bond which the prior of Dunstable declared to be forged and of which Moses could give no satisfactory account.[1] His father would seem to have been the London Jew, Le Brun, who was prominent under Henry II and one of the richest members of the community.[2] The family, therefore, was of high standing and Moses had hitherto been of good reputation.[3] To save him from hanging the English Jewry had to pay a heavy price in consideration of which a sentence of expulsion was substituted for a sentence of death.[4] It will be noted that expulsion is held out as a threat to those who did not pay their taxes promptly. The threat was presumably directed more particularly against those who had recently entered the country. It was in November 1218 that instructions had been given to the authorities at the ports to admit Jews arriving from abroad, provided they gave security that they would register with the Justices of the Jews. At the same time instructions were given

[1] Cole, *Documents*, p. 312; Rigg, *Select Pleas*, pp. 4–5.
[2] Above, pp. 62, 172–4. The description given by Moses fits him: pater eius aliquando diues erat.
[3] Cole, *Documents*, p. 300.
[4] Annals of Dunstable Priory in *Annales Monastici*, iii. 66.

that Jews resident in the country were not to be allowed to leave without licence.[1]

It will be noted that the writ was sent to Cambridge and ten other towns. Presumably a writ in similar terms, assigning perhaps a different day for payment, went to Lincoln, Nottingham, Stamford, Worcester and York: if so, it seems not to have been enrolled.

## 1. WRIT OF 19 NOVEMBER 1219 TO THE BAILIFFS OF LINCOLN, STAMFORD AND NOTTINGHAM

P.R.O., E. 101/249/13(5)

Henricus Dei gracia rex Anglie, dominus Hibernie, dux Normannie, Aquitanie et comes Andegauie Iudeis balliuis suis de Lincolnia, Stanford' et Notingham salutem. Precipimus vobis quod, sicut vos et omnia vestra diligatis, per sacramentum omnium Iudeorum super rotulum diligenter inquiratis qui Iudei aut Iudee de Lincolnia et de Stanford' et de Notingham habeant veteres cartas vel tallias vel cyrographa ante communem capturam Iudeorum confecta et qui Iudei vel Iudee districtiones fecerint super debitores de quibus carte vel tallie vel cyrographa illa loquuntur, et, facta inde diligenti inquisicione, scire faciatis omnibus Iudeis qui huiusmodi habent quod sine omni occasione per manum propriam vel per manum vestram illa habeant coram iusticiariis nostris ad custodiam Iudeorum assignatis apud Westmonasterium a die sancti Hillarii in xv. dies, sicut ad cartas vel tallias vel cyrographa illa vmquam aliquam voluerint habere recuperacionem, quia tunc per consilium nostrum prouidebitur qualiter de huiusmodi melius possit fieri comodum nostrum et ipsorum Iudeorum. Et bene eis ex parte nostra dicatis quod quicumque Iudeus vel Iudea extunc huiusmodi cartas, tallias vel cyrographa protulerit, que ad predictum diem et locum coram eisdem iusticiariis non fuerint exhibita, corpus ipsius in cuius manu inuenta fuerint capietur et de corpore suo et omnibus catallis suis in misericordia nostra erit et carte et tallie et cyrographa illa nostra erunt quieta. Et vos tunc sitis ibi sine omni occasione audituri et facturi preceptum nostrum et inquisicionem factam tunc habeatis ibidem.

Item precipimus vobis quod sicut vos ipsos diligitis sine dilacione per corpora et catalla sua distringatis Iudeos subscriptos ad reddendum

---

[1] *Patent Rolls, 1216–1225*, pp. 180–1.

nobis debita subscripta que nobis debent de tallagio super eis facto apud Bristolliam, ita quod ad predictum terminum inde sufficienter respondere possitis, scilicet:

> De Benliueng' l. marcas et dimidiam
> [*and thirty others*]

Et in fide qua nobis tenemini ita diligenter istud mandatum nostrum exequamini ne pro defectu vestri in aliquo simus perdentes. Et si catalla non habeant unde tallagium nostrum reddere possint, tunc per tales et tam saluos plegios illos ponatis quod de corporibus suis sitis securi quod ibi sint ad predictum terminum. Et habeatis tunc ibi nomina plegiorum singulorum Iudeorum et hoc breue. De illis autem Iudeis qui debitum aliquod debuerunt de tallagio Bristollie qui mortui sunt vel de terra nostra exierunt vobis precipimus quod diligentem faciatis inquisicionem que catalla habuerint in mobilibus, cartis, cyrographis et talliis die quo obierunt vel quo a terra nostra Anglie recesserunt et in cuius manus postea catalla ipsa deuenerunt, ita quod ad predictum terminum predictos iusticiarios super forisfacturam nostram plene certificare possitis. Teste Eustacio thesaurario nostro apud Westmonasterium xvi° die Nouembris.

## 2. RETURN TO WRIT IN RESPECT OF LINCOLN

P.R.O., E. 101/249/13(6)

Hi sunt Iudei qui primo fecerunt sacramentum tenorem litterarum domini regis:

De Beleuing' i. tallia viii. librarum sub nomine Walteri de Fiscart', et i. tallia v. solidorum sub nomine Yngerami filii Symonis, et vnum cyrographum lx. solidorum quod est Helye filii Benedicti et est sub nomine Willelmi de Blithun' per plegiagium Yngerami filii Symonis. Et ipse iurauit fore apud Londonias a die sancti Ylarii in xv. dies.

Deodatus filius Aaron iurauit quod erit apud Londonias: plegius Iosceus filius Abraham. Et habet duo cyrographa: vnum de iiii.<sup>or</sup> libris et aliud vii. librarum de Thoma de Lue.

Vrsellus filius Pucelle iurauit quod erit apud Londonias: Mosseus gener suus plegius.

Mosseus filius Asseri iurauit: Helyas filius Benedicti et Manasserus scriptor plegii. Et habuit quoddam cyrographum xx. marcarum de Andrea de Mauneby quod si poterit perquirere proferret.

Mosseus Bosse iurauit: Iosceus gener Benedicti et Ysaac gener suus plegii. Et per sacramentum suum dicit quod non habet cartam neque cyrographum quod domini iusticiarii sciant.

Angeuin iurauit quod erit apud Londonias per penam ii. marcarum per vadimonium positum in manu Mossei filii Asseri. Et Mosseus respondet de vadimonio vel de ii. marcis si predictus Angeuinus ad diem statutum ibi non fuerit. Et hoc cognoscit Mosseus per vadimonium i. cyrographi.

Iosseus de Colecestria inuenit plegium Beniamin generum suum quod faciet grantum Helyc filio Benedicti antequam eat apud Londonias faciendi vel eundi quo sibi precipiet.

Gersun episcopus iurauit quod erit apud Londonias per penam ii. marcarum sol[uturus] duo cyrographa tradita in manu Mossei filii Asseri, vnum sub nomine Nicholai de Wilinthon' et aliud sub nomine Emme de Tirinthon'.

Plegii Abrahe de Bedeford': Pictauinus filius Manasseri, Pictauinus filius Ioscei.

### 3. RETURN TO LIKE WRIT IN RESPECT OF EXETER

P.R.O., E. 101/249/13(3)

Inquisicio Iudeorum Exonie de veteribus cartis, cyrografis et talliis factis ante communem capturam.

Dicunt quod de partibus illis qui tales cartas, cyrografa vel tallias habent, illas atulerunt vt irrotulantur scilicet omnes illas quas ad presens habere possunt.

De districcione autem facta post communem capturam nichil sciunt neque per cartas veteres, cyrografa neque tallias.

De Iudeis autem mortuis qui debent debita domino regi dicunt quod die quo obiit Samuel de Wilton' omnes carte, cyrografa et tallie quas habuit remanserunt in manu Iuete vxoris sue. De talliis Deodati filii Amiot quod pars est in manu domini regis et quantam partem attulerunt.

De Iudeis autem qui a terra recesserunt dicunt quod nichil sciunt de catallis eorum.

[Dorse]

De catallis Lie Iudee mortue dicunt quod dominus rex ea habet.

## 4. RETURN TO LIKE WRIT IN RESPECT OF HEREFORD AND WORCESTER

P.R.O., E. 101/249/13(11)

Hoc est veredictum Iudeorum de Hereford' et de Wirecestria per sacramentum quod fecerunt super rotulum, scilicet:

De veteribus cartis nec de cyrographis veteribus nec de veteribus talliis ante communem capcionem de Bristoe nullam vnquam districcionem fecerunt nec nullam habuerunt preter has, scilicet, i. cirographum de Ysaac Blundo de xv. libris[1] sub nomine Willelmi de Stanton', vnde idem Ysaac fecit districciones per breue domini regis et per dominos iusticiarios, et i. cirographum de Abraam nepote Auegaie de iii. libris quod est sub nomine Willelmi de Cuberlee per eosdem regem et iusticiarios et i. talliam de lxiii. solidis quam Mosseus Iudeus de Eillesberi habet[2] quam super eum inuenimus.

Nec de catallis Iudeorum nec illis qui mortui sunt nec de illis qui mare transfretauerunt nichil scimus.

## 5. WRIT TO SHERIFF AND JEWISH BAILIFFS OF CAMBRIDGE AND OTHER TOWNS (EASTER TERM 1221)

P.R.O., L.T.R. Mem. Roll 5 Henry III (E. 368/3), m. 1(2)d
P.R.O., K.R. Mem. Roll 5 Henry III (E. 159/4), m. 9d

### CANTEBRIGIA DE IUDAISMO

Rex vicecomiti et balliuis Iudeis Cantebrigie. Precipimus vobis quod statim visis literis istis dicatis et firmiter iniungatis ex parte nostra omnibus Iudeis de Cantebrigia quod, sicut se et omnia sua diligunt et sicut residenciam habere volunt in terra nostra, sine omni occasione et excusacione habeant vel mittant pro vrgentissimo negocio nostro ad scaccarium nostrum in vigilia sancti Iohannis Baptiste[3] omnes denarios qui eos contingunt de tallagio mille marcarum per quas communa Iudeorum Anglie nobiscum finem fecit, de qua medietate nobis soluenda eis terminum nos dederamus in octabis predicti festi sancti Iohannis.[4] Et habeant similiter denarios qui eos contingunt de medietate c. librarum quam nobis dant pro Mosseo filio Brun Iudei de terra nostra eiciendo. Et bene eis scire faciatis quod quicumque Iudeus eo die

[1] de quibus fin[iuit] per xx. marcas *interlined*.
[2] tallia illa non pro tallagio *interlined*.
[3] 23 June 1221.  [4] 1 July 1221.

cessauerit in solucione sua, totum id quod restabit ab eo exigemus ad duplum et insuper ad corpus suum et catalla sua nos grauiter capiemus.

Idem breue missum est apud Herefordiam, Glouerniam, Oxoniam, Norhantonam, Cantuariam, Londonias, Colecestriam, Norwicum, Wintoniam, Bristolliam.

## XII. STATUTE OF THE JEWRY, 1233

THIS STATUTE IS PRESERVED in a collection of documents made by a chancery clerk about the year 1236. It was not entered upon the close roll, where we might have expected it, nor on any other roll of the chancery: neither is it preserved in any extant roll or book of the exchequer.[1]

With the exception of the ordinance of 1194,[2] no earlier legislation governing the English Jewry has come to light, and it will be noted that the statute does not refer to any previous enactment. This, however, is not the only legislation of its kind that was drafted without reference to earlier legislation or that is not to be found in any existing official record: the closely allied legislation of 1239 is an example to the point.[3] It is, therefore, by no means impossible that legislation of a similar type, now lost, preceded it.

If we take the provisions one by one, we shall not find much that is original in them. The use of tallies to secure loans had been forbidden twelve years earlier, for though the text of the prohibition has not come down to us, the payments for licences to continue the practice leave no doubt that a prohibition had issued.[4] The requirement that bonds should henceforward be in the form of triplicate chirographs may be new; but such chirographs were in use previously,[5] though presumably not generally. The prohibition of a penalty clause in Jewish bonds appears to be new and also the prohibition of the exaction of compound interest: at a later date, however, penalties were introduced into bonds as an alternative to specific rates of interest.[6] The next provision, expelling by Michaelmas 1233 penurious Jews who were unable to 'serve' the king is plainly *ad hoc*, though a similar threat had been held out in the writ of 1221, printed above. The

---

[1] *Law Quarterly Review*, liv. 392–4.
[2] R. de Hovedene, *Chronica*, iii. 266–7.
[3] *Liber de Antiquis Legibus*, pp. 237–8.
[4] Above, p. 193.    [5] Above, p. 264.    [6] Above, p. 106.

final provision, that Jews are not to lend money upon ecclesiastical vessels or upon bloodstained garments, goes back to Henry II's charter, though the description of the proscribed articles—bloody or soiled garments or those apparently obtained by force—is now made more precise. The wording should be compared with that of a similar prohibition addressed to the Jews of Poitou and Gascony in 1219: nec aliquis Iudeus accipiant vadium aliquid ut de pannis madidis vel pannis sanguine maculatis . . . unde suspicio aliqua possit oriri.[1]

Harleian MS. 323, fo. 66b
Br. Mus. Additional MS. 25005, fo. 63b
Printed, *Law Quarterly Review*, liv. 393

Anno regni regis Henrici filii regis Iohannis xvij⁰, iiij⁰ die Aprilis in crastino Pasce, statutum fuit ab eodem rege apud Cantuariam quod nullum mutuum de cetero trahatur cum Iudeis per talliam set per cyrograffum, cuius alteram partem Iudeus habeat, cum signo Christiani mutuum contrahentis appenso, et alteram partem habeat Christianus mutuum contrahens. Tercia vero pars que vocatur pes reponatur in archa saluo custodienda per cirograffarios Christianos et Iudeos, et cirograffum cuius pes non fuerit inuentus in archa, sicut predictum est, nullum habeat vigorem.

Nullus Iudeus aliquid det mutuo per penam, set de libra capiat duos denarios per ebdomodam de lucro et non plus, ita quod nichil ponatur in sortem nisi primum mutuum.

Nullus Iudeus remaneat in regno nostro nisi talis sit quod regi possit seruire et bonos plegios inueniat de fidelitate. Alii vero Iudei, qui nichil habent vnde regi seruiant, exeant de regno infra instans festum sancti Michaelis anno regni regis predicti xvij⁰: quod si vlterius moram fecerint detrudantur in carcerem et non deliberentur sine speciali mandato regis.

Nullus Iudeus de cetero aliquid mutuum det super vasa ecclesiastica aut super pannos sanguinolentes aut madidos[2] aut quasi vi confunctos.

---

[1] *Rot. Litt. Claus.*, i. 397.      [2] Harl., *madiatos*.

# BIBLIOGRAPHICAL NOTE

THERE SEEMS NO NEED to burden this book with a full bibliography. The standard bibliographies, such as Charles Gross' *Sources and Literature of English History . . . to about 1485* and Cecil Roth's *Magna Bibliotheca Anglo-Judaica*, include most of the texts and secondary works cited. In any case, no printed book is cited that cannot be found in the British Museum catalogue.

A few explanations may perhaps be desirable. The Pipe Rolls and Memoranda Rolls cited are all published by the Pipe Roll Society, with the exception of the Pipe Rolls for 31 Henry I, 2–5 Henry II and 1 Richard I, published by the Record Commission. Except where otherwise stated, English chronicles are cited from the editions in the Rolls Series. The meaning of the abbreviated titles will, for the most part, be obvious: thus *Cal[endar]* and *Rot[uli]*; while *Rot. Oblat.* stands for *Rotuli de Oblatis et Finibus* and *Rot. Lib.* for *Rotuli de Liberate*. Some excessively long titles have been drastically shortened. *Documents illustrative of English history in the thirteenth and fourteenth centuries . . .*, edited by Sir Henry Cole, appears as Cole, *Documents*; J. M. Rigg's *Select Pleas, Starrs and other records from the rolls of the Exchequer of the Jews*, as Rigg, *Select Pleas*; and the *Calendar of the Plea Rolls of the Exchequer of the Jews*, by Rigg and Hilary Jenkinson, as *Cal. Plea Rolls*. It is perhaps hardly necessary to add that J. P. Migne's *Patrologiae Cursus Completus: Series Latina* is abbreviated to Migne, *Patrologia Latina*.

Adequate references are given to manuscripts and it is unnecessary to list them. Those in the Public Record Office are, where necessary, indicated by the prefix, P.R.O. Those in the British Museum need no prefix.

# INDEX OF NAMES

*Jewish personal names are separately indexed*

William Trentegeruns, 51, 54 n.,
see Rouen, Vicomtesse of
—Turbe, see Norwich, bishops of
— de Warenne, 136
—, son of William of Redburn, 96,
281-2, 284
Wilton (Wilts), 16
Wiltshire, 9
Winchelsea (Kent), 20
Winchester (Hants), 14, 19 n.,
117 n., 128, 179, 220 n., 223,
292
—, citizens of, 54 n.
Wischard Leydet, 101, 272-5
— —, Margery Foliot, wife of, 101,
272, 274

Wischard Leydet, Christiane, daugh-
ter of, see Henry of Braybrooke
Worcester, 14-15, 18, 28, 133, 231 n.,
291
—, bishops of:
Alfred, 67
William of Blois, 187
Godfrey Giffard, 73, 74 n.
Worcestershire, 15


York, 3 n., 14, 19 n., 95, 123, 126,
127 n., 219, 281, 284
—, archbishop of, Walter Giffard,
74 n.
Ypres, 57


## JEWISH PERSONAL NAMES

Aaron (Dunstable), 261, 263
— (Ireland), 221 n.
—, son of Josce (York), 95
— of Lincoln (d. 1186), 8, 11, 45, 47,
59, 61-2, 65, 68-70, 74-6,
80, 89-91, 115-17, 138,
151, 247-53, 259
— — —, Elias, son of, 76, 115 n.
— — —, Vives, son of, 76, 115 n., 249
— — —, Benedict, nephew of, 115 n.
— le prestre (Hereford), 123
—, son of Vives (London), 106, 130,
195
— of York (archpriest), 96, 122,
148 n., 281, 283
— — —, Josce, son of, 283
— — —, Josce, nephew of, 283
See Abraham, Dieudonné,
Hake, Josce, Samuel
Abraham, son of Avigai, 100, 170,
173, 239, 241, 255-6
— —, Aaron, son of, 171 n.

Abraham (early 13th century), Aaron,
son of, 280
— balisterius, 26 n.
— of Bedford, 290
— — Berkhamsted, 17
—, son of Deulecresse (Norwich),
219
—, clerk of Jacob, archpriest, 121
—, son of Rabbi Josce, 2, 60, 62, 121,
126 n., 237-8, 240, 255
—, son of Joseph, 239
— (London: 1130), 25
— (London: 1186), 5 n.
—, bishop (London: 1194), 128
— of Marlborough, 78 n.
— of Norwich, 158
— le Peysoner, 26 n.
—, son of Master Solomon, 279
See Benedict, Deulacresse, Josce,
Joseph, Moses, Samson, Samuel,
Solomon
Adrian (Bristol), 152

Adrian, Richolda, wife of, 152

Amiot (Bristol), 15 n., see Dieudonné

Angevin (Lincoln), 290

Asser (1178), 78 n., see Moses

Auntera (Exeter), wife of Samuel son
of Moses, 18 n.

Avigai, Avigae

— of London, 254–6, see Abraham

—, wife of Sale (Canterbury), 159 n.


Bateman (Nottingham), Hagin, son
of, 106

Belecote (Winchester), 220 n.

Belin of Gloucester, 11 n.

Bendin (Dunstable), 261, 263

Benedict, son of Abraham (Winchester), 27 n.

— of Chichester, 174

— le Chivaler, 26 n.

— of Colchester, 278

— Crespin, 280

—, son of Isaac (Lincoln), 74, 76, 250

— — — Josce (York), 105

— miles, 26 n.

— of Nantes, 282

— le Petit (parvus) of London, 88–9,
246

— brother of Jurnet of Norwich, 40,
43–4, 80–1
of Rochester, 11 n.

— — Romsey, 11 n.

—, son of Sara (1169), 61, 63

— of Talmont, 3 n., 11, 41 n., 117 n.,
135–6, 139

— — Winchester, 220 n.

—, bishop (York: 1221–3), 127 n.
See Aaron, Abraham, Elias,
Isaac, Josce, Jurnet, Solomon

Benjamin (Lincoln), son-in-law of
Josce of Colchester, 290

— of Oxford, 45

Benliveng (Lincoln), 289

Bikot de domo Ysaac (London: 1186),
5 n.

Bonedame (Normandy), 205

Bonenfant (Bedford), 142, 157 n.

—, son of Ursel, 277

— —, Henna, mother of, 277

Bosse, see Moses

Breton (Nottingham), 286

Brun (Le) of London, 40, 41 n., 62,
65, 81, 86 n., 87–9, 172–4, 242–4

— —, Moses, son of, 131, 179 n., 259,
261, 287, 291


Chera, wife of Augustine the convert,
36 n.

— — Isaac chirographer, 30

Coc, Cok (Isaac)

— de domo Abraham (London: 1186),
5 n.

— (Marlborough: 1290), 19

— Hagin, 99 n., 159 n.

Comtesse of Cambridge, 67

— (Exeter), 18

Crespin, see Benedict


David of Oxford, 3 n.

Deulebenie of Juvigny, 2 n.

— — Laigle, 204–5, 211

Deulecresse, Deulacresse

—, l'Eveske (Exeter), 124–5

—, furmager (Bristol), 26 n.

— Morel, 276
See Abraham

Deulesaut, Deulesalt

— of London (1191), 29

—, bishop (London: 1194), 128

— of Stamford, 68, 74, 251

Diai of Worcester, Isaac son of, 73 n.

Dieudonné, Deodatus

—, son of Aaron (Lincoln: 1219), 289

— — Amiot (Exeter: 1219), 290

— l'Eveske (London: 1177), 63,
125–6

# INDEX OF SUBJECTS